AMONG WOMEN ACROSS WORLDS

AMONG WOMEN ACROSS WORLDS

North Korea in the Global Cold War

Suzy Kim

CORNELL UNIVERSITY PRESS   ITHACA AND LONDON

Published with the support of the Rutgers University Research Council.

Copyright © 2023 by Suzy Kim

All rights reserved. Except for brief quotations in a review, this book, or parts thereof, must not be reproduced in any form without permission in writing from the publisher. For information, address Cornell University Press, Sage House, 512 East State Street, Ithaca, New York 14850. Visit our website at cornellpress.cornell.edu.

First published 2023 by Cornell University Press

Library of Congress Cataloging-in-Publication Data

Names: Kim, Suzy, 1972– author.
Title: Among women across worlds : North Korea in the global Cold War / Suzy Kim.
Description: Ithaca [New York] : Cornell University Press, 2022. | Includes bibliographical references and index.
Identifiers: LCCN 2022013394 (print) | LCCN 2022013395 (ebook) | ISBN 9781501767302 (hardcover) | ISBN 9781501767319 (pdf) | ISBN 9781501767326 (epub)
Subjects: LCSH: Women—Korea (North)—Social conditions—20th century. | Feminism—Korea (North)—History—20th century. | Women's rights—Korea (North)—History—20th century. | Women and communism—Korea (North)—History—20th century. | Women communists—Korea (North)—History—20th century. | Women—Political activity—Korea (North)—History—20th century. | Women's rights—International cooperation—History—20th century. | Korea (North)—Politics and government—20th century.
Classification: LCC HQ1765.6 .K5725 2022 (print) | LCC HQ1765.6 (ebook) | DDC 305.42095193/0904—dc23/eng/20220817
LC record available at https://lccn.loc.gov/2022013394
LC ebook record available at https://lccn.loc.gov/2022013395

Contents

List of Figures and Tables	vii
List of Abbreviations	ix
List of Organizations and Personalities	xi
Note on Terms, Transliteration, and Translation	xv
Introduction: Decolonial Genealogies	1

Part 1 **WAR AND PEACE**

1. Women against the Korean War	29
2. Anti-imperialist Struggle for a Just Peace	56

Part 2 **THIRD WORLD RISING**

3. Struggle between Two Lines	97
4. Women's Work Is Never Done	131

Part 3 **CULTURAL REVOLUTIONS**

5. Aesthetics of Everyday Folk	169
6. Communist Women around the World	194
Conclusion: Transnational Solidarities	218
Acknowledgments	239
Notes	243
Bibliography	301
Index	321

Figures and Tables

FIGURES

0.1. World map circa 1959 — xvii

0.2. WIDF Commission meeting to discuss report, 1951 — xviii

I.1. Cover of *Chosŏn Nyŏsŏng*, January 1947 — 5

I.2. Cover of Korean collection of documents from WIDF Founding Congress, 1947 — 6

I.3. Covers of *Women of the Whole World*, circa 1960s — 18

1.1. Hŏ Chŏng-suk attending WIDF Council meeting in Berlin, 1951 — 40

1.2. Cover of *We Accuse!*, 1951 — 42

1.3. Nora Rodd with Pak Chŏng-ae during 1951 visit — 48

2.1. Korean delegates to the WIDF Second Congress preparatory meeting in Budapest, 1948 — 65

2.2. Cover of *Chosŏn Nyŏsŏng*, February 1950 — 66

2.3. Pak Chŏng-ae at the World Peace Congress, 1950 — 72

2.4. Eugénie Cotton with Kim Yŏng-su, 1953 — 84

2.5. "Our little congress" in Berlin at the WIDF headquarters, 1953 — 85

2.6. Cover of *Chosŏn Nyŏsŏng*, September 1954 — 91

2.7. Monica Felton's third visit with Korean women, 1956 — 91

3.1. Women's Peace Caravan and route, 1958 — 99–100

3.2. Pak Chŏng-ae at World Congress of Mothers, 1955 — 102

3.3. Pak Chŏng-ae at World Congress of Mothers with delegates from Côte d'Ivoire and Austria, 1955 — 103

3.4. Emblem of the 1955 World Congress of Mothers — 104

3.5. Korean participation in WIDF Council meeting in Beijing, 1956 — 110

3.6. Lilly Waechter of WIDF with Kim Yŏng-su of KDWU, 1957 — 114

3.7. Korean women at the WIDF Council meeting in Helsinki, 1957 — 115

3.8. Korean women participate in elections, 1959 — 122

3.9. Korean women celebrate International Women's Day, 1959 — 123

4.1. Covers of *Chosŏn Nyŏsŏng* from the 1950s to early 1960s — 134

4.2. Cartoon about changing roles of men, 1959 — 143

4.3. Comic strip criticizing the preoccupation with quantity, 1959 — 152

4.4. Emblem of KDWU first used at the 1965 Third Congress — 157

5.1. National Dance Theater member Pak Kyŏng-suk in dance costume, 1959 — 178

5.2. Choe Seung-hui dressed in the role of Kye Wŏlhyang, 1961 — 180

5.3. Choe Seung-hui preparing dancers for *Kye Wŏlhyang*, 1961 — 181

5.4. Choe Seung-hui at the 1949 Asia Women's Conference — 183

6.1. Painting of Kim Jong Suk defending Kim Il Sung, 1974 — 195

6.2. Roving film car in Chagang Province, 1954 — 205

6.3. Women being organized into militias, 1967 — 216

TABLES

1.1. "Seek those who profit from war and you will find the war-mongers," 1948 — 34

4.1. Wages according to industrial sectors, 1955 — 141

4.2. Number of workers by industrial sector, 2008 — 153

4.3. Demographics of women at the KDWU Third Congress, 1965 — 162

Abbreviations

AAPSO	Afro-Asian Peoples' Solidarity Organization
ACWF	All-China Democratic Women's Federation (All-China Women's Federation from 1957)
AWP	American Women for Peace
CAW	Congress of American Women
CCP	Chinese Communist Party
CEDAW	Convention on the Elimination of All Forms of Discrimination against Women
CSW	Commission on the Status of Women
DPRK	Democratic People's Republic of Korea (North Korea)
Fudanren	Federation of Japanese Women's Organizations
HUAC	House Un-American Activities Committee
KCP	Korean Communist Party
KDWU	Korean Democratic Women's Union
KNPC	Korean National Peace Committee
KUTV	Communist University of the Toilers of the East
KWP	Korean Workers Party
NAW	National Assembly of Women (UK)
NGO	nongovernmental organization
OSPAAL	Organization of Solidarity with the People of Asia, Africa and Latin America
PRC	People's Republic of China
ROC	Republic of China (Taiwan)
ROK	Republic of Korea (South Korea)
SPA	Supreme People's Assembly
SRT	social reproduction theory
UNCURK	United Nations Commission for the Unification and Rehabilitation of Korea
WAF	Women's Anti-Fascist Front of Yugoslavia
WFYS	World Festival of Youth and Students
WIDF	Women's International Democratic Federation
WILPF	Women's International League for Peace and Freedom
WPC	World Peace Council
YWCA	Young Women's Christian Association

Organizations and Personalities

Women's International Democratic Federation (WIDF)

President (1945–1967)

Eugénie Cotton (1880–1967), president, Union of French Women

Vice Presidents (circa 1953)

Nina Popova, president, Antifascist Committee of Soviet Women
Dolores Ibarruri, president, Union of Spanish Women
Cai Chang, president, All-China Democratic Women's Federation
Céza Nabaraoui, Egyptian Women's Union
Rita Montagnana, founder, Union of Italian Women
Andrea Andreen, president, Swedish Women's Organization
Monica Felton, president, National Assembly of Women, UK
Lilly Waechter, secretariat, Democratic Union of German Women
Erzsébet Andics, president, National Peace Committee, Hungary
Funmilayo Ransome-Kuti, president, Union of Nigerian Women

Chronology of Events Covered in the Book

December 1945: WIDF Founding World Congress of Women, Paris
December 1948: WIDF Second Congress, Budapest
April 1949: World Peace Congress, Paris and Prague
December 1949: Asia Women's Conference, Beijing
November 1950: World Peace Congress, Warsaw; formation of World Peace Council
May 1951: WIDF Commission to Korea
October 1952: Asia Pacific Peace Conference, Beijing
December 1952: People's Congress for Peace, Vienna
July 1953: WIDF Third Congress, Copenhagen
July 1955: World Congress of Mothers, Lausanne. Formation of International Mothers' Committee: Andrea Andreen, president; Dora Russell, secretary
May–August 1958: Women's Peace Caravan across Europe
December 1957–January 1958: Afro-Asian Peoples' Solidarity Conference, Cairo
June 1958: WIDF Fourth Congress, Vienna
August 1958: Afro-Asian Film Festival, Tashkent
October 1958: Afro-Asian Writers' Conference, Tashkent
January 1961: Afro-Asian Women's Conference, Cairo
June 1963: WIDF Fifth Congress, Moscow
January 1966: Tricontinental Conference, Havana
February 1966: WIDF Commission to Vietnam
June 1969: WIDF Sixth Congress, Helsinki
June–July 1975: UN World Conference on Women, Mexico City
October 1975: WIDF Seventh Congress, East Berlin

Korean Democratic Women's Union (KDWU)

President (1945–1965)

Pak Chŏng-ae (1907–?), Supreme People's Assembly (1946–1960s?); KWP secretary (1952); KWP vice chair (1953)

Vice Presidents (circa 1950s)

Yu Yŏng-jun (1890–1972), former chair of (South) Korean Women's League; SPA (1948–1950s)

Chŏng Ch'il-sŏng (1897–1958), former vice chair of (South) Korean Women's League; SPA (1948–1950s)

Kim Yŏng-su

Kim Ok-sun

Ch'oe Kŭm-ja

Other Korean Women Leaders

Hŏ Chŏng-suk (1902–1991), minister of culture and propaganda (1948–1957); minister of justice (1957–1959); chief justice (1959); vice chair of SPA (1972); delegation chair to UN World Conference on Women (1975)

Choe Seung-hui (1911–1969), founder of Choe Seung-hui Dance Institute (1946); chair of Korean Dancers Union (1946–1969); president of the National Dance Theater (1946); SPA (1946–1950s); participation in the World Festival of Youth and Students (1947–1957)

Chronology of Events Covered in the Book

November 1945: KDWU Founding Congress
March 1949: Korean National Peace Committee Founding Congress
August 1954: KDWU Second Congress
March–April 1959: National Conference of Women Socialist Builders
November 1961: National Mothers Congress
September 1965: KDWU Third Congress
October 1966: National Congress of Child Care Workers

Note on Terms, Transliteration, and Translation

I use the rather archaic "First," "Second," and "Third World" to refer to the geopolitical divisions during the Cold War. With the so-called end of the Cold War, the Second World has all but disappeared, with the world now divided into the "developed" Global North and the "developing" Global South. Although this latter framing includes critique of inequities in the global capitalist system, conventional uses in developmental discourse tend to depoliticize the relationship between the two poles, eliding the long and continuing history of (neo)colonialisms that undergirds the teleology of "globalization" and "development."[1] Rather, I have opted to use the categories from the Cold War, demonstrating how the world was viewed at the time. Divided between the communist East as a challenger to the capitalist West, the genesis of the Third World was explicitly a political project to unite the marginalized in this bipolar world, harking back to the rise of the Third Estate during the French Revolution. These categories were imprecise and slippery, as countries like Korea moved across different worlds—South Korea moving from the Third World to the First, among the top capitalist economies today, and North Korea moving between the Second and Third Worlds. Although the socialist bloc, including North Korea, rarely if ever used "Third World," preferring instead to identify with the "anti-imperialist" and "revolutionary" forces, the tripartite division became a salient method of theorizing world alignments especially after the Sino-Soviet split, as discussed in more detail in chapter 3.

Communism, socialism, and "the left" are likewise fluid and variable terms. While committed followers and theorists may debate the differences associated with these labels, and state socialist countries themselves were often embroiled in political struggles using these categories to mark differences in the "stages" of history, strategies, and loyalties, these terms were often used interchangeably during the Cold War, and the book follows this convention. I use "state socialism" to refer to the economic and sociopolitical systems put in place by countries in the socialist bloc to differentiate it from "socialism" as a set of ideas.

My usage of "feminism" also requires explanation. While women from state socialist countries often disavowed feminism as a "bourgeois deviation" that prioritized gender issues at the expense of class solidarity, I have opted (admittedly with some unease) to include the arguments and activities of socialist and communist women, including Korean women, under the umbrella of various forms of feminisms, to show both the continuity and the disconnect in the long history of feminisms.[2] As the pioneer historian of the WIDF Francisca de Haan argues, the exclusion of socialist women from the history of the international women's movement has resulted in a lopsided history that privileges the West and liberal feminists as principal actors in the international women's movement, perpetuating the "wave" metaphor of women's history.[3] In order to underscore the significance of socialist and communist women's history in the development of feminist theories and praxes today, I rely on frameworks such as Cold War feminism, communist feminism, and state feminism that show connections among women in their shared commitment to women's liberation, no matter with which world or bloc they were associated. Nonetheless, I also acknowledge that feminism need not be the privileged term by which women's liberation or a pro-women agenda has to be couched, and therefore have tried to distinguish the use of "feminism" in my own analyses while respecting contemporary women's own discourse and framing in their arguments.

I have used the McCune-Reischauer system for the romanization of Korean names and terms, except in quoting original Korean publications in the English language and in cases where the spelling has become common usage, as in "Pyongyang" or "Seoul." I have kept the last name first in referring to Korean historical figures in the text and Korean authors in the footnotes, as is the standard practice in Korean, unless they have their own romanized names. For the romanization of foreign terms other than Korean, I have duplicated the system in the source consulted.

The two Koreas were officially named the Democratic People's Republic of Korea (DPRK) in the north and the Republic of Korea (ROK) in the south with the foundation of separate states in 1948, but following convention, I refer to them in shorthand as "North Korea" or "the North," and "South Korea" or "the South," beginning with the division in 1945 into the present. As the book is focused on the North, I use "Korea" to refer to the DPRK in the rest of the book, unless a clear distinction between the North and South is required.

All translations are mine unless otherwise indicated.

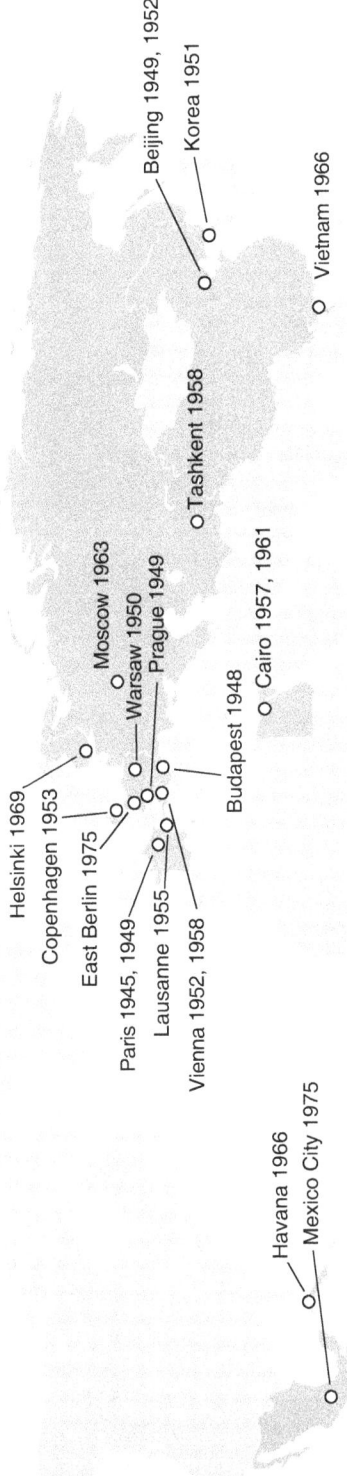

FIGURE 0.1. World map circa 1959, indicating international gatherings covered in the book. Adapted from © Sémhur / Wikimedia Commons / CC-BY-SA-3.0.

FIGURE 0.2. KDWU president Pak Chŏng-ae (*standing against table, center*) convenes the WIDF Commission meeting to discuss its report. *International Women's Delegation in Korea* (Moscow: TsSDF, 1951).

Introduction
DECOLONIAL GENEALOGIES

> Corpses and remains of bodies in mass graves are an ugly sight—
> and an unreal one. These atrocities have been committed less than
> six months ago, but the open graves cannot be actualized for you.
> I wished that I could turn on my heels, walk away and shoot the sight
> out of my mind—because I do not know what to do with it. I do not
> know what to think about it.
>
> Kate Fleron, during the Korean War, 1951

Camera pans a pummeled landscape—desertlike and desolate—but the occasional tree standing solitary amid the crumbling blocks of bombed-out buildings is a testament to an ongoing war. A motley crew of women are led around by locals walking through debris, at times stopping to talk to women and children with tears streaming down their faces. Some stare blankly in shock at the camera, while others are wracked in grief as they clutch the visitors, unable to speak their language. In one scene, as the visitors emerge in white surgical masks from what appears to be a dugout shelter, they are visibly shaken, blood drained from their faces, as the next scene of a mass grave dug open to reveal rows of decaying bodies discloses the shelter to be the site of gruesome killings. The eerie silence of the footage, with only a humming static interrupted by the regular clicks of the film reel looping around is all the more deafening against the vivid remnants of bombings and resounding devastation. How did this group of foreign women end up in the middle of the Korean War? And why is it that they are barely mentioned in any histories of one of the most destructive wars of the twentieth century?

The footage comes from a 1951 archival film stored at the Russian State Documentary Film and Photo Archive on the outskirts of Moscow, at Krasnogorsk.[1] The catalog attributes the film to the Central Studio of Documentary Films (TsSDF) shot by Korean camera operators, but has no further details. Composed of four separate reels for a total length of just over thirty minutes in black and white, the footage was not available for viewing during my May 2018 visit to Krasnogorsk, the archivist told me, because it was on nitrate film, highly combustible and carefully stored in a temperature-controlled building. The film would need to be retrieved and digitally reproduced for viewing, and I would have to pay a fee for this service and wait. The archive reportedly contains approximately fifty-two thousand nitrate films, of which all but 1 percent had been duplicated as of 2008. This one happened to fall in that 1 percent. Why had this particular film gone unnoticed for almost seventy years?

It has become commonplace to understand such erasures as another example of women being written out of history, in this case doubly forgotten as part of a largely unknown Korean War (1950–1953), but there are cascading erasures in this history, as if multiple layers of paint upon paint have to be stripped off in order to see the layer beneath. It would be convenient to strip off all the layers at once, but each layer represents moments in time, and this book proceeds with that metaphor in mind, to appreciate each layer for what it reveals, but also for what was written over, so that our view is not just a long stare into the past but a furtive look with intermittent shifts in focus. The book moves between a microscopic view of specific personalities and events in detail and a telescopic view of the larger context within which these figures moved, for a history of Korea in the global Cold War orbiting around women as key players. Sometimes the layers of paint are not so easy to peel off, and the transitions between layers seem schematic and abrupt. Too often, the personalities and events seem blurry or hard to make out for lack of more detail. My own limitations failed to track every source and draw tighter connections, but the writing of this book raised challenging questions about what it means to write history in the absence of archives and ethnographic sites.

How *do* you write a history without adequate sources, field notes, or access to the very places and peoples whose history should be known and yet is always elusive? Such questions of course are not new.[2] Pride of place given to the written record tends to elide aspects of life that exceed linguistic or other forms of representation—aspects macabre on one extreme, or the everyday relationships and routines of daily life on the other that are an integral part of human lives and yet rarely the stuff of history. Moreover, care work is considered "women's work" through a gendered division of labor, and therefore regarded as somehow less important than the actions of the "movers and shakers" of the world who populate the vast majority of archives. History is too often the story of "victors," and the triumphant narrative about the "end" of the Cold War relegates the histories on the "other side" of that conflict as simply prelude. I open this introduction with Kate Fleron's devastating confrontation with a reality she was not prepared to see, to signal the process by which women like her would come to work in solidarity with Korean women. Despite the impulse to turn away, not knowing "what to do," such examples of transnational solidarities were political struggles to enact a new paradigm of women's liberation.

This book is an attempt to excavate that history to find Korean women in unexpected places. They were part of an international movement of women that combined the cause of women's liberation with that of world peace. In the process, they insisted that family and domestic issues must be part of both national and international debates, pointing out how race, nationality, sex, and class intersect to form systems of colonial and capitalist exploitation. Their intersectional view claimed the personal as the political decades before feminists of the West, with whom such calls have come to be associated. In that sense, the history covered in this book is an archaeology of forgotten movements and ideas that became the foundations for those that would come later. Korean women were part of a global circulation of iconic militant women, a communist archetype as popular as, even if different from, the provocative "modern girl." In the process, Korean women were shaped by, while also shaping, the history of women's liberation and global movements, and yet this mutual contribution is rarely recognized in the historiography, whether produced in Korea or elsewhere, because the worlds of women are often left out, and feminist histories have privileged the experiences of women in the West.[3] This book defies that convention to offer a completely different lineage of the global women's movement to center the "East" as expressly a political, rather than a geographic, category.

Writing in 1960 at the cusp of so-called second-wave feminism but drawing a genealogy different from that of the liberal Western historiography of the women's movement, Korean columnist Yu Ho-jun traced the Korean women's liberation movement to the 1930s national liberation struggles, arguing that Korean women partisans were not waging an isolated struggle but were part of the global women's movement, fighting alongside Soviet and Chinese women.[4] One such personality who would go on to lead the women's movement for two decades between 1945 and 1965 was Pak Chŏng-ae (1907–?).[5]

Despite becoming one of the highest-ranking figures in the North Korean government, arguably with more international renown at the time than even the founding leader himself, there are no known biographies or substantive treatments of her life in Korean historiography, nor has she received much scholarly attention in or out of Korea. In light of the way women are given short shrift in historical research, the gendered bias partly explains her absence, but the continued division and Cold War on the Korean peninsula add to the challenge of writing about a life with limited traces. The division of Korea in 1945 by the Allied powers that was meant to be temporary, to accept the surrender from Japan—with the Soviet Union in charge north of the thirty-eighth parallel and the United States in the south—has outlasted the seventy-year history of the Soviet Union and the Cold War itself. As a result, there is as yet no access to North Korean archives, with the exception of the so-called North Korean Captured Documents from the Korean War, let alone the possibility to do field research in the country for most outsiders.[6]

Born in 1907, on the eve of Japanese colonization of Korea (1910–1945), Pak came of political age as an underground labor organizer in the late 1920s and early 1930s, when out of sheer necessity, for her to remain undercover, no documentation could be preserved, and the only documentation—of dubious validity—of insurgent activities would be left by the colonial authorities.[7] Because of her involvement in underground communist movements, she is absent from any record of women's organizing.[8] She makes a brief appearance in newspaper articles published between September and October 1935, when she and a number of others were arrested by the Japanese colonial police during a crackdown on Korean communists.[9] Although newspaper reports indicate that she was not indicted and therefore released, there is no further record of her activities, except for a brief reference in a news article dated February 1936 to the formation of a women's organization in Harbin, China, that included someone named Pak Chŏng-ae—a common name.[10] It is difficult to know if this was the same person and whether Pak had found refuge in China, as many independence activists did until Korean liberation in 1945.

With these limits in mind, I start with a brief biography of Pak Chŏng-ae as an important yet under-recognized figure, whose career offers a window into the early lives of Korean communist women under colonial rule before they had a state to shape and call their own. Not only would she go on to become chair of the Korean Democratic Women's Union (KDWU, Chosŏn minju nyŏsŏng tongmaeng) for twenty years, from 1945 to 1965, but she would also be active in international campaigns for women's rights and world peace as part of the leadership of the Women's International Democratic Federation (hereafter WIDF, or the Federation, founded in December 1945) and the World Peace Council (WPC, founded in November 1950). Modeling other women's organizations formed in the "people's democracies" of the socialist bloc, the KDWU, founded on November 18, 1945, applied to join the WIDF the following year and was admitted with a unanimous vote by the executive committee meeting in Moscow on October 15, 1946.[11] While the KDWU already had 879,185 members at the time of its application to join the WIDF, membership had almost doubled three years later to 1,404,000, when it was actively organizing around the goals of the WIDF, gathering signatures to ban atomic weapons. As the first international women's organization formed after World War II, the Federation was organized by women who had actively resisted fascism during the war.[12] Based on their experiences, they expressly linked peace as the necessary condition for the advancement of women's and children's rights, and from the beginning, as an extension of their fight against fascism, they defied colonialism and imperialism.

The KDWU periodical *Chosŏn Nyŏsŏng* (Korean women) often carried news about WIDF activities and the struggles of women in other countries through translated articles from the WIDF magazine, *Women of the Whole World*, as well as *Soviet Woman* and *Women of China*. It was not uncommon for publications in fraternal countries to share materials. The February 1950 issue of *Chosŏn Nyŏsŏng*, for example, carried correspondence from Maria Ovsyannikova, the editor of *Soviet Woman*, requesting materials to include in her magazine.[13] An English-language edition of *Chosŏn Nyŏsŏng* was also published from 1964 to 1992 under the title *Women of Korea*.[14] Showcasing this internationalist stance and positioning Korean women within the genealogy of modern revolutions, from the French Revolution down to the Russian and Chinese Revolutions, the January 1947 cover of *Chosŏn Nyŏsŏng* featured women marching together with their respective national flags (see figure I.1).[15] A Korean woman in the foreground was represented by the flag used throughout the colonial period, today

FIGURE I.1.   Cover of *Chosŏn Nyŏsŏng*, January 1947

FIGURE I.2. Cover of Korean collection of documents from the WIDF Founding Congress, 1947

associated with South Korea, because this was before the founding of two separate states in 1948, when the North opted for a different flag. She was accompanied by women from the Soviet Union, China (Republican China, since this was before the founding of the People's Republic of China), and finally France. A similar design graced the cover of the Korean translation of documents from the WIDF Founding Congress (see figure I.2).

Relying on official publications—namely *Chosŏn Nyŏsŏng* and *Rodong Sinmun* (Workers newspaper), the organ of the ruling Korean Workers Party—supplemented by archival traces of Pak and the KDWU in the records of the international organizations in which she participated, I track the contours of Pak's life in this introduction to set the stage for the more detailed histories to come in the rest of the book. Although there is very little record of Pak during the Japanese occupation of Korea, I share examples of communist women's activities during the colonial era in the 1920s and 1930s as a way to situate Pak and her politics, before going on to show her prominence on the international stage. After reviewing Pak's record, I discuss potential methodological issues in using official publications and the availability of sources for research on North Korea in a comparative perspective, and finish with an overview of the chapters to come, with their major themes.

Anticolonial Roots of Korean Communism

Although there are no known personal records left of Pak's early years, a rough sketch of her background can be gleaned through secondary sources illustrating the situation for the majority of Koreans in the 1910s and 1920s. Pak was born on August 23, 1907, somewhere between North Hamgyŏng Province of Korea and the Vladivostok region of Russia, an area with shared borders between Korea, China, and Russia on Korea's northern frontier, facilitating relatively easy migration and receptivity to the influx of new ideas.[16] On the periphery of dynastic power based in Seoul, the region was less bound by Confucian rules of gender and status hierarchy prescribed by the Chosŏn dynasty (1392–1910), the last Korean dynasty before Japanese colonization. Mobile slash-and-burn farmers in the area radicalized to form "red peasant unions" (*chŏksaek nongmin chohap*), which proliferated in Hamgyŏng in the late 1920s and early 1930s.[17] Some estimate that half of the ten thousand political prisoners detained each year during the colonial era came from South Hamgyŏng Province, as the most active region in the organization of peasants and workers throughout the occupation; it would become a strong base for native communists in postliberation North Korea, incorporated en masse into local governments, especially after the Korean War.[18] Between 1928 and 1933, more than half of all arrests for radical peasant organizing came from the Hamgyŏng area, facilitated by the proximity to Kando in Manchuria (present-day Yanbian Korean Autonomous Prefecture in China), which was the center of anticolonial guerrilla forces under the command of Kim Il Sung, North Korea's founding leader.[19] It was in this milieu that Pak came of age.

The first official documentation on her comes from the archives of the Comintern (Communist International, 1919–1943), in which Pak Chŏng-ae is known as Vera Tsoi, of a Soviet Korean peasant family. According to historian Andrei Lankov's reading of the biographical data collected in 1946 by the Soviet occupation forces in Korea, Pak "graduated from a teachers' 'tehnikum' (sort of junior college) in Voroshilov (now Ussuriisk) in the Soviet Far East and went to Moscow to continue her education," where she met Kim Yong-bŏm, another communist, who would become first secretary in the Korean Workers Party after liberation in 1945.[20] Although her own file (if there is one) is yet to be found, Kim's Comintern file indicates that Pak was a Komsomol (Communist youth league) member from 1924 and a Bolshevik Party member from 1931, fluent in both Russian and literary Korean, employed at a highly classified warplanes factory named Moscow Plant No. 39.[21] They returned to Korea in 1932 in disguise as a couple and later married.

This short biography already challenges the simplistic way in which nuanced political differences among Korean figures are often attributed to "factional strife" between the domestic, Soviet, Chinese (Yan'an), and Manchurian factions. Pak may fit into at least three, if not all four groups, if news about Harbin is in reference to her. She had Soviet Comintern experience, domestic labor organizing experience, and ultimately demonstrated a strong affinity to Kim Il Sung and his so-called Manchurian faction. As historian Sŏ Tong-man points out, factions reflected substantive differences in background and attendant political strategies, but could be fluid and varied rather than being rigid allegiances devoid of politics.[22] Different factions could overlap and coexist, especially for the Soviet and Chinese groups with no clear center of leadership. Moreover, while domestic communists were divided into multiple sub-sects, the Manchurian faction had a clear advantage, united around Kim Il Sung with a strong sense of cohesion and loyalty based on their shared guerrilla experience. Pak Chŏng-ae's multiple connections from the 1930s into postliberation Korea challenge the conventional way in which such women have been depicted as tools, serving the interest of more powerful male leaders, rather than as leaders in their own right.[23]

Each of the nodes to emerge from her biography begs us to ask what propelled her there, if not for her own motivations, even as these are undoubtedly shaped by the historical and material conditions beyond any one person's control. After mass protests erupted in Korea against Japanese colonial rule in the 1919 March First Independence Movement, colonial authorities implemented the so-called "cultural rule" to replace "military rule," by which more freedoms of the press and association were granted for Korean-language publications and organizations. Even so, signs of greater political repression were evident in the passage of the 1925 Peace Preservation Law that was used to crack down on political dissent and those considered ideologically suspect. The situation worsened in the 1930s with Japan's renewed militarization and invasion of Manchuria in 1931. As policies for total war mobilization gradually replaced "cultural rule," political repression of leftist movements increased, resulting in the dissolution of the Korean Communist Party (KCP) by 1928, just three years after its founding. Under these circumstances, it would have been prudent to seek training in Soviet Russia, especially if attracted by communism.

Sometime in the late 1920s to the early 1930s then, Pak was in Moscow, possibly at one of the Comintern schools. Although she is not listed among those at the Communist University of the Toilers of the East (Kommunisticheskii Universitet Trudiashchikhsia Vostoka, or KUTV), the school was a major hub of training for communist organizers from colonized regions, attracting notable revolutionary leaders such as Ho Chi Minh, M. N. Roy, and Deng Xiaoping, as well as Pak's soon-to-be partner Kim Yong-bŏm.[24] The "East" in this case was not simply a geographic designation, but referred to those under colonial oppression with whom the Bolsheviks identified in their anticolonial stance since the October Revolution.[25] As historian Masha Kirasirova puts it, "This doubled domestic and foreign quality of the Soviet category 'East' marked a stark contrast with contemporary European approaches to the concept, often as something essential, unchangeable, and fundamentally 'other.'"[26] There were certainly other examples of East-West exchanges in the interwar period, but these were often apolitical associations that used the language of friendship to paper over racial and political differences in the name of "cross-cultural harmony."[27] The peace platform of the International Federation of University Women, founded in 1919, for example, used the language of "neutrality" and "objectivity" to emphasize science and education, claiming that "the right kind of peace was not political peace."[28] This disavowal of any political aim was used to justify the imperialist world order that withheld self-determination from the Third World, privileging public diplomacy through professional networks and nation-state actors. While there is no denying that racism and orientalism existed alongside Soviet ideals to the contrary, at the Comintern schools, "racial problems almost always involved foreign whites, especially Americans, Canadians, and Britons, who not infrequently verbally abused black students and sometimes lashed out at them physically."[29] In this context, the foremost African American intellectual and activist of his time, W. E. B. Du Bois, referred to the "Rising East" as a global movement by the "darker races of the world" against white supremacy.[30]

To be sure, the formation of the Soviet Union as a multiethnic state did not preclude violence. Among the many brutalities against ethnic minorities during Stalin's Great Purge of 1936–1938, countless Korean communist cadres were arrested as Japanese spies and shot, while hundreds of thousands of Soviet Koreans were deported to Central Asia.[31] However, any "backwardness" was attributed to sociohistorical circumstances rather than innate racial or biological traits, in contrast to fascist race theories that relied on biological determinism and eugenics.[32] Likewise, advocating a "proto-constructivist" approach to the emerging concept of ethnic-nation (*minjok*) as a historically produced phenomenon of capitalist modernity, colonial-era Marxists in Korea acted as an important counterweight to the racialized nativism among conservative nationalists of the 1920s and 1930s.[33]

Formed by the Comintern in April 1921 for the purposes of providing communist education to those in the colonial and semicolonial nations, including oppressed minorities, the KUTV admitted its first large cohort of Korean students in 1924–25, with the formation of the KCP in April 1925.[34] KUTV students, such as Kim Tan-ya and O Ki-sŏp, were among the key communist organizers in Korea, and those recruited to train at KUTV would join later efforts to revive the party after the party's demise in 1928. Ironically, the decision to admit the KCP into the Comintern, along with parties in Cuba, New Zealand, Paraguay, Colombia, Ecuador, and the Irish Workers League, came belatedly in September 1928.[35] Later that year in December, the Comintern issued what came to be known as the December Theses, which directed the Korean communists to focus on organizing the large number of peasants alongside workers, rather than intellectuals and students. The Comintern was once again a step behind, however, as this was "mostly a restatement of what was already in progress" at the initiative of the Korean organizers based on their local experience.[36]

Although it is difficult to confirm her precise whereabouts while in Moscow, Pak returned to Korea roughly in the early 1930s to begin organizing peasants and workers for the next few years, until her 1935 capture by the colonial police. With the dissolution of the KCP in 1928 and continued efforts to revive the party thwarted by the arrests of its leaders, much of the organizing consisted of decentralized regional activities that were widespread underground, albeit sporadic and short-lived.[37] Pak was among a group of thirty or so communists with experience studying in Moscow, who attempted to organize workers into "red labor unions" (*chŏksaek nodong chohap*) in northern Korea. This is where the majority of factories were based, and in the aftermath of the 1931 Japanese invasion of Manchuria, Pyongyang emerged as an important center of armor manufacturing.[38] Labor disputes, as well as peasant protests, rose significantly in the region throughout the 1930s.

An oft-cited example in Korean publications of such history of women's labor organizing comes from Pyongyang, already an active site of labor organizing in the 1920s. Unlike in the capital Seoul, where despite the early inception of socialist ideas, intellectuals often led the labor movement, Pyongyang's movement was led by local labor organizers with anarchist and autonomous cooperative tendencies, without relying on ideologically inclined party organizations.[39] As a result, despite the smaller number of workers compared to Seoul, there were more labor unions organized in Pyongyang supported by both nationalists and socialists, as the city became the most active center of the labor movement, with a large number of general strikes and solidarity strikes across different factories.⁴⁰ For example, on May 29, 1931, Kang Chu-ryong, a rubber factory worker, began a strike against wage cuts, with forty-eight other women, on behalf of the twenty-three hundred rubber-factory workers in Pyongyang.⁴¹ The production of rubber shoes worn by Koreans had increased rapidly in the 1920s owing to lowered barriers for Korean-owned businesses after the shift in colonial policy toward "cultural rule." Facilitated by low capital investments and women's labor that cost only half of men's wages, the nascent industry responded to the Great Depression by firing workers and cutting wages. However, Pyongyang had grown to become a major hub of labor organizing throughout the 1920s, and in August 1930, the eighteen hundred workers—of whom two-thirds were women—from the ten rubber factories in Pyongyang waged a general strike against wage cuts, demanding workers' rights to unionization, collective bargaining, and benefits such as paid maternity leave and nursing breaks. When the general strike failed in 1930 and factory owners announced a second wage cut in 1931, the forty-nine women workers at the P'yŏngwŏn Rubber Factory went on strike and were immediately fired, compelling Kang Chu-ryong to climb on the roof of the Ŭlmil Pavilion, a historic structure in Pyongyang, to publicize the plight of the workers. Garnering wide public attention, she continued her protest after her arrest with a hunger strike in prison. Although released on bail because of her weakened state, she died in August that same year at only thirty-two years of age, lionized in Korean historiography as a model labor organizer.⁴²

There are no comparable records of Pak's labor organizing, and it is possible that she survived the harshest years by taking refuge in China from 1936 until Korean liberation in 1945. Prison conditions in colonial Korea were intolerable, leading to many premature deaths like Kang's, while those fortunate enough to avoid imprisonment often joined the ranks of turncoats, who would later come under scrutiny as traitors and collaborators. Especially after the invasion of China in 1937, Japanese authorities were eager to "convert" (*chŏnhyang*) the ideologically suspect through conciliation and intimidation tactics, resulting in large defections from across the political spectrum, ranging from bourgeois nationalists to leftist partisans. In the decade of Pak's absence from public records, Koreans were fully integrated into the Japanese imperial war effort through "imperialization" (*hwangminhwa*) policies designed to root out Korean identity, including the elimination of Korean-language education, coercion to change Korean names into Japanese, and forced worship of the Japanese emperor at Shinto shrines. When Japan's defeat in the Asia Pacific War brought this whole system to a grinding halt, Pak would join the hundreds of thousands returning from exile and the tens of thousands of political prisoners released from their cells with the liberation of Korea on August 15, 1945.

Korean Women around the World

Resurfacing into the limelight upon the end of colonial rule, Pak was immediately swept up in efforts to organize a national Korean government under communist leadership. She became the highest-profile communist woman in Korea to take up multiple positions, first as the only woman among the seventeen Politburo members of the northern branch of the Korean Communist Party newly formed in October 1945 (which merged with the New People's Party in August 1946 to form the Korean Workers Party), and as the chair of the (North) Korean Democratic Women's Union (Pukchosŏn minju nyŏsŏng tongmaeng) upon its founding in November 1945. She was subsequently elected to the Supreme People's Assembly (SPA) in 1946, appointed party secretary in 1952 and vice-chair in 1953, joining a five-member Politburo alongside Kim Il Sung as the only female member of the leadership circle.[43] Hŏ Chŏng-suk (1902–1991) was the only other woman to achieve a comparable status, elected to the SPA along with Pak in 1946 and appointed minister of culture in 1948, serving in that capacity until her appointment as minister of justice in 1957; she became chief justice of the Supreme Court in 1959 and vice-chair of the SPA in 1972.[44]

Centered in areas that had a strong history of red labor unions and red peasant unions, the cities of Pyongyang, Hamhŭng, and Hŭngnam again became the site of active organizing after liberation through people's committees, leftist parties, and labor unions, driven by the release of tens of thousands of political prisoners with organizing experience.[45] This was the basis for a genuine social revolution in the North between 1945 and 1948 that lent legitimacy to the founding of the Democratic People's Republic of Korea in September 1948, one month after the founding of the Republic of Korea in the South through separate UN-administered elections.[46] This history of homegrown anticolonial revolution also explains North Korea's longevity against all odds, similar to revolutions in Cuba, China, and Vietnam, and unlike Eastern Europe. As with other state socialist countries, various sectors of Korean society were organized and mobilized through social organizations that were called "transmission belts," connecting the ruling party to the masses. Among them, women were the first to organize, with the founding of the KDWU on November 18, 1945, under the leadership of Pak Chŏng-ae as chair, holding its first national congress in May 1946 with some eight hundred thousand members and branches in twelve cities, eighty-nine counties, and 616 townships.[47] Open to women from the age of eighteen, when they reached legal adulthood, to the age of retirement at sixty-one, the organization had doubled to 1.5 million members by the end of 1947, of whom 73 percent were peasants, making literacy and educational projects of paramount importance in the early years of its work.

In recognition of Pak's long-standing reputation as a leader in the movement, she was also elected honorary chair in absentia of the first umbrella women's organization formed in the South.[48] Organizers, religious leaders, professionals, and educators active in the women's movement since the colonial period convened a congress of women's groups with the participation of five hundred representatives from 194 organizations in the presence of several thousand observers and guests in December 1945, forming the Korean Women's League (Chosŏn punyŏ ch'ong tongmaeng, hereafter the League), one month after the formation of the KDWU in the North.[49] They advocated women's liberation by overthrowing "feudal remnants" such as polygamy and superstition, and ensuring literacy and economic independence for women. Along with Pak, the group elected Eugénie Cotton, Eleanor Roosevelt, and Soong Ching-ling among its honorary chairs to signal its international outlook, and many of the newly elected leadership traced their activism back to the women's movement and organizations from the colonial era. Now in their forties and fifties, they were poised to become leaders in liberated Korea—Yu Yŏng-jun (1890–1972) was elected chair, and Chŏng Ch'il-sŏng (1897–1958) was elected vice-chair, both of whom would choose to move to the North between 1947 and 1948 because of increasing political repression in the US-occupied South. Both women had experience studying abroad in China and Japan and were founding members of the center-left united front women's organization Kŭnuhoe (Rose of Sharon Friendship Association) in the 1920s, and Yu would go on to represent the South at the WIDF Second Congress in 1948.[50]

At its height, the League had organized 150 branches in cities and provinces down to the villages, counting some eight hundred thousand members in the South.[51] As in the North, the League focused its activities in rural areas, still making up the vast majority of the population, addressing the educational needs of women living in the countryside, 80 to 90 percent of whom were estimated to be illiterate. Its platform tied Korean women's political, economic, and social liberation to the establishment of a progressive democratic country, promoting Korean women to act in concert with the international community for world peace. Demands included women's right to vote; women's economic autonomy by guaranteeing equal wages, paid maternity leave, and social services such as child-care facilities, birthing centers, public canteens and laundries; equal educational opportunities; and abolition of feudal marriage practices such as the sale of brides and arranged child marriage.

These were precisely the measures taken through two pieces of legislation passed one month apart in 1946 in the North—the Labor Law in June and the Law of Equal Rights for Men and Women (hereafter Equal Rights Law, but also known as the Gender Equality Law) in July.[52] In addition to the basic clauses for an eight-hour workday, paid vacations, equal pay for equal work, and improvements in working conditions including health insurance, the Labor Law provided paid maternity leave for thirty-five days before and forty-two days after delivery; lighter work for pregnant women in their third trimester; and nursing breaks for thirty minutes twice a day for women with children under a year old. It also prohibited pregnant and nursing women from working overtime at night. The Equal Rights Law guaranteed economic, cultural, social, and political rights, including the right to vote and be elected to office, property rights, and rights to education, freedom of marriage and divorce, and child support in case of divorce. It voided all previous laws pertaining to women, outlawing polygamy, prostitution, and child marriage. With no comparable reforms in the South and a crackdown on leftists after mass uprisings against US occupation forces in the fall of 1946, the League was forced underground and renamed the South Korean Democratic Women's Union (Namchosŏn minju yŏsŏng tongmaeng) in February 1947, merging with its northern counterpart. The July 1947 issue of *Chosŏn Nyŏsŏng* on the one-year anniversary of the Equal Rights Law (see front cover) identified northern women as leaders of the women's movement—a heroic woman in traditional Korean dress (her hairstyle marking her as a wife and mother) stands atop a miniature globe on the northern half of the Korean peninsula, holding a large red and white flag fluttering behind her inscribed with the Korean acronym for KDWU, or *yŏmaeng*, as she leads throngs of women behind her to liberate the South still wrapped in chains.

While Pak left very little writing of her own, her presence was ubiquitous throughout North Korean publications from 1945 to 1965. Known internationally as Pak Den Ai, following the Russian Cyrillic transliteration of her Korean name, she also appears in the publications of the WIDF. Not only were her speeches from women's events and celebrations of March 8 International Women's Day prominently published in the party newspaper, but she was also the head of delegations to the Soviet Union, Vietnam, Hungary, East Germany, and other fraternal countries of the socialist bloc throughout this period. She, along with Hŏ Chŏng-suk, invited the extraordinary fact-finding women's commission that investigated war crimes committed during the Korean War, as detailed in the next chapter. Her international reputation preceded her; women's commission member Monica Felton described her as "one of the most celebrated personalities not only of North Korea, but of the whole Far East. Her life had been devoted to the struggle for Korean independence, and she had spent many years in Japanese prison camps, enduring like many other Koreans, the most appalling tortures."[53] In the domestic setting, she was often the only woman at the head dais presiding over meetings, sitting next to Kim Il Sung, and her extended speeches published in the party paper delivered major policy pronouncements at this time.[54]

Pak disappears, however, from the published record after 1965, with the possibility that she may have been purged in 1967.[55] Already in 1956, political space for dissenting views had begun to shrink when attempts to critique Kim Il Sung's cult of personality in the aftermath of the 1956 Soviet de-Stalinization were crushed.[56] The effects reverberated throughout society, including the women's movement. One of the leading leftist writers of the colonial era and among the editorial staff of *Chosŏn Nyŏsŏng*, Im Sun-dŭk (1915–?) was no longer listed in the publication as of August 1957, even as Pak celebrated her fiftieth birthday on August 23 that same year with the conferral of the First Order of the National Flag, the highest honor bestowed on its citizens by the Korean state.[57] Beginning in June 1960, the names of the editorial staff were left out altogether from its pages. Meanwhile, Pak was reelected to the SPA on August 27, 1957—one among twenty-seven women elected to the highest governing body, made up of 215 deputies—along with other women leaders, including Yu Yŏng-jun, Chŏng Ch'il-sŏng, Hŏ Chŏng-suk, and Choe Seung-hui.[58] By the following election in 1962, however, women originally from the South who had settled in the North, such as Chŏng Ch'il-sŏng, Chŏng Chong-myŏng, Choe Seung-hui, and Hŏ Chŏng-suk, were no longer members of the SPA (although Hŏ would come back in the 1970s).[59] Although Pak was still listed as a member of the SPA, she was identified only as the minister of agriculture rather than the chair of the KDWU. Without a published obituary, it is difficult to find an exact date of Pak's death, but a memoir smuggled out of the North in 1996 claimed that she was "demoted" from her position sometime in the late 1960s to the position of minister of commerce, with subsequent rumors that she became a factory manager in the outskirts of the city in North P'yŏng'an Province.[60] Her official grave at the Revolutionary Martyrs Cemetery just outside Pyongyang shows that she was laid to rest alongside her husband, who died in 1947, but there are no dates for her on the tombstone.[61]

Because of such tragic ends and afterlives of communist women, they are often figured as victims or pawns subjected to unilateral state manipulation. Even as scholars critique previous research on Korea as a "history without people" centered on the leadership that relegates questions about women and gender to mere top-down policy, there is little discussion about how to overcome limitations in published sources that privilege the official line.[62] Without the international and transnational contexts in which women moved, their strategies, discourses, and identities seem isolated and one-dimensional. As a result, even as scholars cast a critical eye on conventional arguments centered on Confucianism and patriarchy as ahistorical, culturally and biologically deterministic explanations for women's status in Korea, histories of Korean women continue to be portrayed as a top-down process of "granting liberation" from above, quoting official sources that render women as beneficiaries (and thereby victims) of state policy.[63] This book not only offers a decolonial genealogy, different from that of Western historiography of the global women's movement, but also departs from Korean historiographies of the women's movement, either as influenced by Western feminists in the South, or as led by Kim Il Sung and his family in the North.

In her study of 1950s East Germany, historian Donna Harsch notes the centrality of domestic concerns and the role of women in making policy demands, arguing that it was the family-oriented women whose expectations led to the domestication of state socialism toward "a welfare policy with a maternalist core."[64] The crisis of reproduction required state attention to social issues such as consumption needs, marital conflict, and child care. Against feminist arguments that tend to view state socialist maternalism as yet further evidence of paternalism, Harsch sees it as "strategic negotiations."[65] Likewise, historian Wang Zheng has documented in China how women's deference to the benevolence of the party paying tribute to the male leadership was a form of strategy. Using a "hidden script" to couch their feminist agenda in acceptable discourses such as antifeudalism, Chinese women engaged in a "politics of concealment" to minimize their own role while giving credit to the "wise leadership" of the party precisely to achieve their own aims.[66] While scholars of China have the fortune to work with local archives and oral histories to uncover women's ingenuity, and scholars of Eastern Europe and the former Soviet Union have been able to use declassified documents, personal archives, and interviews of surviving women leaders, there are no comparably accessible sources for Korea.[67] The increasing number of North Korean refugees, the majority of them women, are a valuable source of information, but their experiences are limited to the more recent past and cannot adequately cover earlier periods of the Cold War, and scholars have raised methodological concerns regarding the use of such testimony.[68] Therefore, this book tracks Korean women's activities through their interactions in the international arena as they engaged in collective strategy to advocate on behalf of women.

It is true that Korea has had a long history of patriarchal practices and institutions going back hundreds of years, and Korean women in the international forums, like women in other state socialist countries, were "state actors" from a centralized one-party state undergirded by a vast and opaque security apparatus that precluded open dissent and limited independent civil society. The women's magazine and other official publications were state approved and uniformly devoid of any direct criticism of the leadership. Pak Chŏng-ae and Hŏ Chŏng-suk were state officials who invited and welcomed the 1951 international fact-finding commission as official state guests, with receptions given by Kim Il Sung and Pak Hŏn-yŏng (a South Korean communist leader purged after the war).[69] And yet we know that consumer goods and social benefits were often in short supply, travel was variously restricted, and women's roles were curtailed by the sexual division of labor, with women cast as caregivers. These are only the very basic limitations in women's lives that official publications reveal *despite* efforts to paint an optimistic picture, and, as the book shows, much more can be learned if they are read meticulously and persistently to trace changes across time in conjunction with international sources. The point is not to deny the challenges women faced, but to see how they navigated around obstacles to make gains despite these challenges. As historian Maria Bucur judiciously notes in her review of scholarship on women in state socialist Europe, it *mattered* that the communist states publicly staked their position in favor of gender equality, because "new horizons of expectation" were opened up by providing education and jobs for all women, who were not "passive pawns or beneficiaries of top-down policies."[70] Rather than wedded to liberal ideas of "freedom" grounded in individual autonomy and self-expression, communist women identified their liberation with the collective well-being of their families, their communities, and their nation, similar to Third World and postcolonial feminists.[71] In that sense, while individual women such as Pak do make up the story, this book is a history of women as a collective.

Women's Press

One major way by which the women's movement of the transnational left maintained ties across the world was through the pages of the women's press. The WIDF periodical *Women of the Whole World* began publication in 1951 in five languages—English, German, French, Russian, and Spanish—with an Arabic edition added in the 1960s.[72] While other similarly large international women's organizations had published bulletins and newsletters, none compares to the scope and reach of *Women of the Whole World*.[73] It tried to provide geographical coverage of women's issues in every continent, with debates about local problems, biographies of well-known women, histories of women's movements throughout the world, and topical articles on global politics as related to women's rights, children's welfare, and peace. The cultures section included introductions to films, fashion, and cuisine, with recipes from various countries and regions.

In designing the publication, the editorial board explicitly challenged mainstream women's magazines, which more often than not appealed to "glamour, romance, luxury," as a contributing writer from the United Kingdom sharply criticized in a passage worth quoting at length for its continued relevance:

> What is the approach of such magazines? What do they tell the women? First and foremost, they falsify life. The problems of women in Great

Publications

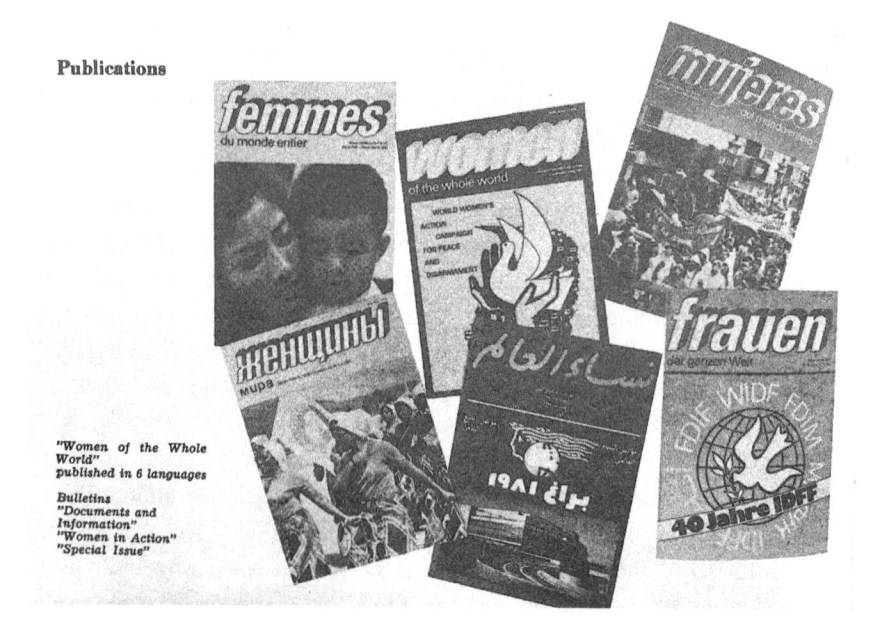

"*Women of the Whole World*"
published in 6 languages
Bulletins
"*Documents and Information*"
"*Women in Action*"
"*Special Issue*"

FIGURE I.3. Covers of *Women of the Whole World* (circa 1960s)

Britain today, the unremitting struggle to feed their families, with the cost of living continually rising, their anxiety about war, the difficulties of young couples without a home to live in—such problems are either ignored completely (as in the case of the women's desire for peace) or surrounded with sentimentality. Glamour, romance, luxury, "love"—these are the stock-in-trade of the women's magazine: How to make oneself beautiful (with tactful references to the cosmetics advertised in the same issue); how to be attractive to men; how to win a man's love; how to keep it when you have got it. Along with this line of approach go, inevitably, reactionary ideas about the status of women: all women want, or ought to want is a husband, home and children; equality and independence are a myth; women are not capable of being more than second-rate in any achievement outside the home; in the marriage relationship, man must be the master; women are emotional and not rational beings, because of their biological make-up. These magazines receive the support they do from the women because they supply vicariously (and in a cheap and falsified way) the colour, adventure and change which the women lack in real life. They provide a dream world into which the women can escape for an hour or so, and in so doing skillfully divert their minds from the possibility of solving their problems, and sap the confidence of the women in their own abilities and consequently, in their capacity to change things.[74]

To address such problems of the women's press, the WIDF called a meeting of editors of women's magazines between April 27 and 29, 1954, at its offices in Berlin. From the ninety-nine magazines of thirty-nine countries published or supported by organizations affiliated with the WIDF, thirty-five representatives from twenty-two countries took part in the meeting.[75] WIDF president Eugénie Cotton underscored the important educational role of the press to show how Indochina, Korea, and Europe are interdependent, so that what is going on beyond one's own borders "are not local problems" but "closely connected and the way in which they are solved can unleash a world war or guarantee peace to all," warning that "too many women still think it is not their business to bother about world events."[76] The editors at the meeting agreed on the need to reach a broad readership and hailed their "great victory" in creating magazines "for the first time in history, that know how to talk to average women about the social and political events which have been changing the face of the world; magazines of current interest which break through the charmed circle of dreams and plunge women into the thick of events; it is a big gain which we must go on and on consolidating."[77] To counter the "enormous circulation of the 'heart-throb' press" in societies where women have few options but to marry for "economic emancipation," the editors called for their own magazines to devote sufficient space to stories, serial novels, and advice columns that women seek in order to provide "a new moral world" of family and gender relations, claiming that "it is wrong to think that these matters are not political and do not help women." Pointing out the importance of practical content dealing with "household matters, needle work, fashions, and articles on medical and educational questions," leftist women already in the early 1950s grasped onto the powerful argument that the personal is political, well before it became the rallying cry of "second wave" feminism.[78] Affirming the need to expand the readership beyond housewives in the cities who made up the bulk of the current audience, WIDF secretary-general Marie-Claude Vaillant-Couturier urged the magazines "to make a special and consistent effort in the direction of women workers, industrial and office workers, etc., especially at factory gates; and also to make a very very great effort—because here our weakness is graver still—in the direction of peasant women subscribers in the countryside."[79]

Successful with their own publications, Italian and French women shared suggestions on how to improve *Women of the Whole World* from their experiences with *Noi Donne* and *Femmes Françaises*. They increased circulation by going "door to door, in the factories, in the offices and in the countryside" to make the magazine the basis for shared cultural activities, recreation, and solidarity actions. As a result, the women could proudly claim that "our press is a powerful element of unity; its circulation is one of the most effective instruments of organization. It makes it possible to set up new local groups, to keep up permanent contacts with women; it introduces into the homes ideas of peace and progress, the consciousness of a new dignity, and confidence in a future of real happiness, won by determination and a common fight."[80] *Noi Donne*'s editor Grazia Cesarini boasted of her magazine, published in color with an impressive circulation of three hundred thousand, distributed by some fifteen thousand canvassers throughout Italy, the best of whom would be presented awards by the Union of Italian Women.[81] Received with more enthusiasm than beauty contests, the awards were organized explicitly against "one beauty contest after another, where Miss This and Miss That, allegedly 'ideal' girls, are chosen but which are actually a glorification of sex or of the false idea of an artificial feminine type with no great aspirations who is satisfied to be nothing but an obedient wife." Dismissing such beauty pageants in which women are judged by their looks, the Union of Italian Women chose eleven women "with their great qualities, which are both traditional and new," to be publicly honored for the first time in Italy: a professor of psychology, a primary school teacher, a widowed peasant manager of a farm with seven children, a worker fighting for equal pay, a member of the solidarity committee and the women's auxiliary of the dockers' union, a factory manager, a doctor, a physicist, a midwife, a caretaker of the homeless, and a writer.

Taking to heart the need to engage the readers and include a variety of voices, *Women of the Whole World* also began a column titled "Women Write to Us," explicitly asking readers for their feedback. The editors wanted to know which articles readers liked and found most helpful, or disliked and found wanting, with reasons and suggestions for improvement. Featured letters often thanked the magazine for providing member organizations with information and resources from the experiences of other women's groups that could be applied to their own organizing among their constituencies. Nora Rodd of Canada, who would go on to forge important connections with Korean women, as we will see in chapters 1 and 2, wrote in frequently. For the June 1956 issue, she wrote in response to the request for feedback that "by bringing articles written by women active in their own lands, articles accompanied more and more by *clear pictures*, we learn the problems and how they are being overcome; even how we can help overcome them, for we learn that all women working together can help overcome their common enemies, poverty and war. We begin to know one another as women; and oceans no longer keep us apart."[82] After referring to specific articles that proved particularly helpful, Rodd ended her correspondence with a plea that special articles "reach us a little earlier," imploring, "We know how busy you are, but if only we could have had the International Women's Day article in early February rather than in April!"

Another Canadian woman, Hazel Wigdor of Toronto, wrote a couple of months later to point out that "the items which stand out most in my mind are those which have given concrete experience of what has happened, and how it was done, rather than those which are dissertations or editorial comments."[83] As examples, she referred to the articles about the women's press in Italy, the experiences of the women of South Africa, and stories about women from the US and Algeria, among others. In reply, Odette Prerret of France wrote with delight,

> To go back to the letter from the friend in Toronto, I was very moved to read the concluding paragraph, because the letter from the French woman to which she refers is the one I sent you during the fight against the European Defence Community. If I refer to my letter, it is not because of any "literary" qualities it may have had, I simply wrote what I felt, and I was surprised and moved to see that a distant friend had found something useful and comforting in it. I must say that this caused me great pleasure, precisely because the work is very difficult at the moment and sometimes one feels like a grain of sand.[84]

Eunice Emilia Concha of Colombia affirmed the important role of the magazine in fostering a sense of connection among the women despite physical distance: "In individual conversations or in meetings we read and comment on one or other of the articles. In addition we point out on the map the country about which the article is written. This helps each woman to feel intimately linked in thought and action with our sisters in distant countries. We must also tell you that when the journal has finished going from hand to hand it is hardly readable."[85]

Overview of the Book

In this book I track the transnational linkages between women of Korea and the world from the late 1940s—just before the official beginning of the Korean War, when the UN flag was first used in an international conflict—to 1975, the year designated by the UN as International Women's Year. In addition to the women's press from Korea and the WIDF, the book relies on the scattered archives of the WIDF in the Sophia Smith Collection at Smith College, and the International Institute of Social History (Amsterdam), as well as pamphlets and publications of the KDWU and other Korean sources at the United States Library of Congress, the National Archives and Records Administration, the Harvard-Yenching Library, the Korea University Library (Tokyo), the Russian State Library, and the Information Center on North Korea at the National Library of (South) Korea.[86]

The book is divided into three parts, each coinciding roughly with two overlapping decades, with specific themes that defined the era. Part 1, on war and peace, encompasses the 1940s to the 1950s as Korea came out of Japanese colonial rule and the Asia Pacific War only to be divided by the Soviet Union and the United States. As the Cold War turned into a "hot war" during the Korean War, women debated the substance of the peace they wanted to achieve alongside questions about what made women uniquely positioned to achieve it. As chapter 1 shows, maternalism was not imposed upon Korean women by maintaining traditional Confucian gender roles or by idolizing Kim Il Sung's mother and wife, but began as an international strategy during the Korean War to demand peace in the name of mothers. It was with this responsibility embodied in maternal feminism to prevent a third world war that twenty-one women from seventeen nations risked their own lives to join a fact-finding commission to investigate firsthand what was happening in Korea and return to tell the truth that would become so politicized with the Cold War.

After seeing in detail the ways in which the international women's movement answered Korean women's call for solidarity to demand a just end to the Korean War, chapter 2 pans out to track the development of the women's movement in Asia that specifically merged anticolonial national liberation with women's liberation. In this context, peace as an emerging political aim already had distinct differences from the history of pacifism in the West. The chapter traces this development through three pivotal, yet little known, gatherings: the 1949 Asia Women's Conference, the 1952 Asia Pacific Peace Conference, and the 1953 World Congress of Women. Well before the 1966 Tricontinental Conference in Havana, Cuba, that forged an anti-imperialist coalition across Africa, Asia, and Latin America, the campaign against the Korean War fomented a transcontinental alliance to demand an anti-imperialist peace with justice, or what Nobel laureate Gabriela Mistral would call the "militancy of peace." Just as later radical intersectional analyses tying the personal to the political had institutional forerunners covered in this book, calls from the civil rights era down to social justice movements today connecting justice with peace—as in the slogan "no justice, no peace"—had antecedents in the declarations and movements that came earlier.

With the emergence of the Third World as a powerful bloc complicating the bipolarity of the First and Second Worlds, part 2, on the rising Third World, focuses on the 1950s into the 1960s, as women's attempt to unite in the name of mothers faltered with divisions within the socialist bloc itself. Chapter 3 begins with the 1955 World Congress of Mothers, which brought together an unprecedented group of women across ideological lines, building on the momentum of the peace campaign during the Korean War. But within a year, the 1956 Hungarian Revolution exposed the fragility of Soviet hegemony, ultimately leading to the end of the Cominform (Information Bureau of the Communist and Workers' Parties). Eclipsing the Second World then, the 1958 Afro-Asian Peoples' Solidarity Conference signaled the emergence of the Third World as a rival force. Simplistically termed the Sino-Soviet split, the division was in reality much more than a conflict between states, representing genuine ideological and political differences about revolutionary strategy, apparent in the left international women's movement during the 1963 World Congress of Women in Moscow. Chinese women explicitly challenged Soviet détente as a betrayal of the anticolonial struggle, and withdrew their WIDF membership. Although Korean women remained in the WIDF, they sided with the Chinese and other Third World women, delineating the "political" that would give women the leverage and authority to demand a just peace. These debates were a remarkable precedent echoed in later slogans "the personal is the political" and "women's rights are human rights." In effect, the international left women's movement of the 1950s and 1960s carved out the space for these movements to come.

With this international context in mind, in chapter 4 I direct my attention back on Korea through three parallel national gatherings: the 1959 National Conference of Women Socialist Builders, the 1961 National Mothers Congress, and the 1965 Third Congress of the Korean Democratic Women's Union. Discussions during these conferences and throughout the pages of the Korean women's magazine show that the conceptual division between production and reproduction often made in economic theories attributing sexual inequity to the gendered division of labor is woefully inadequate. In fact, the experiences of Korean women challenge the very categories of production and reproduction by posing fundamental questions about what constitutes "proper work" for women and men, and how to value different forms of labor and distribute the fruits of such labor under socialism. While it is true that state socialist countries rarely questioned the nuclear family as the primary unit of society, the emotional and material work of the family and the redistribution of domestic labor within the family were recurring topics in the women's press. Women debated how to juggle their multiple roles and address the contradictions between demands for their labor force participation in production and competing demands to organize consumption and fulfill their reproductive work in ever greater capacities. Ultimately, lively discussion on such topics during the 1950s and 1960s would give way to the 1967 Monolithic Ideological System that consolidated authoritarian rule in Korea, sublimating all forms of labor as individual sacrifice for the collective.

Having covered in the first two parts of the book the political and socioeconomic spheres through debates about women's role in world peace and in national development, in part 3 I move to the cultural sphere of the 1960s and 1970s. Globally understood as a time of cultural shifts with parallel movements in the East and West marked by the Great Proletarian Cultural Revolution in China and the countercultural movement in the United States, chapter 5 decenters these foci to examine the most influential figure behind early cultural developments in Korea, the dancer and choreographer Choe Seung-hui (Ch'oe Sŭng-hŭi, 1911–1969).[87] Following her career after her move to the North in 1946, the chapter traces the emergence of folk aesthetics as part of a transnational cultural movement influenced by socialist realism and a decolonial aesthetics of everyday life centered on women's activities. A close reading of her aesthetic philosophy also underscores the extent to which important arguments made by women such as Choe have been appropriated by men, in this case the leader himself, to erase the women's contributions. Her example confirms yet again the need to trace political and cultural movements and the circulation of ideas transnationally across time, rather than taking claims of state power at face value. This is especially true in the case of women, who are too often relegated to the periphery and whose ideas are either lost or misattributed.

Building on such transnational currents, chapter 6 further demonstrates how even nationalist works conventionally associated with solidifying the leadership in the 1970s find influences and resonances across the socialist world with the global circulation of militant women archetypes from works such as *Mother* (Russia), *The White-Haired Girl* (China), and *Sea of Blood* and *The Flower Girl* (Korea). Although the desexualized aesthetics of female characters in such works have come under criticism as the "erasure" of femininity and womanhood, the chapter argues that such critique inadvertently relies on a binary concept of gender that reifies sexual differences. Challenging oppositional binary definitions of gender, communist feminism understood gender *as* sex difference to be performative and thus subject to manipulation and change. Instead of viewing communist women archetypes as inauthentic for their lack of sexuality, I suggest that the proliferation of such figures heralded the emergence of a new feminine ideal that was not tied to sexuality.

Finally, the conclusion explains the significance of 1975 as a bookend to this history. The year marked the turn toward "gender mainstreaming" with the UN International Women's Year, concurrent with the rise of neoliberalism, the end of decolonial movements, and the waning of the Cold War. This period also marked a shift within Korea, with a designated hereditary succession of leadership and increasing economic hardships that contributed to a more insular posture. While such results and the ups and downs of the international women's movement highlight the challenges of bridging the global and the local toward a truly transnational sense of solidarity, this history of Cold War feminisms deserves recognition for its impact on the development of the international women's movement and the Cold War.[88] After all, the Cold War has not yet ended, and the Korean War remains in a state of unendedness with a precarious truce. Transnational solidarity continues to be as important as ever, and the first chapter takes us to those beginnings during the Korean War.

Part 1
WAR AND PEACE

1
WOMEN AGAINST THE KOREAN WAR

> **Do not believe that you will be spared, that New York and the other American cities will never have to endure the wrongs that our cities and villages are now suffering. Fight harder against the sending of your sons and husbands to Korea!**
>
> Hŏ Chŏng-suk, 1951

> **Jagged walls, twisted girders, vast piles of shapeless rubble tangled the skyline, composing a picture of such absolute destruction that it seemed to transcend reality, to leap away from the special and individual tragedy of whatever had happened here, in this particular place, and to become a symbol. . . . A woman separated herself from the crowd and, thrusting a bouquet into my hand, became a person, throwing her arms around me, looking into my eyes, smiling and then suddenly turning from smiles to tears.**
>
> Monica Felton, 1954

In June 1953, just before a cease-fire finally halted the Korean War (1950–1953), the World Congress of Women convened by the Women's International Democratic Federation met in Copenhagen. The head of the Swedish delegation, Andrea Andreen, greeted "our sisters from Korea, Viet-Nam and Malaya who are fighting alongside their whole peoples to expel the aggressors, to defend their right to life, national independence and peace," calling on women as mothers, workers, and citizens to struggle for women's rights and toward world peace.[1] The congress produced two documents: an Appeal to Women of the Whole World, and a Declaration of the Rights of Women, indicting the Cold War for its detrimental effects on women's rights. The appeal called for "an armistice [to] be signed on a just basis and that the cessation of hostilities in Korea be followed by a just and lasting peace," in addition to a general reduction in military expenditures by the great powers and a complete ban on all weapons of mass destruction.[2] These demands were justified on the basis of women's rights as mothers.

While historians of the Cold War in the United States have argued that both feminism and pacifism receded in the 1950s with the twin rise of domesticity and McCarthyism, the Korean War galvanized international women to promote women's rights and launch the first global peace campaign during the Cold War.[3] Cold War historiography has skewed our understanding of the international women's movement and dismissed serious efforts against the Korean War as "bogus peace ventures."[4] Situating Korean women within international currents, this chapter excavates buried histories to show how leftist women tried to bridge the Cold War divide through maternal strategies. Doing so challenges the "containment" thesis on the retrenchment of radical movements during the early Cold War to reveal the dynamic possibilities opened up *by* the Cold War, offering an alternative transnational history of the Korean War that includes women as peacemakers.[5] Even when its origins as a civil war are acknowledged, the Korean War is most commonly framed in Western diplomatic and military histories as a "proxy war," waged on the whole by male politicians and soldiers.[6] When women enter the picture at all, it is usually as victims, survivors, or sometimes fighters, but rarely does this change the overall history of the war itself. It has come to be known in the United States as a "forgotten war" for the allegedly muted response it received during and since.[7]

The origins of the Cold War may have predated the Korean War, but the Korean War was the "crucible" of the Cold War, shaping the postwar world order.[8] A situation that was at best described as "a cold war" or the "so-called cold war" in the late 1940s became *the* Cold War in the process of the Korean War, whereby the mutually perceived threat actualized the worst outcomes in a self-fulfilling prophecy.[9] The stalemate of the Korean War ended in an armistice rather than a peace settlement, leaving the conflict between the two Koreas, and also between North Korea and the United States, unresolved to date. While the Korean War is conventionally dated between 1950 and 1953, there were hundreds of thousands already dead through guerrilla fighting and extrajudicial killings since at least 1947.[10] Although I too have relied on the 1950-to-1953 years as rough markers of when the domestic conflict turned into an international war, it is important to keep in mind that the war predates 1950 and has never ended. The Korean War therefore opens this book to examine the gendered effects of the *long* Cold War and women's attempts to deploy maternal feminism to intervene in it. The Korean War was the crucible of the Cold War precisely as the first test of international solidarity among transnational women calling for peace. To be clear, these women were not an anomaly who went against the tide of rising domesticity and McCarthyism. Political scientist Marjorie Lansing argues that women in the US have been a significant voting bloc at least since 1950, when "foreign policy, far more than any other issue, has divided men and women," describing "women as more opposed than men to American involvement in Korea."[11]

In fact, at the height of the Korean War in 1951, civil rights leader Eslanda Goode Robeson emphatically claimed that "there are no points which do not refer back to Peace."[12] As historian Jacqueline Castledine has shown, a progressive definition of peace as more than the "*absence* of violence but also the *presence* of social and political equality" led women like Robeson to fight for "Peace, Freedom, and Abundance" under the platform of the short-lived US Progressive Party (1948–1955), at a critical juncture of the Cold War when women on opposite sides of the conflict debated the position of women in politics. A growing body of scholarship led by historian Francisca de Haan has rightly emphasized the importance of left feminism in the development of the international women's movement, challenging the "wave" metaphor of feminist history.[13] Left feminism as a global movement was certainly important, but central to this history are the women of *Asia*, not so much a geographic category as a political one that figured the "East" as an alternative to the "West" in a constellation of Third World solidarities led by women years before Bandung. That history will be fully fleshed out in the next chapter, but this chapter begins with the Korean War as a foundational moment in how left feminism in the context of a global peace movement facilitated a productive understanding of *difference*—whether gendered, racial, ethnic, or national—toward a transversal politics of solidarity.

To be sure, social reformers grappled with the dilemma of difference long before the Cold War. For women, the question centered on whether to celebrate their alleged differences from men as offering a more emancipatory potential or to challenge those differences as man-made in the process of delineating modern sexed subjects.[14] Although the divide was never as stark as it might appear in hindsight, and many women's rights advocates rejected "feminism" as a label before the 1960s, the clash was most contentious early on in regard to special labor legislation over whether measures such as prohibition of night work for women protected or discriminated against women. In the United States, for example, conflict erupted between the National Woman's Party and the Communist Party over the Equal Rights Amendment, first proposed by the former in 1923 and opposed by the Communists because the stress on equality threatened the hard-won protective legislation for working-class women to prevent excessively long hours and night work.[15] Communists countered with an alternative proposal for a Woman's Charter, which codified gender equality while still recognizing the need to protect women from exploitative labor practices. They saw no contradiction in advocating gender equality even while advancing special protective legislation because their structural analysis took aim at inequalities and material differences that would be the target of social reform.

Historically, the "woman question" is therefore part of the larger dilemma of difference that confronted social reformers and revolutionaries alike: what to do with difference in the age of social revolution and the rise of mass society when mobilizing for change? How to unite under a common cause despite perceived and material differences? Communist feminisms that stretched across the Cold War divide were no less conflicted about what to do. Maternal strategies, according to Castledine, "helped to bridge the schism" over whether emphasizing difference would empower or impede women through the "commonly held commitment to the concept of political peace and to the role that postwar women's organizations could play in bringing it to fruition."[16] In reaction to the horrors of the two world wars, women activists gave birth to the international peace movement, proclaiming women to be the "natural" instruments of peace as mothers and caregivers.[17] By looking specifically at the international mobilization of women as mothers against the Korean War, this chapter introduces the promises and challenges of the women's movement during the Cold War. I begin with the Women's International Democratic Federation (WIDF), which took an early position against colonialism, before examining in detail the work of the women the WIDF commissioned to investigate war atrocities during the Korean War. Emerging from their work are debates about how best to understand women's power in relation to maternalism, complicating the concepts of peace and war. War and peace could not easily be separated in the hot zones of the Cold War where "peace" could mean maintaining the status quo, an intolerable condition for those exposed to the "balance of terror."[18]

The Women's International Democratic Federation and the Third World

The WIDF was the largest international women's organization to form after the end of World War II with the aim of advancing women and peace, and yet it has received relatively little attention.[19] With efforts to overcome this neglect, new scholarship highlighting the organization's work has continued to emerge since 2010.[20] The WIDF was formed in Paris in November 1945 at the first World Congress of Women, with some 850 women from forty countries in attendance.[21] In an interview, founding president Eugénie Cotton described how the idea for the WIDF began when the Union of French Women held their first congress in 1945 and drew up a program for women's rights, peace, and the welfare of families. With guests from other countries including Dolores Ibarruri, Nina Popova, Tzola Dragotcheva, Ada Gobetti, Mary Pritt, and Anezka Hodinova-Spurma, Cotton thought "there are no frontiers to our programme. What would it mean, if we could transform it into an international programme?"[22] They decided to set up a preparatory committee to explore the possibility, and later that same year the first congress was convened, where Cotton, as someone without party affiliation, was elected president, "to stress the fact that the federation is open to all women."

The group denounced imperialism and racism as responsible for World War II, arguing that peace, anticolonialism, and antiracism were necessary for the protection of women's rights. As the scholar of women and gender studies Elisabeth Armstrong notes, "In 1945, WIDF was the only transnational women's organization that explicitly condemned colonialism," and the linkages between imperialism, racism, and fascism were made yet sharper by African and Asian women struggling against American, British, Dutch, and French imperialism.[23] Other women's peace groups, such as the Women's International League for Peace and Freedom (WILPF), in existence since 1915, dropped their critique of capitalist exploitation as an obstacle to peace and freedom in the 1950s because of fears of red-baiting, and did not take up decolonization work until the 1960s.[24]

Committed from the beginning to solidarity against Western imperialism, the WIDF sent its first fact-finding delegations to South America in 1946 and to Southeast Asia in 1948.[25] Subsequently, in a 1949 report, the US House Un-American Activities Committee (HUAC) labeled the WIDF a "Communist-front organization" and branded the group "a specialized arm of Soviet political warfare in the current 'peace' campaign to disarm and demobilize the United States."[26] As a result, the US affiliate of WIDF, the Congress of American Women (CAW), had no choice but to disband in 1950, but during its three-year life between 1946 and 1949, it established three commissions—on Peace and Democracy, the Status of Women, and Child Care—the most active of which was Peace and Democracy.[27] Founded by American women who had attended the 1945 WIDF Congress in Paris, CAW chose March 8 International Women's Day in 1946 for its first meeting. By 1948, CAW had 250,000 members, with twelve branches in seven states, sending a delegation of twenty-four women, including Black women leaders, to the WIDF Second Congress in Budapest.[28] CAW persevered for three years despite being placed on the "subversive" list by the Justice Department, with members losing their jobs, investigated by HUAC, deported, and imprisoned.

CAW chapters formed in New York, Cleveland, Chicago, Pittsburgh, Los Angeles, Detroit, Milwaukee, and Seattle with funds raised through membership dues and fund-raising bazaars that featured home-baked goods, handicrafts, holiday candies, and baby clothes. Organizational affiliates included the American University Women's League, the National Association of Colored Women, and eighteen other organizations. Not only were members active in social justice movements, but they actively campaigned to place female candidates in office in state legislatures, with such slogans as "48 Congresswomen in '48," and a pledge to organize "women of every race, every creed, every nationality, for peace; for social, economic, political and legal advancement; for the betterment of the lives of their children, for common action to meet the problems of their daily life—backed by the strength and vision which our world tie with millions of women gives us."[29] Irène Joliot-Curie, a renowned chemist and peace activist, speaking at a reception organized by CAW soon after its founding, noted the special responsibility of American women in the global peace movement to "organise women more than in any other country in the world—to stop the drive towards war—because you are the only country in the world which has the atom bomb. You are the only country which can make war today."[30] The first CAW national convention took place in New York on May 6 to 8, 1949. Reporting on the work of the three commissions, the Status of Women Commission countered the Equal Rights Amendment with the Women's Status Bill to "wipe out discrimination against women without doing away with protective legislation." CAW also decided to support the 1949 Conference of the Women of Asia in Beijing (see chapter 2) by sending delegates and fund-raising under the name "Pennies for Peace."[31]

There is clear evidence of communist sympathies and Soviet support among the WIDF leadership and affiliates at the organization's inception. For instance, WIDF president Eugénie Cotton compared the "peace-loving" USSR to the "warmongering" United States. Calling for the "unity and action of democratic women of the whole world," the organizational bulletin contrasted the impact of World War II on the US and the USSR in stark terms, as shown in table 1.1. Concerned about such polarization along Cold War lines, one of the Swedish delegates, Andrea Andreen (WIDF Council member from 1945 and executive committee member from 1948), warned during the 1948 Second Congress, held in Budapest, that "she was afraid there was a certain amount of distrust existing between the East and the West, which might become a cause of war."[32] Andreen advocated revising the content of WIDF materials to show more diplomacy, "so that the non-democratic women [outside the WIDF orbit] should not be made suspicious" presumably that the Federation was a Soviet front rather than an independent organization. However, the Soviet delegate and WIDF vice president since 1945, Nina Popova, replied that "the East–West distrust . . . is directed towards the reactionary imperialists . . . and against these elements the fight has to be intensified." Comparing the Soviet demobilization of World War II soldiers by 1947 with the increasing militarization and ambitions of the US and the UK, Popova argued that the Soviet Union "fights unceasingly for peace," as proven by

TABLE 1.1 "Seek those who profit from war and you will find the war-mongers"

USA	USSR
Cities destroyed: 0	Towns and villages destroyed or burnt: 71,710
Profits of trusts: 70 million dollars	Losses (roubles): 679 milliards

Source: WIDF *Information Bulletin* 32 (November 1948), 1.

its proposed UN resolution in 1946 to ban atomic weapons. Unabashedly aligning itself with the Soviet bloc, the WIDF Second Congress concluded that it was "impossible to be an enemy of the Soviet Union and at the same time to declare oneself a defender of peace: enemies of the Soviet Union are enemies of peace as well."[33] The Korean women's magazine *Chosŏn Nyŏsŏng* reported on these proceedings in Budapest, siding with the Soviets and dismissing Andreen's concerns as groundless.[34]

The WIDF indeed had strong connections to the communist world, with Soviet-sponsored conferences, organizations, publications, and festivals, but the Federation's overall membership grew to include a diverse array of groups from the Third World.[35] While the First Congress in 1945 represented 40 countries, with only a handful from Asia and Africa, the Fourth Congress a decade later brought together some 70 countries, and by 1985 the Federation included 135 member organizations from 117 countries.[36] India, Egypt, and Algeria seem to have had the largest representation at the First Congress from among the Third World in 1945, and by the Second Congress in 1948, both North and South Korea were represented on the executive committee, with Pak Chŏng-ae for the North and Yu Yŏng-jun for the South.[37] With the growth in membership, the WIDF tried to secure financial independence through membership fees, sales of publications, and various fund-raising campaigns that included large bazaars at the world congresses featuring arts and handicrafts from member organizations.[38] As the Federation grew, incorporating greater numbers of women's groups from across the world and especially the Third World, the world congresses became an impetus by which women learned to organize their local communities. In turn their growing ranks increased the WIDF's racial, ethnic, and political diversity.

The statutes formulated during its First Congress show why the WIDF attracted such a broad base of support, forging a global membership. Four interrelated principles, of antifascism, peace, women's rights, and children's rights, advanced the right to self-determination and democratic freedoms, with calls for an end to war and militarism, and equality between the sexes through equal pay for equal work, equal opportunities in education and professional training, social services for women, and the protection of mothers irrespective of marital status.[39] The Federation drew a clear connection between rising military expenditures and cuts in social spending, arguing that "women more clearly grasped the relation between their personal financial problems and the increased military budgets."[40] It made peace an explicitly feminist issue by analyzing the ways "pro-war" propaganda relied on "anti-woman" messaging, citing a 1947 issue of *Life* magazine, which allegedly argued, "Only in wartime do the sexes achieve a normal relationship to each other. The male assumes his dominant, heroic role, and the female, playing up to the male, assumes her proper and normal function of being feminine, glamorous and inspiring."[41] True to its peace mission, the WIDF called on the UN for a general arms reduction and a ban on atomic weapons beginning in December 1946.[42] The Federation also campaigned early on against the French colonial war in Vietnam, under the leadership of founding president Cotton (who was also president of the French affiliate, the Union of French Women). For this, the WIDF was expelled from France in January 1951 and forced to relocate to East Berlin, where it remained until 1991.[43]

Undeterred, in the same year as the expulsion from Paris, the Federation also investigated war atrocities committed in the Korean War, sending a fact-finding delegation of twenty-one women from seventeen countries to Korea in May 1951.[44] The subsequent report accused the US of war crimes, and in retaliation the United States took the initiative to strip the WIDF of its consultative status at the UN in April 1954. Obstructed by the US from attending the UN meeting in New York at which its status was to be decided, the Federation asked British peace activist Dora Russell to attend on its behalf, but she was given a visa only in the third week of March, with strict restrictions on her movement to the area around the UN. She was appalled at accusations that the Federation's collection of signatures for peace opposed the UN work in Korea, and distraught at how the WIDF's report on Korea was received as "vile," "*cynical, destructive, barren . . . exploiting women for propaganda purposes.*"[45] The decision to revoke the Federation's consultative status barely passed a majority vote, with four abstentions among the eighteen member states of the UN Economic and Social Council, and the remaining votes more or less evenly divided, with India, the USSR, Czechoslovakia, Egypt, and Yugoslavia in favor of the WIDF. By a sliver of a margin, the final vote cast against the WIDF came from Chiang Kai-shek, representing the Republic of China (Taiwan). Russell was stunned that the WIDF could be expelled from the UN in this way for calling attention to the plight of women, while "the debate went on, here in this spacious, richly carpeted and curtained conference hall, [where] these men talked on about things which they had no wish to understand." While the consultative status given to nongovernmental organizations (NGOs) provided a modicum of people's voices to enter the fray at the UN, including those from countries without state representation, this hardly gave them much power, and Russell lamented that this precedent would have a chilling effect on the ability of NGOs to criticize governments or the UN itself, asking "what sort of democratic representation exists at the United Nations, if the largest women's organization, world-wide in its membership and influence, fighting everywhere for the rights of women and children, has no place there?"[46]

After the Federation's expulsion, its consultative status would not be reinstated until June 1967.[47] Despite such reprisals, the WIDF valued its members in the Third World from the beginning, reserving a seat for a Chinese vice president during its founding in 1945, filled only in 1948. In 1953, the number of vice presidents was expanded from four to ten to include Third World women from the People's Republic of China (Cai Chang), Egypt (Céza Nabaraoui), and Nigeria (Funmilayo Ransome-Kuti), with seats reserved for India, Japan, and Brazil.[48] The rest included members from the Soviet Union (Nina Popova), Hungary (Erzsébet Andics), West Germany (Lilly Waechter), Spain (Dolores Ibarruri), Sweden (Andrea Andreen), Italy (Rita Montagnana) and the United Kingdom (Monica Felton). Its monthly journal (quarterly from 1966), *Women of the Whole World* began publication in 1951 at the height of the Korean War, and therefore the first several years of the magazine dealt extensively with coverage of the war and the campaign to stop it.

The Korean War as Crucible

As the first major international conflict after World War II to test the organizational effectiveness of groups like the WIDF, the Korean War received prominent attention in many Federation publications. The February 1951 issue of *Women of the Whole World* contained detailed reports from various countries on their antiwar actions. Newspapers in Greece distributed leaflets with slogans such as "Korea for the Koreans!" and "No Greek in Korea." Mothers' Committees in Cuba opposed the sending of troops to Korea, and there were demonstrations in Argentina and Israel demanding "Hands off Korea."[49] Marie-Claude Vaillant-Couturier, WIDF secretary-general, member of the French parliament, and prisoner at Auschwitz and Ravensbrück during World War II, implored, "The voice of the Korean women must be heard!" reporting that "in a large number of countries which were to supply mercenaries for [the US commander, General Douglas] MacArthur, the women are in the front ranks of the movement for the recall of the soldiers and against the sending of troops to Korea," including "in the United States of America itself."[50]

In fact, many US women protested against the Korean War in the Save Our Sons campaign. Founded in 1952 in Illinois by families of soldiers fighting in Korea, the Save Our Sons Committee demanded a cease-fire in Korea and the establishment of a lasting peace. The chair of the committee, Florence Gowgiel, who was moved to action when her son-in-law returned paralyzed from the war, received hundreds of support letters from other parents and relatives of US soldiers from all over the country.[51] One seventy-five-year-old printer wrote, "What our army has done in Korea and still does there is a crime. In my opinion the war in Korea is the greatest stain on the history of the U.S.A."[52] Reflecting this sentiment, the US representative to the WIDF Council meeting in February 1951, Betty Millard, wrote,

> As I sat listening to the terrible, burning words of the Korean delegate this morning, I was overcome with waves of shame and horror. I tried to tell myself that there are two Americans: there are those who wage war, and against them, those who fight for peace and a better world in the spirit of Paul Robeson and of our many heroes such as Joe Hill, of whom he sings. This is true. I have great faith in my people. And yet, it is we, the American people, who are responsible for the crimes committed in Korea, and we who will be responsible if another terrible war engulfs the world.[53]

Citing the threefold increase in military spending as a result of the Korean War, "the biggest war budget in history" at $52.5 billion, Millard detailed the work of US women, 350 of whom went to the UN to demand the withdrawal of US forces from Korea. Subsequently, they formed the American Women for Peace (AWP) in August 1950, leading a national pilgrimage of one thousand women to Washington, DC, on the anniversary of the bombing of Hiroshima, representing eighty organizations from forty states and forty-six cities to demand a ban on atomic weapons and an end to the Korean War.[54] Active from its founding on August 8, 1950, through 1953, precisely during the years of the Korean War, AWP membership overlapped with CAW, suggesting that former CAW members remained active through other organizations even after they were forced to disband.[55] The AWP issued five thousand copies of public service pamphlets calling on Congress for an immediate cease-fire in Korea.[56] Millard went on to report,

> All over the country "Women for Peace" groups have grown up.... They go door-to-door with peace petitions ... they build floats and hold motor-car parades with peace signs.... Young mothers organize baby-buggy parades. They write letters, send telegrams to President Truman and go in delegations to local politicians, radio stations and newspaper editors. And in all this, Negro women play a leading part. For they know that preparations for war go hand in hand with increasing discrimination and violence against the Negro people. It is a bitter irony to the Negro people to be told that while they are segregated, given the meanest jobs and lynched at home, they are expected to support a war for "freedom" against the colored people of Asia.[57]

Enabling such critique linking racist violence at home with imperialist wars abroad, the Korean War was instrumental in shaping radical theory and praxis, especially in the United States. Castledine credits the US involvement in Korea for confirming critics of Cold War policy who warned against its dangers as early as 1948, and Africana studies scholar Robeson Taj Frazier notes the "racial implications of the Korean War" as a "war of color . . . more than a struggle over communism . . . an Asian rejection of white supremacy and Western imperialism."[58] Likewise, historians Dayo Gore and Erik McDuffie recognize the McCarthy era as the period when "black Communist women pursued their most sophisticated work."[59] Beulah Richardson (aka Beah Richards) was one of those women, a poet and actor, whose 1951 poem "A Black Woman Speaks of White Womanhood, of White Supremacy, of Peace" explicitly connected the issues of racial justice with global peace. Her poem was a "smash hit" among the left in 1951 during the height of the campaign against the Korean War.[60] In that same year, W. E. B. Du Bois and Paul Robeson were among those who organized the American Peace Crusade, lobbying against the extension of the draft and militarization, and leading another national pilgrimage to Washington, DC, on March 15, 1951, of more than two thousand people to demand that the US "abandon the futile conflict in Korea" and withdraw its forces.[61]

The WIDF argued that it was owing to many such actions, led by women all over the world, that public opinion was swayed against the war in Korea. Indeed, Herbert Goldhamer, who had the opportunity to observe the US armistice negotiation team for several months in 1951, remarked that "the UN seemed to spend much more time worrying about the public than it did about the Communists."[62] He noted the extent to which Admiral C. Turner Joy, at the head of the US negotiation team, "was considerably worried by these letters [from the public] because they implied that a heavy moral responsibility for further deaths and for continuation of war would rest on him."[63] For such reasons, international relations scholar Rosemary Foot concludes that "the UN involvement required a responsiveness to international opinion (and especially to the views of America's most important allies), which could sometimes cut across the demands . . . from those in the bureaucracy who preferred force and inflexibility to diplomatic compromise."[64]

As cease-fire negotiations dragged on, however, the WIDF also campaigned to aid Korean children. Soviet, Romanian, Chinese, Czechoslovakian, and German women welcomed thousands of children into their homes.[65] A WIDF pamphlet opened with the following appeal on their behalf: "MacArthur has been able to sow death on a scale hitherto unknown in the world. Here are the terrible figures: in a country whose population is 26,000,000, in the first 8 months of war one million Koreans were killed, of whom 33% were children and 45% women."[66] Quoting various news outlets, the pamphlet borrowed the words of journalists and war correspondents to describe the war's devastating effects. The United Press International observed that "one must be here to realise exactly what this 'scorched earth' tactic means," pointing to the total leveling of Korean cities, towns, and villages.⁶⁷ A *Chicago Daily News* correspondent reported that the US Air Force was given orders "to kill everything that moves."⁶⁸ No wonder that Cold War sutures were necessary to stitch shut the horrific violence perpetrated in the name of "freedom" and to drill anticommunism into the very fabric of American consciousness. The thousands upon thousands of pages of records left by HUAC grilling its own citizens for simply standing against the war are a resounding testament to how much opposition there was and the amount of force required to bully it into silence.

The WIDF pamphlet concluded with the words of Hŏ Chŏng-suk, Korea's minister of culture and highest-ranking female cabinet member. Appealing to the women assembled at the WIDF Council meeting in Berlin on February 3, 1951, she made a point to speak directly to the women from the US: "American friends! You must know of the atrocities committed by your sons and husbands in Korea. You cannot escape the responsibility for the murder of completely innocent people. It is your sons and your husbands who are committing these deeds. Do not believe that you will be spared, that New York and the other American cities will never have to endure the wrongs that our cities and villages are now suffering. Fight harder against the sending of your sons and husbands to Korea!"⁶⁹ She pleaded similarly to the British women that they demand the return of their sons and husbands, as "the English troops fighting in Korea have gained only death and the hatred of the Korean people." It was in this context that she asked "that representatives of the WIDF be sent to Korea so that they can see with their

On the rostrum: Marie-Claude Vaillant-Couturier, General Secretary of the W.I.D.F. Che Den Suk, Korean delegate, Lu Tsui, Chinese delegate.

FIGURE 1.1. Hŏ Chŏng-suk attending the WIDF Council meeting in Berlin. *Women of the Whole World*, February 1951.

own eyes the inhuman cruelties the American barbarians have inflicted on our country."

As noted in the introduction, Korean women were affiliated with the WIDF through the Korean Democratic Women's Union (KDWU), which was founded in November 1945 and joined the WIDF in October 1946. At the invitation of Hŏ Chŏng-suk and Pak Chŏng-ae, chair of the KDWU and a WIDF executive committee member since 1948, the WIDF sent an international delegation, representing women from the Americas, Europe, Asia, and Africa, not all of whom were members of organizations affiliated with the WIDF. The international women's commission of twenty-one women from seventeen countries, with ages ranging from twenty-eight to sixty-five, consisted of the following members:

Chair: Nora K. Rodd (Canada)
Vice-chairs: Liu Chin-yang (China; administrator), Ida Bachmann (Denmark; librarian)
Secretaries: Miluse Svatosova (Czechoslovakia), Trees Soenito-Heyligers (Netherlands; lawyer)
Members: Monica Felton (Great Britain; city planner), Maria Ovsyannikova (USSR; editor in chief of *Soviet Woman*), Bai Lang (China; writer), Li K'eng (China; educator), Gilette Ziegler (France; journalist), Elisabeth Gallo (Italy; parliamentarian), Eva Priester (Austria; journalist), Hilde Cahn (East Germany), Lilly Waechter (West Germany), Germaine Hannevard (Belgium; biologist), Li-thi-Quê (Vietnam), Candelaria Rodriguez (Cuba; lawyer), Leonor Aguiar Vazquez (Argentina; lawyer), Fatma ben Sliman (Tunisia), Abassia Fodil (Algeria)
Observer: Kate Fleron Jacobsen (Denmark; journalist and editor in chief of *Free Denmark*)[70]

While the women hailed from diverse political and cultural backgrounds, they had all experienced the horrors of colonial occupation and World War II, having been active in antifascist and anticolonial movements. Kate Fleron had worked at the underground newspaper *Frit Danmark* (Free Denmark), founded by nationalists and communists in a united front against the Nazi occupation, and had been detained at the Frøslev prison camp by the Gestapo for eight months before escaping in April 1945; twenty years after her mission to Korea, she would also join a women's delegation to Vietnam in 1971.[71] Most of Lilly Waechter's family had been killed by the Nazis, and Hilde Cahn had been a prisoner at Ravensbrück.[72] Gilette Ziegler had served in the French resistance, while Abassia Fodil was a leader in the Union des femmes d'Algérie (Union of Women of Algeria) against French colonialism—she and her husband would be assassinated in 1962—and Trees Soenito-Heyligers had married an Indonesian independence

FIGURE 1.2. Cover of *We Accuse! Report of the Commission of the Women's International Democratic Federation in Korea, May 16 to 27, 1951*. Berlin: WIDF, 1951.

leader against Dutch colonialism and would be jailed in Indonesia in 1968 for defending communists.[73] At least two members of the delegation had previously served in the military during World War II: Ida Bachmann was a colonel in the US Army at the head of the Danish section of the US Office of War Information, and Maria Ovsyannikova was a colonel in the Soviet Red Army in Stalingrad.[74]

With extensive experience of war and conflict zones, the commission compiled its report *We Accuse!* in five languages—English, French, Russian, Chinese, and Korean—to be published subsequently in many more. It provided a harrowing account of death and devastation from city to village, as noted in its introduction: "Every page of this document is a grim indictment. Every fact speaks of the mass exterminating character of this war. More homes have been destroyed than military objectives, more grain than ammunition, more women, children and aged than soldiers. This war is war on life itself."⁷⁵ It concluded that war crimes had been committed in Korea in contravention of the Hague and the Geneva Conventions "by the systematic destruction of food, food-stores and food factories . . . by incendiary bombs," "by the systematic destruction of town after town, of village after village . . . dwellings, hospitals, schools," "by systematically employing . . . weapons banned by international convention i.e., incendiaries, petrol bombs, napalm bombs, time-bombs, and by constantly machine-gunning civilians from low-flying planes" and "by atrociously exterminating the Korean population . . . tortured, beaten to death, burned and buried alive."⁷⁶

Although the report would be red-baited as communist propaganda in the polarized context of the Cold War, the accounts of utter destruction and violence were by no means an exaggeration. Strikingly similar depictions of extreme cruelty and unimaginable forms of torture accompanied wartime conduct during the Asia Pacific War and its aftermath, as demonstrated in the Nanjing Massacre and the anticommunist counterinsurgency campaigns on Cheju Island. The commander of the US-led UN forces General Douglas MacArthur himself testified during a congressional hearing in the same month that "I shrink with a horror that I cannot express in words. . . . The war in Korea has already almost destroyed that nation of 20,000,000 people. I have never seen such devastation. I have seen, I guess, as much blood and disaster as any living man, and it just curdles my stomach, the last time I was there. After I looked at that wreckage and those thousands of women and children and everything, I vomited. . . . If you go on indefinitely, you are perpetuating a slaughter such as I have never heard of in the history of mankind."⁷⁷

The women's delegation visited Sinŭiju, Pyongyang, Anak, Sinch'ŏn, Namp'o, Kangse, Wŏnsan, Ch'ŏrwŏn, Hŭich'ŏn and Kanggye, covering some of the worst affected areas. They gathered meticulous data, with the reported numbers of dead recorded at each site, as well as the markings on bombs and weapons dug out from the debris, noting the use of napalm as a "new destructive weapon."⁷⁸ The report also recorded individual stories of loss in graphic detail: "Kim Sun-Ok, 37, mother of four children killed by a bomb, stated that . . . the Americans led [the secretary of the local women's union] naked through the streets and later killed her by pushing a red-hot iron bar into her vagina. Her small son was buried alive."⁷⁹

Despite the ghastly and emotional testimonies and the gruesome scenes of death, the report is detached and methodical, illustrating the delegation's efforts to be precise and systematic, as exemplified in the following excerpt:

> The mother told members that she had been tortured by having red-hot knitting needles pushed into her finger nails. Members of the

Commission observed the marks of disfigurement. The witness stated that when she was led to be tortured she saw people being thrown alive into a pit in the yard outside. The members of the Commission inspected this pit, which was an unused well. It was surrounded by a concrete wall about 60 cm high and about 1 meter in diameter. It appeared to be about 7 or 8 meters deep, and in the strong morning light human remains could clearly be seen at the bottom. Members noticed nearest to the surface the body of a child dressed in a dark coat with shining buttons.... The bodies that remained were too mutilated for identification. Apart from these remains, the members could see children's shoes, tufts of women's hair, books and small personal possessions, and also the ropes with which people had been bound together.[80]

From the number of farm animals, schools, houses, and hospitals destroyed, to the number of women raped and children killed, the report was a scathing account of the war's effects, particularly on women and children. For the commissioners, whose investigation was limited to the North, it was clear who was most responsible for the atrocities. The report ended with a letter to the president of the UN General Assembly and Security Council, and the Secretariat of the UN, demanding that the document be examined with the utmost urgency on behalf of the ninety-one million women represented by the WIDF. The letter called on the UN to stop the bombings in Korea to reach a peaceful settlement according to the principle of self-determination for the Korean people without interference from foreign troops.[81]

While the commission's diverse composition led at times to heated debate, the Cold War divide was already inscribed into the scope of its investigations limited to the North, thus affecting the reception of its work. Some members of the delegation, such as Monica Felton and Kate Fleron, proposed to visit the South, without success. Whether to request the UN to allow the commission to visit South Korea was a contentious issue, which divided the delegation from the outset.[82] Consequently, the report makes no mention of possible crimes committed in the South, and was susceptible to charges that it was a one-sided propaganda ploy. As Felton argued, however, "the fact that we still have to learn more about what has happened in the South does not—and cannot—invalidate the truth as we established it for ourselves in the North."[83] She further noted that racism against "Asiatic peoples" by the West not only resulted in the use of the atom bomb against Japan but also led to violations of the Geneva Conventions, withholding the right of China and North Korea to claim their own prisoners of war. As armistice negotiations dragged on for two years over US demands for "voluntary repatriation," Felton pointed to the hypocrisy of holding their own soldiers hostage for political ends.[84]

Fearful of public opinion being swayed by such accusations, the US government tried to discredit the report by red-baiting its authors as communist agents in order to deflect charges of war crimes. The State Department and the Women's Bureau of the US Labor Department were particularly concerned about accusations of germ warfare.[85] Concerns raised by the women's commission had led to further investigation in March 1952 by the International Association of Democratic Lawyers regarding allegations of bacteriological and chemical warfare categorically denied by the West.[86] In this Cold War information war, the CIA covertly funded US women's groups such as the Committee of Correspondence, which was "established as a direct response to the Soviet peace campaign and the activities of the WIDF."[87] Moreover, a coalition of over thirty US women's groups that formed the Women United for United Nations (WUUN) waged a "patriotic" defense of "collective security," standing against pacifist and peace groups that campaigned against war and armament.[88]

Under such circumstances, and despite its focus only on the North, the international women's commission and its report provided a crucial platform by which to discuss possible war crimes. The newly created UN could not provide such a forum precisely because it was itself accessory to the war.[89] South Korea fought under the UN banner, as part of a joint command made up of sixteen member states led by the United States. Countering the male-led UN coalition fighting in the name of "freedom," without asking for whom, the WIDF's all-female fact-finding commission specifically reached out to women affected by the war and included rape and sexual violence as war crimes decades before the UN would do so in the 1990s (see conclusion). Subsequently, the WIDF international network and member organizations demonstrated global opposition to the Korean War as another disastrous war on the heels of World War II. Condemning the "criminal military intervention of American imperialism against the legitimate rights of the Korean people" in a telegram sent to the KDWU on June 30, 1950, WIDF president Cotton concluded in the organization's information bulletin that "the provocation in Korea and the American intervention show that the warmakers will be driven back only by the united might of the peoples."[90]

The dangers and risks that the women took upon themselves to join the fact-finding commission cannot be overstated. Not only were some women maligned as "traitors" even before their departure, as those willing to go behind "enemy lines," but the women had to consider the very real possibility that they might not return alive, leading them to prepare letters to their families in the event of death.[91] They repeatedly had to take cover from aerial machine-gun fire and bombings during their twelve days in Korea, as well as in northeast China en route to and from Korea. Many of the women had lived through World War II and yet found the Korean War to be far more destructive because napalm combined with time-bombs made rescue operations nearly impossible.[92] For their efforts to shed light on the realities of the war, women from countries allied with the US paid a heavy price for their work.[93] Monica Felton was expelled from the British Labour Party and fired from her government position as head of urban planning in the Stevenage Development Corporation. Candelaria Rodriguez lost her job with the National Bank of Cuba and was jailed, as was Lilly Waechter by the US occupation forces in West Germany. Bombarded with vitriol and criticism at her "red propaganda" and treated with "disgust" and "contempt" by those who found the women's "consorting with the enemy" treasonous and worthy of capital punishment, Felton was "overtired" of being labeled Communist on one side and a reactionary Social Democrat on the other, forcing her to cancel speaking events.[94] Meanwhile, Fleron faced a "storm of indignation," with angry reactions from those unwilling to believe that the UN and its soldiers could be responsible for war crimes.[95]

This was just a few years after the Allied victory against the Axis that was as much a moral triumph as a military one, and years before civilian massacres became headline news during the Vietnam War. As a result, even when Felton delivered mail from British POWs to their families through her peace work in Korea, this was considered a "peculiarly vile form of Red propaganda."[96] Despite such reactions, the Korean War and Felton's intervention galvanized the organization of the National Assembly of Women (NAW) in the UK, where "the heavy involvement of British troops in Korea" led to their rallying cry "Bring Our Boys Home"; the slogan was "taken to the streets in almost every town and city where women, respectably dressed in hats and with not a hair out of place, defiantly marched with their banners, risking, at times, physical attack from the passing crowds."[97] Felton was elected chair to lead the group, and Pak Chŏng-ae was among those who sent a telegram of congratulations to NAW's first meeting, held on International Women's Day in 1952.

The urgency to act was especially acute because the threat of nuclear war loomed large. Shortly after the beginning of the Korean War, WIDF Executive Committee member and vice president of the Union of French Women Jeannette Vermeersch wondered in anguish, "Will the Americans use the atom bomb against Korea?"[98] The WIDF condemned US president Harry Truman for his threat to use atomic weapons "if the need arises," and called out the US for its hypocritical application of democracy: "What they say about 'democracy' is that they have so much of it that they want to export it to the rest of the world.... Meanwhile his government shows what it means by the word 'democracy' by imprisoning men and women who fight against this policy of mass murder, who fight for true peace and true democracy."[99] The Federation therefore lauded women's organizing efforts against the war, pointing to those jailed for opposing

US war policy (among them three women: Charlotte Stern, a labor leader and member of CAW; Ruth Leider, an attorney and widow of an aviator killed fighting fascism in Spain; and Marjorie Chodorov, a housewife). The Federation also cited the Harlem Women's Committee for Peace and Freedom, which gathered twelve hundred signatures from its Black residents in one day, thanks to the work of women like Amy Mallard. Mallard's husband had been lynched in Georgia, and she told the WIDF that "the same forces who killed her husband were the ones who want to murder millions of other people by starting another war."[100] In January 1953, thirteen members of the Communist Party USA were sentenced to five-year prison terms for their opposition to the war; among them were Claudia Jones, Elizabeth Gurley Flynn, and Betty Gannett.[101] As one of the leading Black left feminists, Jones spoke out against the war, and faced deportation to Trinidad, from where she had immigrated.[102] Writing in the *Daily Worker* in November 1951, Jones described the Korean War as "a white supremacist lynch mob passion against the darker peoples of Korea and Asia."[103] Flynn was one of the American delegates to the WIDF founding congress and a long-standing labor organizer, leading the campaign in defense of Sacco and Vanzetti in the 1920s. Gannett was an educator and an organizer in the labor movement.

Despite challenges of maintaining communication during wartime, *Women of the Whole World* served as an important conduit to share news, as articles were translated and adapted to be included in local women's magazines, while local news made its way to the Federation through the national affiliates. The KDWU organ *Chosŏn Nyŏsŏng* likewise carried translated excerpts from *Women of the Whole World*. In one such excerpt, Korean women learned that Ruby Davis and Patricia Kerry (or Kelly), who had sons in Korea, and Mona Thomas, whose son was sent to Alaska to be trained, had organized a national campaign to bring their sons back from the war, supported by the broader US peace and labor movements.[104] Another article relayed news about Lilly Waechter, one of the delegates of the 1951 fact-finding commission.[105] Waechter had been expelled from the Social Democratic Party in West Germany and arrested by the US occupation forces at a demonstration on September 6, 1951, for speaking out against US war crimes in Korea. After serving an eight-month sentence and paying a fine of 15,000 marks, through donations from supporters, she was released following a storm of protests.

The women of the 1951 commission also exchanged letters and made additional visits when they could. Women from Belgium wrote about their activities against the war, including news about Germaine Hannevard, the Belgian member of the 1951 delegation.[106] Ashamed at the deployment of Belgian troops to Korea, the women were actively campaigning to bring them home, widely distributing their report and sending medical supplies to Korea. Monica Felton visited Korea for the second time before going on to Beijing for the 1952 Asia Pacific Peace Conference (see chapter 2), holding a roundtable with the Korean women's union in Pyongyang.[107] Vice-chair Kim Yŏng-su opened the meeting with hope pinned on international peacemakers like Felton, who "evokes great trust among Korean women, widely loved with an internationally recognized name." They hoped that "her enormous achievements in the peace struggle will rapidly end the war in Korea and contribute greatly to the world cause for peace." Felton thanked the warm welcome and the roundtable gathering, conveying the support of British women for the Korean women's struggle. Since her visit in May 1951, she had wanted to reconnect with the Korean women and was alarmed to see the added hardship and destruction. She relayed how the letters she was able to take back home from British POWs from her previous visit enabled the mothers and wives of the POWs to become committed peace activists against the war, calling for the withdrawal of troops from Korea. Joining the roundtable was Chinese author Bai Lang, also a member of the fact-finding commission, who had returned to Korea

FIGURE 1.3. Nora Rodd, *left*, with Pak Den Ai (Pak Chŏng-ae) during the 1951 visit. *Women of the Whole World*, February 1955.

many times since. Bai echoed Felton's observations, praising Korean women's strength.[108]

When the fighting stopped in a stalemate, the WIDF continued to call for a lasting peace to replace the armistice. When the cease-fire led to periodic clashes, the WIDF sounded alarm bells at the growing tension, with fingers pointed squarely at the United States for "continuing its policy of domination, in league with the reactionary forces at present in power [in the South], who themselves placed the population under complete oppression."[109] Based largely on information provided by the KDWU, the WIDF accounts of the situation in Korea duplicated the official North Korean narrative of the war as an attack instigated by the South with US support, against charges that the North "invaded." While the origins of the Korean War, from crude questions about who first pulled the trigger to complex structural causes, continue to be a source of contentious historical debate, undeniable is the fact that division was imposed by external forces upon Korea, and when all-out civil war broke out as a result, outside forces once again intervened.[110] This prolonged what would have been a relatively quick end to the fighting, thereby exacting untold suffering with millions of civilian deaths, as witnessed by the women's fact-finding commission. As discussed in the next chapter, a long view of the Korean War places it alongside other wars of national liberation. In the years after the armistice, the WIDF therefore made consistent reference to continued solidarity with Korean women "fighting along with their people for the unconditional, total and immediate withdrawal of US troops stationed in the southern part of their country, so that the Korean people can themselves proceed with the peaceful reunification of their homeland without any foreign interference."[111]

Vicissitudes of Maternal Feminism

The Federation devoted its work to advocating peace and curbing militarism during and after the Korean War, and it did so by appealing to maternalism. The wartime commission's report, for instance, called on the "women and mothers" of the world to heed the "voice of the tortured and heroic mothers of Korea":

> We call upon the women and the mothers, to make this document known to every home, factory, field—to every man and woman of goodwill. It is the voice of the tortured and heroic mothers of Korea. It is the voice of peace itself.... We especially call upon women and mothers of the USA, Great Britain, and other countries of the world whose governments have sent troops to Korea to intensify their efforts to get their sons and husbands out of Korea.... If we continue to let this war of mass destruction to go on in Korea, it will spread to all parts of the

world and what is happening in Korea will be repeated elsewhere. By saving the mothers and children of Korea we save our own families.[112]

The 1953 World Congress of Women with which this chapter began likewise called on all women to unite as mothers, workers, and citizens for world peace. Bringing together 1,990 representatives from sixty-seven countries, including 613 delegates, 1,312 guests, and sixty-five observers, the WIDF placed the importance of the congress not only on the increase in the number of participants but also on the participation of women's organizations not affiliated with the Federation, such as WILPF and the Young Women's Christian Association (YWCA), which brought diverse perspectives to the congress. Nine women attended from the United States, among them Lillian Levine, chair of the Brooklyn Peace Committee, and Dorothy Burnham, a noted civil rights leader.

Assessing the global mobilization of their members against the Korean War in the previous three years, member organizations reported that the antiwar campaign had made significant headway. For example, the Union of Italian Women had asked young girls to make peace flags with small squares of fabric in rainbow colors, with their names embroidered on them; by February 1953, twenty-five thousand flags had been made with two hundred thousand names; and Hungarian women collected peace pledges door to door, designating outstanding streets and apartments with the most pledges as "Peace Street" or "Peace Apartment."[113] Levine of the Brooklyn Peace Committee reported that thirty thousand letters against the war were reaching the US president Dwight Eisenhower every day, and Ryo Oyama of Japan wrote on behalf of the "Japanese masses, who are now firmly determined not to fight our Asian neighbors," criticizing the San Francisco Treaty that established "American war bases all over Japan, totaling over 700," from where "American war planes have taken off, carrying bombs for killing our Korean brothers and sisters en masse."[114]

Even as delegates celebrated the expansion and effectiveness of the Federation, discussions at the congress showed subtle differences in the way its members conceptualized the source of their power as women, harking back to debates earlier in the century about women's equality and difference. For instance, French participant Colette Jeanson rejected "women-specific" issues and appealed to human universality: "Women are absolutely aware that their economic, social and political demands are part of the general problem," and therefore "their demands far outreach their own special needs. . . . Their struggle is the struggle of the whole of society. That is why the 'feminist' conception is now out of date."[115] On the other hand, Thel Murrel of Britain highlighted the experience of women as mothers, emphasizing women's common cause for peace despite their differences. Remembering the congress as a "wonderful moment when we . . .

found ourselves among hundreds of women of many races and colors all talking fast in different languages, many wearing national costumes," she concluded that despite these differences, "we knew that we were all there for the same thing—to defend peace and our children."[116] Maternal strategies that emphasized the need to fight for the rights of mothers and children helped unite different groups of women, appealing to the "universality of motherhood."[117] As historian Judy Wu notes in the context of the US war in Vietnam, "maternalist and gender essentialist justification for women's engagement in international politics" was particularly salient in the context of the Cold War because women's political activism could be couched as "commonsense" and "nonideological," carried out for the sake of their children.[118]

However, women also advocated *for* war as "militant mothers."[119] While appealing to US and British mothers during her meeting with the WIDF Council in February 1951, Hŏ Chŏng-suk made a point to demonstrate the fighting spirit of Korean women, comparing them to the Soviet heroine Zoya Kosmodemyanskaya: "The patriotism and heroism of our women has been no less than that of the men . . . . Young women and girls have asked to be sent to the front. Many of them are fighting today in the front lines of the People's Army."[120] In the face of threats to family and country, Korean women actively joined military mobilizations throughout the Cold War. Indeed, the WIDF distinguished its own active pursuit of peace from pacifism, criticizing the latter as bourgeois for its passive rejection of war.[121] The WIDF's own publications often used militaristic language, describing women activists as "soldiers of peace" and as "heroines" in the "fight for national independence."[122] Likewise, Korean women rejected pacifism, asking women of the world to join the "Month of Joint Anti-imperialist Struggle for the Withdrawal of the US Imperialist Aggression Army from South Korea" between June 25 and July 27, on the anniversary dates of the formal beginning of the Korean War and the signing of the armistice. They were skeptical that the UN could be an instrument of peace, recalling its role during the war, and demanded the dissolution of the United Nations Commission for the Unification and Rehabilitation of Korea (UNCURK, 1950–1973), established concurrently with the UN Command.[123] In fact, the fact-finding commission during the war faced traumatized women who demanded retribution rather than peace by asking, "What are you going to do to help us get our revenge? I cannot live without revenge."[124] Such reactions dramatically illustrate the ambiguities of war and peace during the Cold War, under which maternalism could be deployed for both war and peace.[125]

Leading the first major global antiwar campaign during the Cold War, the WIDF greeted news of the Korean armistice with pride as "a great victory for the forces of peace, among whom women occupy a leading place."[126] At the next WIDF

Executive Committee meeting in January 1954, Cotton opened the meeting by again crediting the women's peace movement for the cease-fire in Korea, proving "the efficiency of collective action."[127] Encouraged by the news of the armistice, the executive committee worked in two commissions to draft the appeal for International Women's Day and a resolution calling on member organizations to mobilize for disarmament and for the conclusion of peace in Vietnam and Korea.[128] The Federation knew that the Korean cease-fire was a temporary solution and called for a permanent peace settlement, at a time when others were simply relieved that the fighting had stopped. In fact, Felton, elected as one of the WIDF vice presidents in 1953, observed that "during these campaigns a growing realization developed of the connection between rising prices and the policy of rearmament, but the feeling of relief engendered by the Korean Armistice, instead of spurring people to fresh activity for peace tended to lead to a diversion of efforts from the international field."[129]

Despite the personal consequences of her work in Korea, Felton maintained her connections to Korean women and peace activism throughout the 1950s, moving to India in 1956, where she continued to work with peace activists until her death in March 1970.[130] While her 1952 Stalin Peace Prize and WIDF vice presidency pegged her as communist, her writings clearly indicated her desire to overcome Cold War divisions and her frustrations at the deep hostility on both sides. Her move to India is telling. As we will see in chapter 3, she along with several other members of the fact-finding commission would ultimately leave the Federation in 1956. But before that, Felton described her trip to Korea as "the longest and most significant journey of my life," a sentiment deeply affecting those in Korea who heard of her persecution.[131] In homage to her courage and solidarity, Korean poet Ri Yong-ak dedicated a poem to Felton.[132]

> To Ms. Monica Felton: Upon hearing of [Prime Minister Clement] Attlee government's persecution of Ms. Monica Felton, British member of the WIDF fact-finding commission (translated by Flora M. Kim)
>
> > To peace raises truth
> > Consciences of the world,
> > Calling them to its guard posts.
> > And that is what
> > Attlee fears the most.
> >
> > Dear Ms. Monica Felton
> >
> > In Pyongyang, where you used to roam
> > Enraged, again pour down
> > Crazy bombs today
> > Upon hospitals and schools

Of which only brick chimneys remain,
Upon shacks that already rejected sorrows.

My gray-haired mother is gone,
My beloved siblings are lost,
And I tell you with all my heart—
You are righteous.

You couldn't part without pain
From these people with thick hair:
Ten-year-old Kim Sŏng-ae,
Who was killed with a livid bayonet,
Whose father was bound and thrown into water,
Whose mother's breasts were cut out;

Eight-year-old Pak Sang-ok, who,
When asked, "Who killed your mom and sis?"
Answered with glaring eyes shaded by wet lashes:
"Americans."

On behalf of him, on behalf of her,
On behalf of too many people with cruel fate,
I tell you with all my heart—
You are righteous.

Dear Ms. Monica Felton,

On a May afternoon, on a nameless hilltop
In Hwanghae Province,
When the "Big Grave" was dug up, unearthing
Countless children in the tens and twenties,
Countless women in hundreds,
Buried alive in ochre pits,
Even the passing clouds stopped;
Even the birds could not continue singing.

From our Sudol, Pongnam, and Okhŭi,
Their faces not even recognizable,
You couldn't help seeing your Johns and Marys
Who were dear to you in your land.

Dear Ms. Monica Felton,

Although the Attlee faction judges you as "traitor,"
Even the waves of the Thames

That course through the darkness know
The scathing judgment of the people
Of the world will come upon them.

The light of truth has lit the front line of peace
On the crossroads of the century;
Who dare extinguish the light?
Truth has called the consciences
To the crossroads;
Who dare silence truth?

Dear Ms. Monica Felton,

Hills are steeped in the blood of our brothers.
They are burning with vengeance for our brothers.
Till the day we put down the last of invading
American and British troops,
We will not even wail bitterly.
And we tell you with all our hearts—

As our fight will surely win,
Your struggles will prevail.

July 1951

Despite the triumphant celebration of women's capacity for united action to achieve peace, unity was a consistent challenge, already tested in the varied approaches to the question of difference between liberal and communist women earlier in the century. The Cold War further divided and reified this clash. While the liberal West prioritized individual rights, the communist East emphasized collective rights based on structural analyses of inequities. As attested to by the early and active inclusion of Third World women in the WIDF, the organization integrated the analyses of gender, class, and race long before the term "intersectional" came into vogue.[133] Looking beyond national borders to apply such critique internationally, the WIDF condemned imperialism and colonialism. Rather than relying on universal concepts such as human rights, the WIDF paid attention to the particularities of women's lives, such as religious prescriptions and traditional laws on marriage and children, the economic conditions of working women, and racist practices that perpetuated segregation and apartheid. Unity would be forged by collective struggle against such systemic problems.

The convergence of Cold War ideologies, however, in the form of the welfare state—both capitalist and communist—preserved the ideal of domesticity and its gendered division of labor, exemplified most by maternalism itself.[134] Maternalism therefore became one of the defining features of Cold War feminism in order to bridge the ideological divide, but conflict also arose on how to conceptualize peace. Moving from the specific debates and activities that women engaged in during the Korean War, the next chapter traces the complex history of preceding discussions about women's roles in politics, the place of Asian and Korean women in the international women's movement, and how to define peace—issues that would become so contentious as to split the WIDF in 1963. But first we examine how peace in the colonial and semicolonial world was different from pacifism, contingent on *justice* that required struggle against imperialism.

2
ANTI-IMPERIALIST STRUGGLE FOR A JUST PEACE

> There was no difference in our willingness to be in unity with one mind and common purpose against US imperialist aggression for the sake of peace, against war, and for national independence. The noble ideology of internationalism eradicates all foul feelings of human hatred and ethnic discrimination.
>
> Chang Sun-il, 1953

> By defending her own child against war, against the atomic menace, and against misery and servitude, a mother also defends other people's children. . . . Every one of the women, clasping the baby against her heart, thought of her own child. Whether a baby is white, yellow or black it is the future of the world and the sweetness of life. The things that divide us are trifling compared to the things which unite us.
>
> WIDF, 1955

The sense of urgency at the immediate disaster of the Korean War catapulted the first global peace campaign during the Cold War. On the one-year anniversary of the signing of the 1953 Korean Armistice, women celebrated the vastly increased capacities of women in Asia and Africa, pointing to the 1954 Geneva Agreement on Indochina as yet another sign that the "forces of peace have triumphed over war."[1] Especially impressive in their "size and authority" among the national delegations at the 1953 World Congress of Women, women's organizations in Asia had grown through their participation in the global movement. The Federation of Japanese Women's Organizations, or Fudanren, fought to ban military conscription and atomic weapons, while the Congress of Indonesian Women showed a dramatic growth in membership from eight thousand to eighty-eight thousand women; the National Federation of Indian Women was founded with over one hundred thousand women at the founding congress in Calcutta (Kolkata), and the Union of Vietnamese Women united over three million women. Listing these achievements while celebrating the development of the postwar Japanese women's movement, the president of Fudanren and one of the WIDF vice presidents, veteran feminist Raicho Hiratsuka, noted the significance of the outbreak of the Korean War for Japanese women.

News of the war had broken in Japan during the visit of the US secretary of state, John Foster Dulles, just one day after Fudanren had submitted to him an appeal against the installation of US military bases in Japan, urging peaceful coexistence and friendly relations with China.[2] Alarmed by news of the war in Korea, the women of Fudanren had received widespread support across a diverse spectrum for their appeal for disarmament, and yet their call went unheeded by the US occupation forces—an affront that only gathered more women's organizations under the Fudanren umbrella. Over thirty member organizations from different strata, including "women workers, office girls, and even mothers and wives of workers and farmers, in co-operation with the intelligentsia," had joined by the next year, expanding the movement beyond national issues and across ideological lines to acquire "a spirit of international solidarity."[3]

Joining this women's movement was the Korean Democratic Women's Union of Japan (Chaeil Chosŏn minju nyŏsŏng tongmaeng), formed on October 12, 1947, by the Korean women residents there.[4] While other leftist Korean groups in Japan did not survive the US occupation, as they were forced to disband by 1949, and the General Association of Korean Residents in Japan (Ch'ongryŏn) would not be formed until 1955, the KDWU of Japan continued its work, demonstrating the resilience and significance of women's organizing under the auspices of the peace movement and the WIDF.[5] They tried to send delegates to the international women's meetings despite repeated oppression, calling for a peaceful resolution to the conflict in Korea and against any remilitarization of Japan as a threat to Asia. In solidarity with the WIDF, they emphasized peace, children's education, and the protection of families, reiterating many of the same calls from the Stockholm Peace Appeal to ban atomic weapons. As of August 15, 1951, five million signatures for the appeal came from Japan, of which 75 percent were reportedly collected by Korean residents.[6] Warning against a simple numbers game, however, organizers emphasized the need to connect peace to concrete issues such as women's rights, social welfare, and Korean unification.[7]

This chapter traces the women's movement for decolonization in the years roughly coinciding with the Korean War through three pivotal gatherings—the 1949 Asia Women's Conference, the 1952 Asia Pacific Peace Conference, and back to the 1953 World Congress of Women in Copenhagen that opened and closed the last chapter—which illustrate not only the lead that Asian women took in this movement but also the international solidarity that was an integral part. Neither the histories of Third World solidarity nor the histories of the international peace movement have positioned Asian women at the center of the story, but the history of colonialism shaped the definition of peace in the postcolonial world. When the 1919 Versailles peace negotiations failed to include representatives from the colonized nations, Wilsonian principles of self-determination proved anemic next to the more militant calls to fight imperialism.[8] Definitions of peace and its substantive content would hence be intricately tied to movements for decolonization, causing rifts in all "Three Worlds" between peace activists, between communists, and between women. The peace sought by the women of Asia was therefore a key response to the Cold War, as historian Rachel Leow has argued, "against 'global north' ideas of peace activism as nonviolent nuclear disarmament movements," so that "popular anti-colonial Afro-Asianism itself [became] one of the largest peace movements in history."[9]

Anticolonial Afro-Asianism had roots among communists during the early days of the Comintern in the context of Japanese imperialism. An important catalyst in the development of anticolonial struggles in Asia, including Korea, was the Comintern-sponsored Congress of the Toilers of the Far East, which opened in Moscow on January 21 and concluded in Petrograd on February 2, 1922.[10] Although this was not a women's congress per se, the congress minutes included significant interventions by Korean women that would come to define the role of women in Korean liberation. Out of the 150 delegates, the largest contingent, with 54 delegates, represented Korea, which had been under Japanese colonial rule since 1910. Most of the remaining delegates came from China (44), Japan (16), and Mongolia (14), with a handful from the Dutch Indies (1), India (2), and the minority nations of Siberia. With slogans such as "Peace and Independence of the Country," "Land to Those Who Till It," and "Factories to the Workers," the main aim of the congress was to create a communist party in Japan, not through a proletarian revolution, but by shifting to an anti-imperialist united front of the masses against the Japanese Empire. As reflected in the much larger proportion of intellectuals (46) and peasants (46) attending the congress compared to workers (24), the congress included bourgeois democrats and nationalists in order to organize the broad masses against Japanese imperialism.

The Korean delegation was chaired by Kim Kyu-sik, former foreign minister of the Korean Provisional Government in Shanghai formed after the 1919 March First Independence Movement, the first large-scale mass protests against Japanese occupation in Korea. Also among the Korean delegates was the charismatic Yŏ Un-hyŏng, who would go on to lead the short-lived Korean People's Republic (KPR) after the Japanese defeat in 1945.[11] The Korean contingent was the largest and best-organized among the delegations, partly because of the over one hundred thousand Koreans settled by then throughout the Russian Far East.[12] They had migrated at the turn of the century, not only in search of opportunities, but also to escape the economic and political devastation caused by the Japanese imperial incursion into the region. Thousands of such Koreans in Russia had enlisted in the Red Army and other independent militias during the Russian civil war, particularly after the Japanese intervention.[13] According to American journalist Ernestine Evans, who covered the congress, "The Korean delegation gave the most encouragement to those who wanted to take the affair seriously as a representative conclave. There were fifty-two [sic] Koreans, representing various organizations and classes. They came from Vladivostok, from Manchuria, from Shanghai. Fifteen with prices on their heads, had slipped out of Korea."[14]

While only seven among the 150 delegates were women, and the woman question was not the main agenda, four of the seven women came from Korea, one from China, and two from Mongolian Buryat.[15] Despite their small number, they insisted on the crucial role of women in any revolution. Kim Wŏn-gyŏng, a communist member of the Korean Women's Patriotic League (Aeguk puinhoe), assured the assembled delegates that "the women of the East have been awakened," especially noting the Korean women's "valour and devotion to the revolution" as demonstrated during the 1919 March First Movement. She went on to suggest that "the October Revolution in Russia was the impulse that called forth the revolutionary movement of the Koreans in 1919," and proclaimed that "Korean women have long since shaken off the oriental traditions which confined them to the hearth and kept them in the bondage of their parents, husband and children."[16] Claiming women's liberation to be an integral part of the revolutionary struggle, communist women insisted that it should not be made a separate question. Kwŏn Ae-ra, another Korean communist woman at the congress, reminded the delegates that "the true emancipation of the peoples of the Far East does not consist in the emancipation of the men only, but also of the women."[17] Wary of being misunderstood, she argued that women's liberation should not become "a separate question" and that the movement for the emancipation of the peoples of the Far East be one in which women and men work cooperatively together. It nevertheless was up to both men and women, she reasoned, to provide women with the independent space to exercise their full capacity by giving them "a separate place in the movement," to "have their proper work, separated into proper departments." Redolent of later calls for women's autonomous space protected from male chauvinism, Kwŏn concluded her address with a searing warning to the congress that "women should not be looked down upon with contempt, and that they should not be looked upon slightly."[18]

Chŏng Ch'il-sŏng reminisces about the March First Independence Movement[19]

As a former *kisaeng* (courtesan) who left the profession and became a socialist after the March First uprising, Chŏng offered a description of the protests that is worth quoting at length. She describes the impact of this movement, especially on women like her in the lowest social strata at the time.[20] She vividly remembers the morning of March 1, 1919, when she heard loud uproars of crowds from the direction of the city center. As the funeral of Kojong, the last king of the Chosŏn dynasty, was scheduled for this day, a crowd of some three hundred thousand in their horse hats and white jackets were already milling around central Seoul. Running out, she was swept up in the mass of protesters as they made their way from the East to the West Gate, from the West to the South Gate, and then out the West Gate toward Independence Gate. While the protests continued for months throughout the country, spreading beyond the peninsula to overseas Koreans in Kando, Shanghai, and Japan, the nonviolent struggle ultimately failed to topple Japanese colonial rule. She left Korea shortly thereafter to study in Japan. Despite being over sixty years of age at the time of writing in 1957, she affirms her commitment to continue to struggle for the peaceful reunification and independence of Korea.

> Our country became a Japanese colony when I was 11 years old. Ten years after that, in March 1919, the independence movement rose up all across the country. At the time, our house was in Ch'ŏngjin-dong, close to Chongno Street in Seoul. . . . I heard legendary stories about the Russians in the midst of children's chatter. . . . It was the story of the victory of the great October Revolution in Russia in 1917. This legendary story became a beacon that reflected the dawn of the anticolonial struggle for national liberation, having a decisive influence on the Korean people's struggle for national liberation against Japan. It was the night of February 29, 1919. Younger brother in his senior year of Posŏng Middle School came back home late from school, holding a large sack along with his book bag. . . . The sack contained a declaration. It was the size of a traditional paper scroll written powerfully in ink, and I can still clearly recall the contents of the declaration in hundreds of copies.
>
> Long live Korean independence!
> Korea belongs to the Korean people!

Japanese troops go home!

Long live freedom and equality!

Mother and I folded the hundreds of declarations as my brother instructed us, in the shape of a paper plane that children make these days, folding one side to make a point so that they can be thrown silently. That night, my mother and I went around the alleys of Ch'ŏngjin-dong and sent the declaration flying over fences and through open gates and doors left ajar. We didn't miss a single house in Ch'ŏngjin-dong. According to my brother, male and female students from across Seoul were mobilized that night to distribute 300,000 copies of the declaration. . . . Next day, it was the morning of the first day of March. That day was the state funeral for the Chosŏn king, so the streets were crowded since dawn with the 300,000 residents of Seoul and those coming up from the countryside wearing white mourning caps and white robes. I was in a hurry to eat breakfast, when the sound of bursting cries, "Ah!" piercing the sky came repeatedly from the direction of T'apgol [Pagoda] Park and Chongno intersection. . . . Seeing the protest procession, I couldn't suppress the excitement swelling in my heart. No matter the scourge from the oppressors, I made up my mind to follow the patriots of Korea, mixing among the crowd.

On this day, any Koreans with blood flowing [in their veins] were choked with tears, cursing Japanese imperialism and its collaborating traitors, and joined the struggle to reclaim the country. Even grandmothers with a cane in one hand raised their other hand shouting "Long live" [Manse] until their throats became hoarse, and even young women who couldn't go outside freely came out and shouted for independence. Everyone lost themselves and shouted "Long live independence!" Water buckets were lined up along Chongno Street, which women kept filling to quench the throats of the protesters. . . . I heard from my brother that a Japanese policeman attacked a woman shouting independence, cutting off her right hand that held the Korean flag [T'aegŭkki], at which the woman picked up the fallen flag with her left hand shouting independence, when the officer also cut off her left hand. . . . Women fought with rocks, sickles, and swords, the same as men. In Haeju, even the *kisaengs* followed the female students and fought bravely. A *kisaeng* named Mun Yŏng-sin was

> imprisoned and tortured for six months but did not give in. The people's uprising continued like this for almost three months.... This lesson of the March Uprising showed the future path for the Korean people that the independence of our country must be achieved by "struggle" and not by "petition," and that a spontaneous fight without the leadership of the working class cannot be successful. Afterward, I went abroad in September of that year, joining a Marxist group to find a path for Korean independence through a revolution of the propertyless class.

Chŏng's position, and those of others at the congress, reflected ongoing discussions among early socialist feminists in Korea organizing against Japanese colonialism. Capturing a key difference between such leftist women from the liberal "New Women," or "modern girls" of the era, a 1929 periodical published their opposing views on the most appropriate hairdo for women. In a fiery debate that erupted across the pages of the current events magazine *Pyŏlgon'gŏn*, Kim Hwal-lan (1899–1970) advocated the short bobbed hair to foster hygiene while saving time grooming, in accordance with global fashion trends, as a basic condition for women's self-realization. Also known as Helen Kim after earning her PhD at Columbia University in 1930—one of the first Korean women to earn a doctorate—she was a founding member of the YWCA in Korea.[21] As one of the quintessential New Women, she embodied the liberal feminist ideal at the turn of the century—educated and liberated, upending traditional norms with new hairstyles and sartorial practices.[22] By contrast, the socialist Chŏng Chong-myŏng (1895–?), a nurse, midwife, and founding member of the center-left united front women's organization Kŭnuhoe (Rose of Sharon Friendship Association), argued that in order to appeal to the majority peasant women in Korea, organizers must be approachable and familiar, attending to everyday basic needs, which had been especially ravaged by the influx of modernization. Chŏng categorically dismissed Kim's arguments about hygiene by arguing that short loose hair could fall into food more easily, unlike the traditional long hairstyle tied up in a bun.[23] Kim would go on to become dean of Ehwa College (founded by American missionary Mary F. Scranton) in 1931, whereas Chŏng was sentenced to a three-year prison term that same year for her political organizing.[24] Such different life trajectories and clashing views on feminisms continued into postliberation Korea after the end of World War II, hardened by the division of the peninsula and emerging Cold War blocs.

Rather than treating these histories as a "failed" project of nationalism, the story of anti-imperialist women in this chapter paints the feminist futures they imagined through their international connections that in many ways were a continuation of colonial-era struggles.[25] As historian Vladimir Tikhonov argues, the 1920s–1930s "Red Age" of global communist militancy against both capitalism and imperialism was unprecedented in its scope for *mass* liberation and *international* coordination through the Comintern.[26] An important antecedent for later Third World solidarities, socialist women's commitment and allegiance to the oppressed peasant masses became a through-line in the birth of the Third World. To be clear, this is an entirely different genealogy from the liberal feminist tradition with imperialist connections.[27] For example, British women active in the international arena after World War II replaced their focus on peace and feminism with international development, because this was "a 'safe' subject that drew on older colonial and philanthropic Western female traditions," sustaining the imperialist ideology that continued to see problems in the Third World as a civilizational issue rather than a structural one.[28] No wonder that there seemed to be a hiatus in the women's movement between two "waves," as liberal women in the West focused on domestic issues in the postwar period, disavowing peace as too "political" precisely because it entailed decolonization and a reckoning with imperialist violence. The fact that peace had to be linked to communism and red-baited to the extent it was signals just how threatening it became to Western hegemony built on imperialism.

The West increasingly pathologized communism as a disease and orientalized it as "Asiatic" or the "yellow peril" that justified acts of violence in Asia as a defense of "freedom." Historian Young-sun Hong aptly calls this Western coalition against communism a form of "white solidarity." She points, for example, to the 1954 Geneva Conference, in which German chancellor Konrad Adenauer referred to the Russian, Chinese, Vietnamese, Korean, Cambodian, and Laotian delegates at the table as a "horde" that sent a "shudder through him and his white colleagues," incensed that they should be given equal seating.[29] Indicative of this East-West divide, Soviet bloc development aid to the Third World provided credits that could be used to buy capital goods and technical services at rates far below those of the World Bank or private Western banks, with relatively easier programs of repayment through the export of primary products, whereas capitalist aid sought profits through financing schemes, unequal terms of trade, and exploitative transfer of technology.[30] Etched in the very origin of the term "Third World" when French demographer Alfred Sauvy coined it in a 1952 article titled "Three Worlds, One Planet," the emergence of this Third World was thus predicated on the imperative for decolonization during the Cold War.[31] In that sense, the Third World was a political project rather than a geographic category, with precursors that predated the term.[32] Before the 1955 Bandung Conference, which is commonly associated with the beginnings of the Third World project, there were earlier roots laid by women.

The 1949 Asia Women's Conference for Decolonization

Six months before the official outbreak of the Korean War, the WIDF sponsored its first conference of Asian women in December 1949, attended by representatives from both sides of the recently divided Korea. As noted by Elisabeth Armstrong, the WIDF and its national affiliate organizations spearheaded the anti-imperialist mass coalition led by women seven years *before* Bandung.[33] Holding its Second Congress in Budapest in the first week of December 1948, the WIDF had included in its agenda a discussion of the "development of a women's democratic movement in the countries of Asia and Africa" as part of its ongoing work.[34] For this discussion, the WIDF prepared a preliminary report on women's conditions, including information from the WIDF delegation to Southeast Asia earlier that year. Although the delegation intended to study conditions in India, Burma, Malaya, Indonesia, and Vietnam, they were unable to visit Vietnam and Indonesia because of visa denials by the French and Dutch colonial governments.[35] But the report did include information on both Koreas, provided by Korean women who had participated in drafting the report: Cho Yŏng and Kim Hong-ok from the North, and Yu Yŏng-jun and another woman from the South.[36] Ending with a message to the women of Asia, the report linked fascism, racism, and imperialism as the origins of war by tracing the motivation for the founding of the WIDF to the experience of World War II: "When our Federation was formed, women, crushed by the sufferings inflicted by a fascist war, took the path of gathering together the women of every country in the world; to struggle for their rights, establish a genuine democracy and insure a durable peace, only guarantee of the prosperity of the home and of the happiness of the children; to defend the vital interests of women, *whatever the color of their skin, their nationality, their place in society, their religion, their political opinion.*"[37]

Unable to hold the gathering in Calcutta as originally proposed, the WIDF Secretariat wrote to governments of all Asian countries with a request to host the conference in the first months of 1949.[38] Ho Chi Minh replied personally to convey that Vietnam would have been honored to host but that "the stain of war dragged on by the French colonialists prevents you from coming to our country."[39] In the end, the impending Communist victory in China allowed Beijing to serve as the conference site, announced in June 1949 after the first

THE PREPARATORY COMMITTEE IN BUDAPEST AT WORK

FIGURE 2.1. Korean delegates to the WIDF Second Congress preparatory meeting in Budapest, Hungary, 1948. *The Women of Asia and Africa: Documents* (Budapest: WIDF, 1948).

national congress of Chinese women met between March and April to found the All-China Democratic Women's Federation (ACWF) with a membership of 22.6 million women.[40] Subsequently, an International Preparatory Committee began work months before the opening of the conference, composed of delegates from China, India, Indonesia, Korea, Mongolia, Vietnam, and the Soviet Asian republics.[41] Having joined the WIDF in October 1946, the KDWU was scheduled to send fifty delegates, including partisan women from the South.[42] Also attending in solidarity with the women of Asia were trade unionist Marian Ramelson, from Leeds, representing the British Committee of the WIDF, along with African American activists Ada Jackson and Eslanda Robeson of New York, the Roman Catholic Françoise Le Clerc of France, and Edith Buchaca of Cuba, making the long journey to Beijing on the Trans-Siberian Railway.[43] The conference was aptly held in the Hall for Strengthening Humanity in the formerly Forbidden City, now open to the masses after the Chinese Communist victory.

In an "appeal to the women of the imperialist countries," the Conference of the Women of Asia (hereafter, Asia Women's Conference) specifically addressed mothers, as they were to do during the Korean War: "Mothers of France, Britain and Holland! The imperialists are utilising your sons to force us to submit, through terror, to a thankless war. They are sending your sons off to die in defence of their profits. Mothers of the United States! It is the tanks and airplanes from your factories which come to burn our villages, destroy our meagre resources, massacre our children and further increase the indescribable horror of our lives."[44] One of the renowned delegates to the conference was Soong Ching-ling, vice president of China, who declared the women of Asia to be model examples of a powerful force for liberation. Even while acknowledging, "we must learn from the Soviet Union," she argued, "countries like the newly formed People's Republic of China, the People's Republic of Korea and the Democratic Republic of Viet Nam can be an example for those countries not yet able to liberate themselves and their women." Placing Asian women in the lead, she affirmed that "on the road to peace, the women of the world are the most potent force."[45]

The Korean women's magazine *Chosŏn Nyŏsŏng* devoted special coverage to the conference as an important juncture in the anti-imperialist united front. With a long history of struggle against imperialism, Asian women had a significant role to play in sharing their experiences internationally, as emphasized in the months leading up to the conference.[46] Returning from the conference on

FIGURE 2.2. Cover of *Chosŏn Nyŏsŏng*, February 1950, with Pak Chŏng-ae at the Asia Women's Conference

December 30, Korean women shared news of their trip during the All Korean Women Enthusiasts Congress on January 21, 1950, and adopted their own resolution affirming the Korean women's commitment to fulfill the conference resolutions.[47] With some two thousand women in attendance at the Enthusiasts Congress, the presence of South Korean women partisans added extra zeal to the gathering.[48] Extolling the conference for uniting the power of Asian women to advance democracy, women's rights, and world peace toward a better future for all children, they especially thanked the WIDF for the active support. Their resolution once again affirmed national liberation movements with close ties to movements for women's liberation.[49]

In a moving first-person account in the pages of the Korean women's magazine, Kim Im-sŏng provided a more intimate and detailed narrative of her experience than that conveyed by the resolutions and conference proceedings.[50] Attending the meeting with a ninety-eight-person delegation of forty representatives and fifty-eight performers, Kim had left for Beijing on November 29 from Pyongyang Station on the three o'clock train. Not only was this the first international gathering in which so many Korean women participated after the end of the Japanese occupation, but the reality that the group was going to "New China" left them "flush and bereft with joy." The delegation represented the diversity of "women warriors representing all walks of life," with labor heroes, peasant leaders, cultural workers, guards and soldiers, college students, teachers, and women activists, including underground partisans from the South.[51] They arrived in the border town of Sinŭiju at midnight, crossing over the Amrok (Yalu) River into China after a warm sendoff from the local villagers. Here Kim was poignantly reminded of the anticolonial partisans who would have crossed the same river into exile during the Japanese occupation. Across the river, the delegation was welcomed in the Chinese border town of Dandong by the mayor and local women's union, with a band playing below a large red banner that greeted the Korean women on behalf of the Liaoning Province Women's Federation. They switched to a Beijing-bound train, arriving in Shenyang on the morning of November 30, where they were also met by a large welcoming group of the local women's federation, along with Korean students singing the "Song of General Kim Il Sung." After a breakfast banquet, they left on the two o'clock train, joined by sixteen of the Chinese women from the local federation headed to the conference. They arrived in Beijing on the afternoon of December 1, spending the next several days taking in the sights of New China.

The historic meeting began on December 10 at four o'clock in the afternoon, with 165 Asian women representatives and an additional thirty-three guests from twenty-three countries, including Burma, China, Korea, India, Indonesia, Iran, Israel, Madagascar, Mongolia, Malaya, the Soviet Union, and Vietnam, as well as leftist women from Britain, France, the United States, and the Netherlands—four of the imperialist countries in Asia. As shown by the inclusion of Iran, Israel, and Madagascar, an expansive vision of Asia as the "East" encompassed not only East, South, and Southeast Asia as part of the "Far East," but also the Middle East and East Africa. However, with the US occupation of Japan, and the Cold War blocs beginning to form in the Asia Pacific, there were no women from Japan, Australia, or New Zealand at the conference. The Korean delegation included, from the North, Pak Chŏng-ae, who participated in drafting the main report, as well as Yu Yŏng-jun and Hŏ Chŏng-suk, who were among those drafting the report on children's rights; and from the South came Hŏ Ch'ŏl, an underground partisan whose family members had reportedly been killed by US occupation forces and South Korean authorities.[52] Citing such examples, the conference took aim at imperialism in Asia as obstacles toward peace and democracy, and adopted a resolution demanding the withdrawal of the UN Commission on Korea as a tool of US imperialism and sent a letter of protest to General Douglas MacArthur for prohibiting Japanese women from attending the conference.

Using a recurring expression of solidarity that deemed race, culture, or language as no obstacle, Kim Im-sŏng was struck by the presence of women from all over the world, united in common struggle:

> Women from all over the world with different faces in white, yellow, and black, wearing different clothes, and speaking different languages gathered together with burning hearts for the common goal of national independence, people's freedom, and world peace, singing together the *Internationale*. At the center of the main podium hung the emblem of the Asia Women's Conference, with a globe on which sat a dove symbolizing peace. Flanking the stage were thirty-one splendid national flags, surrounded by a variety of fragrant flowers and beautifully potted plants, all tangled warmly abloom as if it was spring.[53]

The first day of the conference opened with a welcome from Cai Chang, followed by the introduction of each delegation and a report from the WIDF secretary-general Marie-Claude Vaillant-Couturier. The day ended with the adoption of the agenda, the exchange of gifts, and several congratulatory messages from Chinese officials, including the famed writer and peace activist Guo Moruo.

The second day proceeded under KDWU president Pak Chŏng-ae's leadership, with a report by ADWF vice president Deng Yingchao, followed by reports from India, Iran, and Korea on the imperialist aggressions in Asia. The highlight of the conference for Kim came on the third day, with the solidarity shown by the Dutch and French delegates toward the Indonesian and Vietnamese women in their shared struggle to end Dutch and French imperialism. Exchanging flags of solidarity, Kim observed that the French delegate Jeannette Vermeersch embraced the younger Vietnamese delegate as if she was her own sister, writing that "their comradely embrace forged in tears was a beautiful memory that would live in our hearts for a long time."[54] Recalling her encounter with the Korean delegation at this conference, Vermeersch in turn recounted that the women from both North and South Korea "were firmly united in the struggle for the unification of their country. These women were painfully unhappy, as are all peoples in countries where civil war is fanned and supported by American imperialism.... The delegate from South Korea, overcome with emotion, had to leave the meeting. She was thinking of the fratricidal war perpetuated in her country by the American imperialists and sobbed forth the flood of tears held back for so many years in her tormented heart."[55] Worth underlining is that these assessments came *before* the official start of the Korean War. In that sense, like the war in Vietnam, the Korean War at its roots was a war of decolonization.

The next two days of the conference addressed the impact of imperialism broadly on women's and children's rights. The last day on December 16 resulted in a final resolution, with the famed Chinese feminist Ding Ling underscoring yet again the importance of international solidarity that would overcome racial divides. Kim Im-sŏng concluded her reflections by reiterating how "in the hearts of the Asian women who have lived through hardship, the scenes of each other's passionate kiss as an expression of pure and sublime international comradeship that completely overcomes any racial and ethnic discrimination will always live on as a beautiful memory."[56] The Korean War would become the first crucible to test the strength of these sentiments and women's commitment to international solidarity.

From Beijing to Warsaw and the Birth of the World Peace Council

Cold War historiography has habitually dismissed the left peace movement as a Soviet "offensive" or "front." However, its radical significance lies in the evolving conceptualization of peace, not as a pacifist endeavor, but as one that required active struggle for justice against imperialism. Prioritizing decolonization as a necessary condition for peace, Pak Chŏng-ae declared that the Korean War was an anticolonial war of national liberation for world peace: "Today, peace-loving peoples all over the world are enthusiastically supporting the Korean people struggling in blood against the US invaders. I witnessed this myself at the Second World Congress for Peace, confirmed by the fact that the representatives of each country embraced me, cheering enthusiastically because I was the representative of the Korean people.... The Korean people's struggle for justice to defend the country's independence, freedom, and honor is part of the struggle for the consolidation of world peace."[57] She concluded her 1951 press statement with a direct quote from the declaration made at the 1950 World Congress of Partisans for Peace in Warsaw, affirming that "we cannot wait for peace, but it must be won. Let us join forces to stop the war that is destroying Korea and may turn the whole world into flames!"

The first World Congress of Partisans for Peace had met in Paris (with a parallel meeting in Prague for those denied French visas) in April 1949, followed by a second meeting in Warsaw in November 1950, resulting in the formation of the World Peace Council (WPC), led by Nobel Prize–winning French physicist Frédéric Joliot-Curie.[58] The WIDF was a major partner in these efforts, and representatives from Korea actively participated from the beginning. *Chosŏn Nyŏsŏng* relayed the call for the first world congress for peace from the WIDF and the International Liaison Committee of Intellectuals for Peace, reporting on the Korean National Peace Committee's own declaration in support of the call, signed by thirty renowned figures, including women such as Pak Chŏng-ae, Yu Yŏng-jun, Choe Seung-hui, Pak Yŏng-sin, and Mun Ye-bong.[59] Gathering some 1,550 writers, actors, artists, scientists, engineers, professors, workers, farmers, entrepreneurs, religious leaders, women, youth, and activists, the Korean National Peace Committee (KNPC, Chosŏn p'yŏnghwa ongho chŏn'guk minjok wiwŏnhoe) held its founding congress on March 24, 1949, in preparation for the world congress. Its founding declaration specifically referred to armed struggles in Indonesia, Vietnam, China, Palestine, and Greece because of wars instigated by "imperialist aggression, war profiteers, and monopoly capitalists."[60]

Returning from the 1949 World Congress, Pak delivered her report back to women in Pyongyang. Thrilled to represent her own country at an international meeting after decades under colonial rule, she was touched by the warm welcome in Paris and especially stirred by the speech and serenade from a "black singer," who was none other than Paul Robeson.[61] Even as Pak was moved by the popular support of Parisians for the congress, with a mass rally of half a million people, she also noted the great disparity in wealth, where the homeless begged outside restaurants and a typical hotel charged 2,000 francs for a night's lodging, while workers made only 50 francs a day in wages.[62] Pak and Korean writer Han Sŏl-ya were elected to the 140-member WPC leadership committee, and the first WPC meeting in February 1951 in Berlin gathered representatives of some eighty nations, including the Asian and African countries under colonial rule not yet represented at the United Nations.[63] As a result, the WPC represented a much larger coalition of nations alongside the fifty-some UN member states, highlighting their broad anticolonial agenda.

The momentum for the formation of the WPC was the launch of the Stockholm Peace Appeal in March 1950, calling for a ban on all nuclear weapons. This made front-page news in Korea, with the launch of a national campaign to gather signatures, and gained fuel after the start of the Korean War as the threat of a US nuclear strike loomed.[64] As of June 1950, just before the start of the war, 5,680,000 people had already signed the appeal, with Korean women playing an active part in the campaign with the participation of leaders Yu Yŏng-jun and Chŏng Ch'il-sŏng.[65] Affiliated with the WPC, the KNPC, led by Han Sŏl-ya as chair and Pak as vice-chair, spearheaded the signature drive, which included high-profile individuals and celebrities such as composer Kim Sun-nam and film star Mun Ye-bong.

Celebrated author Ri T'ae-jun, originally from the South but who had moved to the North in 1946, had joined the Korean delegation to Warsaw in 1950. He published an evocative reflection—unusual for the party newspaper—on his impressions of Pak at the congress.[66] With some two thousand representatives from eighty-one nations gathered at the congress, Pak's international reputation, her ability to command an international audience with her fluent Russian, and her level of comfort in navigating such contexts seem to have left a deep impression. Ri's observations as a famed writer were detailed and descriptive:

> Ms. Pak Chŏng-ae has long devoted herself to international projects to consolidate peace between countries. She has spent more time on trains and airplanes than at home, and her news has appeared more often in foreign newspapers and magazines than in Korean ones.... Last winter, I attended the Second World Congress for Peace with Pak Chŏng-ae. At that time, I was left with a unique impression from Ms. Pak. She seemed familiar to any one of the representatives from the 81 countries, well acquainted with the formalities of all nations of the world, and was proficient in all procedures of international meetings. Ms. Pak's multifaceted international presence, rarely seen within Korea, poured forth at once. Rather than the Pak Chŏng-ae of Korea, she gave the impression of a "Pak Chŏng-ae of the World." But she was nonetheless Korean, and therefore the best representative of the Korean people.... She was also comfortable with any mode of living. In the train or on a plane, in a Chinese-style room or in a Russian-style one, at a Polish table or at a Hungarian table, she quickly adapted and acted naturally as if she were at her own home.... She wore white top to bottom. Her hair was combed simply. Her whole being gave a tranquil impression, and yet when she appeared in front of the auditorium of 3,000 people, they all rose from their seats cheering.... When her report was over, they all rose

again. It wasn't just the applause and cheers. As Pak Chŏng-ae in her white clothes came down from the podium, the representatives nearby competed to lift her up as if greeting a white dove of peace descending from the sky. The Chinese delegate ran over to take over and lift her up. The Soviet delegate rushed over too.... Some representatives sang their revolutionary songs and the bloodstained songs of partisans. Finally, the entire throng of 3,000 sang the *Internationale*.

Ri was not alone in his praise. The Russian poet and writer Nikolai Tikhonov, having met Pak at the congress, and himself also elected to the newly formed WPC, dedicated a poem to Pak Chŏng-ae from their time in Warsaw, titled "Pak Chŏng-ae at the Second World Peace Congress."[67]

Il saluto di Pak Den Ai
delegata della Corea Popolare

FIGURE 2.3. Pak Chŏng-ae at the World Peace Congress. *Polonia d'Oggi* [Poland today] 5, no. 7–8 (November–December 1950).

For her role in the international peace movement, Pak made headlines in 1951 as one among seven recipients of the inaugural Stalin Peace Prize (renamed the Lenin Peace Prize after de-Stalinization in 1956), which included a gold medal and prize money of 100,000 rubles.[68] The award ceremony was held in Moscow from April 2 to 6, 1951, in the presence of the award committee, which included French writer Louis Aragon and Chilean poet Pablo Neruda. The six other recipients included WPC president and French physicist Frédéric Joliot-Curie, vice president of China Soong Ching-ling, the dean of Canterbury Hewlett Johnson, the president of the WIDF Eugénie Cotton, US Episcopal bishop Arthur Moulton, and former Mexican ambassador Heriberto Jara.

Calls for peace, however, did not mean the total rejection of violence, as shown by parallel efforts on the war front. Eschewing pacifism, Pak lauded the efforts of the Korean People's Army and the Chinese People's Volunteers, who together had slain 260,695 enemy soldiers and captured 65,368 prisoners of war in the nine months since the outbreak of war.[69] Confident that such strides would lead to national reunification, Pak attributed the "wins" to the significance of the war as a "just war" for the Koreans and the Chinese in their anti-imperialist struggle, whereas it was an "unjust war" for their enemies. She was assured of victory because rather than an army of "mercenaries" like the US side, her side was a "people's" army, fighting not only for the reunification and independence of the Korean people, but to prevent a new world war in defense of peace. Despite the brave face put on to boost morale, however, the war was far more devastating for the North than the South. Carpet-bombing by the unrivaled US air force in a "scorched earth" campaign destroyed an estimated 75 percent of North Korean cities and industries; according to North Korean statistics, the population had decreased from 9.62 million in 1949 to 8.49 million by 1953.[70] As the war came to a stalemate by mid-1951, efforts for a just settlement were as important as the fate of the war. Rather than contradictory terms, war and peace came to signify points along the same continuum, in which the struggle against imperialism was the only way to truly guarantee peace, as articulated during the 1952 Asia Pacific Peace Conference.

The 1952 Asia Pacific Peace Conference against Imperialism

With the war in Korea and the ensuing rearmament of Japan, Asia now stood at the epicenter of the global peace movement. Beijing again became the site of another major international gathering, this time during the war itself. Concerns of remilitarization that had been focused on Europe during the previous peace congresses shifted to Asia, with the newly formed WPC suggesting that the next conference be held there.[71] The key significance of this shift was that anti-imperialism and decolonization became central not only for women's liberation, but also in definitions and practices of peace, so that rather than a pacifist leaning, as in the history of peace movements in the West, in the East peace became a militant project. As we will see in the next chapter, these developments in the peace movement in Asia became, in countries like China, Vietnam, and Korea, the backdrop to a critique of "peaceful coexistence" as appropriated by the Soviet détente from the mid-1950s to the mid-1960s. At a time of heightened anti-imperialist struggles throughout the Third World, such a calculated program of peaceful coexistence seemed a farce. By contrast, initiated at the 1949 Asia Women's Conference, the 1952 Asia Pacific Peace Conference would define peaceful coexistence in principled terms as attainable only through armed struggle against imperialism, rather than rapprochement. This was the *original* articulation of peaceful coexistence before the famed 1955 Bandung Conference, and at the root of the subsequent split between the Second and Third Worlds.

A four-day preparatory meeting for the Asia Pacific Peace Conference had been scheduled for May 1952 in Beijing, but because of travel delays, the meeting was held from June 3 to 6, with the participation of forty-seven representatives from twenty countries: Australia, Burma, Canada, Ceylon (Sri Lanka), Chile, China, India, Indonesia, Japan, Korea, Malaya, Mexico, Mongolia, New Zealand, Pakistan, the Philippines, Thailand, the United States, the USSR, and Vietnam.[72] As the participants took turns sharing their country's situation, Pak Chŏng-ae appealed to the delegates to oppose the US war in Korea, which threatened "to make the world a second and third Korea."[73] She reiterated arguments from the World Peace Congress in the context of Asia that decolonization to end colonial violence was a requirement for peace:

> Peace does not come on its own but must be won. The Korean people, who have already recognized this truth, are fighting at the forefront of the struggle for peace, sacrificing blood and life with weapons in their hands. The Korean people are well aware that the struggle against the US invaders for freedom and independence of their homeland is part of the struggle for world peace. The world historical victory of the Chinese people today, and the courageous and just struggle of the Vietnamese and Korean peoples, demonstrate that the imperialists can no longer successfully carry out their war of aggression to conquer the weak nations as before.[74]

Subsequently, the preparatory meeting proposed agenda items that included broad questions of ways to guarantee national independence, freedom, and peace in the Asia Pacific through cultural exchange and economic relations on an equal basis with mutual respect, opposing all sanctions and trade restrictions in order to improve people's livelihood and the welfare of women and children.

Building on the relationships formed at the 1949 Asia Women's Conference and the important role of the WIDF in organizing the World Peace Council, women made up a third of the 1952 Asia Pacific Peace Conference, many of whom were affiliated with the WIDF.[75] The conference lasted for eleven days, from October 2 to 12, 1952, claiming to represent the 1.6 billion people throughout the Asia Pacific that spanned not only the Far East and the Middle East but also the Americas as part of an expansive coalition of the trans-Pacific region. Attended by 367 representatives from thirty-seven countries, 34 observers, and 23 special guests, the conference included a total of 429 participants from diverse countries, ethnicities, religions, organizations, and occupations, encompassing workers, farmers, technicians, scholars, writers, poets, artists, journalists, lawyers, medical workers, entrepreneurs, and politicians.[76] Participating countries were Australia, Burma, Canada, Ceylon, Chile, China, Colombia, Costa Rica, Cypress, Ecuador, El Salvador, Guatemala, Honduras, India, Indonesia, Iran, Iraq, Israel, Japan, Korea, Laos, Lebanon, Syria, Malaya, Mexico, Mongolia, New Zealand, Nicaragua, Pakistan, Panama, Peru, the Philippines, Thailand, Turkey, the Soviet Union, the United States, and Vietnam. More than a decade before the 1966 Tricontinental Conference in Havana, Cuba, that brought together the three continents of Africa, Asia, and Latin America as an anti-imperialist coalition that would become the Global South, the peace movement against the Korean War forged a transcontinental alliance.

While the agenda addressed questions of national independence, cultural and economic exchange, women's and children's rights across the Asia Pacific, the conference specifically raised the alarm at the remilitarization of Japan as a major threat to peace, the need for a peaceful resolution to the Korean conflict through a just outcome, and a peace treaty among the Five Great Powers—the US, Britain, the USSR, China, and France—that would put an end to all war propaganda and future hostilities.[77] By setting the agenda in this way, the conference made explicit the need to safeguard the independence of all nations against imperialism as the very foundation for a lasting peace.

Among the Korean women attending the conference was the KDWU vice-chair Kim Yŏng-su, who shared detailed reflections about the trip through her women's magazine.[78] Leaving Pyongyang on September 17, the delegation's journey to Beijing took several days, made especially difficult by the war. Despite arriving in the early morning of September 22, the delegates were greeted at the station by a large crowd wearing red signs with the Chinese characters for welcome, *hwanyŏng*. The group was "moved to tears," Kim Yŏng-su related, "when young children came running to give us bouquets of flowers and hung on our necks with warm welcome."[79] From across the Asia Pacific, almost five hundred peace activists had come together in Beijing, although some delegates had trouble arriving in time because of obstruction in their home countries. When the conference began on the afternoon of October 2, an enlarged painting of Picasso's peace dove hung above the podium, with the national flags of the participating delegations decorating either side of the main stage. Among them stood the Korean flag with its five-pointed star, which according to Kim left her delegation speechless with emotion.[80]

In her opening address, Soong Ching-ling made clear the Asian roots of the conference, which followed in the footsteps of a peace conference in September 1933 held in secret in Shanghai. Organized by the Anti-imperialist League, the first Asia Pacific Peace Conference, Soong claimed, represented some thirty million people of Asia.[81] Tracing the history of colonial oppression in Asia, she expressed grave concern over the renewal of imperialist ambitions by the US, France, and Britain after the end of World War II, pointing to aggression in Korea, Vietnam, and Malaya. In that sense, the 1952 Asia Pacific Peace Conference aimed to stop the ongoing wars and demand a peaceful solution through talks, prohibition of weapons of mass destruction, and accountability for their use under international law.[82] Not only did she call for international trade and cultural exchange to foster peaceful relations between nations, but she advocated friendship and understanding, rather than war and hatred, between peoples of the world, "by achieving ethical conditions favorable to peaceful coexistence." The "ethical conditions" favorable to peace required nothing less than true national liberation as a necessary condition, "because true peace can never be established on the basis of one country's subjugation by another or the arbitrary encroachment on the sovereignty of another country."[83]

Following Soong, Guo Moruo's report laid responsibility for current hostilities squarely on the US government for disturbing the peace in Asia with its and its allies' military intervention in the Far East (in Korea, Vietnam, and Malaya) and sanctions against the Middle East (in Iran, Turkey, Iraq, Syria, and Lebanon).[84] The 1951 San Francisco Treaty that legally ended the US-led Allied occupation of Japan after World War II excluded the Soviet Union, China, Mongolia, Korea, India, and Burma from the talks, and was seen as the initial step toward rearming Japan, with some 612 US military bases, 300 of which would be permanent, violating the terms of the surrender. Guo noted with alarm the creation of a US-led "Pacific alliance" that included Australia and New Zealand, which would lead to the revival of the "Greater East Asia Co-Prosperity Sphere"—a euphemistic slogan for Japanese imperial rule over Asia between 1931 and 1945. Guo pointed to the release of some 184,000 Japanese war criminals, including those responsible for bacteriological warfare in the Asia Pacific War, who were now to blame for germ warfare in Korea.[85] Arguing that the people of the Asia Pacific cannot accept another threat of war when the memories of the Asia Pacific War were still so fresh, Guo argued that "the struggles for national liberation and peace movements are inseparable." Reviewing the peace movements across the region, he noted that in China, 340 million people had signed the appeal calling for a peace treaty among the Five Great Powers, claiming that "we cannot wait for peace; peace must be won through the unity of the peace-loving peoples."[86]

With the war ongoing in Korea, all speeches at the conference referenced the conflict, especially on the second day, as the head of the Korean delegation Han Sŏl-ya called for an end to the war with a peaceful and just solution. Han condemned the indiscriminate bombing and germ warfare by the US forces, calling for an immediate cease-fire in order to prevent the war from spreading throughout the Asia Pacific.[87] He repeatedly referred to ending the war as a linchpin to avoid similar dangers elsewhere, arguing that "to prevent the suffering and misery falling on the heads of the Korean people today from falling on the heads of the people of other countries in the future, we must first end the Korean War on an equitable and reasonable basis."[88] Critical of the stalemate around the armistice negotiations, Han proposed three conditions for a peaceful resolution to the war: the exchange of POWs according to the 1949 Geneva Conventions; an immediate stop to indiscriminate bombing and germ warfare and the prosecution of those responsible for war crimes; and the withdrawal of all foreign troops from Korea so that Koreans may solve their own problems.

The Vietnamese representative concurred, pointing out that like the US-led UN coalition in Korea, seventeen countries had contributed troops to the French forces in Vietnam, and just as the US had bombed the hydroelectric dam in North Korea on January 13, 1952, eighty French B-26 bombers had destroyed dams in North Vietnam.[89] Maintaining that the Korea question was a concern for all peoples, he argued that "the American imperialist bloc's war of aggression against Korea is the first step in their plan to provoke a new war of aggression against Asia," as shown by the US policy in support of the British in Malaya and the French in Indochina.[90] The head of the Colombian delegation, Diego Montaña Cuéllar, added that countries like his—the only Latin American country to contribute troops to the UN forces in Korea—were used as a reserve military force by the US and pressured to contribute soldiers, in violation of the national constitution and the will of the people.[91] Observing the detrimental effects of submitting to US pressure, Cuéllar argued, other Latin American countries resisted; Guatemala and Mexico refused to contribute troops, and in Argentina, Brazil, Costa Rica, and Chile there were strikes, protests, and petitions against participation.

Despite all the criticism leveled against US policy, a seventeen-member US delegation attended the conference. Longtime peace activists Isobel and Edwin Cerney were among them, as well as two Japanese Americans—US Army veteran-turned-peace-activist Lewis Suzuki and formerly interned Tomoko Ikeda Wheaton, who was accompanied by her spouse Louis Wheaton, an African American labor activist.[92] Isobel Cerney thanked the conference participants for making a distinction between the government and the people of the United States, recognizing the responsibility of the people to stop the government's actions committed in their name.[93] Despite limited reporting in the country that kept the public in the dark, Cerney argued that the increasing death toll and worsening economic conditions were becoming a major campaign issue in the upcoming presidential elections, with growing public concerns that the conflict would escalate into another world war. More people were beginning to speak out, she claimed, especially the working class, with an unprecedented increase in the number of strikes in the last year calling for a return to peace. Another US delegate, Anita Willcox, agreed that a recent Gallup poll showed 70 percent of Americans supported an immediate stop to the war.[94] Attributing the use of napalm and other war atrocities to racism, as demonstrated by the lynchings and police brutality within the United States, she blamed the delayed opposition to the war on the mistaken public assumption that disarmament and a reduction in military spending would lead to mass unemployment and economic recession. The US delegates condemned their country's intervention in Korea and vowed to strengthen efforts to galvanize the peace movement back home. Sharing stories of a Korean War veteran who had donated his savings to help with the delegation's trip to participate in the conference, and another veteran who, in opposition to the war, had returned his medal of valor, the Americans went over to shake hands with the Korean delegation, gifting a potted plant in the spirit of friendship, with a note asking that the tree be planted in Korea to symbolize their friendship, "growing to become a large tree of life with lush green leafy branches, under the shades of which your sons and daughters may play."[95]

Monica Felton's presence at the conference as a special guest was especially meaningful given her participation in the 1951 WIDF fact-finding commission to Korea. Arriving in Beijing just after making a second visit to Korea in September, Felton observed just how much worse the devastation had become since her previous visit. Whereas there had been some semblance of life in 1951, today there was nothing left but destruction.[96]

> Now the old ruins show a new face. In all of Pyongyang, there are no buildings with walls or roofs. Not even ordinary areas have been spared damage from the recent barbaric bombings. . . . On the morning of

September 16, I went to see for myself the effects of the previous night's bombing. Around the city, in the countryside, in fields lush with crops without any military targets or buildings, the bombs struck onions and cabbages, leaving them pockmarked, and another thirteen bombed-out holes in a field of less than a half hectare. Most of the injured were women, still being transported to the hospital, and some of the dead were already settled in crude coffins. Two women were weeping as they watched the last of their father's face being buried. Beside him were two other bodies, and people's torn limbs remained where the explosion had swept them away. The peaceful face of a dead girl was next to a headless body torn apart into pieces.... The future of Korea—no matter what happens—is our future. We must not forget that the terror that has crept in there is the terror that can destroy the world. But, if we can capture the hope that exists there, it's not just hope for the future of the Korean people, but also hope for the entire human race. The Korean War has been going on far too long. The time has come for the people of the world to take action.[97]

Echoing the spirit of solidarity, a Belgian woman at the conference gave Kim Yŏng-su a blue kerchief with a kiss from the mothers of Belgium, "sending their thoughts and love to the heroic mothers and war orphans of Korea."[98] For Kim, the second day proved to be most memorable, as "the whole day felt as if it had been dedicated to welcome and support the Korean delegation." When the delegation delivered Pak Chŏng-ae's congratulatory message, the conference gave a standing ovation, "sending love and respect with a storm of applause to this great daughter and peace fighter born to the Korean people," and Han Sŏl-ya elicited a similar response at his report on the Korean situation. When the Indian delegation presented the Koreans with a gift at the end of the day, "they held us in embrace for a long time while the whole hall stood in standing ovation to cheer us, with the accompanying magnificent music in the hall that left us with a flood of emotion hard to describe." Delegates from New Zealand brought baby clothes for Korean children, at which "two women from Korea threw their arms round Rita Smith and me [Margaret Garland], their cheeks wet with tears."[99]

In the end, after intense discussions that sometimes lasted all night, the conference produced a cascading set of resolutions addressing both international questions and domestic conditions that together affirmed the importance of respect for national sovereignty and equality, in the belief that different political systems and ways of life could coexist without imperialism.[100] On the international side, the conference called for the removal of all foreign troops to prevent the remilitarization of Japan and a peace settlement toward the normalization of relations in the region, in support of the Japanese people in their struggle for independence, peace, and democratic rights. The conference also called for an end to the Korean War based on a just armistice, including the return of POWs to their home countries according to the Geneva Conventions, the cessation of indiscriminate bombing and germ warfare, and the withdrawal of all foreign troops, including the Chinese Volunteers, so that the Korean people could solve their domestic issues autonomously. Likewise, a peaceful resolution to the conflicts in Vietnam, Laos, Cambodia, Malaya, and the Middle East required respect for the independence of these nations without foreign intervention in domestic affairs. In order to undergird a general peace regime throughout the world, the conference called for a peace treaty among the Five Great Powers toward international disarmament and the banning of all weapons of mass destruction, including atomic, bacteriological, and chemical arms.

On the domestic side, the conference affirmed the importance of national independence for all nations, with the right to freely choose the desired political system and way of life, opposing the construction of foreign military bases as a violation of national sovereignty. To govern relations between independent nations, the conference advocated trade and cultural exchange based on the principles of equality and mutual benefit. It called for the immediate cessation of all artificial obstacles to trade, such as blockades and sanctions, monopolies, price fixing, and overblown military budgets, which have led to inflation and economic imbalance, decreasing the standard of living while increasing unemployment and in some cases serious food shortages and famine. This call for open trade and economic exchanges based on principles of equality may seem to contradict autarkic communist economic policy. However, post–Cold War scholarship has demonstrated just how important global trade was in both principle and policy, so much so that the economic constraints placed on the socialist bloc from integrating into the global economy may have led to political constraints that exacerbated the Cold War standoff.[101]

The conference further blamed war propaganda for fomenting hatred among peoples, including racism and discrimination against people of color, and for suppressing all forms of peace movements. It called for eliminating suspicion and countering hatred through cultural exchanges such as youth festivals, student exchanges, athletic competitions, and exchanges of music, arts, theater, films, and literature as the best method of achieving peaceful coexistence. Noting that women and children were most impacted by war, the conference called on peace-loving Asia Pacific women of all political and social backgrounds, regardless of ethnicity, language, or religion, to unite to achieve women's peace, safety, and equality. These would be attained by ensuring that international conflicts were solved fairly and peacefully, that the world's abundant resources were used to improve the people's welfare by shifting expenditures away from the military and toward social welfare, and that women's status was improved by guaranteeing their political, economic, educational, and social rights.

Ending with the performance of Prokofiev's oratorio *On Guard for Peace*, as three hundred Young Pioneers entered the hall throwing confetti, the conference issued its final appeal on the last day, underscoring the heavy responsibility of Americans to steer their government away from the path of war against the interests of the American people.[102] A letter was drafted to the UN General Assembly, denouncing its failure to uphold the UN Charter by intervening in Korea in violation of national sovereignty.[103] It also condemned the UN for its partisanship in refusing to admit the PRC into the UN Security Council despite representing 475 million people. It reiterated the UN's responsibility to respect and guarantee national sovereignty by ensuring the cessation of foreign interference, racial discrimination, and suppression of national liberation movements, to remove all obstacles in regular economic and cultural exchange in affirmation of peaceful coexistence among countries with different systems. The conference resolved to create a permanent liaison office and secretariat in Beijing to publicize and implement the decisions of the conference and to facilitate communication across different countries in the global peace movement.[104]

Attesting to the urgency for peace, the Asia Pacific Peace Conference was quickly followed by the People's Congress for Peace, hosted by the WPC in December 1952, just two months after the meeting in Beijing. Held from December 12 to 19, the congress brought to Vienna 1,857 representatives—about 500 of them women—from eighty-five countries, including Soong Ching-ling of China, Monica Felton of Britain, Lilly Waechter of West Germany, and Elisa Blanco of Brazil.[105] The three main issues addressed at the congress were again the questions of national liberation and security guarantees; ending current conflicts, especially in Korea; and international governance to ease tensions. As the ongoing war was an urgent issue, every one of the approximately two hundred speakers at the congress referred to it in some form. As in Beijing, the nineteen-member Korean delegation was moved by expressions of support during its stay in Vienna. Schoolchildren came to see the delegation, bringing donations of clothes, gloves, and handkerchiefs they had personally made and embroidered with doves of peace, along with letters for Korean children. Women from Uruguay gave the delegates a flag with signatures of those against the war as an expression of their solidarity; the Swedish women donated medical equipment; the English women contributed tablecloths and flags of peace; and the Soviet women offered clothes for Korean children. When Kim Yŏng-su, as KDWU vice-chair, spoke on behalf of all Korean women and children, there was reportedly not a dry eye in the hall.

The twenty-seven-member US delegation expressed the desire of Americans for peace, vowing to stop sending their husbands and sons to Korea and to bring the rest back home. A young veteran from Canada who had been sent to Korea made an urgent plea to the congress to stop the terrible calamity in Korea: "What have I seen in Korea, 50,000 km away from our country? As a young man, I saw what no one should have to see, the devastation caused by napalm, hard to see as a human being. If we do not immediately stop the terrible sins that Americans are now committing in Korea, that misfortune will sweep the world. Mothers and fathers of the whole world! In order to prevent your sons from being crippled like me, fight against the war!"[106] The congress ended with a unanimous resolution demanding an immediate end to all conflicts, including the Korean War, a peace treaty to be signed by the Five Great Powers, and the cessation of all foreign interference. The meeting assured the Korean delegation of "ultimate victory in our heroic struggle," because "the Korean struggle for independence is not an isolated one."[107]

After attending the congress in Vienna, the Korean delegation went on to Moscow and Leningrad, traveling by train between December and January for some ten days, visiting institutions such as libraries, museums, universities, and factories, in which women took up key positions as conductors, doctors, teachers, and managers.[108] Moved at the empathy shown for the Korean people at the congress, one of the Korean participants poignantly recounted their departure from Moscow along with the other delegates from the Asia Pacific region:

> In the train, there were people of various colors and races with different languages. Among them were people's representatives from Australia and the Philippines, whose armed forces were confronting us with guns at the 38th parallel due to their own reactionary governments. We greeted each other, sharing a table and eating together. There was no difference in our willingness to be in unity with one mind and common purpose against US imperialist aggression for the sake of peace, against war, and for national independence. The noble ideology of internationalism eradicates all foul feelings of human hatred and ethnic discrimination.

In the repeated references to unity despite differences, the antiracism of the antiimperialist front paradoxically reinforced racialized traits, as skin color and facial features came to represent ethnic diversity in a kind of "racial rainbow."[109]

WIDF materials also deployed varieties of traditional women's costumes such as kimonos, saris, and cheongsam to denote cultural and ethnic diversity, alongside stylized depictions of racialized groups colored "yellow," "black," and "white." To be sure, such practices of understanding humanity as essentially divided into different "races" were ubiquitous in this period, buttressed by the UN itself. The

1950 UNESCO "Statement on Race" took for granted the existence of races, even as the dangers of such a concept became self-evident after the genocidal violence of World War II.[110] As Young-sun Hong argues, the UN Charter affirmed the general principle of self-determination but did not guarantee rights to it, thereby betraying the imperialist origins of the international order, including human rights and humanitarian law. A case in point is the 1949 Geneva Conventions that govern conduct in war, including the treatment of POWs and their return to their home countries, over which the armistice negotiations in Korea had stalled. The conventions limited the purview of humanitarian agencies to civilian and military victims of "international armed conflicts," recognizing only those conflicts between sovereign states, while provisions for other armed conflicts applied only to noncombatants, thereby excluding insurgents fighting for national liberation from basic protections, despite the fact that such conflicts were precisely created by colonial wars and crises of decolonization.[111] Declaring the Korean conflict "an attack on the United Nations itself," the US bypassed the required congressional approval to officially declare war, instead using the banner of the UN to claim its intervention a "police action"; a UN Security Council resolution led to the formation of the UN Command under US authority, with General MacArthur as the commander-in-chief.[112] Without recognition of North Korea or China as sovereign states, the 1949 Geneva Conventions became a piece of paper in Korea, as in other colonial wars.

A Reunion in Copenhagen at the 1953 World Congress of Women

In the face of such limits to the new UN system, the women who joined the 1951 fact-finding commission risked their lives to answer the call of Korean women during the Korean War, and the WIDF provided an important platform through which women could come together. As noted in the previous chapter, the third World Congress of Women met in Copenhagen from June 5 to 11, 1953, over the course of seven days. Although the Korean, Vietnamese, and Malay delegates were denied visas to enter the country, they were nonetheless greeted by the congress "as if they were present" as they waited to meet with the WIDF Executive Committee in East Berlin.[113] Compared to the previous 1948 congress in Budapest with 385 women from fifty countries, participation had swelled to over 2,000 women from sixty-seven countries with the global mobilization of women against the Korean War. The Federation reported that

> for five days, all the delegates and guests at the Congress had kept up the hope of seeing the delegates from Korea and Viet-Nam arrive in Copenhagen. They were so near, in Berlin, less than 2 hours by plane.... When Mrs.

Baldwin, whose son had just come back from Korea and Mrs. Watmouth, wife of a soldier who has been a prisoner in Korea for two and a half years, carried the Korean flag; when an English working woman and the wife of a miner carried the flag of Malaya; when Mme. Challin, whose son had been killed in Viet-Nam, and Mme. Margerie, wife of a Marseille docker, held up the flag of Viet-Nam, all the women at the Congress pledged themselves to join their efforts to unite all women to put an end to these cruel wars.[114]

When Yu Man Oe (Yu Man-ok), one of the Korean delegates, spoke at the later meeting in Berlin, "Tears misted people's eyes, hearts were torn, when they heard her painful story of a family of 16 persons, of whom she is the only one left.... Appealing to the participants at the meeting, and through them to all women in the world, she said: 'You must not forget that if you relax the fight for peace for one minute, the horrors of war in Korea will reach out to you.'"[115]

FIGURE 2.4. Eugénie Cotton with Kim Eun Sou (Kim Yŏng-su), *left*, from Korea and Hoang Thiai, *right*, from Vietnam. *Women of the Whole World*, June 1953.

The Korean delegation, conducted by Madame Kim En Sou first on the right, is received at the headquarters of the WIDF in Berlin.

FIGURE 2.5. Korea's "little congress" in Berlin at the WIDF headquarters, June 13–16, 1953. *Women of the Whole World*, June 1953.

Despite the disappointing absence of Korean delegates in Copenhagen, a number of those who had been part of the 1951 fact-finding commission to Korea attended the 1953 congress, and Kate Fleron, the Danish journalist and observer in the delegation, invited them personally to her home. A rare and intimate account of the reunion by Maria Ovsyannikova, the Soviet delegate, was translated and printed in *Chosŏn Nyŏsŏng*.[116] Along with Fleron and Ovsyannikova, the reunion brought together eight of the twenty-one commission members, including Candelaria Rodriguez of Cuba, Abassia Fodil of Algeria, Ida Bachmann of Denmark, Monica Felton of Britain, Bai Lang of China, and Lilly Waechter of West Germany. Andrea Andreen of Sweden also joined them. Although not among the original members of the delegation, she had returned from a 1952 visit to Korea as part of a scientific delegation to investigate charges of germ warfare. In the following recollection, I follow Ovsyannikova's use of first names to refer to the women at the reunion as a sign of their friendship and intimacy.

In her account of the congress, Maria first set an evocative scene. The streets of Copenhagen were filled with excitement as ordinary Danes lined up outside the conference hall in order to get souvenir signatures from the international visitors. Taxi drivers offered free rides to show the foreign guests around town. The Egyptian delegate, an older peasant woman in gray hair, opened the congress:

> Her old clothes were worn out by the sunlight of the southern country. On her wrists with protruding veins toughened by hard work

hung jeweled bracelets, each of her fingers held rings, and each of her long ears wore long jewel-embellished earrings twinkling like dew drops. She spoke of the poverty in her country and the unprecedented abuse of peasants. As she said this, she took off the rings one by one from her fingers, took off the bracelets, and carefully took off the earrings from her ears. She gathered the jewels together and put them on the podium table. "Please use this toward the Federation's funds," she said. "We are poor. But we are many. It is a small token, but this is what we collected. We went from house to house. From each family, from each hut, they donated with sincerity. Rather than bringing it as money, we bought jewelry with that money. Please allocate some of these to the children of Korea. This is the wish of the women of our country."[117]

Despite the absence of the Korean, Vietnamese, and Malay delegates, Maria's account still shows how central their struggles were at the congress. The reunion of the women who had taken part in the 1951 trip to Korea was a moving testament to how women, separated by long distances and ideological divisions, managed to stay in touch and work in common cause through the bond of their shared experience. I quote at length Maria's own words to describe the scene of the reunion:

We reached a two-story house with pylons and tiny windows. The house was also covered in ivy. It seemed an uninhabited house. But when the doorbell rang, Kate came out and opened the door. Kate Fleron Jacobson! When I first faced her in the Moscow airfield, I never thought we would meet again like this two years later. . . . We went up to the second floor. A girl in white pajamas jumped out of the [door of the] second floor room that was prepared to greet us. She wrapped around her mother's knees and cautiously looked at us with curiosity. Kate took her daughter's hand, and said, "For whom did I go to Korea!" We were beside ourselves when we saw the girl. Candelaria called her a young angel, and was already twirling her around the room by her wrists. It occurred to me that when Kate Fleron left for Korea, this girl would have been barely a year old. As a mother, it's not so easy to leave a child of this age at home. Next to the long sofa, the low coffee table held glasses filled with champagne. Kate offered a toast to celebrate our friendship forged in the small and distant Korea. We continually cheered our friendship, for a victorious cease-fire in Korea, for world peace, and for our fellow friends who weren't there—our delegation members who were unable to participate in the Congress.[118]

But such camaraderie was not without challenges, as Maria recounted her first impression of Kate. She referred to her as a "bystander" who "was a biased observer trying to see everything from the notorious 'red propaganda' point of view." As a reporter, Kate had refused to join the delegation as an official member but did so as an observer, and she had been the only member of the group who did not sign the commission's report charging the United States and UN forces with war crimes. Maria interpreted Kate's actions as "extreme wariness" driven by ideological prejudice, but observed upon their reunion in Copenhagen that it was the "sadness of the Korean people and the tragedy in Korea" that ultimately brought everyone together, with Maria herself now able to "share a firm handshake with this Danish woman with satisfaction."[119]

As the women went around sharing stories from the two years since their 1951 trip, it was clear that the persecution and hardship the women faced as a result of their actions further solidified their resolve. While six of the eight delegation members at the reunion had not had any connection to the WIDF just two years earlier when they visited Korea, now Monica Felton, Candelaria Rodriguez, and Lilly Waechter were all vice presidents of the Federation. The three women suffered some of the worst consequences for their actions. In addition to losing her job and being expelled from the Labour Party, Monica was refused entry to several countries, including Canada, and was unable to reconnect with Nora Rodd, who had chaired the commission to Korea. After returning to Canada, Nora, the sixty-five-year old grandmother of three young men, had toured the country, campaigning for the return of Canadian soldiers. She spoke about what she had seen in Korea, making recordings to be distributed throughout the country, writing essays and poems against the war. Lilly had been arrested five times by the US occupation forces in West Germany, released each time after wide public protests. Monica had testified on her behalf during the last trial, and supporters attending the trial had penetrated past the guards to shower flowers upon Lilly and Monica. The latest sentence imposed on Lilly prohibited her from participating in any gathering of over five people, or from leaving her town of residence, and yet she defied these bans to attend the congress.

Candelaria had recently visited the Soviet Union, where she had reunited with Maria and left her her most prized possession—the national flag of Cuba.[120] In 1951, as Candelaria had prepared to leave for Korea, people had warned her that with this single trip she would be branded a national traitor. So she left with a small Cuban flag that she kept on her at all times, including when she signed the report documenting what she saw in Korea. She was arrested in transit on US orders, even before she set foot back in Cuba. While in jail, everything she had seen in Korea, the scenes of massacre in Sinch'ŏn and Anak, flashed before her eyes. It seemed that the dead got up at once and commanded, "You must speak." She began to speak first to the prison guards and police, and continued speaking to whoever was there among the prisoners, about the death of children, the use of napalm, the torture of women in Korea. When the guards tried to stop her, accusing her of being a communist traitor to the Cuban nation, she took out her flag and insisted that her actions were motivated by her love of country, and that it was imperative to stop the war in Korea to prevent Cuba from being engulfed and destroyed beyond recognition as Pyongyang had been. She would continue to carry her flag close to her heart as she traveled around the world to speak about what she had seen, until leaving it with Maria.

At Candelaria's story, the women shared their memory of witnessing the destruction of Wŏnsan, the countless bombs dropped on the wet rice patties and dry fields, the plowing oxens injured or burned to death, the dark and damp makeshift huts dug into the ground in which people lived, and the temporary office made of mud underneath the hills near Pyongyang where they had stayed during their visit.[121] Having visited Korea for the second time in 1952, Monica informed the group that this building was no longer there, so destroyed was the area by US bombing. She fondly remembered the interpreters and guides, especially Sin Hyŏn-ok with jet black hair and bright eyes, who as a student had dreams to go back to university to improve her Russian, and was often embarrassed by her mistakes. The thought of her and memories of the war's devastation blanketed the group in silence as Abassia Fodil from Algeria wiped tears from her face. Her husband was in prison, leaving her to raise their two young children and make a living by sewing. When things became difficult, she reminded herself of the Korean mothers and their pain, and now she was disappointed that Pak Chŏng-ae was barred from joining them in Copenhagen.

Breaking the silence, Monica asked the group if they had seen Austrian Eva Priester's book about Pak Chŏng-ae and germ warfare in Korea. The commission had debated whether to include the issue of germ warfare in their report. Although Monica had felt that there was not enough evidence to do so at the time of their visit, Lilly argued that they should have included warnings of this. Maria agreed and remembered how much the Vietnamese delegate Li-thi-Quê was affected by evidence of germ warfare and advocated to include it in the report, breaking her usual quiet demeanor. Ida Bachmann interjected that the French delegate, Gilette Ziegler, was busy writing against the war in Vietnam, and Lilly chimed in that Gilette had also been active during her trial as part of her defense committee, reporting on her case for the French newspapers. The group went down the list of other commission members, wondering about Elisabeth Gallo of Italy, Trees Soenito-Heyligers of the Netherlands, Hilde Cahn of Germany, the two other Chinese delegates (Liu Chin-yang and Li K'eng), the lawyer from Argentina Leonor Aguiar Vazquez, and Germaine Hannevard of Belgium.

Maria remembered how Germaine had explicitly warned the delegation at the beginning of the trip that her visit was motivated by humanitarian reasons, as she did not consider herself to be "political." However, after her return to Brussels, she joined numerous rallies on Korea calling for peace. Based on their exchange of letters, Maria described the embroidery hanging in front of Germaine's desk, on which was stitched in colorful thread a rose of Sharon, the Korean national flower.[122] Monica confessed that she was skeptical at first whether women from such different backgrounds, divergent as "water and fire," could work together. But time had proven to her that those with different views *can* come together and arrive at an agreement for the sake of truth and justice.[123] Kate concurred: "The visit to Korea became a great milestone in my life.... I came home and saw my little daughter. As I kissed her face, hands, cheeks and hair countless times, I couldn't help but cry. Facing my daughter after such a long while, I thought of the massacres by US soldiers in Sinch'ŏn and Anak, the shoes of young children here and there tossed up with the dirt at my feet. Alas, I really could no longer be a simple bystander."[124] Her publications after the trip indicting the Danish government for participating in the war had placed her on a blacklist. As Kate stood up to put her daughter to bed, the group bid their farewells, and Chinese delegate Bai Lang bowed with her hands on her heart to convey her thanks on behalf of Korean women, as a fellow woman of Asia and friend to Korea.[125]

Maria's account of the reunion is a mixture of both the highs and lows of their international solidarity, inescapably colored by her own political allegiances. Like her initial impression of Kate as "extremely wary," Maria remembered both Lilly and Candelaria to have been "reserved," noting that they had become more active through their peace work. Even as Maria recognized Candelaria to be a "delightful person who enjoyed dancing and singing most of her waking hours," she contrasted this with what she perceived to be her initial challenges in getting along with the group. But Candelaria also assessed Maria to have grown more "humane" and "honest" as a result of their shared experience. While the 1951 commission was clearly composed of women critical of Western imperialism, they were far from a homogeneous group, and the very intimacy of the 1953 reunion suggests there were substantial differences in social background and political approaches that required earnest discussion, negotiation, and compromise that ultimately brought the women closer together.

Monica's 1954 memoir *That's Why I Went* offers an added perspective that complements Maria's account. From her disagreement that there should be a "chair" for the commission, to the divisive issue of whether the delegation should try to visit the South, Monica recalled that at the outset "arguments were dividing the whole delegation into factions, and we were all growing more and more suspicious of each other."[126] Insisting that the delegation had to be as objective and impartial as possible to be effective, Monica and Kate were two of the most vocal members in the group, who insisted that the commission refrain from making politicized speeches about "capitalist tigers" and "imperialist aggressors" in the interest of finding the truth.[127] Although Kate, as an independent observer, declined her nomination to the editorial committee made up of professional writers in charge of drafting the final report, Monica volunteered to join the other nominees, Maria, Gilette Ziegler, Eva Priester, and Bai Lang, to bridge the East-West divide.[128] While Maria and Monica had each been wary of the other in the beginning, Monica recounted how that relationship had changed:

> Our public disagreement had given us a starting point for private discussion, and it had not taken me long to realise that, however great the difference in our personalities and in our experience of life, we had nevertheless both come to Korea with the same purpose: which was to find out the truth, and having found it to report it with unimpeachable accuracy. . . . Now that we had become friends our arguments started with the assumption that each of us was trying to understand the other's point of view, and that we usually—though not always—managed to reach agreement.[129]

Their shared experience forged a lasting sense of solidarity that was maintained through occasions when they could meet, as in Copenhagen, and through the exchange of letters that often took several intermediaries to get delivered and yet continued throughout the 1950s.

When the Korean War halted with a temporary cease-fire, international women renewed their efforts for a lasting peace and continued to build relationships, maintaining connections through both formal gatherings and informal letters. In October 1954, for example, Korean women were invited by Chinese women to celebrate the five-year anniversary of the founding of the PRC, where they were reunited with Lilly Waechter.[130] In April 1956, the Korean women attending the WIDF Council meeting in Beijing took the occasion to send a letter to Nora Rodd via the Canadian representative at the meeting. This was following Pak Chŏng-ae's 1953 letter to Rodd via the Korean delegation to the Red Cross meeting in Canada. Without formal diplomatic relations, communication between Korea and Canada had to be delivered through informal channels, and with no address available, Rodd sent her latest reply through her contacts at the Chinese women's federation via the Canadian affiliate of the WIDF.[131] Rodd's letter finally arrived at the Korean women's union office via Beijing. Although she

FIGURE 2.6. The KDWU Second Congress, with foreign guests. Cover of *Chosŏn Nyŏsŏng*, September 1954.

만경대 농업 협동 조합원들에게서 옥수수 선물을 받는 모니카 펠톤 녀사

FIGURE 2.7. Monica Felton's third visit with Korean women. *Chosŏn Nyŏsŏng*, October 1956.

was unable to read the Korean letter, she had fondly greeted the sight of Korean script with memories of the banners at the underground Moranbong Theater in Pyongyang, where the Korean women had made their moving appeals for peace. Remembering her time in Korea, she took another look at the silver spoon gifted to her in Anak with the words "In genuine friendship of women of the world" engraved on it.[132] Sending her regards to Pak Chŏng-ae, Hŏ Chŏng-suk, and Kim Kwi-sŏn, she recalled the faces of the Korean women she met in 1951 with the following poem.

> To the Women of Pyongyang (translated into Korean by Kim Chong-uk, back-translated into English by Flora M. Kim)
>
> May comes again, and apple blossoms fall in silence.
> Dancing gently, they fall on the dewy grass.
> New sprouts murmur; gentle songs of doves promise
> That a summer's day will come with a new dawn.
>
> White petals falling on the hills of Korea—
> Scent of Acacia filling the village entrance—
> Children playing in the streams of spring—
> Farmers leading their bulls to the field—
>
> Oh the dawns you constantly faced with fear!
> Oh the flower-patterned pillows strewn on the ground!
> Oh the desolate villages and hills filled with ashes!
> Oh the days you never saw your children again!
>
> You live on; though napalm no longer falls
> on the land of Korea, the bird of peace cries out still.
>
> May 22, 1956

Two years later, in May 1958, Nora Rodd again wrote from Canada in reply to a New Year's greeting card and International Women's Day postcard she had received from Korea.[133] Although the package had arrived too late for her March 8 women's meeting, Rodd shared the material with other Canadian peace women, to display at the International Children's Day picnic in June. Thanking the Korean women for the materials, Rodd again resolved to work for peace, as she had promised "in front of the graves of the children who were cruelly slaughtered in Sinch'ŏn."[134] The experiences of the Korean War and other struggles for decolonization connected women not only in places directly affected, but also in geographically far-flung places through global movements of solidarity. These networks were sustained against all odds through international gatherings where women could physically meet, and through personal letters as well as bulletins and magazines that shared news from across the world on women's efforts in their common struggle for peace. But the idea of a *just* peace as part of decolonization was interpreted very differently, depending on the local context—a difference over which the international women's movement would split, as the next chapter shows.

Part 2
THIRD WORLD RISING

3
STRUGGLE BETWEEN TWO LINES

Even if we build cities many times more splendid than before the war, and build an economy many times larger with great factories, our little ones lost in the last war will never live again. For the lives of these precious children who, once lost, will never return, we oppose war to the end.

Pak Chŏng-ae, 1955

As a result of the activity of all the women who, expressing it together, have found a new policy, mother-love is no longer an isolated and fearful emotion, a purely sentimental phenomenon caused by the biological function of women as mothers. It has become "human consciousness" and has acquired a force hitherto unknown in the world.

Gisella Floreanini, 1958

On May 26, 1958, eighteen women—the youngest being twenty-one and the oldest seventy-nine—set out from London to travel throughout Europe, making their way east all the way to Moscow and back, in a Women's Peace Caravan.[1] Their route would take them first through France, Belgium, Holland, and Germany, but when they got to Switzerland, they were arrested and held for two hours before being expelled from the country and told not to return for twenty years. Their trip was hardly easy, made on an eighteen-passenger coach that looked like a small school bus, packed with camping gear to make simple meals on the road. Sometimes the vehicle served as their lodging, since the trip was funded almost entirely through personal contributions from the participants. Despite the harsh treatment from the Swiss authorities, they were warmly welcomed wherever they went, with a demanding schedule of lectures, interviews, and rallies in support of peace. Their bus broke down in the mountains of Albania, but they continued their journey, with the help of provisions from local women, to visit Yugoslavia, Bulgaria, Romania, Hungary, Czechoslovakia, and Poland. They were finally airlifted to Moscow at the end of August before making their return route home by train and bus, again visiting local women and calling for peace throughout their three-month trip.

Dora Russell, a lifelong feminist and peace activist, proposed the idea for the unprecedented journey. At the third meeting of the Permanent International Committee of Mothers in Sofia, Bulgaria, from February 20 to 22, 1958, Russell, as the committee secretary, had proposed that a women's caravan of peace be organized to travel across Europe "to strengthen the bonds of friendship between the women of different countries."[2] In just three months after the proposal, the caravan of eighteen women was on its way, with each member paying £100 toward expenses. Russell provided her own camping coach for transport, and one of the two male drivers provided a truck for the luggage, folding beds, and cooking utensils. Among the caravan were Jane Wyatt, the oldest member and a well-known suffragette; Edith Adlam, a Quaker and leading member of the Women's International League for Peace and Freedom (WILPF); Doris Adams and Hilda Lettice, members of the British Women's Cooperative Guild; Wynsome Marshall, a journalist from New Zealand; two Irish-born sisters, Rosaleen and Paula Popp; Josephine Warren, a member of the Peace Pledge Union; and Julia James, actress and filmmaker, who was one of the youngest in the group and took the footage that would become the documentary *Women's Caravan of Peace*.[3]

Stressing the significance of the peace caravan, Gisella Floreanini, a deputy in the Italian Parliament and member of the WIDF Council, declared that men will have to follow women's example by adopting "mother love" as a new policy of "human consciousness" rather than as a biological function.[4] Explaining that the women's peace movement, as demonstrated by the peace caravan, presented a "new type of people's diplomacy" that offered "new forms of understanding and conversation," she asserted that the history of this movement will be "difficult to write" because "the historian who is preparing to write this history will find in his path thousands upon thousands of meetings, flags, doves, conferences and congresses." Although "women enthusiastically and courageously [made] a stand, proving more and more that they are capable of outstanding action," Floreanini suggested that such acts would not receive the attention they deserved. Indeed, were it not for Dora Russell's efforts and scattered records such as those left by the WIDF, the 1958 peace caravan would have been almost entirely forgotten, receiving little press coverage at the time or attention since, despite its unparalleled voyage. As Russell attests, "During all that journey there had not been one day when we were not speaking, meeting people or travelling; we were never more than three nights in one place, at times driving all night to keep appointments.... Although we were tired, we were still exalted, carrying back with us the memory of so many different friendly faces; courteous speeches from many men; and from women words that moved us so deeply because they fully echoed the aspirations and hopes within our own hearts."[5] Paradoxically, the very success of the trip and the enthusiastic welcome in the communist world sowed Cold War

FIGURE 3.1. Women's Peace Caravan members and their route. *Women of the Whole World*, October 1958.

The Women's Peace Caravan in Berlin

by Ruth DISTLER

The Caravan on its departure from London. Dora Russell, left, and Mabel Ridealgh, secretary of the Women's Cooperative Guild, right, (this organisation sent a delegate and helped in the preparation for the Caravan).

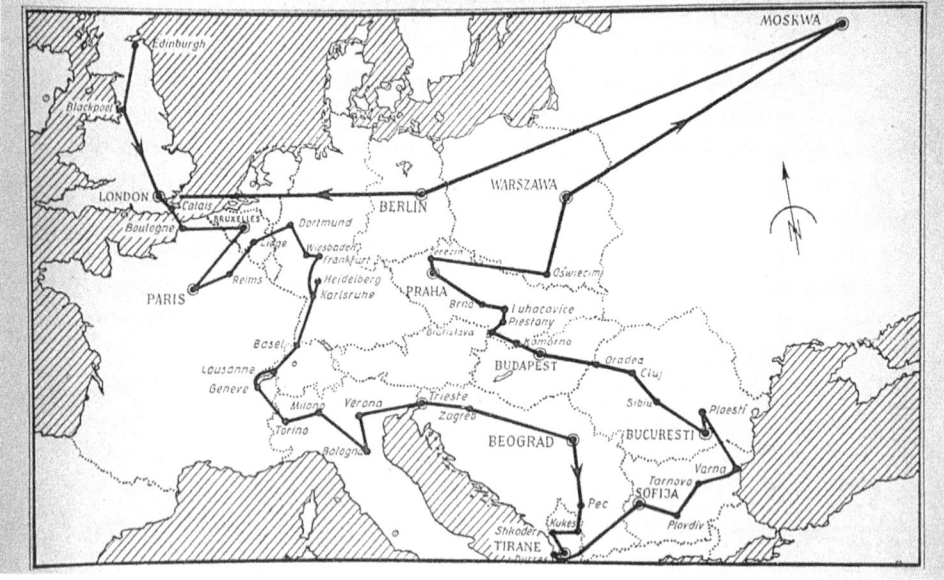

FIGURE 3.1. (Continued)

suspicions that the whole enterprise was propaganda, despite the nonpartisan ranks of the caravan, making publicity and advocacy efforts in the West challenging. Russell was exasperated by papers that refused to run even paid advertisements about the caravan, while Western governments, wary that peace advocacy would drive down public appetite for military budgets and Cold War policies, denied that communists could want peace.

As shown in the previous two chapters, maternalist strategies to bridge the Cold War divide had begun during the antiwar campaigns against the Korean War. The culmination of these efforts, some three years before the peace caravan, led to the 1955 World Congress of Mothers, organized by the WIDF in order to reach across partisan divisions, where the participants decided to set up the Permanent International Committee of Mothers. However, such attempts could not thwart conflicts even within the same bloc. Earlier in 1949, Yugoslavia was attacked for its "nationalist" policies and censured by the Soviet bloc, including the Federation, which expelled the Yugoslavian women's organization from WIDF membership. In 1956, the Hungarian Revolution was squashed by Soviet intervention, in violation of principles of sovereignty that Soviet leaders so highly espoused. Exposing the fragility of the socialist bloc and Soviet duplicity, the Cominform dissolved in 1956. This chapter traces the ups and downs of the international women's peace movement in which Korean women took part, to illustrate the theoretical debates about the proper definitions of peace and womanhood that would ultimately fracture the movement between "two lines." I first look at the 1955 World Congress of Mothers in detail to examine women's efforts to overcome ideological divisions, before mapping the debates that ensued with the rise of the Third World and the 1958 Afro-Asian Peoples' Solidarity Conference. The increasing friction between those still struggling against colonial violence and the shift in Soviet policy after the 1956 Twentieth Party Congress toward détente ultimately led to the Sino-Soviet split.[6] Rather than registering this conflict simply as a power struggle for hegemony over the socialist bloc, the history of the international women's movement reveals precisely what was at stake in this split that led to the Chinese women leaving the WIDF after the 1963 World Congress of Women.

Women Unite at the 1955 World Congress of Mothers

The WIDF Council meeting in Geneva in February 1955 unanimously agreed to convene a world congress of mothers in July of that year "to defend life against death, friendship against hatred, peace against war."[7] "In the name of the mother love that unites us all," the WIDF called on its duty to protect children "from the evils menacing them—hunger, cold, misery, disease and war which brings with it all other evils." While the World Congress of Mothers was only held once, in 1955, and the Permanent International Committee of Mothers became inactive by 1959 owing to heavy red-baiting in the West, the Japan Mothers' Congress that was an outgrowth of the World Congress continues to exist today as an active part of the women's peace movement against Japanese militarism in East Asia.[8] To prepare for the World Congress, national organizations actively raised funds for their delegations. The French sold flowers and pastries, organizing raffles with items collected by the women; the Swedes sold postcards; the Dutch sold bookmarks and handkerchiefs; and the Austrians issued special stamps.[9] Thousands of gatherings, large and small, were held all over the world, "in meeting halls of the big cities as well as in private homes and the farthest villages," publicizing the appeal for the congress, "which had been translated into twenty-three languages, to collect penny by penny the money for the journey, in spite of poverty and often in spite of repression."[10] Finally, from July 7 to 10, 1955, the World Congress of Mothers convened in Lausanne, Switzerland, "in defence of their children against war, and for disarmament and friendship between the peoples," as publicized in the official tagline for the congress.

A giant reproduction of a mother-and-child sculpture by the Romanian artist Lelia Zuaf became the towering symbolic backdrop to the meeting, at which the vast majority of participants were in fact mothers. But what made a lasting impression on many who were there was the strength of diversity amid the appeals to the universality of motherhood. WIDF reports noted the "most beautiful aspect when all the delegates were seated—those dark, fair, or silver-haired heads, the bright coloured costumes all made a symphony which harmonized perfectly with the blue scarf of Congress designed by Marie-Anne Lansiaux. Merely to say that there were 1,060 participants—964 delegates, 73 guests and 23 observers—would be insufficient to give a real picture of the immense force Congress represented."[11] Of those 964 delegates, many of them elected through their neighborhoods, workplaces, and schools, 835 were mothers, and 266 of

FIGURE 3.2. Pak Chŏng-ae (*second from left*) at the World Congress of Mothers with Cai Chang of China (*second from right*). *Women of the Whole World*, August/September 1955.

FIGURE 3.3. Pak Chŏng-ae, *right*, at World Congress of Mothers with delegates from Côte d'Ivoire and Austria. *Ssoryŏn Nyŏsŏng*, March 1956.

them had more than three children. Two-thirds of them had never before been to an international meeting. The age of the delegates ranged from those under thirty (128 of the delegates) to those over sixty (68 of the delegates), with the majority in between. Although the largest group—398—of the delegates were housewives, a variety of occupations were represented at the congress, with 32 members of parliaments or local governments, 150 workers (including farmers and office workers), 97 teachers, 57 doctors, 41 writers, 23 culture and science workers, 11 students, and 9 lawyers. Of the total delegates, 119 publicly spoke at the congress, some of them for the first time at such a large gathering. Their speeches were translated simultaneously into twelve languages.

In her opening speech, WIDF president Eugénie Cotton explained the rationale for holding such a congress by declaring that "mothers who gave life want to defend it. . . . We are here because we are convinced that our prime duty is to

FIGURE 3.4. Emblem of the 1955 World Congress of Mothers with sculpture by Zuaf

safeguard peace, because we know that we can work effectively if we all stand up against war, instead of resigning ourselves to it and weeping as women have done for so long whilst they believed that wars were inevitable evils. Today mothers no longer accept the inexorability of war. They demand the banning of atomic weapons, the peaceful use of atomic energy, disarmament and negotiation."[12] Assisted by 183 translators and typists, meetings throughout the congress covered general issues of health, the protection of children, education, culture, and the press, while other meetings were specific to various professions and religions.[13] A permanent international mothers' committee, made up of mothers nominated by different national organizations regardless of their membership in the WIDF, would continue the work of the congress. A manifesto was adopted declaring that the gathering had unleashed the power of women: "Coming from sixty-six countries and from all continents, with different languages, customs, religious beliefs, opinions and social conditions, we women and mothers have gathered together for the first time in history in a World Congress of Mothers . . . . We have discovered what an immense force we are. The things that divide us are trifling compared to the things which unite us. We understand better that the peoples of the world have no reason to be enemies. The world is big enough for everyone to find his place in it and live in peace."[14] Indeed, while women from the United States had difficulty participating in WIDF meetings with the disbanding in 1950 of the US affiliate, a wide array of peace activists from the US were able to attend the World Congress of Mothers, including Eslanda Goode Robeson; Charlotte A. Bass, vice presidential candidate for the Progressive Party in 1952; Anna Ganley, Peggy Wellman, and Helen Winter from Detroit; Florence Gowgiel with the Save Our Sons Committee from Illinois; Idell M. Umbles and Dorothy M. Hayes from the Chicago Women for Peace; and Valeric Taylor, the president of Women's Auxiliaries of the International Longshore and Warehouse Workers' Union from California.[15]

Among the presidium of the congress was Pak Chŏng-ae as chair of the Korean Democratic Women's Union. Standing at the podium on the opening day of the congress, Pak addressed an emotion-filled hall. Mindful of postwar reconstruction efforts in Korea at the time, Pak poignantly noted how such rebuilding would never bring back the lives lost during the war, as noted in the chapter's epigraph.[16] Inspired by Doris, the "ten-month-old baby girl from the Congo who came from Brazzaville to Lausanne with her very young mama . . . passed from one pair of arms to another," and who came to personify the very reason for the congress, Korean reporting reiterated the common desire among mothers of the world for peace.[17] Appealing to a shared motherhood that united mothers of the "black, white, and yellow races," *Chosŏn Nyŏsŏng* relayed the story of Doris's nineteen-year-old mother, the Congo delegate Véronique Bouesso, who was the only one to "run to this venue despite threats and blackmail from the oppressors" with a baby on her back, after leaving her older child with a friend back home.[18] References to "black, white, and yellow races" would be a running theme in textual and visual imagery throughout WIDF and KDWU publications.[19]

Underscoring the diverse languages, social status, customs, religions, and beliefs represented at the congress, the Korean women's magazine published a full translation of the resolution that emphasized the collective power of mothers to reiterate that "the things that divide us are trifling compared to the things which unite us."[20] Attributing the end of the wars in Korea and Vietnam to the "will of the people," the congress affirmed the ten principles adopted at the Bandung Conference just three months earlier in April 1955 as evidence that countries with different institutions can coexist peacefully with progress toward disarmament. Crediting such victories "to the indomitable joint efforts of the peace-loving people," the congress resolved to "dedicate the great power of our maternal love to those who are advocating for life and peace," avowing that "all children, whether yellow or black, are equal and have a right to life" and must be protected. To do so, the congress agreed to set up a Permanent International Committee of Mothers.

The correspondent for *La semaine de la femme* declared the significance of the congress as "a human tide, a tide of mothers speaking different languages and wearing gorgeous or humble dress, saris, sarongs, embroidered skirts, kimonos, plain frocks, under the material of which beat the same generous heart—for love shared and a hand outstretched across frontiers, across iron or gold curtains, across political convictions, so that in the near future the living forces of humanity can be embodied in the core of dreams come true."[21]

Subsequently, at the first meeting of the Permanent International Committee back in Lausanne in early February 1956, sixty-two delegates representing thirty-six countries brought together local organizations that had not previously been members of such international coalitions, including the Save Our Sons Committee in the US, the Polish Catholic organization Pax, the Italian Catholic Action, and the Belgian Co-operative Women's Guild.[22] The committee adopted three documents at the end of its first meeting: a Declaration of Mothers for the defense of children and against the danger of war, an appeal to mothers of the world for support of the declaration, and a message to the three nuclear-weapons states—the US, the USSR, and Great Britain—demanding that they come to an agreement to put an end to all nuclear testing. Dora Russell, who would go on to organize the 1958 Women's Caravan for Peace, was elected secretary, while Andrea Andreen was elected president.

Declaration of Mothers for the Defence of Children, against the Danger of War, February 1956

All mothers, all women, know from experience what terrible sufferings war brings to their families: misery, poverty, the destruction of homes and of millions of promising lives. In the course of the last war, some 40 million children were made orphans. . . . As mothers, we have the duty to demand the end of this threat and we have the right to be heard. Our first responsibility is the defence of human life. By their work in field and factory, in professional life and in the care of the family, women contribute their full share to the creation of wealth and will no longer endure the squandering of that wealth on armaments and war preparations. . . . We are convinced that all disputes can be solved by negotiation in a spirit of friendship and co-operation.

- We mothers call upon all statesmen and all peoples of the world to observe the spirit of the United Nations Charter, to abolish all military pacts which threaten peace, and to renounce the instrument of war as a means of settling disputes.
- We demand general, progressive, substantial and simultaneous disarmament, essential to remove the immediate danger of war.
- We demand, pending the prohibition of atomic weapons and complete disarmament, that all governments sign a Convention not to use weapons of mass destruction, and that they at once cease from experiments with nuclear weapons.
- We demand that the resources of the world be used for the well-being of humanity and above all for our children to ensure for them health, education, the social services necessary to safeguard their development and promote their happiness. We demand the education of our children in the spirit of friendship, justice and peace.
- We want all men and women to work for increased understanding, friendship and exchanges between the peoples of the world, in mutual respect for each other's sovereignty and national independence.
- We demand that the dignity of mothers, so often the inspiration of the artist and poet, shall be fully respected in our society, and that the views and wishes of women be given due weight in all places where decisions on the present and future of mankind are made.

Convinced that the love of mothers for their children, the desire that they should live and grow up in peace and security, is common to all women, no matter what their race or creed, nation or political and economic system, we, the mothers of all continents, call upon women to join with us.[23]

The declaration forcefully laid out precisely what Gisella Floreanini, in referring to the 1958 Women's Peace Caravan, would call "a new policy of mother-love" that would go beyond the biological function of women as mothers to become "human consciousness." Demanding dignity for mothers and that their commitment to humanity be a model for world governance, the declaration denounced war and militarism to prioritize social welfare for the sake of future generations.

Despite the declaration's radical attempt to denature motherhood from its conventional association with biological sex, motherhood was as politically fraught as sex itself. The inspiration of artists, referenced in the declaration, continued to dwell on motherhood as a biological function rather than as a new "human consciousness." Maxim Gorky's use of motherhood, for example, was a constant resource not only in print publications, but also as symbolic language in filmmaking and cultural production (see chapter 6). In the publicity for the World Congress of Mothers, an excerpt from one of Gorky's essays addressed to mothers, written in 1925, made its way into the WIDF magazine, despite the three decades separating them:

> Why do you remain silent, you who bear them in pain, why do you not raise your powerful voice against the madness that is threatening once more to envelop the whole world in a poisonous cloud? You, mothers, are the sole eternal force that replenishes the earth devastated by death. . . . Mothers! Wives! You have the say, you have the right to lay down the law. From you life comes and it is you who must rise, one and all, to defend Life against Death. You are the eternal enemies of Death. You are the power that ceaselessly fights and conquers it. Why, then, in these days of approaching madness, do you not save your sons from foul massacre? Why do you not raise your powerful voice in the defence of life, against those who thirst for destruction and annihilation? Why?[24]

While Gorky's words were used deliberately by the WIDF to mobilize women for the congress, they nonetheless betray the ambiguity inherent to any gendered language that slips between "nurture" and "nature." Hailing the success of the congress, West German peace activist Clara-Maria Fassbinder likewise appealed to women's "nature" that "negotiations may take a long time and put our patience to a hard test. But isn't it precisely in the *nature* of woman to know how to wait? She has to wait for her child and all the science in the world is incapable of cutting short the time it takes to make a man."[25] Arguments about women's difference and equality therefore coexisted, not as contradictory but as reinforcements in which women's specific experience mandated equal, if not elevated, status.[26]

As a result, the unavoidable twin image that went alongside mothers was that of children, ubiquitous throughout WIDF events and publications. The campaign against the atomic bomb was especially active in Japan and resonated widely with the public, Japan having been the only country to experience the horror of nuclear attacks. As a result, a quarter of the Japanese population of eighty million had signed the petition against the bomb, in which images of injured and dead children were dominant, accompanied by texts such as that by the famed Turkish poet Nazim Hikmet.[27] Titled "The Little Dead Girl," the poem appealed for signatures in the name of child victims in Hiroshima "knocking at your door ... so that children shan't be slain."[28]

Despite such nonpartisan appeals by which the Mothers' Committee hoped to organize a broad segment of women worldwide for peace, independent of the WIDF, anyone calling for peace was ostracized in the West as communist. Dora Russell wrote exhaustedly to Andrea Andreen in 1957, "I feel I cannot go on doing this job.... And I feel terribly lonely, as maybe you do too. For 37 years now I have spent a great deal of my time trying to build a bridge between communist countries and the west and the wreckers win every time."[29] Reflecting on the reception of their work, she commented on just how "tired" they were "of seeing how, in everything that we touched, the opinions of women counted for so little.... Women were always 'on the outside looking in.'"[30] Partly in an effort to distance the Mothers' Committee from the WIDF, Andreen, who was one of WIDF's vice presidents, resigned and handed the presidency over to Russell in 1958, just before the peace caravan; but there would be no further meeting of the Mothers' Committee after the trip. Despite the all-out effort by the committee members throughout Europe, especially by "the women behind the Iron Curtain, [who] had used every effort and probably dug deeply into their resources, to welcome and support our rather limited and not very efficient attempt to bridge the gulf," Russell lamented that "on our return, we continued to be ostracised and frustrated. As I remembered those peasant women who had embraced us and thanked us for 'coming all this way' to bring a message of peace, I felt like a fraudulent saleswoman offering goods that I could not deliver."[31]

Nonetheless, the strategy of rallying around maternal feminism partly succeeded in bringing together previously disparate groups—such as the two largest international women's organizations advocating for peace, the WILPF and the WIDF—to work cooperatively, especially in solidarity with the Third World. Indicative of this shift, the WIDF Council held its first meeting outside of Europe in 1956. In the last week of April, 184 delegates from forty-eight countries met in Beijing.[32] The WIDF Council member from India, Safia Begum, asserted that "a new situation" had arisen in Asia and Africa, where several nations had succeeded in or were in the process of gaining their national independence. She argued that for centuries the colonial powers had tried to maintain their rule through "wars, terrible oppression, extreme poverty and deliberate attempts to create discord and disunity among different sections of the people." But, she declared, "women of Asia and Africa are not the same today as they were ten years back. Gone forever are the days when they could be forced into subjugation. They are coming forward with raised heads and with growing confidence that they are a great force."[33]

FIGURE 3.5. Korean participants Yu Yŏng-jun (*far left*) and Kim Yŏng-su (*middle*) with Indonesian delegates at the WIDF Council meeting in Beijing. *Chosŏn Nyŏsŏng*, June 1956.

From Korea, Yu Yŏng-jun as chair of the National United Front and Kim Yŏng-su as vice-chair of the KDWU participated in the council meeting.[34] While previous gatherings had focused on strengthening the unity and friendship among women throughout the world against war, the meeting in Beijing discussed concrete ways by which to implement a peace program that was based on the common struggles of the Third World against imperialism. In fact, the WIDF Secretariat explicitly included in its invitation of the KDWU to the Beijing meeting a request for help in inviting South Korean women to attend as observers. Yu, as the former chair of the South Korean Women's League, used the airwaves of the Korean Central News Agency to broadcast her message to the South, urging that the southerners join them in Beijing in the struggle for women's liberation and the protection of women's rights.[35] The women in the South would not be able to hear such a message, nor would they be able to visit Communist China, let alone meet with their counterparts from the North; all these actions were banned by the National Security Law. But the gesture from the WIDF was the first of its kind since the WIDF Second Congress in Budapest in 1948—the last time that both Koreas were represented.

Rejecting a pacifist understanding of peace as a disavowal of justified militancy, the Korean delegation renewed calls made during the Korean War for a *just* peace based on principles of sovereignty and equality that would require active struggle. After the meeting, the Korean women joined twenty-three other delegations, including those from India and Indonesia, to visit Shanghai, Nanjing, Guangzhou, and Hangzhou at the invitation of the All-China Democratic Women's Federation. Chinese women affirmed their joint struggle with Korean women against Japanese and US imperialism. Women who had fought in the Korean War as part of the Chinese People's Volunteers were especially keen to meet the Korean women. At a large public rally in Beijing, a former female Volunteer who had been in Korea since 1951 and discharged the previous year to become a student at Peking University "waded through the crowd toward us, shedding tears overcome by emotion upon meeting us Koreans again."[36] Sharing a sense of common purpose throughout their visit, the Korean delegates were moved by the "spirit of unbreakable friendship" with the Chinese women, who were especially impressed by the successes of the Korean women's literacy campaign.

Third Worldism from Bandung to Cairo

The 1956 WIDF Council meeting in Beijing signaled the rising tide of Third Worldism on the heels of the 1955 Afro-Asian Conference in Bandung, Indonesia.[37] While Bandung is often regarded as the historic watershed when Third Worldism became a political project, the story of global left feminisms in this book makes clear that there were unrecognized antecedents to Bandung led by women.[38] As shown in the last chapter, Third World women had met in Beijing already in 1949 and 1952, and the international communist movement had been a close ally of those subjected to colonialism as far back as the Bolshevik Revolution and the birth of the Comintern.[39] In fact, eleven days before Bandung, the Conference of Asian Countries on the Relaxation of International Tensions convened in New Delhi largely thanks to the organizing efforts of Indian women active in the peace movement, bringing together a much greater constellation of bottom-up, mass-based, non-state actors through the mobilization of the World Peace Council.[40] Pak Chŏng-ae led the North Korean delegation, while the South was absent.[41] The New Delhi conference was nary worth a mention in the women's press back in Korea, however, unlike the other international meetings Pak attended; she reportedly did not bother to address the conference's main agenda but called for another meeting on the Korea question.[42] Her position, while awkwardly out of step, was understandable, given that the 1954 Geneva negotiations failed to resolve the Korean cease-fire with a peace settlement. Besides, the 1952 Asia Pacific Peace Conference had laid out the principled contents of peaceful coexistence in much greater detail and universal application than the Five Principles of Peaceful Coexistence that became the cornerstone of Bandung. These five principles were based on the 1954 Panchsheel Treaty between China and India that agreed on mutual respect for territorial sovereignty, nonaggression, noninterference, equality, and peaceful coexistence. And yet, the Koreas were not invited to the Bandung Conference, despite the conference's aims to overcome Cold War bipolarity, precisely due to the Cold War division of Korea. Despite its absence and in contrast to the South, which looked askance at the whole program, North Korea built on this momentum to expand its relations with Asian and African countries, opening diplomatic offices or making trade and cultural agreements with Algeria, Burma, Egypt, India, Indonesia, Iraq, and Syria between 1957 and 1958.[43]

Meanwhile, the Soviet policy shift toward détente under Khrushchev in this period directly collided with rising Third World militancy in the context of escalating conflicts in Vietnam and Algeria. In the face of continued colonial violence, the neutrality of the nonaligned provided little relief, and Third Worldism was radicalized through the globalization of Maoism.[44] As an alternative to Stalinist excesses and Soviet dogma and bureaucracy, Maoism in part was a response to the problem of revolutionary agency in Western Marxism that privileged the working class, turning a blind eye to the peasant "masses" and imperialist violence in the Third World.[45] Maoism as a global theory of revolution upended the urban-vanguard-led Western Marxism with a mass-peasant-based guerrilla warfare, which not only underpinned the Chinese revolution but could be applied internationally, according to its proponents. With his theorizing, Mao redrew the geopolitical map, placing both the US and the Soviet Union in the First World, while the "middle powers" such as Japan, Canada, and Europe fell in the Second; the Third World would lead the global revolution through mass liberation struggles in Africa, Asia, and Latin America in an agrarian "people's war" against imperialism.[46] Maoism's appeal to the 1960s social movements was not limited to revolutionary theory; radical feminists in the West adopted Chinese women's practices of "consciousness raising" and "speaking bitterness" in their program of women's liberation, linking the personal to the political.[47] With the Sino-Soviet split and criticisms against "revisionism" emerging in Korea beginning in 1958, Korean publications replaced references to "peaceful coexistence" with renewed struggle against imperialism, even while demurring from any overt support of the Chinese position over the Soviets.[48]

But the year 1956 turned out to be full of contradictions. On the one hand, the WIDF finally reconciled with the women of Yugoslavia after their 1949 expulsion.[49] In the earliest evidence of schisms within the socialist bloc, the WIDF Secretariat had expelled the members of the Women's Anti-Fascist Front of Yugoslavia (WAF) as reactionary nationalists for their support of premier Josip Broz Tito, who had opted to receive US aid.[50] Vice president of the WIDF Jeannette Vermeersch had rejected the Yugoslav refusal to join the Cominform and instead go their independent way as a betrayal under the bloc politics of the Cold War, arguing that "it is not possible to claim to stand alone. The world is divided into two camps."[51] The Yugoslavian women rightly regarded their country's expulsion a clear indication of Soviet hegemony in violation of the principles of independence and sovereignty, a "consequence of the subjugation of [the WIDF] to the aims of the Cominform, of the transformation of an international organisation into a tool in the struggle for the imposition of the USSR's hegemonistic policy upon other countries."[52] They deemed the decision "an arbitrary and hostile action toward the Yugoslav women" that was passed in "an undemocratic and unjustifiable manner" in the absence of WAF delegates at the council meeting before the full congress, which ultimately held the power to expel a national section from the WIDF. Now in Beijing at the 1956 council meeting, the WIDF issued a public apology. Reversing the 1949 expulsion at the council meeting in Moscow, WIDF president Cotton "recognized that this decision was unjust," and the 1956 meeting in Beijing unanimously decided to rectify the error, admitting that the Federation had "made mistakes" and that they should "learn to respect points of view which are not our own, and remember to preserve the special character of our Federation."[53] In a nod to the diversity of views, the vice president of the ACWF and executive committee member of the WIDF Deng Ying-chao reiterated the importance of national independence for countries, "for without peace, national independence and democratic freedom, it would be futile to talk about women's rights and children's well-being."[54]

On the other hand, the 1956 Hungarian Revolution left the WIDF once again caught in a bind about how to respond. Events in Hungary erupted in the midst of the Suez Crisis after Egyptian president Gamal Abdel Nasser nationalized the Suez Canal in the name of self-determination. Having condemned the bombing of Egypt by Israel, France, and Great Britain as interventionist, the WIDF was keenly aware that the same critique could be applied to Soviet intervention in Hungary. After all, the "death and destruction" in Egypt was happening "at the same time other tragic and regrettable events are taking place in Budapest," which prompted the WIDF to "sincerely hope, at this time of going to press, that they will not be the means of transforming Hungary into a centre of war, and that the social achievements gained by the Hungarian people will not be endangered."[55] With members in disagreement about the best course of action, the WIDF was ultimately stymied from any overt condemnation of

Soviet actions in Hungary. As a result of such debilitation and the revelations at the Soviet Twentieth Party Congress regarding Stalin's crimes, several leaders of the WIDF and its affiliate organizations who had been members of the fact-finding commission to Korea would leave the Federation, including Lilly Waechter of West Germany, Ida Bachmann of Denmark, and Monica Felton of the UK.[56]

Despite the challenges of navigating Cold War geopolitics, the WIDF took seriously the lessons from its 1956 council meeting to "respect all views" and used

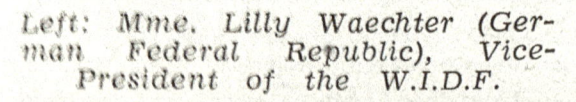

FIGURE 3.6. Lilly Waechter of the German Federal Republic, vice president of the WIDF, poses with Kim En Sou (Kim Yŏng-su), vice president of the KDWU. *Women of the Whole World*, August–September 1957.

리사회에 참가한 외국 대표들과 함께…

FIGURE 3.7. Korean women at the WIDF Council meeting in Helsinki. *Chosŏn Nyŏsŏng*, August 1957.

the next council meeting in Helsinki in June 1957 to draft a revised constitution with a new preamble, delineating the aims, program, organizational structure, and finances of the organization, to extend the possibilities for membership and cooperation.[57] This included allowing forms of collaboration and participation in WIDF programs without full membership, as well as providing membership with greater autonomy for those organizations and individuals only in partial agreement with the Federation's aims; a more flexible executive bureau replaced the former executive committee.[58] The draft of the revised constitution was to be finalized by the bureau and put up for discussion among the member organizations before being voted on at the next WIDF congress. With the WIDF's greater flexibility in conditions for membership and a concerted attempt to include greater numbers of women outside Europe, a number of new organizations would join in 1958. These included the National Federation of Indian Women, the Federation of Japanese Women's Organizations, the Union of Sudanese Women, and the Democratic Union of the Women of the Cameroons; and there was interest from groups in Senegal, Ceylon, Nepal, Panama, and Haiti.[59] The May 1958 issue of *Women of the Whole World* also announced that a new Arabic edition of the magazine was forthcoming, in addition to the English, French, German, Spanish, and Russian editions. Internal WIDF documents at this time show increasing concerns about the predominance of European representation in the WIDF Secretariat and the executive bureau, leading to more recruitment of Third World women, who came to constitute the majority of the bureau and the council by the 1970s.[60]

In Helsinki, KDWU vice president Kim Yŏng-su again echoed Deng Yingchao's earlier emphasis on national independence, arguing that peace in Korea required the withdrawal of US troops to allow Koreans to peacefully unite their country on their own.[61] Returning from the meeting, Kim shared how the representative from Jordan brought her two sons, three and five years old, who became the "little reps" (*kkoma taep'yo*), and who would run away from anyone who spoke English as "bad Americans" (*nappŭn miguk saram*).[62] Korean women also began actively preparing for the Fourth World Congress of Women scheduled for June 1958. They made Korean dolls in colorful traditional dresses, embroideries with scenes of Pyongyang rebuilt after the war, textiles, and celadons to take as gifts to the congress.[63] Committed to the collective power of women's international solidarity, *Chosŏn Nyŏsŏng* poetically compared the strength of the peace movement to "a single drop of rain that gathers to become a stream and streams flowing to become a river, so that the river of peace created by people all over the world who oppose war and pray for peace only grows as the days and moons go by."[64]

Alongside preparations for the WIDF congress, Korean women joined the global campaign in support of a nuclear test ban.[65] International outrage over radioactive fallout from Soviet and US nuclear testing had been building, especially since the contamination of the Marshall Islands and the Japanese fishing boat *Lucky Dragon* in 1954. This prompted Indian prime minister Jawaharlal Nehru to propose a moratorium on nuclear testing, followed by calls from Albert Einstein and Pope Pius XII for a total ban on nuclear tests.[66] What started out in 1957 as the Appeal by American Scientists to the Government and Peoples of the World, initiated by Nobel Prize–winning chemist Linus Pauling, became a global petition to ban nuclear testing signed by over nine thousand scientists from forty-four countries, addressed to the UN secretary-general.[67] International groups were quick to endorse and support the petition, including the WIDF, the WILPF, and the World Council of Churches. Joining them, Korean women gathered 6,458,000 signatures in support of a total ban on the production and use of nuclear weapons, demanding the withdrawal of US troops and nuclear bases from South Korea.[68] This was not empty rhetoric, as it is now known that the US had violated the Armistice Agreement almost as soon as it was signed and secretly introduced nuclear weapons into South Korea in early 1958.[69]

In the face of such threats, the Afro-Asian Peoples' Solidarity Conference heralded the potential of the Third World to broker peace. Held in Cairo, Egypt, from

December 26, 1957, until January 1, 1958, with delegates from almost fifty countries, the Cairo Conference claimed to represent 1.8 billion people across two continents, "to struggle against all forms of imperialism and colonialism in order to ensure the complete independence of their countries."[70] In addition to resolutions on general disarmament and the elimination of nuclear weapons in favor of social development to improve living standards, the conference passed a resolution specifically against French genocidal actions in Algeria. It called for the observation of March 1, 1958, as Algeria Solidarity Day, with demonstrations across the world and the formation of solidarity committees to aid Algerian refugees. In the end, the conference gave rise to the Afro-Asian Peoples' Solidarity Organization (AAPSO), with a permanent secretariat in Cairo.

The secretary-general of the WIDF, Carmen Zanti, gave her impressions of the Cairo Conference as one dominated by a shared sense of struggle and the power of solidarity: "The unity of these two continents against colonialism dominated all the proceedings. Every one of the speakers, whether from one of the already independent countries or from one struggling for its freedom—everyone made it clear that the peoples of these countries have an ever-increasing awareness of their right to independence and to choose their own government and their own life."[71] Staking its claim to an independent path, the conference decided to organize a group of historians to prepare an encyclopedia on the countries of Asia and Africa in order to "reinstate the truth about their histories, their national culture and the often very ancient civilisations which colonialism ravaged and destroyed . . . often not known in Europe." Although it is unclear whether the project ever materialized, such cultural movements to advance the power of Afro-Asian solidarity picked up momentum throughout the year.

In August 1958, the Asian-African Film Festival was held in Tashkent, the capital of Uzbekistan, attended by screenwriters, directors, and actors from all over the world. Paul and Eslanda Robeson were among the attendees. Reflecting upon her trip, especially when her husband spontaneously danced the jitterbug to the tune of local folk music, Eslanda Robeson found cultural and spiritual affinity between Africa and Asia in their communality of everyday folk:

> The Uzbek people are very Asian, with black hair and dark copper coloured skin. As the musicians played and the singer sang the simple rhythmic folk music, it became more and more familiar to us, and Paul began to hum along with them. When the dancer began, the music became more rhythmic, and even more familiar, and made us think of our own real folk-jazz. . . . To my own surprise and great satisfaction, Paul proceeded to do a most graceful, spirited, and dignified jitterbug, while the dancer and musicians adapted themselves perfectly to him.

The whole thing lasted about five minutes, and everyone was delighted. We found much in Uzbekistan which reminded us of Africa: the mud-brick houses in the rural areas; the warmth, simplicity and thoughtfulness of the hospitality, the darkness of skin, and the shy friendliness of the children.[72]

Just two months later, in October 1958, two hundred writers from forty-eight Asian and African countries and the Soviet Asian republics met again in Tashkent to discuss problems of national culture and "their common historical background of oppression and struggle."[73] Calling it the Writers' Bandung, the "poets and authors reaffirmed the essential unity of the spiritual values of the human race, in contrast to the racist ideology which denies the possibility of understanding between east and west."[74] Like the Cairo meeting that ended with the proposal to produce an encyclopedia, the Tashkent meeting agreed to set up a joint publishing house in order to produce English and French translations of the works of the most important African and Asian writers.[75]

The Militancy of Peace and the Dilemma of Maternalism

In the attempts to forge solidarity and chart a "third" way, women faced a double dilemma in their international work, first in arriving at a common definition of peace, and second in positioning women as a vital part of that definition. The core of these questions had to do with the ultimate aim of the movement and the best strategy to get there. On conceptions of peace, two views were diametrically opposed: pacifists argued that violence begets more violence, and thus advocated nonviolence as the best method for achieving ultimate peace. But others involved in anticolonial struggles insisted that there was no peace without justice, and that nonviolence in the context of colonial violence was a ruse to pacify resistance. Representing the African American press at the All-African People's Conference in Accra, Ghana, in December 1958, Eslanda Robeson, for example, expressed disappointment at the lack of women delegates, observing that the Western powers tried to "divide the Conference . . . to persuade the participants to adopt Non-Violence as a method—at a time when Algeria, the Cameroons, Kenya and South Africa are experiencing force and violence."[76] Ultimately, the participants agreed that nonviolence would be desirable if *all* parties adopted it, "especially the Colonial Powers and white settlers." Such arguments further stigmatized what was already regarded as a communist "peace offensive," and Chilean poet Gabriela Mistral, winner of the 1945 Nobel Prize for Literature, bemoaned the way peace had become an accursed word, "a label which, even if it doesn't kill, spoils the reputation of the writer and brands him."[77] Reassuring readers to have courage, however, she called for a "militancy of peace," which "is not the sweet jelly some people imagine, [but] it gives us a driving conviction which cannot remain static." In the face of red-baiting employed as subterfuge against anticolonial movements for a *just* peace, Mistral argued for a militant peace movement driven by active struggle, rather than the passive rejection of war, reiterating arguments made against pacifism during the Korean War.

Alongside debates about the meaning of peace, the use of maternalism to unite women proved to be another point of contention.[78] Not only could such a strategy potentially peg women to traditional gender roles, but it could also reinforce a pacifist conception of peace. The president of the Swedish branch of Open Door International, Ina Möller, for example, supported state protections for mothers but insisted that "these should be part of the social services and should not be mixed up with restrictions on the right to work or on wages."[79] Repeatedly hammering this point in the pages of the *Women of the Whole World*, lest state protection for mothers preclude women from working in occupations deemed hazardous to them, Möller forcefully argued against any type of discrimination against women, so that "a woman shall be free to work and protected as a worker on the same terms as a man, and that legislation and regulations dealing with conditions and hours, payment, entry and training shall be based upon the nature of the work, and not upon the sex of the worker; to secure for a woman irrespective of marriage or childbirth, the right at all times to decide whether or not she shall engage in paid work, and to ensure that no legislation or regulations shall deprive her of that right."[80] Although critical of night work, Swedish women campaigned to abolish the prohibition of night work for women as a "handicap" to women in the labor market looking for better wages. However, others, like Dora Russell, emphasized the advantages of "old traditional values" that gave women a special standing. Russell lamented how the women's liberation movement, in stressing women's rights and equality with men, was missing the "old traditional values for which women and mothers must stand." Calling out the WIDF for not adequately standing "in the right way for *women's* values," she explained that it was indeed her concern for mothers as "the most neglected and oppressed of her sex" that led her to fight for birth control, since "liberation must begin with and for her."[81] As we will see in a moment, Russell was not advocating gendered roles, so much as insisting that women, including their "traditional" roles, be socially valued, rather than dismissed and neglected as "private" concerns.

This debate took center stage during the WIDF study session "on the protection of motherhood as a right of women and a responsibility of society" held in Potsdam, in East Germany, from September 27 to October 1, 1957, two years after the 1955 World Congress of Mothers.[82] One of the participants described the need for the meeting "to re-examine the conception of maternity, because the social order has often used this as an excuse to limit woman to her task as a mother, and so to deprive her of her initiative and the possibility of action."[83] Even as such voices expressed concern for the limitations imposed by maternalism, others noted the urgency of nationally implementing the International Labour Organization (ILO) Convention 103 on maternity protection to ensure paid maternity leave. What both sides of the debate could agree on was that "the arrival of a new human being is not a private event which concerns the mother exclusively, even if indeed the baby needs the mother's milk and her care and attention."[84] Insisting that children are the responsibility of the whole "human family" and that women are endowed with capabilities and qualities beyond motherhood, the Potsdam meeting pragmatically concluded that the movement was still in its infancy "towards the effective liberation of woman and the construction of the new family."[85] In building the movement, women agreed that motherhood should be a source of joy and empowerment rather than a "fresh source of worry," as was the case for most women around the world. Practical recommendations included national ratifications of the ILO principles on pre- and post-natal care of mother and child; adequate medical attention for mother and child in both cities and rural areas; education of women on existing laws, hygiene, and reproduction, including advice on nutrition, health, and child upbringing; and the establishment of nurseries, playgrounds, and recreational facilities located conveniently for mothers.[86]

Synthesizing these positions to offer a remarkably prescient view on women and peace as fundamentally a *political* question, Dora Russell argued that the private and the personal are indeed political, more than a decade before the slogan was popularized in the 1970s.[87] Decrying how her advocacy of a woman's right to decide on the number of children was construed as a personal "sex question" rather than a political one, she pointed out that the death rate of mothers in childbirth was four times the death rate of miners from fatal accidents in coal mines. She blasted the women's organizations that failed to support the 1958 Women's Peace Caravan as too "political," insisting that "today we have total war, to which the only answer is total peace. And there is no individual who is not influenced in almost every event of his daily life by war and preparations for war." Reasoning that the danger of radioactive fallout was a question of public health, much like the question of childbirth, she pointedly asked whether "the 'non-political' man or woman ever reflects that the refusal to be concerned about other human beings is in itself a political act." She pinpointed how the very definition of the *political* was in itself political, and that this very boundary was used to forestall change by justifying apathy. Arguing that no one "can really shirk individual responsibility for what our Government does at home and abroad," she offered as example the dangers posed by "non-politically-minded" scientists, who had become "the instruments of the most deadly political power," namely nuclear weapons.

Riding the tide of Third World ascendancy with the conviction that women had a political role in advancing a militant peace, the 1958 World Congress of Women in Vienna included the highest number of participants to date from over seventy countries. National independence became a prominent agenda of the congress, and "the representatives from Asia and Africa were also the most sought after subjects for the photographers," with the mother and child from Madagascar taking the spotlight.[88] The congress praised women throughout the world fighting in the ranks of national liberation armies, and Korean women proudly shared advances made in their national compulsory education, as well as in postwar reconstruction efforts with the building of apartments outfitted with the latest household appliances and modern furniture.[89] Returning from the congress, KDWU vice-chair Kim Yŏng-su placed particular significance on the start of the five-day congress on June 1, International Children's Day, as women struggled in solidarity, "united hand in hand despite different skin color and language."[90] To illustrate her point, she shared the story of a Cameroonian woman who broke down in tears when she took to the podium to speak about the status of women and children under French colonial oppression. The solidarity of women at the congress gave her strength to continue, as she "pounded on the podium with her fists, declaring that the only way to escape the yoke of colonialism was to stand up and fight." Kim emphasized the shared women's struggle against colonialism from Korea to places as far-flung as Algeria, Morocco, Yemen, Cuba, Madagascar, and Tunisia.[91]

Following the numerous gatherings in 1958, the conference of Asian and African women from thirty-five countries met again in Cairo from January 14 to 19, 1961, underscoring the need for national independence and peace in order to guarantee the complete liberation and rights of women, with specific references to Algeria, Congo, Laos, Korea, China, and Vietnam.[92] Interestingly, Korean sources referenced this conference as the "first" such gathering, despite the earlier 1958 Asian-African Conference of Women in Colombo. This was likely due to the reformist nature of the latter, focused on women's welfare, organized by women of Sri Lanka, Burma, Indonesia, Pakistan, and India who tried to stay clear of any explicit political position, invoking the nonaligned spirit of Bandung.[93] The 1961 meeting, by contrast, was focused on women workers, with a large contingent from state socialist countries. Despite the impassioned pleas for political unity on the role of women in the struggle for peace, however, the next World Congress of Women in Moscow exacerbated schisms between the Second and Third Worlds as China and Albania dissented against the Soviet position. While Korea

FIGURE 3.8. A Korean woman participates in elections, in a photo appearing in a special issue on the fiftieth anniversary of International Women's Day. *Women of the Whole World*, October 1959.

remained somewhat inconspicuous in these debates internationally, its domestic publications positioned it clearly on the side of the Chinese and the Albanians in their rejection of peaceful coexistence.[94] The 1963 congress would be touted as the largest WIDF congress, outdoing the previous one in absolute numbers of participants, but it became the occasion for the sharpest rift in the global left women's movement, with the Chinese women officially withdrawing their membership from the WIDF.[95]

The Sino-Soviet Split at the 1963 World Congress of Women

Featuring the first woman cosmonaut, Valentina Tereshkova, who had just returned from her space flight five days earlier, the 1963 World Congress of Women began in Moscow on an optimistic note.[96] Convened from June 24 to 29, 1963, at the Kremlin Palace of Congresses, the gathering brought together 1,543

FIGURE 3.9. Koreans celebrate International Women's Day. The original caption to the photo reads, "At many of the demonstrations held to celebrate International Women's Day, Korean women demanded the peaceful reunification of their country and the cessation of nuclear tests. . . . Two million signatures were collected to the Appeal launched by the WIDF last March for disarmament and the banning of nuclear weapons." *Women of the Whole World*, June 1959.

women—1,291 delegates, 116 guests, and 136 observers—from 113 countries, "assembling women of the whole world, without distinction as to race, countries, social conditions, opinions or religion, to work together at the realisation of their common ambitions: the happiness of their children, the improvement of the status of women in all fields and peace."[97] Among the 181 women's organizations at the congress, thirty-seven were from Africa, twenty-two from Asia, nineteen from Latin America, seven from North America, and four from Australia and New Zealand; only a third of all organizations were affiliated with the WIDF.[98] Women came from a variety of backgrounds and occupations, including 288 housewives as the largest single group, 211 in science and education, 85 workers, 78 journalists, 72 in medicine, 59 students, 53 parliamentarians, 41 farmers, 38 lawyers, 34 artists, 25 writers, and 4 in religious positions.[99] Not only were the usual partner organizations such as the World Peace Council, the World Federation of Trade Unions, the World Federation of Democratic Youth, and the International Student Union represented at the congress, but newly formed organizations such as the Pan-African Women's Conference, Women Strike for Peace (from the US), and Voice of Women (from Canada) were also present, as was the US section of the WILPF, the Committee for International Co-operation Year, the International Cooperative Guild, and the International Red Cross Committee, making the 1963 congress one of the most diverse since the Federation's founding in 1945.[100]

Dissenting views were not covered in the official proceedings, which focused on the benefits, rather than the pitfalls, of meeting face to face to learn from each other and unite under a common cause. But there were hints that "this process is never smooth and the World Congress of Women naturally showed evidence of certain differences of opinion."[101] Despite the welcome of newly independent states and support for those "suffering from the brutality of racism, colonialism and imperialism, as in South Africa, Angola and South Vietnam," the congress placed emphasis on the recent push for disarmament.[102] Several major international meetings on disarmament had taken place since the 1958 congress, including the International Assembly of Women for Disarmament in Sweden (December 1959), conferences on the Responsibility of Women in the Atomic Age in Brunate, Italy (July 1959), and Salzburg, Austria (October 1960), and the 1962 World Congress for Peace and Disarmament in Moscow.[103] The Soviets had resumed nuclear testing in 1961 after declaring a unilateral moratorium in 1958, and the 1962 Cuban Missile Crisis made ongoing negotiations for a nuclear test ban treaty particularly urgent. In this context, peaceful coexistence became the central theme of the congress, with positive references to its leading proponents such as Khrushchev, Kennedy, and Pope John XXIII.[104] Continued conflicts in the Middle East and Indochina served to underscore the need for peace, and the more militant critiques of colonialism, racism, and imperialism were diluted as a generalized condition of the world, in which "oppressions of all kinds and of all degrees still exist in all continents!"[105]

Consequently, China took the lead in attacking the congress as reformist and undemocratic. Left out of the proceedings and blocked from delivering their statements at the congress, the Chinese women had their statements and reports published separately in Beijing under the title *The Struggle between Two Lines at the Moscow World Congress of Women*, showing the major fault lines over the question of peaceful coexistence that had been widening since the late 1950s.[106] Calling on the WIDF to keep alive its anti-imperialist tradition, the leader of the Chinese delegation, Yang Yun-yu, accused the Kennedy administration of weaponizing peace through such programs as the Peace Corps, Alliance for Progress, and Food for Peace to infiltrate the Third World and continue a "special warfare" against countries like Vietnam, Laos, Korea, China, and Cuba, while within the US, "monopoly capital is bleeding the working people white, and cruelly slaughtering our Negro brothers and sisters."[107] Invoking earlier debates about the proper role of women in politics, Yang argued that "those who claim that anti-imperialism is the task for the political parties and not for the women's organizations, and emphasize that the central tasks now facing the women's movement are general and complete disarmament and peaceful coexistence, fail to see, nor wish to see the excruciating miseries of women under imperialist oppression."[108]

Yang used examples of Western intervention to argue that calls for disarmament in the face of armed suppression amounted to surrender:

> While mothers and children in south Viet Nam are being massacred by the US imperialists, can the people there be told to accept general and complete disarmament instead of taking up arms to fight against imperialism? Among the peoples of those African countries which have not yet attained independence, some are being subjected to armed suppression by imperialism and old and new colonialism at this very moment. How is it possible for them to sit and wait for the realization of disarmament instead of rising to fight for national liberation? To strive for general disarmament at a time when the imperialists are carrying on general arms race, it is imperative to direct our struggle against imperialism and to expose and oppose the imperialist policies of arms race and war preparations. To do otherwise is deliberately to lull and dupe the peoples of the world and to divert their attention from the real target of struggle.[109]

Redolent of the principles laid out at the 1952 Asia Pacific Peace Conference, Yang defined peaceful coexistence as "a relationship between states with different social systems," governed by mutual respect for sovereignty and territorial integrity, nonaggression, and noninterference in internal affairs, and based on the recognition of the equality of all races and all nations. Therefore, she concluded, it "must not be extended to cover relationships between oppressed and oppressor nations, between oppressed and oppressor countries, or between oppressed and oppressor classes. At no time is it possible for the oppressed nations and peoples to coexist peacefully with the imperialists, nor should the former be told to do so. To ask the oppressed nations and peoples to coexist peacefully with imperialism is to force them to give up their struggle and to keep them forever in the position of being oppressed and enslaved."[110]

Chinese women urged the congress to affirm struggles against imperialism, explicitly condemning US imperialism as the most dangerous to world peace and demanding the complete ban and total destruction of all nuclear weapons, including the dismantling of foreign bases and the withdrawal of troops. However, such demands were nonstarters under bloc politics, in which nuclear weapons states—the US, the USSR, and the UK—were unwilling to give up their military advantage. The Chinese position was also marred by its own geopolitical interests. In the following year, China would become the world's fourth nuclear weapons state, with its own testing in October 1964, and continuing Sino-Indian border disputes had been yet another source of conflict at the congress.[111] Although eighteen different Asian and African countries, including Korea, Vietnam, Indonesia, Japan, Laos, Mozambique, and Kenya, had signed a joint statement supporting the Chinese delegation's right to respond, ultimately they were prevented from presenting their position by sheer force; when they took the floor, a bell declared the session adjourned, the speakers were disconnected, and the lights switched off.[112]

Upon her return to Beijing, Yang Yun-yu charged the WIDF Bureau of "undemocratic" procedures, indicting the WIDF leadership for "serv[ing] the needs of the foreign policy of the Soviet Union" at the expense of long-standing principles.[113] Yang argued that rather than standing together with the delegations from Albania, Korea, Indonesia, Vietnam, and other Third World countries to wage "a common struggle against the enemy," the WIDF leadership placed their hope on "big powers" such as the Soviet premier, the US president, and the pope, weakening the anti-imperialist position of the congress. She charged the congress with striking wording from documents, including the Japanese report on disarmament and the Cuban report on the crimes of US imperialism, removing passages that referred to US military bases, imperialist exploitation of Africa, and Algeria's anticolonial struggle.[114]

Balking at the suggestion that understanding among "the leaders of a few big powers" was a way to ensure world peace, the Chinese delegation countered allegations that they were a lone voice by pointing to "Albania, Korea, Viet Nam, south Viet Nam, Indonesia, Laos, Zanzibar, Southwest Africa, Mozambique, Angola and Venezuela" as those who expressed similar positions against imperialism in their speeches and written statements.[115] While the record of their participation in the official proceedings is thin, the Chinese report included excerpts of statements from sympathetic countries. The Korean delegate affirmed that "it will only harm the struggle for national liberation to preach that disarmament is the task of primary importance for the oppressed peoples who are now waging struggles and at the same time to insist that if we ensure peaceful coexistence and realize disarmament this will naturally bring national independence with it. We must never beg imperialism for independence, freedom and peace; we must win them through struggle."[116] The Indonesian delegate agreed that "the demand for disarmament cannot be easily realized because it meets with strong opposition from imperialism. We maintain therefore that there is a pressing need to launch an unrelenting struggle against the aggressive forces of imperialism, a struggle in which women must take an active part." The Japanese delegate went further to suggest that peaceful coexistence and disarmament were mere subterfuges of imperialism itself, which "while paying lip-service to peace and disarmament, is actually pursuing a dual policy; it is carrying on aggressive wars and an arms race." Therefore, the Japanese women warned, "the women of the whole world must have enough vigilance not to be fascinated by fine words." The Zanzibar delegate concurred that "we should not allow ourselves to be fooled by the imperialist 'policy of peace,'" warning that "to hope that imperialism will disarm is like expecting a man-eating tiger to go to a dentist to have its fangs removed."

Sidelining such voices amounted to "sectarianism, splittism and great-power chauvinism," according to the Chinese, turning the WIDF into an elitist "club" of upper-class women from European and North American capitalist countries.[117] As proof, Yang charged that nearly 700 of the total 1,289 delegates came from twenty-seven European countries, more than 100 from North America, and another 115 from East and West Germany, whereas fewer than 100 came from thirty-four African countries and fewer than 250 from twenty-three Asian countries; in short, almost 75 percent of the delegates had come from the West, by Chinese accounts. This was the most damaging critique, which attacked the very core identity of the WIDF as a broad anticolonial, antiracist coalition of progressive women from all over the world. The Chinese counter-report placed the responsibility of these failures of the 1963 congress squarely on the hosting Soviet Women's Committee, which had ignored some member organizations in favor of others who would assure them the majority vote, erecting obstacles to limit the number of delegates and participation from Third World countries while facilitating with travel subsidies the participation of those deemed suitable. Soviet documents meanwhile claimed that each country was allotted an equal maximum of twenty-five delegates.[118] Although difficult to confirm from the existing record how votes were actually tallied, delegation size would have been a key issue, since it ultimately influenced the congress's decisions, as each delegate could cast one vote. According to WIDF rules, the size of the delegation was supposed to be a proportional representation of the national population. But the Chinese had unsuccessfully proposed one vote per country, likely to add weight to the Third World as a voting bloc, as was to happen at the UN with the formation of the Group of 77 in 1964.[119]

The Chinese report also accused Soviet women and WIDF leaders of refusing to allow the organization's bureau and council to discuss the reports and other outstanding issues in advance because "daughters could not discuss their mamma's report."[120] The four reports—the first on peace and disarmament by the Japanese delegate, the second on national independence by the Mali delegate, the third on children by the Cuban delegate, and the fourth on women's rights by the Italian delegate—became controversial, as pressure mounted to replace references to anti-imperialism with general disarmament. When the Japanese and Cuban delegates refused to succumb to pressure, they were told that the two reports could be given only in their individual names. As a result of these conflicts and disagreements, only one document was ultimately issued in the name of the congress, the Appeal to the Women of the World. Even this single appeal failed to pass unanimously, as the Chinese, Albanian, and Korean delegations voted against its adoption, with the Vietnamese delegation abstaining from the vote. Finally, when it was time to elect a new executive bureau, the WIDF leaders unilaterally announced that the former bureau members would retain their positions, with the addition of just a handful of new members. Although Korea nominated Vietnam, and China nominated Korea, seconded by a number of other countries, these motions were ignored by the presiding officers, who refused to put them to a vote.

Chinese criticisms aside, the final appeal of the congress did in fact focus on peaceful coexistence and general disarmament, but it also referred to the importance of anti-imperialist struggles for national independence. Contrary to blanket Chinese condemnation, the appeal tried to walk a delicate line, describing the work of the WIDF toward "the establishment in the world of peaceful coexistence between States with different systems on the basis of mutual respect, national integrity and sovereignty, of non-aggression, non-interference, of equality and reciprocal advantages, for the achievement of general disarmament, complete and rigorously controlled, and of thermo-nuclear disarmament in particular," adding that "the cause of disarmament and peace is inseparable from the cause of people's struggles for their national independence" and that the WIDF must "support the women and peoples who struggle against all kinds of imperialist oppression and all forms of colonialism and the remnants of feudalism, for their liberty and national independence."[121] In fact, the WIDF was one of the few international organizations to raise the alarm when its affiliate Indonesian women's organization, Gerwani, came under attack after anticommunist violence swept across the country in 1965.[122] Over the next few years, tens of thousands of people were massacred at the hands of the Indonesian military under Suharto. The WIDF supported Gerwani in this struggle, despite the fact that the Indonesian Communist Party had by then become decidedly Maoist, which led the Soviets to ignore the "destruction of the largest communist party in the non-communist world."[123] Trees Soenito-Heyligers, the Dutch lawyer who had joined the WIDF delegation to Korea in 1951, was arrested at this time, in 1968, after defending one of the Indonesian communists in the 1966 military tribunal.[124]

Meanwhile, reporting back to the Soviet Women's Committee in Moscow, the Soviet delegate to the congress Nina Popova in turn railed against the Chinese delegation for "the most sharp dissonance." Against Chinese allegations of undemocratic procedures and revisionism among the WIDF leadership, Popova charged the Chinese delegation of "thrusting its own opinion on the Federation" and the "propaganda of their opinion," without any support save the Albanians.[125] Accusing the Chinese of libel and of weakening "the front of the struggle for peace against imperialism and colonialism," Popova threw the same attack right back at the Chinese as the ones "who broke the democracy and order, demanded the floor at the Congress out of turn and *even tried to seize the rostrum*, broke the time-limit, propagated various materials among the delegates regardless the established order at the Congress."[126] But Popova was mistaken. The Albanians were not the only ones who supported the Chinese.

Back in Korea, the July 2 issue of the *Rodong Sinmun* published unusually detailed news about the congress, with a copy of a statement issued by the Korean delegation on the last day of the meeting, June 29.[127] Declaring that they felt a responsibility to the international women's movement to state their principled objections against the wrongful statements and "irregular" (*pijŏngsang*) actions taken at the congress, the Korean women reiterated the charges made by the Chinese, further claiming that they were also prevented from exercising their right to speak:

> The leadership of the World Congress of Women must conduct the meetings fairly to ensure the free exchange of rightful opinions of the congress delegates based on the spirit of equality, mutual respect, friendship, and unity. However, some members of the leadership ignored these principles and international customs, running the congress in a non-democratic way in a chaotic atmosphere of slander, disorder, and coercion. We recognize that some members of the leadership were prejudiced, betraying the trust of the congress, and did not perform their duties faithfully, negatively impacting the success of the congress. The Korean women's delegation, along with delegations of certain other countries, had our rights suppressed to fully state our opinions.[128]

Although the Korean women voiced their objections during the congress, they were silenced, and thus the need to issue a statement of protest, which specifically criticized the way the congress was used as a venue to air anti-Chinese sentiments. Mindful that the WIDF was not a "social gathering" but a global women's organization, the statement went on to express "deep regret" that the adopted appeal did not reflect the fundamental issue confronting the women's movement, ignoring the "just demands" of the women of Asia, Africa, and Latin America. Led by Kim Ok-sun, one of the vice-chairs of the KDWU, who would go on to succeed Pak Chŏng-ae as chair at the KDWU Third Congress in 1965, the Korean delegation consistently voiced its protest to the congress that the foremost task for the women's movement was the struggle against imperialism and colonialism, and that peace could only be achieved through such struggle. In solidarity with the Chinese women, the Korean women held their own report-back in July, paralleling the Chinese counter-report with a similar critique of the congress.[129] By October, a full three-page editorial in the party newspaper staked Korea unmistakably on China's side. Obliquely criticizing Soviet policy as interventionist, the *Rodong Sinmun* opined, "Some people have moved far from Marxism-Leninism and the principles of proletarian internationalism, and have fallen into the muddy waters of revisionism. . . . Some people are using foreign aid as an excuse to interfere in the international politics of fraternal parties and countries and are unilaterally imposing their wishes."[130]

As a result of increasing conflicts, not only between China and the Soviet Union, but also between China and other Third World allies such as Indonesia and India, the second Afro-Asian meeting after Bandung scheduled in Algiers for 1965 was postponed indefinitely, and the Union of Italian Women also ceased active participation in the Federation after the 1963 congress.[131] Meanwhile, the politics and turmoil of the Cultural Revolution in China that centered class struggle above all else led the Chinese women's federation to disband and its organ *Women of China* to cease publication in 1966, not to be revived until 1978.[132] Even as the 1960s' global movements coalesced against the US war in Vietnam, and the 1966 Tricontinental Conference in Havana, Cuba, combined Afro-Asian solidarity with Latin American concerns in an enlarged coalition, the decade proved as challenging as ever for the international women's movement.

By the 1970s, Anwar Sadat reversed Nasser's foreign policy, defunding the "infrastructures of solidarity" based in Cairo that restricted further opportunities for Afro-Asian connections.[133] The end of the Cultural Revolution and the beginning of Sino-US rapprochement in 1972 also muted the militant anti-imperialist stance that China had earlier insisted upon, shifting toward a focus on economic development and "modernization." Decline of Third Worldism in Asia was as stark as its rise with the turn to market reforms in China and Vietnam and the emergence of conservative "Asian values" rhetoric.[134] It is no surprise then that a more insular position took root in Korea too. Before this turn, however, and paralleling the debates about women's role in politics among the pages of *Women of the Whole World*, spirited discussion also ensued in the pages of *Chosŏn Nyŏsŏng* about what it meant for Korean women to both work inside and outside the home, as unprecedented numbers of them joined the labor force from the 1950s into the 1960s. This is the subject of the next chapter.

4

WOMEN'S WORK IS NEVER DONE

> The proud journey we have taken is not at its end today, since we have farther to go than the road we have already traveled.
>
> Chang Ŭn-dŏk, 1966

> Whatever the social form of the production process, it has to be continuous, it must periodically repeat the same phases. A society can no more cease to produce than it can to consume. When viewed, therefore, as a connected whole, and in the constant flux of its incessant renewal, every social process of production is, at the same time, a process of reproduction.
>
> Karl Marx, 1867

A 1959 issue of the *Women of the Whole World* ran an article headlined "Who Says Women's Work Is Never Done?" featuring the National Institute of Information on Consumer Products based in Stockholm, Sweden.[1] Founded in 1940 by a group of housewives, domestic science teachers, and architects "to help rationalise housework and household utensils," the National Institute was government-funded with a staff of forty, including specialists and engineers. Although Sweden never entered the theater of conflict of World War II, women there were drawn into production too, requiring ways to solve the problem of housework. "To save valuable time and energy," the National Institute aimed "to work out the most economical and least tiring methods of doing housework ... leading to a standardisation facilitating rational production of kitchen equipment at a low price, having sufficient working space to ensure comfort, and a suitable arrangement of cupboards easy to keep clean and in order."[2] With mid-century designs that have become ubiquitous in affordable assemble-it-yourself furnishings today, the items in the photos accompanying the article could have easily come from an IKEA catalog in our time. Despite the promise of such modern homes to ease domestic burden, the article concluded in a skeptical tone that "doubt came into our minds after seeing so many pleasant and practical models: are these household implements going to free women or are they going to enslave them even more?"[3] The question sharply captures the dilemma faced by women throughout the world, including those in Korea. The strategy to "liberate" women through work became a "double burden" of combining productive and reproductive labor.

As harsh wartime conditions began to shift to reconstruction efforts in Korea, rather than women's burden being eased, their Herculean efforts seemed to know no bounds. According to a profile of eight women "labor heroes" (*roryŏk yŏng'ung*) in a March 1953 issue of *Chosŏn Nyŏsŏng*—four months before the armistice was signed—Tang Un-sil met her production target by 200 to 400 percent above quota, and Ko Yŏng-suk produced more than one hundred thousand meters of textile in a year.[4] Model rock driller Kim Ch'un-hŭi broke all records, producing thirty-five tons of rock, 500 percent above the six-ton quota, and model weaver Kim Chŏng-ok saved, on average, sixty-seven meters of thread per day. Despite losing sixteen members of her family in Sinch'ŏn during the war, Yu Man-ok tilled five thousand *p'yŏng* (just over four acres) of land on her own, producing 360 sacks of rice, offering 22 sacks of her best rice to the government and donating 80 sacks to the war front. Paek Sin-jŏn also tilled five thousand *p'yŏng*, producing 17 tons and 740 kilos of grain. After submitting her tax-in-kind, she donated thirty-six sacks to the war front. Kang On-sun took up plowing, traditionally considered men's work, training 624 other women to plow and donating twelve sacks of rice, and Hwang In-ae used advanced farming techniques to cultivate 477 *p'yŏng* of cotton field, producing six hundred *kŭn* (almost eight hundred pounds) of cotton. These women were nationally decorated for their achievements, which represented the pinnacle of productive work. As the war had enlisted most men to the front, women's labor had filled the places left empty on the production lines. Women had been mobilized during the Asia Pacific War too, but unlike the Japanese Imperial War, the Korean War was billed as a war of liberation, to free the South from US occupation, including the liberation of South Korean women. Women's entry into the workforce, not just in production efforts in the rear, but directly at the fighting front as medics and soldiers, therefore had become symbolic of women's expanded roles that would in theory continue after the war's end. However, when the armistice halted the fighting, women continued to face challenges because of sexism and entrenched gender roles.

In a 1957 collection of women's stories, ship captain Pang Chae-suk had to deal with sexism from her male subordinates as her leadership came under constant scrutiny. The older first mate of the ship would disobey her decisions, with belittling comments based on gendered stereotypes and superstition that viewed women as bearers of bad luck and physically unfit to operate a ship.[5] Despite the first mate's experience as a seasoned seafarer, the female captain ultimately navigated the ship more effectively during a storm, based on her education and scientific training abroad in China. As with many of these kinds of stories, her effective leadership became a turning point for the first mate when he realized the gravity of his mistakes and abandoned his sexist ways. The entire setting of the story in which the ship and its crew had to struggle against nature symbolically paralleled women's struggles against sexism and sexual hierarchy often justified as "natural." Chae-suk's successful navigation of the ship enabled the first mate to realize that "her disciplined three years had advanced her far beyond my ten years [of experience]," as the story cathartically concluded with the declaration that "the era in which women were looked down upon is over."[6]

Other work conventionally performed by men, such as mail delivery, plowing, and maintaining security, were also carried out by women after the war, changing the very landscape of the countryside. A mail carrier from South Pyong'an Province relayed her experience of disapproving looks from older villagers, who regarded her public presence as unsightly, with children following her around as if observing a strange spectacle.[7] But she took pride in her new position as "a proud correspondent of the party, relaying the voice of the party to the people," rather than a simple delivery person making a living. Eventually, rather than being treated awkwardly as a courier (*paedalbu*), she was welcomed as the "correspondent auntie" (*t'ongsinwŏn ajumŏni*) wherever she went. Likewise, upon returning to his hometown after four years of military service, a soldier observed in awe how women had taken up security and agricultural work previously performed by men.[8]

The most iconic symbol of liberated socialist women embodying the ideals of rural industrialization was "the tractor girl," first circulated in Soviet Russia and ubiquitous throughout the socialist bloc. Indeed, the first labor heroes were the 1930s Soviet Stakhanovites, named after a coal miner who exceeded all production targets to initiate a "shock workers" movement that was emulated throughout the communist world, including China and Korea.[9] In the aftermath of the Korean War, tractors in Korea were Soviet imports, just like the image of the women driving them, but that made them no less impactful. Wartime labor heroes were eager to become tractor drivers, inspired by their Soviet counterparts, and deliberately modeled themselves after Soviet tractor drivers like "Pasha" Angelina Praskovya, celebrated as the first Soviet woman tractor driver.[10] In the following decade, tractor drivers had become such heroic figures that a "city girl," the daughter of artists and with a keen literary and artistic sensibility of her own, chose to become a tractor driver in the countryside rather than go to university, even at the risk of disobeying her parents' wishes.[11]

How do these models of women in production as workers stand next to the pervasive image of women in reproductive roles as mothers and homemakers? What constituted "proper work" for women and men? How should the gendered division of labor be valued? While capitalist exploitation extracted surplus value,

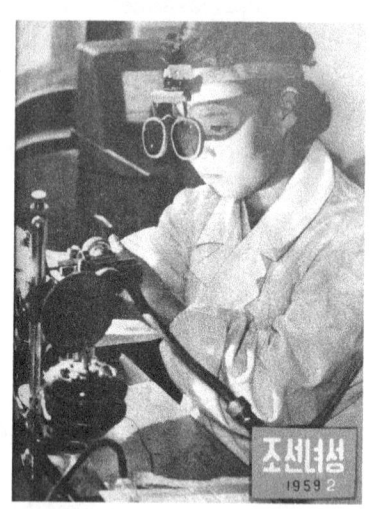

FIGURE 4.1. Covers of *Chosŏn Nyŏsŏng* from the 1950s to the early 1960s, featuring a tractor driver, a metalworker, an engineer, a scientist, welders, and sailors—all of them women.

profiting from the productive labor of the working class, how would socialist Korea value different forms of labor, and how would the fruits of such labor be distributed? What would happen to the capitalist division between waged productive labor and unwaged reproductive labor under state socialism? These are the questions animating this chapter. Rather than viewing women's "double burden" in Korea as the lack of attention to gendered oppression over class or the result of a patriarchal state merely paying lip service to women's liberation to extract their labor, I problematize the distinction between productive and reproductive labor. Conventionally, productive labor is associated with paid waged work that is "value-producing" according to capitalist relations of production, while reproductive labor is considered unpaid, unwaged work without surplus value, owing to its traditional locus outside capitalist circuits. As Marxist feminists have long shown, however, the very idea of social reproduction originated in classical economic theory to naturalize and thereby normalize the gendered division of labor between "productive" work outside the home and "reproductive" domestic work.[12] Waged labor was entirely dependent on the unpaid work by women, not only in the biological reproduction of future generations of workers but also in the socially necessary recuperative care work of cooking, cleaning, and generally tending to the well-being of families and communities. And yet theorists often conflate "paid" and "productive" as synonyms, ignoring the way reproductive activities shape relations of surplus extraction, thereby replicating the capitalist division and hierarchy of labor.[13]

The cult of domesticity, or *housewifisation*—as sociologist Maria Mies explains, "the externalization, or ex-territorialization of costs which otherwise would have to be covered by the capitalists" that was part of Western cultural and territorial colonialism—propagated this gendered division of labor as a necessary component of industrialization.[14] While Marxists and other radical thinkers critiqued the exploitation of waged workers, few of them saw the extent to which such waged work was underpinned by the creation of the fictive "private" sphere as yet another "hidden abode" of *reproduction* by unwaged labor. Although Mies's analysis thus materially grounds the history of women's oppression, she devotes only one short chapter to state socialist countries, mainly focusing on the capitalist accumulation process through women's exploitation in the First and Third Worlds.[15] Because of her disregard for state socialism and dismissal of communist women, her narrative duplicates the history of "wave feminisms," to render invisible the 1930s to the 1960s, calling socialist feminists such as Clara Zetkin "anti-feminist" for her focus on women's roles as mothers and wives.[16] Contrary to her claims that the public-private distinction went unchallenged by leftist women, socialist and communist women raised housework as a political issue well before "second wave" feminists.

Although state socialism did not explicitly target the productive-reproductive binary, it did challenge the divide between public and private spheres as a form of bourgeois ideology, and introduced mass campaigns to collectivize and socialize child care, cooking, and cleaning through public investments in nurseries, communal canteens, and laundries. The private sphere was dismantled through public programs focused on social welfare and the distribution of basic necessities such as food and housing. Western critique of the dwindling private sphere in state socialist societies has too often focused on the encroachment of privacy and individual rights without appreciating the extent to which these policies freed women from their domestic "prisons." Although the communist strategy of liberating women through their entry into the labor force had clear limitations, as the gendered division of labor was often maintained in both the home and at work, state socialist women did in fact experience greater work opportunities and social benefits, compared to gains from liberal feminist movements.[17] While state socialism continued to distinguish between productive and reproductive work along gendered lines, both forms of work were explicitly valued as integral components to overall social functioning and collective well-being, and women often voiced their demand that men share in this reproductive work.

Using examples from *Chosŏn Nyŏsŏng*, this chapter illustrates the way *housewifisation* was replaced by *workingclassization* to support women's entry into the workforce, not only by including women as part of the working class but also by elevating the value of reproductive work. This involved creating positions such as child care workers and cooks as part of a general class of service workers, while also providing benefits to support women's reproductive labor by institutionalized nursing breaks at workplaces; a workday shortened from eight hours to six hours, with the same pay, for mothers with three or more children; and paid maternity leave. This in effect dismantled the false juxtaposition between work and life, which under capitalism served to extract yet more surplus. For example, textile workers under capitalism were forced to live in dormitories on factory grounds in order to minimize time "wasted" on commutes, while wages were withheld as payment for room and board. Rather than such subsidies to capital accumulation through the unpaid and unaccounted reproductive work among individuals, families, and communities, state socialist policy specifically invested in social reproduction through state-run retreats and vacation homes, the Public Distribution System that disbursed food and other necessary consumables, nationalized health care, public housing, and education. Before any official state ideology of self-reliance, "self-production, self-determination" (*chasaeng chagyŏl*) became a key slogan in mobilizing villages to take the initiative for collective subsistence, including reproduction *as part of* production through forms of domestic sericulture and animal husbandry to meet local consumption needs.[18]

Examples of a similar strategy for women's welfare were already evident among socialist feminists throughout the colonial era. Discourses about reforming everyday life continued with renewed energy in the aftermath of national liberation, and in December 1945, the journal *Saenghwal Munhwa* (Everyday life culture) held a roundtable on the topic, with a variety of professionals including educators, doctors, and artists.[19] While most participants noted the need to address "underdevelopment" in Korea through the simplification of clothing and food preparation attuned to hygiene and nutrition, such suggestions had also been made by modernizers under Japanese occupation, with parallels in the conservative New Life Movement across East Asia. A more radical proposal was suggested by Chŏng Ch'il-sŏng, the socialist feminist and former *kisaeng* who chose to settle in the North in 1948. Linking the immediate task of women's liberation to class liberation in light of her own experiences, she demanded that women be supported to enter the workforce by remodeling the kitchen for anyone to use, whether husband or wife, so that whoever returns home first could cook, with priority placed on the creation of nurseries for working mothers.[20] She went on to demand public laundries, maternity wards, and other state facilities to address women's needs. This is precisely what happened as state policy in North Korea.

In the following sections, I first return to theories about social reproduction to show how reproduction became a part of production in Korea, not only in theory but in practice, as women called for the valorization of reproductive work. Toward this end, two key women's meetings took place in Korea paralleling the international conferences discussed in the last chapter. The National Conference of Women Socialist Builders in 1959 and the National Mothers Congress in 1961 focused on women's productive and reproductive work respectively. Even as the two meetings appeared to segregate women's labor as two distinct forms of work, the content of both gatherings affirmed women's experiences that blurred any strict division between the two. The chapter ends with the conservative backlash against women's radical demands that reproductive work be valorized and that men do their share of it. Women's work became symbolic of pure sacrifice, resuscitating traditional virtues as markers of Korean womanhood.

Nature of Work and the Valorization of Reproductive Labor

Although Marx did not fully theorize the implications of his own observation in the chapter's epigraph, Marxist feminists have grasped his point to argue that women's reproductive work undergirds capitalist accumulation. While theorists have differed on whether to push the argument to claim that reproduction itself is productive to create surplus value or rather that it merely creates the necessary conditions to enable capitalist accumulation, social reproduction theory (SRT) as an evolving body of feminist theorizing has made insightful connections between the realm of production and reproduction toward a unitary framework. While early SRT feminists in the 1970s, represented by the works of Mariarosa Dalla Costa, Selma James, Silvia Federici, Leopoldina Fortunati, and Maria Mies, understood reproduction to mean unpaid domestic labor, advocating that this be regarded as productive and be paid wages (e.g., the "wages for housework" campaign), this risked homogenizing and making equivalent different forms of labor, inadvertently attributing normative value to the category of production.[21] Lise Vogel's work in the 1980s tried to address this problem by arguing that reproductive work was *not* in fact surplus-value producing, falling outside the purview of capital's immediate "gender blind" profit motive, so that the drive to minimize social reproduction and maximize labor force participation ultimately would lead to a crisis of capital by its inability to address social reproduction needs.[22] However, Vogel's position advocating the socialization of reproductive labor for gender equality did not ultimately solve the gendered division of labor, as shown by outcomes in state socialist countries despite their attempts to socialize reproductive work, and global capitalism has only further segmented and moved reproductive labor to the bottom of the labor hierarchy across the world.

Even as SRT engages with Marxist theory that would lend it a useful lens with which to examine gender relations under state socialism, SRT has rarely been used to critically assess state socialist systems because of the theory's explicit aim to understand "everyday life under capitalism" and its autonomist roots that reject statist models.[23] Owing to the different, often contradictory interpretations of Marxist theory itself, SRT has at times led to a conflation of three different albeit related processes of reproduction: one, as "societal reproduction" within capitalist relations of production through mechanisms such as Althusser's ideological state apparatus or Bourdieu's *habitus* that serve to reproduce the system; two, as the "social reproduction" of labor power as noted by Marx in this chapter's epigraph; and three, as the "biological reproduction" of the species, often the main target of critique by radical feminists. Among the three forms of reproduction, the latter that focuses on women's roles as child-bearers is often dismissed as biologically deterministic, overlooking its nuanced historical account of the way biological reproduction and its attendant meanings have always been a "socially organized" outcome.[24]

As indicated by the conflation in the different forms of reproductive processes, the fundamental problem has to do with how to understand production, reproduction, work, and labor, all ambiguous terms laden with normative and subjective meaning. When linguistic differences are added to the mix, the problem can be infinitely more challenging. For example, in the Korean language, different connotations associated with "work" as *il* encompass a wide variety of activities, including events as in "did something happen" (*musŭn il issŏyo*). Meanwhile, "labor" as *rodong* or *kŭllo* is often associated with physical labor, and hence the Korean translation of proletariat as *rodongja* or *kŭlloja* that is used to refer to both worker and laborer without an equivalent derivative of *il*. "Work" and "labor" in English are equally capacious; work can denote any act of effort, while labor includes the process of childbirth based on its Latin roots for toil, apart from its later associations with production. Recognizing these nuanced differences across languages and cultures, I use "work" and "labor" interchangeably throughout the chapter according to contemporary usage.

Helpful in this regard is the April 1950 issue of *Chosŏn Nyŏsŏng*, in which socialist feminist Im Sun-dŭk offered her conception of labor (*kŭllo*) as creative work.

> Creation from nothing—this, in other words, means "construction" [*kŏnsŏl*] and "production" [*saengsan*], which is a sublime mark that cannot exist apart from the fondness for everyday life of good people, who are faithful and diligent, and love labor [*kŭllo*]. That is, the fact that a person does not spare one's own body, moves steadily, and works hard [*roryŏk*], no matter how small or large, contributes to a more abundant life for our human society and is a plus. In this way, the presence of labor [*kŭllo*] fosters a beautiful sentiment for those who see it, and we discover that the spirit of labor [*kŭllo*] is accompanied by infinitely high creativity.... Moreover, today, when work [*rodong*] or labor [*kŭllo*] is dedicated not to fatten any greedy capitalist or landowner, but to our own life and happiness ... they are autonomous expressions of a worthwhile life united in the mission for production and labor [*kŭllo*].[25]

Exalting work and labor as acts of creation, Im nonetheless acknowledges that capitalism also depicts labor as sacred in order to further exploit workers, in contrast to the feudal past when labor was debased as lowly and extracted through the enslavement of peoples. Therefore, she argues, it matters *for whom* labor is sacred under the different systems. In a new society where working people are the masters, she concludes, their work, including women's labor, determines the wealth and prosperity for all.[26]

Following a similar logic, some SRT feminists have advocated an expansive conception of labor as "broadly productive—creative not just of economic values, but of society (and thus of *life*) itself" as a way to valorize all forms of work.[27] But under capitalism, gender inequality persists because capitalism disavows reproductive labor as "non-value-producing." In an innovative iteration of SRT, theorists Maya Gonzalez and Jeanne Neton therefore show how "value" itself operates to separate out different activities between those regarded to produce surplus value and those that do not.[28] In so doing, they offer a necessary critique of the "wage fetish" that inadvertently emerged from Marxist analyses of capitalist exploitation. Their insight not only makes women's labor visible but, for my purposes, also underscores the extent to which work under state socialism is poorly understood. Wages in state socialist economies function differently from those in capitalist economies, because in principle, much of the costs of social reproduction, whether in the form of housing, food, education, health care, or child care, are assumed by the state.[29] In other words, the focus on the wage as a by-product of surplus creation (and therefore exploitation, in the gap between the price of labor power and the cost of living labor, extracted as profit) not only ignores informal and unwaged labor under capitalism, but cannot capture the varied forms of labor and the different functions they serve in an economic system that is not driven by private profit. As Gonzalez and Neton emphasize, "wage itself is not the monetary equivalent to the work performed by the worker who receives it, but rather the price for which a worker sells their labour-power, equivalent to a sum of value that goes one way or another into the process of their reproduction.... It is imperative to remember that Marx demonstrated that no actual living labour is ever paid for in the form of the wage."

This is why Korean terminology came to favor "labor remuneration" (*rodong posu*) or "living expenses" (*saenghwalbi*) rather than "wages" (*imgŭm*) to refer to payments made for work.[30] Despite the holdover use of "wage" as a term in a 1955 text produced by the Institute of Labor Science at the Ministry of Labor (Rodongsŏng rodong kwahak yŏn'guso), economists there explain how socialist and capitalist wages were fundamentally different:

> Under capitalism based on the private ownership of the means of production and the exploitation of employed workers, wages are the monetary expression of the value of labor power as a commodity. However, wages under socialism are fundamentally different from wages under capitalism in their essence, which is based on relations of socialist mutual aid and comradely cooperation of workers freed from exploitation in the production process. In a socialist society, wages are the monetary expression of the share of social products that the state allocates to workers in order to distribute them according to the quantity and quality of each worker's labor.... In other words, our labor becomes a source of social wealth and the continuous improvement of the material and cultural standard of living of the working masses. In imperialist countries, workers are completely subordinated to capitalists as they are

subjected to harsh exploitation in their pursuit of maximum profit.... The basis for the continuous growth of labor productivity and the systematic improvement of workers' material, cultural living standards lies in the fact that in socialist production, labor is not divided into necessary and surplus labor. In our country, the labor provided to the state for the expansion of production, education, development of health care, and the organization of national defense is as necessary to the workers, as the country's masters, as the labor expended to satisfy their individual and their families' needs. In this way, the concept of necessary labor is extended to the entire labor invested in production, and the social product is distributed according to the quantity and quality of the labor spent by each worker after deducting the part that is needed for the expansion of production and other social needs.[31]

Accordingly, labor was categorized into different levels of difficulty and skill required, with the most dangerous occupations in underground coal mining given the highest remuneration (table 4.1).[32]

Pay was also guaranteed for time off work, such as vacations, holidays, and maternity leaves; periods of national or community service, including training and accreditation; and lighter assignments for pregnant women, with nursing breaks for women with infants.[33] While the realm of reproduction was in this way indirectly "paid," reproductive labor was not included in calculations of the total national income, which only included "productive services" directly related

TABLE 4.1 Wages according to industrial sectors, 1955

SECTORS	BONUS (%)	WAGE STANDARD BASED ON 100
Textile, paper, rubber (light labor)	26	100
Transportation (hard labor)	25	106.5
Electrical (hard labor)	25	106.5
Construction (hard labor)	25	106.5
Cement and construction material (hard labor)	26	107.4
Machine-making (hard labor)	30	110.8
Fishery (hard labor)	30	110.8
Forestry (hard labor)	30	110.8
Shipbuilding (hard labor)	40	119.3
Chemical (underground harmful labor)	30	119.6
Railway (hard labor)	45	123.6
Regular mining (underground harmful labor)	35	124.2
Special mining (underground harmful labor)	40	128.8
Metal (underground harmful labor)	40	128.8
Coal (underground harmful labor)	55	142.6

Source: Reproduced from Yun Ŭi-sŏp and Ch'a Sun-hŏn, Konghwaguk esŏŭi imgŭm chojik hwa rodong ŭi kijunhwa [The organization of wages and labor standardization in the republic] (Pyongyang: Kungrip ch'ulp'ansa, 1955), 41.

to the production and distribution of commodities.³⁴ This in effect maintained the productive-reproductive distinction, and continued to leave a large portion of domestic labor unaccounted for.

Despite the continued emphasis on women's entry into the labor force, women therefore found it challenging to integrate productive work alongside their reproductive role. For example, an agricultural cooperative composed of sixty workers, fifty of them members of the women's union, had trouble with absenteeism in 1954.³⁵ While men's attendance was almost at 100 percent, the women's stood at only 60 percent, owing to perceptions that men were the primary earners. Unable to convince the women of the principled merits of work solely based on collective welfare for the cooperative, the leader of the local women's union decided to approach the person with the lowest attendance record, engaging her in a casual conversation during work hours about how much one absence could impact her household income. She explained how labor contributions by each of the co-op members were used to calculate the distribution of income to each household. When the woman realized that points deducted for her absences could add up to a substantial loss in her family revenue, the word spread among the rest of the women, and without further convincing, the attendance rate shot up from 60 to 95 percent within two days. The inability to reach the full 100 percent was attributed to child care needs among some women, so the women used the experiences shared in an issue of *Chosŏn Nyŏsŏng* to organize a child care facility in their cooperative.

Such experiences of organizing at the local level spurred women to make more radical demands for new ways to organize productive and reproductive labor. In an essay about combining work, family, and child care explicitly from a woman's perspective, O Yi-suk advocated the need for everyone in the family to take charge of reproductive labor.³⁶ Declaring an end to times when domestic work was considered solely women's domain, she cited the works of Soviet child educators and their emphasis on the critical role of fathers. Refuting assumptions that work and family are incompatible, she attributed current difficulties to the inadequate availability of child care facilities. Urging people to tackle problems without simply relying on the state, she credited the mothers who had been able to juggle work, family, and child care for their "advanced ideology" (*sŏnjin sasang*). Even as O gave examples of women who meticulously planned their schedules to manage all three spheres of their lives, she argued that the whole family is responsible for domestic labor. She offered as example a model family, in which the husband made dinner and put the children to bed when the wife was home late from work.³⁷ In another example, a local women's union dealt with husbands who frowned upon their wives' participation in after-work "circles" (*ssŏk'ŭl*) by organizing weekly meetings of husbands urging them to take

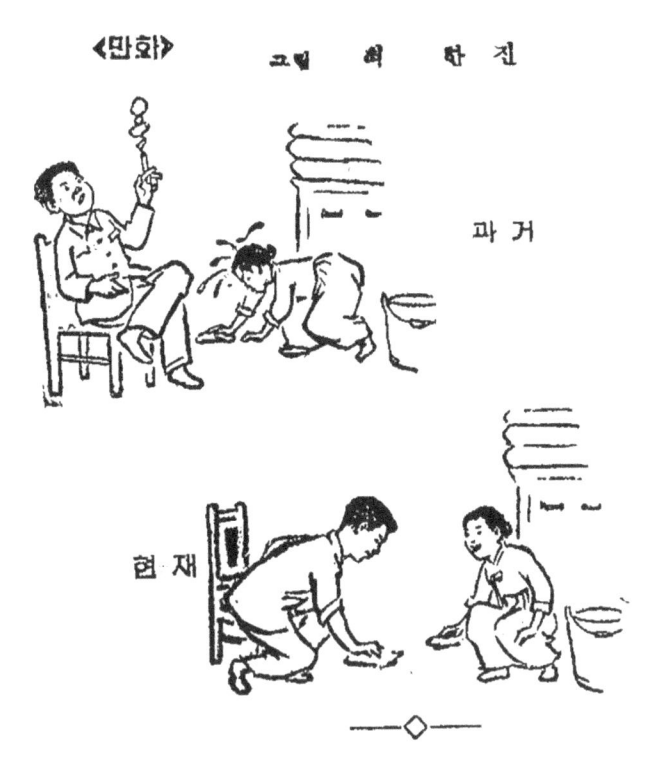

FIGURE 4.2. Cartoon about the changing roles of men. *Chosŏn Nyŏsŏng*, May 1959.

on domestic work.[38] As a result, reformed men began to look after the children in their wives' absence and started cleaning up around the house before work in the morning, creating an ethos of helpful husbands.

However, problems persisted in the retention of women workers, especially after marriage. Article after article in the women's magazine appealed to married women to return to work, as illustrated in the "letters to comrades" in *Chosŏn Nyŏsŏng*, encouraging them to return while chiding husbands for their lack of support for their wives. In one letter, a former teacher wrote about her experience of marrying someone who had promised to support her continued career as an educator.[39] The newlyweds embarked on their lives together soon after the Korean War, "filled with hopeful resolve to discuss all things together, replenishing and helping each other." She expected that her husband's help and support would allow her to become a better teacher, but as the days went on, her husband seemed to dislike her working, complaining that breakfast was late or that there was no hot water after he returned from work. His nagging increased daily, with comments like, "Why is the table so untidy?" "How can I go out with [unmended] socks like these?" "Didn't you see that the button on my suit needed stitching?" She lamented that his facial expression and voice got coarse over time, irate at the thought that he wasn't the only one working. They would bicker without holding back. When she demanded to know why he couldn't help out when she was juggling so much, he coldly questioned, "What important work could women do when they can't even do proper housework?" Concluding that her husband had never truly supported her work, she quit her teaching position in the end, but upon a visit to the school, she realized her mistake in leaving. Talking with her husband, she found that he had also arrived at the same conclusion after seeing how she had lost her cheer and confidence without her career.

As captured by the unreformed husband's remark questioning "what important work could women do when they can't even do proper housework," the core issue had to do with the nature of work and how the different forms of gendered labor would be valued under state socialism. According to the social hierarchy of the Chosŏn dynasty (1392–1910), work as physical labor was associated with the peasantry and slaves, butchers, shamans, and female entertainers or *kisaeng*, at the bottom of social classes, providing services considered too debased for others. The *yangban* scholar-officials defined their superior status precisely by their distance from physical labor. Sustained by the work of peasants and slaves within their households, they were unwilling to take up work, even at risk of starvation, as an affront to their very identities as *yangban*. Some of this changed with the onset of Japanese colonial modernization and increasing class polarization. But it was the previously landed elites who were able to use their wealth to become a new class of capitalists, and even the ranks of the emerging labor movement were by and large led by intellectuals who had the resources to study abroad in Japan, where they were exposed to the influx of Marxism and other radical ideas.[40] Adding to the stigma against labor, strict segregation between men and women throughout the social hierarchy, with *yangban* women mostly confined to the "inner" domestic realm, meant that women working outside the home were marked with low status.[41]

Despite the changes brought by social revolution and war, a 1955 essay by a canteen worker illustrates the kind of continued shame attached to working women.[42] An Kŭm-sŏn had no choice but to work after her husband died eight years earlier, but found this disgraceful, as she regarded working women as selling themselves for wages (*p'ump'ari*). As a result, she viewed her work at the canteen washing dishes and preparing food for others as difficult and menial, took frequent breaks, and put in as little effort as possible. She contemplated whether it might be less humiliating to open a small business instead. Upon hearing this, her son threatened to stop attending middle school, as his mother's business would bring him shame among his classmates, rather than the pride he felt at his mother's public service at the canteen. After this exchange, she was able to distinguish her present work from waged labor at private restaurants because work under socialism provided an essential service to the people, contributing to their collective well-being. Realizing her mistake, she began to take pride in her position, thinking about ways to improve her work. While these kinds of stories undoubtedly served to mobilize women to work, they also convey the reluctance and ambivalence women felt about working, and the impact of previous conceptions about work on their ability to accept new roles.

Negative attitudes were pervasive even regarding domestic work, prompting some housewives to adopt "petit bourgeois" attitudes by hiring servant girls, as in times past. After three years of married life as a housewife, for example, a former teacher in Pyongyang had become so accustomed to a leisurely life that she had abandoned any aspirations she had before marriage, becoming a "dull" woman, especially after having children, when she stopped reading altogether.[43] She found herself "satisfied with things in stasis," according to the article, with a limited view of women's work confined to keeping house, raising children, and obeying her husband. Worried that her hands would become too rough from housework, she decided to hire a servant girl for tasks around the house such as laundry, cleaning, and shopping, so as to avoid getting her face tanned during the summer months. She hired a sixteen-year-old country girl from her hometown, who came with hopes of studying in the city, but the girl hardly had time to leave the kitchen, much like servants of the past, even to eat at the same table as her employer. It was a cautionary tale of fates to be avoided, whether as the urban lady of the house or as the country girl looking for opportunities in the city.

But negative attitudes toward work were not the only obstacles, since women's expanded positions required them to juggle multiple roles. In order to hear directly from working women about the challenges of combining family and work responsibilities, the Pyongyang women's union held a roundtable with six working women in February 1956.[44] While everyone agreed that it was difficult combining work and domestic chores, especially at the outset, Chŏng Ok-suk, a mother of three and eager to contribute to society in her work as a bookbinder at a printing press, found her work rewarding and easier to manage with disciplined planning. Others added that, in addition to time management, family and state support were critical to working women. Chin Ok-sun returned to teaching middle school only after her mother-in-law moved in with the family to help manage the household; and Chi Chŏng-ja, a forty-two-year-old housewife with no previous work experience outside the home, was able to secure a position as a salesclerk with the support of her local women's union, enjoying the improved standard of living with her additional income. Factory worker Kim Rak-ju enjoyed the weekly film showings at her workplace that provided entertainment after work.

For working mothers, public child care and education were paramount concerns. Child care worker Kim Saeng-gŭm spoke of her sense of obligation to make sure that mothers could leave their children without worry, attributing the threefold increase in the number of children left in her care since the previous year to her effectiveness at work. Primary school teacher Pak Suk-hyŏn underscored the importance of all family members pitching in to ease the burden on women while creating better family relations. When she was asked for an example of such family cooperation, others were surprised to hear that her young children could cook. Sharing details of her method, she explained how she prepared a pot of uncooked rice in the morning, which the children would place inside a larger pot with water to steam the rice without danger of burning it. She noted how her children had matured to become more helpful now that she was busy with work, learning to study on their own.

As women entered the workforce and the problem of domestic work became an urgent issue, housewives and their reproductive labor emerged as key parts of building socialism. In a letter to the editorial office of *Chosŏn Nyŏsŏng*, a reader emphatically rejected the idea that housewives were "unliberated," arguing that women's reproductive labor was just as vital to economic development and must be valued as an integral part of socialist construction.[45]

> Everyone has a family, and this family requires a good manager. Then who will be in charge of this domestic labor [*kasa rodong*]? The public canteen, child care centers, and kindergarten facilities cannot meet the overall demand, so the housewife and mother should take charge. However, we must not forget that these kinds of facilities are provided in line with the country's economic development. Therefore, women's domestic labor is essential work, and cannot be regarded as "eating without work" but must be viewed as an important force in promoting the construction of socialism. . . . Some say that "women cannot be liberated without economic independence," arguing that housewives are "liberated" by entering the workforce, but this is a serious mistake, reflecting the view of the women's rights movement cried out by upper-class women in bourgeois society. The question of women's liberation is a part of social liberation, and it is impossible to talk about women's liberation apart from the social system.

Not only did she call on housewives to take pride in their work as an integral part of building socialism, but she encouraged mothers to regard their role in raising children as a significant endeavor in creating a new kind of family. In order to offer a new model of women as socialist workers who would combine productive and reproductive work, two major meetings were convened after the official end of postwar reconstruction. The first meeting focused on women as *socialist builders*, and the second focused on women as *mothers*.

Women as Socialist Builders

The end of 1958 marked a shift in postwar recovery. Not only did the last of the Chinese People's Volunteers who had stayed after the war to help with reconstruction efforts depart, but private farming was phased out with the completion of agricultural collectivization, as were private commercial businesses and handicraft production.[46] Reconstruction had consisted of two economic plans, a Three-Year Plan (1954–1956) and a Five-Year Plan (1957–1961), which took advantage of socialist bloc allies and their material and technical aid to prioritize heavy industries such as steel, machine tools, shipbuilding, mining, electricity, chemicals, and construction, all foundational for a self-sustaining economy.[47] Foreign aid that had amounted to as much as 34 percent of the state budget in 1954 dropped to 4.5 percent by 1958, which had to be made up by yet greater mobilization of labor through such campaigns as the Chollima Movement, named after a mythical winged horse that could travel long distances, with parallels to China's Great Leap Forward.[48] Even as official policy claimed to simultaneously develop light industry along with heavy industry, the overall priority placed on heavy industries dominated by men meant that women made up for the shortage in other sectors, especially to meet consumption needs.

In this context, the KDWU organized the National Conference of Women Socialist Builders, held from March 28 to April 2, 1959, in Pyongyang, with seventeen hundred model women workers.[49] Convened in order to share and learn from the best of the "socialist builders," the meeting began with opening remarks by KDWU vice-chair Kim Yŏng-su and proceeded to Pak Chŏng-ae's report as chair of "enhancing the role of women in building socialism."[50] Forty women innovators from various sectors participated in the discussion; thirteen of their stories were included in the conference proceedings. Those thirteen included four industrial workers—two from mining and two from textiles—and four farmworkers from agricultural cooperatives. The rest consisted of a women's union official, a post office worker, a fisherwoman, a train station manager, and a plasterer in a construction "trust" (*t'ŭresŭt'ŭ*).[51] Many of the women were widows who had lost their husbands during either the colonial era or the Korean War.

One of the party decisions in 1958 was to increase the participation of women in the workforce, a goal that was repeatedly highlighted throughout the 1959 conference. Pak Chŏng-ae reported that the participation of women in the labor force had already doubled as a result, and that women made up 70 to 80 percent of the workforce in local industries, including commerce and distribution.[52] Moreover, there were 6.8 times more specialists and skilled women workers in 1958 compared to 1953.[53] As of 1959, almost 90 percent of the students at the newly formed workers schools (kŭlloja hakkyo) were women.[54] In order to facilitate the entry of women into the workforce, the state had greatly expanded child care services, so that by 1958 there were forty thousand beds in 591 facilities, as well as an additional 383 nurseries and kindergartens set up by agricultural cooperatives.[55]

A photo essay in Chosŏn Nyŏsŏng boasted of other domestic aids complementing the increase in public child care. There was a rice factory run by an independent income-generating store in Pyongyang, from which cooked rice could be ordered and delivered to any home in the city, as advertised in the essay, or sent to public canteens for working couples who preferred to dine there rather than at home.[56] Moreover, two new seven-horsepower washing machines and five large laundry tanks were recently acquired by the laundry department run by the Pyongyang City Department of Facilities Management, and the Ryongsŏng Meat and Vegetable Processing Plant had industrialized the making of kimchi, enabling working women to purchase it without having to make it themselves.

Claiming that women had been "liberated from the kitchen," another photo essay, featuring working mother Kim Sang-gi, copiously described the ideal schedule for a family reaping the benefits of socialized reproductive labor.[57]

> After a comfortable night's sleep in a cultured apartment where steam heats the room, the family greets the morning in a pleasant mood. Husband and wife help each other, and the children are accustomed to self-reliant behavior, grooming themselves and cleaning the house happily within a short time. After they get ready and arrive at the family canteen near their house, the receptionist comrade welcomes them with warm soup, rice, and side dishes without delay. There are over twenty kinds of side dishes that one can ask for, boosting one's appetite to eat in plenty. Younger children are fed lunch and snacks at the kindergartens and nurseries, so only older children and adults receive lunches to take.... After dropping off the children at the nursery, mother and father devote themselves to their work without worry, and after work, they freely participate in study sessions before returning home.

Despite the ebullient depictions, the availability of such facilities was insufficient to meet demand, and some women continued to resist calls to combine productive and reproductive labor. To address the shortage of state facilities, the women's union independently organized communal kitchens, laundries, and child care to help working women. KDWU chair Pak Chŏng-ae urged local initiative, rather than relying on the state, to set up collective canteens, laundries, and sewing shops to lessen individual women's domestic burden. She praised the example from Ich'ŏn County in Kangwŏn Province, where members of the women's union organized 206 canteens, giving each woman in the county five extra hours of time per day as a result.[58] Women were also encouraged to take up various positions in the service sector, at restaurants, hotels, hair salons, and bathhouses, "eradicating outdated ideology that looks down upon service work."

Nonetheless, some women chose to remain "buried in the home" (*kajŏng e p'amuch'yŏ*), preferring to be conventional housewives supported by their husbands.[59] Pak pointed out that even women with technical skills were frequently changing their place of work in search of "easy work," and many women workers behaved too "freely," often tardy or absent without proper work discipline. In the light industry and service sectors, household items were not aesthetically mindful, and prepared foods did not taste good, leading to "useless" and "tasteless" consumer goods. There were also problems with hygiene and cleanliness. All of these, Pak argued, were the result of outdated ideological remnants among women and their low technical standards. Pak pointed to the way some women devoted attention to color and fabric in making clothes for their own families or made delicious foods according to their family's preferred taste, but failed to devote as much care in their work outside the home because of "an employee-like attitude and individual selfishness" (*koyong sarijŏk t'aedo wa kaein rigijuŭi*) rather than working "in the service of society and the people from a mass perspective with a collective ideology." Pak pressed women to improve their technical expertise "from unskilled to skilled, from skilled to multi-skilled," eradicating the "mysticism" (*sinbijuŭi*) surrounding technology that perpetuated the idea that women have no business obtaining skills.

"Outdated practices" (*nalgŭn insŭp*) had to be rooted out to increase women's educational levels and improve the economy through local production of everyday staples by raising livestock such as rabbits, chickens, cows, and pigs, as well as silkworms and honeybees. In doing so, Pak emphasized the importance of improving the quality rather than just the quantity of products. Whereas incomes had increased by 40 percent, she argued, people had nowhere to spend their money, as there was a shortage of vegetables, meats, and other consumables in high demand.[60] If traditional well-being was associated with tiled-roof houses, silk clothes, white rice, and meat soup, then these demands would have to be met through local production. Raising rabbits was one way, since children could also help while learning responsibility. Rabbits could fill multiple needs, providing delicious meat and good-quality fur for winter coats and blankets. Chickens would meet additional demand for protein, with the goal of providing everyone with at least an egg a day. Cows would provide children with milk, and vegetables and legumes would enable people to enjoy tofu and other nutritious side dishes with their meals.

Alongside the emphasis on local production as part of reproduction (and vice versa), a special column of *Chosŏn Nyŏsŏng* was devoted to the party's renewed emphasis on the importance of innovative technology in order to complete the new Seven-Year Plan (1961–1967).[61] According to one article, women workers at the Namp'o Machine Factory came up with forty-three new creative techniques that reduced labor time for 8,342 workers, saving 16,160 won in expenditures while making work easier and improving the quality of the products. But compared to the accomplishments of their male colleagues, this was small progress. While women put in place forty-three new labor-saving innovations, men at the same factory implemented 685 new techniques. Although women made up almost half, or 47.2 percent, of the workforce at the factory, the article bemoaned that they were responsible for only 6 percent of the innovation. The leader of the factory's women's union, Yun Pun-ok, wondered about the reasons for this large discrepancy between men and women's creativity, when the proportion of workers by gender was roughly equal and the women worked just as hard as men.

A work team leader suggested that technical innovation required using one's head, but that women just do as they are told rather than thinking about how to improve their work, because they are accustomed to relying on men, "a habit from the feudal past when women were slaves to men."[62] A technician further observed that too many women leave their workplace after three or four years of solid work, just as they are gaining experience.[63] For instance, two-thirds of factory women left for another town after getting married, relocating to their husbands' place of work. While women often avoided marrying a coworker as they got to know their flaws firsthand, the technician suggested that it was better to fully know their future husbands, including their faults, since no one is perfect. Another work team leader compared the rate at which new workers advanced their skill levels.[64] Of the 113 new workers who joined the factory in the previous year, men were able to advance three times faster, which she attributed to women not making as much effort, with the expectation that they would have to leave the factory and go elsewhere upon marriage. Like the technician, the team leader suggested women marry coworkers to avoid moving. To drive this message home, the advice column in the same issue of the magazine featured a question from a level-five technician, who wrote to ask what she should do about a marriage proposal from a school friend who was now teaching at a technical school in another town, as she was reluctant to give up her work experience.[65] The columnist answered that it was out of date to assume that "women have to follow men" (*yŏp'iljongbu*), asking in reply, "Can't a man follow the woman?" Urging her to solve her marriage problem "actively, so that you can have a happy family without leaving your beloved workplace," the columnist suggested that if her job was tied to the factory, her prospective husband should move, since he could easily find a teaching position near her factory.

Rather than placing the responsibility solely on women, several contributors also pointed to problems of sexism faced by women both in and out of the workplace. A lathe operator explained that women often lacked confidence because experienced male workers belittled younger workers. New women workers were understandably shy, unable to ask questions that would help them innovate. She encouraged women to proceed boldly and fearlessly, to develop a thick skin, reciting the old saying that water collects only on hard surfaces.[66] Likewise, a press worker called on mothers to raise their daughters and sons equally, fostering curiosity to tackle problems and a sense of openness to new things in order to cultivate a spirit of innovation.[67] Juxtaposing her own mother against others who would scold their daughters for "playing like a boy" and limiting them to "womanly" tasks, she credited her mother for challenging her to make things with her own hands from a young age, when she and her sisters made simple household furnishings like a bookshelf, a shoe closet, and a clothes rack. Rather than scolding her for taking apart her mother's sewing machine or telling her to stay away from electrical equipment as dangerous, her mother complimented her for taking an interest in machines and showed her how they worked. It was thanks to such an upbringing that she was able to advance to become a level-five technician in just two years of work. She blamed the discriminatory practices in child-rearing for the "mysticism" some women felt toward technology, and praised her own mother for raising her three daughters to all become "masters of creativity" (*ch'ang'ŭi koan myŏngsu*).

Despite such examples of model women, undesirable attitudes continued to surface in the women's magazine as targets of critique. Counseling a "sincere attitude toward labor," one vignette after another decried the way young women with career ambitions got stuck at home after marriage, and how frequently workers moved to look for "easier" work.[68] Furthermore, the lack of respect for collective resources and quality led to shoddy products in the rush to meet production quotas that emphasized quantity. A comic strip poignantly captured the preoccupation with statistics in the form of "percentage illness" that led to bad quality—products turned out defective and came back to haunt the worker, and the patterns on poorly made textile faded in the sun.[69]

FIGURE 4.3. Comic strip criticizing the preoccupation with quantity leading to low quality. The original caption of the figure reads, "Sick with the Percentage Illness." *Chosŏn Nyŏsŏng*, March 1959.

As in other state socialist countries, labor provided the means by which to build socialism toward the ultimate goal of communism. But until that goal was achieved, when materials could finally be distributed according to need, official policy demanded strict adherence to the socialist principle of distribution based on the amount of work performed, as a way to increase labor productivity.[70] Socialist distribution entailed allocation of resources according to the quality and quantity of work regardless of age, sex, or race, by accurately evaluating the amount of work performed based on its difficulty and the skills required.[71] Critical in this process was how precisely and fairly work was assessed by the work team leaders, but they were often found to rely on estimates and averages rather than calculations after daily site visits. They often based their calculations simply on the number of family members to feed rather than work performed, sometimes unfairly giving preferential treatment to their own family and friends, affecting morale.

Generally, labor sectors segregated by gender placed women in the light and service industries, whereas men took up more positions in the heavy industries, with higher pay and greater benefits under the Public Distribution System.[72] While this coincided with patterns of gendered hierarchy across global labor markets in which women made up a significant proportion of the informal sector, as well as lesser-paid positions even in formal work, there was less dramatic a difference than one might expect in Korea, given the gendered division of labor. Although gender-disaggregated data for this period was difficult to find, the 1993 census (before the economic crises of the 1990s) showed that the labor force participation rate was 84.6 percent among men and 68.9 percent among women, with the gap significantly less for those in their forties, at the peak of labor force participation—98.7 percent among men and 91.1 percent among women.[73] Even as later statistics show that 78 percent of male industrial workers were in heavy industry, as opposed to 22 percent in light industry, more women were also in heavy industry, at 55 percent, than those in light industry, at 45 percent.[74] In fact, the top three sectors employing the largest number of industrial workers in 2008—light industry, machine building, and mining—were the same for both women and men (table 4.2).

TABLE 4.2 Numbers of workers by industrial sector, 2008

SECTORS		WOMEN	MEN	TOTAL
Light industry		747,177	461,357	1,208,534
Heavy industry	Machine building	280,586	547,653	828,239
	Mining	262,579	463,872	726,451
	Chemical	152,241	155,952	308,193
	Construction	84,188	167,579	251,767
	Metal	76,591	141,975	218,566
	Energy	32,164	117,405	149,569
	Electrical	39,365	64,197	103,562
TOTAL		1,674,891	2,119,990	3,794,881

Source: Cho Young-Ju, "Pukhan yŏsŏng ŭi silch'ŏn kwa chendŏ rejim ŭi tonghak" [The practice of women and dynamics of gender regime in North Korea] (PhD diss., Ewha Women's University, 2012), 74. There is a mistake in the original calculation of the total number of workers, which I have corrected here.

Although these numbers reflect later conditions and cannot directly speak to the 1950s and 1960s, they parallel other state socialist economies with larger proportions of women in the light industries.[75] What is important to keep in mind is that in comparison to market economies, commerce and retail in socialist economies are comparatively small sectors, so relatively fewer of the total women working are employed in those sectors. As a result, while there were certainly more men in the industrial sector overall, women made up 44 percent of industrial workers and 36 percent of heavy industry workers, confirming the consistent priority placed on these sectors.

In addition to problems in the valuation and distribution of industrial labor, there were also issues related to the appropriate disbursal of funds among agricultural cooperatives. Ideally, a cooperative's total income should be suitably divided between the distribution fund (*punjae p'ondŭ*) that would disburse payments to the cooperative members according to their labor input, and the accumulation fund (*ch'ukjŏk p'ondŭ*) that would set aside savings toward infrastructure improvements. An inadequate amount allotted to the distribution fund could negatively impact the livelihood of the cooperative members, whereas an insufficient amount saved for reinvestment in the accumulation fund reduced the material foundations for improving the cooperative's future production. This would have been an especially important issue to address in the women's magazine, since women made up a substantial proportion of membership and leadership in agricultural cooperatives. Many men had lost their lives during the Korean War, and surviving men went into heavy industries, leaving agricultural work to women.

With priority on accumulation for reinvestment, various forms of saving labor time and material inputs by reducing or recycling waste became yet another way in which productivity was calculated. Especially prominent beginning in the 1960s, examples of saving and reducing waste around the house were extended to workplaces, with textile workers gathering broken thread for reuse in their "red pouch" (*pulgŭn chumŏni*) and collecting leftover paraben to make candles.[76] A new *Chosŏn Nyŏsŏng* column called Frugal Housekeeping (*alttŭlhan sallimsari*) in the first half of 1966 featured essays devoted to saving and treating collective property as preciously as one's own, lauding such acts as "patriotic."[77] Owing to problems of scarcity, recycling to get the most out of materials was an early practice, adopted before environmental concerns made recycling a common practice in the First World. Recycling strategies ranged from gathering leftover cloth and threads in textile factories for repurposed industrial use to everyday practices like the use of leftover pencils (*yŏnp'il kkongdari*).[78] For example, Ch'oe Chŏng-ok, salesclerk at the Sinŭiju Department Store, was particularly innovative and diligent about finding uses for things that other people would throw away. She collected old shoes left at the store after new shoe purchases to send back to the factory for recycling. She found a way to reuse wrapping paper as book covers, even using the cutout scraps from the book covers as labels (*kkorip'yo*) for packaging. She collected plastic waste to send back to the factory, and at her request, students brought back the packaging of their crayons, which could be reused to package new crayons.

Others, like Ch'oe Ho-suk, took to heart the old Korean saying that "specks of dust can collect to become a mountain" (*t'ikkŭl moa t'aesan*). Ch'oe used her outings to gather medicinal herbs and plants, ranging from five-flavor berries, winter cherries, white bellflowers, atractylodes roots, motherwort, apricot seeds, and green onions, to perilla leaves, which made her room resemble a small herbal pharmacy.[79] Another essay detailed how to properly use the coal briquette (*kumŏngt'an*) for heating without any waste.[80] And another described the mind-set of a recycling center worker, who firmly believed that there was not a single thing to be thrown away, always carefully looking around her surroundings to collect even the most minor scraps.[81] She picked up bottle caps from the street and dug up rusted nails from the ground, washing them off and gathering them in her pouch. She even collected used oil from various places in the belief that even a small bucketful could be useful. Likewise, Kim Chŭng-nyŏ, a frugal housewife and mother of eight, and vice-chair of her local women's union in Kanggye, Chagang Province, didn't let a single hair go to waste.[82] She collected loose hairs and used them to fill a shoe mat; collected threads of only two to three centimeters, fallen out from clothes, to twist them together to make a hanging ribbon for items like brooms and dustpans; and reused the plastic from wrappers and torn rain gear to make covers for her furniture legs. She put each of her children in charge of a type of item to collect for recycling, such as paper, metal, and rubber, and she dried her food waste to use as feed for her household pigs.

As these examples make clear, productive labor and reproductive labor were difficult to distinguish in practice, as women's labor both outside and inside the home was an integral part of building socialism. Even as labor was differentiated between domestic labor (*kasa rodong*) and social labor (*sahoe rodong*), without proper accounting of the former in national statistics, housewives were organized into domestic work teams (*kanae chagŏpban*) tasked with meeting local consumer demands: in the actual practices of work, the conventional division between productive and reproductive labor all but broke down.[83] As a product of capitalist developments, the public-private distinction was meant to be abolished as anachronistic, but this proved inadequate to dismantle the productive-reproductive binary that placed a double burden on women. This was also evident at the National Mothers Congress.

Women as Socialist Mothers

Just over two years after the National Conference of Women Socialist Builders, the National Mothers Congress convened from November 15 to 17, 1961, in Pyongyang, with some twenty-one hundred women, including exemplary mothers, child care workers, labor heroes, and innovative socialist builders. The meeting began with a report by the first vice-chair of the KDWU Central Committee Kim Ok-sun and ended with medals and awards given out to model mothers.[84] A Mothers Exhibition accompanied the congress, showcasing daily schedules of children in the care of public kindergartens, the wide array of musical instruments available at child care facilities, and fashionable clothes available to children and mothers. The year in which the congress was held, 1961, is often associated with the culmination of top-down state centralization through the completion of rural collectivization and party control over workers.[85] In this context, previous scholarship on the National Mothers Congress tends to view it as state co-optation of the women's agenda, in which their traditional roles as mothers became a focal point to displace earlier socialist models, such as the "tractor girl" with transnational linkages.[86]

Placed in the international context of the earlier 1955 World Congress of Mothers, however, the Korean Mothers Congress was part of the international movement to valorize maternalism. Neither of the mothers congresses limited participation solely to mothers or restricted discussions about women's roles simply to motherhood, instead offering maternalism as a form of socialist practice that combined productive and reproductive labor. In fact, the women who participated in the congress were not stay-at-home mothers but were also workers outside the home. Of the seven women's statements included in the collection of documents from the congress, two were from workers in agricultural cooperatives, two from textile workers, and one each from a pharmacist, a middle school teacher, and a mother with a disabled child.[87] The last three women are especially good examples of blurring conventional boundaries between productive and reproductive labor. The pharmacist combined her work in health care with taking care of her blind husband, who was honorably discharged from the military. The middle school teacher formed study sessions for mothers in her local area, reforming mothers who "blindly" loved their children and thereby were unable to provide discipline or foster autonomy. Meanwhile, the mother with the disabled child spoke of her child's severe burns, healed thanks to skin grafts from 250 party members, vowing to give back to society through her hard work in her domestic work team.

Many of the experiences shared at the congress combined productive and reproductive work in such ways. A cooperative member with nine children brought in added income for her household and alleviated food shortages by putting her children in charge of raising domestic livestock such as pigs, chickens, and rabbits. This also served to instill the value of labor among her children. Several women spoke of their earlier unproductive habits, cursing and yelling at their children and forcing them to do things without proper instruction. One mother detailed how she ran such a strict household that her children were afraid of her, fearful of spoiling their clothes and unable to have any fun.[88] Whereas traditional parenting had focused on providing basic physical security through shelter, food, and clothing, mothers were now urged to provide more hands-on guidance to nurture children by attending to their specific personalities and characteristics, tailoring their education accordingly. With the shift in expectations on the role of the family in productive and reproductive labor, the KDWU launched a nationwide "movement to create model families" (*mobŏm kajŏng ch'angjo undong*). Model families would combine the daily study of revolutionary texts (especially the memoirs of anticolonial partisans) with the raising of at least two pigs and thirty rabbits in each family, all the while maintaining proper hygiene and cultural standards; children would aim to become best students at school, and every family member would aspire to perform at least one good deed per day.[89] Proper

FIGURE 4.4. Emblem of the KDWU, first used at the 1965 Third Congress, with parallels to the 1955 World Congress of Mothers (see figure 3.4). *Chosŏn Nyŏsŏng*, August 1966.

child care was an important way to help prevent children from getting sick, which was a major factor impacting the rate of women's work attendance.[90]

Three years after the National Mothers Congress, the KDWU celebrated the integration of an additional 313,000 women into the workforce so that almost all housewives participated in "domestic industries" (*kanae kongŏp*), for example raising livestock using homegrown pumpkins as feed for pigs, rabbits, and chickens.[91] By 1966, Cabinet Decision No. 23 on the Regulation of Work Hours for Working Mothers (Mosŏng rodongjadŭl ŭi rodong sigan e kwanhan kyujŏng) stipulated that, for mothers with three or more children under the age of thirteen, work hours be reduced from eight to six hours without any reduction in salary, rations, social insurance, pension, or vacation time, shortening the workweek from six to five days for those unable to shorten the workday owing to work requirements.[92] To follow up on the National Mothers Congress and its aim to increase the role of women in children's education and strengthen the connection between schools and families, a National Congress of Child Care Workers convened from October 20 to 22, 1966, five years after the National Mothers Congress. The 1966 congress showcased best practices at nurseries and kindergartens in the education and health care of children from newborns to children under eight years of age before primary school. Rejecting traditional views of child care workers as "simple babysitters" (*tansunhan aibogae*), the congress awarded certificates, prizes, and medals to over a thousand child care workers for achievements as labor heroes and model merit workers.[93]

The Seven-Year Plan reportedly placed socialist construction on a firm footing with the 1966 abolition of agricultural tax-in-kind and the start in 1967 of a nine-year compulsory education system, after successfully providing middle school education since 1958.[94] In fact, by the mid-1960s, the rate of industrialization and urbanization was comparable to parts of Eastern Europe.[95] In this context, nurseries and kindergartens were not just places to "look after children," but important in their early education as a way to instill a collective spirit "to liberate women and eradicate inequality between men and women."[96] With the push to expand the number of child care facilities, 23,251 nurseries and 15,218 kindergartens were opened by 1966, caring for 877,000 babies, or 70 percent of this age group, and 790,000 children, or 60 percent of kindergarten-age children. This was reported to be an eighty-three-fold increase in the number of nurseries, and a sixty-four-fold increase in the number of kindergartens over the previous ten years.[97] The number of child care personnel and educators had also increased, to 130,000 workers.[98] As a result, women now constituted almost 50 percent of the workforce, making up the majority of workers and managers in light and local industries. In order to provide sufficient medical care for mothers and children, 34 percent of hospital beds were reserved for mothers and children, and more birthing centers and pediatric hospitals were being built. Child mortality had decreased to a quarter of the rate from the colonial era, and in the twenty years since national liberation, life expectancy had been extended by twenty-two years.[99] Consumer goods also expanded, with more investment in culture, education, housing, public facilities, and social services.[100] Outside economists observing such changes with awe attributed the rapid growth of the Korean economy in the 1950s and early 1960s to the effective use of foreign aid and investment in human capital with a compulsory nine-year education focused on science and technical training, "the first such program in the Far East."[101] Despite such improvements, the Seven-Year Plan had to be extended for three years owing to setbacks and slowdowns, as industrial output declined for the first time in 1966, with impacts across all sectors.[102] Diminishing returns on existing resources demanded greater labor productivity and efficiency while cutting costs and forcing savings.

The emphasis on women as socialist builders and mothers is not unique to Korea. The valorization of women in their productive and reproductive work parallels programs of the left international women's movement. The WIDF and the KDWU deployed maternalism not only to advocate for the militancy of peace, as shown in the previous three chapters, but also to underscore the double burden of working mothers to demand support for women in their productive *and* reproductive roles. Despite this, prominent male critics launched competing narratives about women's work couched in the language of sacrifice. They were only too eager to draw upon traditional stories and folktales of sacrificial heroines as a way to shore up nationalist narratives about Korean women, even as such appeals to tradition were dissociated from feudalism and Confucianism.

Work as Service and Sacrifice

Conceived in terms of "moral character" (*todŏkjŏk p'umsŏng*) serving the collective rather than individual fulfillment, both productive and reproductive labor were presented as service (*pokmu*) and sacrifice (*hŭisaeng*) regardless of sex. But the rhetoric of sacrifice often used examples from "tradition" that centered on female characters as interpreted by male critics. In a serialized 1955 column in *Chosŏn Nyŏsŏng*, critic and literary scholar Yun Se-p'yŏng traced the moral character of Korean women back to figures from the Three Kingdoms period (57 BCE–668 CE).[103] He noted that the main characters of classical literature consisted mostly of women such as Princess P'yŏnggang of Koguryŏ, Jiŭn of Silla, and Tomi of Paekje. Reminding readers of the historical context for such stories bound by the "patriarchal family system privileging male power" (*namgwŏn chŏnje ŭi kabujangjŏk kajok chedo*) that restricted women to the "inner" sphere cut off from society, Yun argued that despite such limitations placed on women's freedom, they showed their intrinsic moral character through their service and sacrifice. Prime examples included beloved characters like Simch'ŏng and Ch'unhyang from eponymous folktales, and historical figures like Kye Wŏlhyang and Non'gae, who sacrificed their lives to protect their communities from foreign invaders. Pointing to women's use of cunning strategy that surpassed their male peers, Yun read these stories as implicit critiques of gender inequality to make a case for women's liberation, even as this liberation was dependent on self-sacrifice.[104]

Yun offers the story of Simch'ŏng as the most representative. Rather than the tale being an exemplar of Confucian filial piety, as it is commonly understood, he argues that it exemplified self-sacrifice and humanist empathy for the people.[105] Attributing these sentiments to Simch'ŏng's experiences growing up with a blind father, Yun contends that had Simch'ŏng not lost her mother at birth, she would not have developed such strong attachments to her father, for whom she sacrifices herself to restore her father's sight. This sacrificial spirit, Yun insists, is a reflection of her "sublime humanism" (*sunggohan indojuŭi*), rather than filial piety. Moreover, comparing Simch'ŏng to Ch'unhyang, Yun claims that while Simch'ŏng's sacrifice was limited to her own father, Ch'unhyang's self-sacrifice for her lover is representative of the people's liberation movement when she resists the governor's sexual advances.[106] Again rejecting the conventional interpretation of Ch'unhyang's chastity as emanating from Confucian ethics, Yun maintains that this fidelity is a native custom, intrinsic to Korean women's moral character.[107] Citing Ri Su-kwang, compiler of the first Korean encyclopedia, between 1614 and 1634, Yun reiterates Ri's arguments that Korean women valued chastity so much that at the risk of death and mutilation, they refused to be "sullied" (*tŏrŏp'ida*) by enemies during the Japanese Hideyoshi Invasions (1592–1598).[108]

As further examples of Korean women's fidelity, Yun also points to several folktales, including that of Princess P'yŏnggang and her choice to marry Ondal, the town "fool." As the story goes, whenever she caused trouble as a child, her father had threatened to marry her off to Ondal, despite his commoner status. Rather than treating these as empty threats, the grown-up princess decides to marry Ondal against her father's wishes. This, Yun regards, was a sign of her steadfast fidelity and purity (*chŏljo wa sun'gyŏlsŏng*), expressing her love of labor by joining the commoners. Yun interprets similarly the tale of Paegun and Chehu from the 1485 *Annals of the East* (Tongguk t'onggam), about two families that give birth to a son and a daughter on the same day. The fathers, bound by friendship, promise their children for betrothal, but when the son goes blind in an accident, the daughter's father tries to break the engagement. The tale ends with the son and daughter running off together to live happily ever after. While Yun condemns the practice of arranged marriage as an old tradition violating individual rights, he praises the purity of the daughter in keeping her engagement, *not* as a Confucian practice, but as the result of her humanism.[109] Yun's serialized column and his attempts to reinterpret the history of gender relations in Korea illustrate similar strategies to condemn harmful sexist traditions even while avoiding a blanket negation of the past. While the adoption of Confucianism under the Chosŏn dynasty would be condemned, traditions predating this would become a wellspring to celebrate Korean women's "traditional" values.

As a contemporary of Yun, Cho Byŏng-ryun followed on the heels of Yun's column to attack the division of the sexes and sexist traditions in Chosŏn Korea that extended to all levels of society so that women were kept indoors, unable to participate in society.[110] When going outside, Cho argued, upper-class women had to cover themselves, and even the famed *kisaeng* of Pyongyang and Haeju had to cover their faces with a large hat. Cho contrasted this period of Korean history with the previous era of the Koguryŏ (37 BCE–668 CE), Silla (57 BCE–935 CE), and Koryŏ (918–1392 CE) Kingdoms when women held important positions and often participated in horseback riding and archery. In Koguryŏ, Cho explained, every October was celebrated for the new harvest, with days of song and dance, including both women and men in their best clothes. In Silla, women and men gathered together every August, dancing around a pagoda inside the temple with prayers to fulfill their wishes. Under Silla and Koryŏ, women engaged in commerce in the marketplace, and during Koryŏ, records reportedly show that women competed in horseback riding. As evidence, Cho pointed to scenes of women on horseback in the paintings by Kim Hong-do and Sin Yun-bok before these practices were completely banned by the "blind adoption of Confucian morals." Despite these difficulties, Korean women continued to shine "like little stars and fireflies," Cho claimed, as in the poetry of Hŏ Nansŏlhŏn and the paintings of Sin Saimdang. Indeed, while *yangban* men abhorred labor, Cho argued, women were the main drivers of production in their daily domestic work, with their needlework and weaving to make beautiful textiles and in the raising of chickens and geese for food. Cho claimed that beautiful and practical craftwork was the result of women's diligence, demonstrating Korean women's love of labor handed down into contemporary times.[111] In stark contrast to the women's voices examined earlier in this chapter, such essays about Korean women's sacrifice were all written by male authors in order to argue that traditional gender roles were not the same as remnants of feudalism and its sexual hierarchy, but rather "lofty tradition" (*kosang han chŏnt'ong*). While difficult to confirm without access to the debates behind the scenes, such insistence on the tradition of gendered labor may be read as an attempt to sublimate women's more radical demands that men also take up reproductive labor.

Passing the Baton at the 1965 Third Congress

By 1962, when the Supreme People's Assembly elections voted thirty-five women into office, the newly elected women representatives included Pak Chŏng-ae but none of her previous female peers.[112] By this point, Pak was passing the baton over to the next generation of leadership for the KDWU. At its Third Congress, Kim Ok-sun was elected new chair, replacing Pak to conclude her twenty-year presidency.[113] Opening on September 1, 1965, for four days in Pyongyang with 1,165 participants, the Third Congress began with Pak Chŏng-ae's opening remarks. Vice-chair Kim Ok-sun delivered the main report, with three agenda items: first to review its work, especially in regard to women's participation in the

TABLE 4.3 Demographics of women at the KDWU Third Congress, 1965

	SOCIAL CLASS (SŎNGBUN)			
	WORKERS	FARMERS	OFFICE WORKERS	HOUSEWIVES
Percent	36.4	45.8	14.7	3.1

	OCCUPATION					
	FACTORY	AGRICULTURAL COOPERATIVE	EDUCATION, CULTURE, HEALTH	COMMERCE, DISTRIBUTION	PARTY, GOVERNMENT, WOMEN'S UNION	MISC.
Number	379	335	69	6	363	13
Percent	32.6	28.6	6	0.5	31.2	1.1

	AGE			
	BELOW 30	31–40	41–50	OVER 51
Number	98	653	353	61
Percent	8.4	56	30.3	5.2

	EDUCATION		
	PRIMARY OR SECONDARY SCHOOL	COLLEGE OR TECHNICAL SCHOOL	PARTY OR POLITICAL SCHOOL
Number	622	268	547
Percent	53.4	23	46.8

Source: Chosŏn minju nyŏsŏng tongmaeng che-3-ch'a taehoe munhŏnjip [Documents of the Korean Democratic Women's Union Third Congress] (Pyongyang: Küllo tanch'ae ch'ulp'ansa, 1965), 112–13.

Seven-Year Plan; second to revise its procedural rules; and finally to elect a new slate of officers to lead the union. Table 4.3 shows the characteristics of the 1,165 women attending the congress.[114]

The vast majority of women active in the union were young workers or farmers in their thirties, with some level of schooling. Moreover, 479 women (41.1 percent), or almost half of all the participants, came from "patriotic families" with someone either killed during the Korean War or currently serving in the Korean People's Army, and 282 (24.1 percent) of the women had received some kind of medal or award from the government for contributing to socialist construction and national unification, while 27 had received the highest honor as Hero of the Republic or Labor Hero.

In the twenty years of Pak's leadership, union membership had grown to 2.73 million women.[115] Of them, some forty-seven thousand women had received national medals of commendation, twenty-five thousand women had been elected to people's committees at various levels of government, and sixty-three women were decorated labor heroes.[116] There were now seventy thousand women who were experts, engineers, technicians, doctoral and master's graduates.[117] With the 1958 party directive to foster married women's participation in socialist construction, married women now made up as much as 80 percent of textile workers in some factories, whereas previously few married women had jobs outside the home.[118] The congress celebrated this expansion of women's entry into the workforce since the last congress in 1954, welcoming women's work in solving the labor shortage by replacing "outdated ideology" (*nalgŭn sasang*) with communist collective labor.

The congress also revised the articles of the women's union based on discussions at the National Mothers Congress and the Fourth Party Convention.[119] The KDWU, like other social organizations, was officially designated the party's "transmission belt" under the leadership of Kim Il Sung to promote women as both communist mothers and builders of socialism. Juche ideology was included as a guiding principle, alongside Marxism-Leninism and proletarian internationalism. The KDWU renewed its commitment to organize entry-level chapters (*ch'ogŭp tanch'e*) in all factories, cooperative farms, government institutions, schools, hospitals, and social enterprises, instituting new union dues at ten won upon initial membership and five won monthly thereafter.

A year later, celebrating the twenty-year anniversary of the passing of the 1946 Equal Rights Law, Kim Ok-sun, as the new chair of the women's union, traced the achievements of the last twenty years, including the graduation of thirty-five thousand women from university since liberation and the institution of seventy-seven days of paid maternity leave.[120] She attributed such rights and benefits to the sacrifices made by those who came before, urging women to devote their wisdom and strength to further progress. As a member of the women's union, Chang Ŭn-dŏk shared her memory of the day that the draft Equal Rights Law was introduced:[121]

> Twenty years ago on July 28, 1946, a historic meeting was held at this very theater. The theater building was destroyed during the war, and even though twenty years have passed, the meeting is fresh in my mind's eye as if it was yesterday. It was an unusually hot day, two days before the official declaration of the Equal Rights Law. Many women rushed over upon hearing that there was to be a meeting of women enthusiasts in Pyongyang to discuss the draft statute, unable to calm their swelling hearts. It was my first time at a meeting with so many of us women, and more so because of the presence of *kisaeng* and nuns who were not even valued as persons back then. "What is the Equal Rights Law?" I wondered, not knowing its content yet, but I felt as if there would be something refreshing that would open up my heart. "Thanks to everyone for your efforts to come despite such hot weather." Unexpectedly, the meeting began with a casual greeting. Comrade Pak Chŏng-ae went up to the podium and began to explain each section and provision of the draft statute.[122]

Listening to Pak and each of the articles of the Equal Rights Law, Chang was reminded of the terrible conditions at the sock factory where she had worked during the Japanese occupation. She remembered the sixteen-hour workdays, the unhealthy working conditions in crammed spaces with little to eat, being fired for giving birth, while only getting paid half the men's wages. When Pak explained that the statute would guarantee equal wages for equal work, maternity leave, and sick leave for all workers, Chang "just fell over crying." She remembered, "Although it was just a few words, they released all the bitter sorrow [*wŏnhan*] burrowed in my heart. All the factory women who had endured hardship like me sobbed." After the release of such emotions, the women in tears beamed with smiles, clapping as if their hands would burst. Chang continued:

> To be sure it was a wailing of joy, a happy cry at the feeling of excitement boiling over in my heart. The *kisaeng* women sitting there just wept. "What is this day! It's not the day I lost my mother, nor is it the day I lost my father. But why do tears keep coming? I'm crying for joy. I'm crying for joy. We women, who have lived bounded for 4,000 years without knowing life, met liberation today. These are clogged tears. These are embittered tears. These are tears rotted into the skirt over generations. All we could do was cry." When discussion began, a woman ran out and

expressed her tumultuous feelings this way, crying with tears streaming down her face as she stood holding on to the podium. All we could do was cry.[123]

The repeated references to *kisaeng* women overcome with emotion were no exaggeration, as these women were situated at the bottom of the social hierarchy, rarely treated as part of the working class, even by labor organizers. Working in the education department of the local women's union in Pyongyang, Chang was determined to make a copy of the Equal Rights Law to post that very night. She sat herself down at a table, but as someone who had not even finished primary school, she remembered how challenging it was to properly manipulate the writing brush, so that "the ink fell here and there, leaving stains on my hands and face, and I struggled to barely write the two pages all night. Two pages! The letters were crooked, but my honest sentiment was that each letter seemed to be dancing with joy."[124] Marking the anniversary of the landmark legislation with such vivid memories twenty years later, Chang nonetheless concluded that the "proud journey we have taken is not at its end today, since we have farther to go than the road we have already traveled."[125]

From the existing sources, it is difficult to know whether this was a veiled critique about work left to do to guarantee equal rights for women in Korea, but similar references to progress yet to be made were (and continued to be) a consistent theme throughout the international women's movement. Indeed, women's work was never done. Rather than spurring further radical demands, however, the disappearance of the first generation of women leaders such as Pak Chŏng-ae from the scene coincided with the consolidation of authoritarianism. Kim Il Sung took credit for leading the women's movement, and the women in his family became models for others to follow. In 1967, as the hagiography around Kim and his family gained renewed significance, a campaign was launched to study and follow the model of Kim Il Sung's mother, Kang Pan Sok (*Kang Pansŏk ŏmŏni ttara paeugi*). Although Kang had occasionally been mentioned since the early 1960s, she was then one among many other models of heroic mothers celebrated in official publications.[126] The Monolithic Ideological System (Yuilsasang ch'egye), formalized during the May 1967 Politburo meeting of the Korean Workers Party, institutionalized the authoritarian leadership system.[127] Replacing Kim Ok-sun, who had only just taken over the leadership of the women's union in 1965, Kim Il Sung's then wife Kim Sŏng-ae took charge of the KDWU in 1969, largely as a figurehead.[128] The next National Mothers Congress would not be held until 1998, almost forty years since the first in 1961, and by then the membership of the KDWU had shifted to mostly housewives, as professional women joined their respective work organizations.[129] Although official discourse thereby shifted to put a man at the center of the Korean women's movement, this book has insisted on listening to the varied and buried voices of women before 1967 that come through *despite* the official rhetoric. As we will see in the final part to this book, this kind of displacement and appropriation of women's contributions and leadership also took place in the cultural sphere.

Part 3
CULTURAL REVOLUTIONS

5

AESTHETICS OF EVERYDAY FOLK

> **What pride that not only professional artists, but also many working masses, young students, and even the Young Pioneers participate in autonomously creating great works of art. . . . That is why our era can be referred to as the age of people's creation.**
>
> Choe Seung-hui, 1961

Groups of women step gingerly into formation as they whip open and shut a pair of folding fans. The gentle gliding steps are a sharp contrast to the strong extended arms, even as the lilting up-and-down motions of the wrists lend a tenderness to the movement. Such juxtapositions of hard and soft, tough and tender, are diverse expressions of femininity and womanhood that also formed the first two parts of this book. Korean women called for a militant peace while combining their reproductive labor as mothers with their productive work as socialist builders. This valorization of social labor, including reproductive work, was infused into the arts when everyday tasks—harvesting grain, gathering fruits, fetching water—became sublime movements in the world of arts and culture through what I call an *aesthetics of everyday folk*.

Rather than treating such examples as political theater, this chapter positions women at the center of aesthetic developments in Korea. I have insisted throughout the book that state socialist women were not simply tools for mobilization used by male leaders, but were part of the long history of the women's movement. Likewise, Korean women in the arts were not merely used for propaganda but were part of an aesthetic movement led by the creative hand of the modern dancer Choe Seung-hui (Ch'oe Sŭng-hŭi, 1911–1969). While both Koreas regularly feature the fan dance as part of "traditional" Korean culture, it was thanks to dancers like Choe that it became a canonical part of the Korean repertoire. Less well known are her striking poses as a woman warrior performing the sword dance as she pirouettes and leaps with double swords to vanquish her oppressors in a narrative dance-drama that fused classical ballet technique with folk motifs.

Featuring colorful costumes with long flowing sleeves and skirts that drew on folk culture, Choe's dance-dramas were critical in setting the foundation for later revolutionary operas in Korea.

Hailed for adapting traditional dance for the modern stage, Choe Seung-hui became the first Korean woman to achieve global fame, touring the United States, Latin America, Europe, and Asia in the 1930s. A striking figure at five feet, seven inches tall (170 cm), she stood well above average male height in East Asia at the time. Her effective use of lighting with sequined and accessorized costumes, accompanied by her charisma, drew throngs of crowds to her performances—for many, a novel experience of enjoying dance in a theater, instead of in the pleasure quarters or palace courtyards.[1] Her success as the "dancer of the Orient" under colonial occupation was therefore aligned with Imperial Japan's own ambitions to assimilate Korea, leading to charges after World War II that she had collaborated with Japan. Complicating her status even more, a divided Korean peninsula has left mixed legacies of her artistic contributions in both Koreas. Soon after national liberation, Choe settled in the North, relegating her to persona non grata status in the South. In the 1960s, she fell out of favor in the North too, and as a result, neither the North nor the South gave her proper recognition until decades later with the thaw of the Cold War. In the late 1980s, the ban on North Korean materials in the South was partially lifted with the end of military rule. Meanwhile, in the early 1990s in the North, Kim Il Sung began publishing his memoir, which included references to Choe, crediting her as the founder of modern dance in Korea. As a result, not only does Choe's personal biography ebb and flow with the currents of modern Korean history, but the aesthetic choices she faced and ultimately made were shaped by the contradictions and supposed binaries attributed to these currents—between so-called tradition and modernity, East and West, North and South, nationalist and socialist—no matter how slippery these categories could be in reality.

Since the revival of popular and scholarly interest in Choe Seung-hui, a growing number of biographies have been published in Korean, as have more academic analyses of her work in both English and Korean sources, with particular attention being paid to her formative period in the 1920s and 1930s.[2] By contrast, this chapter assesses her role in the development of dance in Korea as part of a socialist realist aesthetics of everyday folk. Her theorization of form that tried to combine ballet technique with folk dance navigates the complicated politics of aesthetics between "high" (elite) and "low" (mass) art—a topic that continues to provoke passionate debate in the arts today. This tension and emphasis on folk aesthetics can be found throughout other artistic fields, from painting to music, as a new amateur arts system encouraged the masses of people without formal training to actively take part in the creation of new proletarian arts. This chapter focuses on dance because Choe, like Pak Chŏng-ae, is another woman whose contributions have been subsumed by official state narrative. By comparing the prolific history of women artists like Choe with later pronouncements and treatises published in the name of the second North Korean leader Kim Jong Il, we see yet again how women's work has been sidelined, in this case appropriated by the state. But it was Choe who resolved her aesthetic dilemma through a renewed commitment to folk dance as the quintessential embodiment of "national in form and socialist in content" with a lasting legacy, not only in Korea but also in China.[3]

In that sense, Choe Seung-hui's oeuvre subverts multiple conventional historiographies. Her work reverses the usual Chinese hegemony over Korea to show how she as a Korean dancer shaped Chinese dance. She also challenges conventional scholarship and official discourse that center the "Kim dynasty," in which different aspects of culture, from stage performances and films to military parades and mass games, are understood purely functionally as propaganda to control people's lives.[4] The most seductive and overused analogy is to regard Korea a Potemkin village, in which all aspects of life and culture become theatrical and fictional, fake and illusive, simply staged for the glorification of the leader. Instead of an application of aesthetic criteria to Korean performances, performativity itself becomes problematic. This chapter disrupts this usual reading to uncover how ideas first advanced by Choe were eventually appropriated as the official line. Such a method rejects a simple dichotomy between the disciplinary powers of the state and the parameters for individual choices. All choices—creative or otherwise—are made within given rules, and Choe's aesthetic choices were no different. She had to negotiate binary worlds in which she lived. Although the story of her expert navigation may appear seamless here, this is so only in hindsight, as folk aesthetics proved durable, enabling her resuscitation in both Koreas.

Art in the "Age of People's Creation"

Previous studies of Choe's early career have described her adaptation of traditional Korean dance as a form of tactical orientalism—an attempt at an alternative modernity through the exotic embodiment of a superior East over the West.[5] In fact, these adaptations of Korean dance were not traditional at all, but new creations by modern Korean dancers of "New Dance" (*sinmuyong*), influenced by movements in Germany and Japan in the 1930s.[6] Choe's mission paralleled developments in the history of twentieth-century aesthetics, specifically the issues Walter Benjamin laid out in his 1936 essay "The Work of Art in the Age of Mechanical Reproduction." What is art when new technologies allow infinite reproductions? If artworks can be mass produced to facilitate accessibility and strip art of its singularity and authority, or what Benjamin calls the "aura," then how do we identify the creativity and originality upon which artworks garnered value? As dance scholar Emily Wilcox shows in regard to modern Chinese dance, the major aesthetic preoccupation for artists of nascent countries emerging out of colonial and semicolonial status centered on questions of new form rather than content.[7] Instead of experiments in abstract form or a strict adherence to formalism, however, form was sought in the interstices of everyday life, because the question of form was so closely intertwined with questions of national identity.

In reaction to the homogenizing forces of industrialization, the beginning of the twentieth century saw a major preoccupation with "folk" and the varied possibilities offered by its diverse forms.[8] In the heyday of nation-building, the term came to increasingly represent the masses, going beyond concerns of simply preserving the past, in order to discover everyday practices of the common people as a new form of national culture.[9] After her return from her 1937–1940 world tour, Choe Seung-hui spent much of the remainder of the Asia Pacific War in China, where her most significant work was the opening of the Oriental Dance Institute in Beijing in 1944. Here she played a central role in systematizing dance adapted from Chinese opera. Choe received praise for her adaptation of folk-dance rhythms for the modern stage, and one of her lasting contributions to Chinese dance was a conceptual distinction between the "folk" (*min*), identified with peasants and agrarian culture in performances such as the masked dances, and the "classical" (*kojŏn*), associated with elite urban culture represented by the fan dance.[10]

While the attention to "folk" was certainly global in scope, folk culture as representative of nationalism was notably incorporated into the Soviet cultural policy of socialist realism, which regarded it as the source of art in its collective expression of communal living. As early as the 1920s, soon after the 1917 October Revolution, socialist realism as a new aesthetic practice focused on *novyi byt*, or the new everyday life, which was supposed to supplant the "homogeneous empty time" set by the pace of industrial clockwork.[11] Rather than the mundane dictates of productivity and efficiency imposed by the priorities of capital that stripped everyday life of any spontaneity or creativity, the socialist everyday would be imbued with a sensuous materiality in which people could connect with things aesthetically. Instead of people becoming commodified as labor power to produce yet more commodities in the capitalist process of alienation, *novyi byt* would enable people to interact with their material environment in socially and aesthetically meaningful ways. The Constructivist movement among the Russian avant-garde arose with this express goal in mind, as artists took up design of quotidian objects such as kitchen utensils, textiles and clothes, furniture and architecture, as well as posters and theater sets, eschewing the classical arts as elitist, in favor of an applied and practical approach to the arts.[12] In this way, socialist realism was expressly born with the aim of combining elite and mass culture by giving expression to socialist ideas. Even if largely developed by the intellectual elite, socialist realism would depict scenes of daily life accessible to the working class. Elevating the creative impulses as heroic and revolutionary, the arts became the arena to express a new worldview, combining aesthetics with an ethics that dignified the masses.

The attention to folk culture was also closely tied to the Soviet project of consolidating a multiethnic state by collecting and controlling ethnographic knowledge through inventories of local lands, peoples, and customs.[13] With the valorization of ethnic cultures in a combination of political radicalism and artistic experimentation, in what literary scholar Steven Lee has called the "ethnic avant-garde," everyday folk took the lead in visions of a world revolution that was both inclusive and decolonizing.[14] Likewise, literary scholar Sunyoung Park notes the role of Korean writers in advocating a "dialectical realism" that would center proletarian life on a "people's culture."[15] While she rightly notes differences between later socialist realist dogma and the dialectical realism in colonial Korea as a critique *against* dogma, the common focus on a "people's culture" facilitated continuities from Choe's use of folk dance in the 1920s to its later appropriation in the development of national culture.[16]

Indeed, state-supported folk dance ensembles became a worldwide phenomenon in the 1950s in response to the popularity generated by the Moiseyev Dance Company, which officially became the State Folk Dance Ensemble of the Soviet Union.[17] New forms of writing emerged too, such as reportage, *ocherk* (literary sketch), and the "wall novel"—short stories written by workers for their workplace to be posted on the wall for others to read.[18] Rather than segregating the different artistic fields as in the classical arts, folk culture facilitated a new amateur art system open to mass participation, combining dance with music, song, and theater that went hand in hand with folk traditions. In sum, a new valorization of folk culture and the incorporation of peasants and workers as artists democratized the arts, in how art came to be defined and who had the resources to produce it. Dance took pride of place in this amateur art system precisely because it was "relatively apolitical compared to other genres that were based on textual messages."[19] As such, it became an important way to demonstrate national culture and cultivate "friendship among the peoples," embodying the socialist realist epithet "national in form, socialist in content."

On Korea's national liberation in 1945, dance circles and other mass culture and arts circles flourished throughout the North, and in March 1946, the North

Korean Literature and Arts Union was founded, including the Dancers Union.[20] Saddled with her two young children and living in China at the time, Choe did not return to Korea until July 1946. But when she arrived in her native Seoul, criticisms of her pro-Japanese collaboration began to resurface. In an interview she gave with reporters on her arrival, she announced that she planned to work on developing a form of "Korean ballet" (*K'orian palle*), which was roundly criticized as opportunistic. Detractors railed that "she danced Japanese dances under the Japanese and now that they are defeated, she wants to dance Western dances."[21] Her reference to Korean ballet was misunderstood as Western dance, whereas Choe likely meant a form of dance-drama (*muyonggŭk*), much like the Chinese opera she had been studying in Beijing. Dance-drama was to become her major legacy, as well as the core of the challenges she faced. With the lifting of Japanese censorship, grievances and sharp denunciations were now aired in public, and Choe opted to follow her socialist husband to the North.

According to a 2012 biography published in Pyongyang, Choe received a letter of invitation from Kim Il Sung soon after her arrival in Seoul.[22] Although publications after the 1967 introduction of the Monolithic Ideological System must be taken with a grain of salt, such an invitation is plausible, given the cultural Cold War in which Choe's request for help to establish a dance school was reportedly ignored by the US occupation forces in the South; many artists and intellectuals did choose to head North.[23] Despite the strong anticolonial rhetoric, the North proved much more tolerant of colonial-era intellectuals, artists, and educators, not only because of the historically lower population there compared to the rich rice-producing centers in the South, but also because of the united-front strategy, which sought to rally the majority peasants against the minority of landlords and collaborators who had actively supported the colonial regime. With Choe's arrival in Pyongyang, a rare three-story building with a view of the Taedong River became the Choe Seung-hui Dance Institute (Ch'oe Sŭng-hŭi muyong yŏn'guso), fitted with student dormitories, offices, and a dance hall.

Her school was to become a permanent institution, receiving the status of a national school in 1953. There were several name changes after its founding; it became the National Dance Academy (Kungrip muyong hakkyo) in 1956, the Pyongyang Arts University (Pyongyang yesul taehak) in 1965, and finally the Pyongyang Music and Dance University (Pyongyang ŭmak muyong taehak) in 1972.[24] Thanks to Choe's fame, her first class enrolled forty students in the fall of 1946, and she quickly garnered the most prestigious posts in her field.[25] She was named chair of the Central Committee of the Korean Dancers Union (Chosŏn muyongga tongmaeng), a position she held until her death in 1969 except for a brief hiatus when she was politically censured, and she was also named president of the National Dance Theater. She gained political status too, being elected as representative to the Provisional People's Committee (to become the Supreme People's Assembly) of North Korea in the first election of November 1946.[26]

In 1957, Choe celebrated the thirty-year anniversary of her debut with great national fanfare. She was awarded a national medal, with full coverage in newspapers, magazines, and radio, and her work was lavishly praised.[27] A centerfold photo spread in *Chosŏn Nyŏsŏng* was dedicated to commemorate her achievement, with the latest update on her children's career following in her footsteps. Her daughter An Sŏng-hŭi had recently returned from her five-year study of dance in Moscow, and her fourteen-year-old son Mun-ch'ŏl was to study music in Moscow, having learned piano and *kayagŭm* (a traditional Korean plucked zither) from his mother while growing up.[28] Praising Choe's resolve tirelessly committed to her arts, the article listed her accomplishments as a dancer, choreographer, producer, and educator. This was when Choe began publishing some of her most important texts, including the two-volume *Basics of Korean National Dance* and *Collection of Dance-Drama Scripts*, both issued in 1958, and the *Basics of Korean Children's Dance*, published in 1964.[29]

The dance circles created after liberation came together to compete in the National Arts Festival (Chŏn'guk yesul ch'ukjŏn), often reviewed by Choe Seung-hui herself. A good description of the festival comes from a 1954 report in *Chosŏn Nyŏsŏng*.[30] The featured works were based on the activities of ordinary workers, as reflected in the titles, such as "Furnace Ablaze," "Bowl Dance," "Song of Young Innovators," and "Maidens of the Orchard." The reviewer lauded that "a brilliant outcome of the festival is that working women created such great works with their own hands, demonstrating yet again the superiority of the people's democratic system [in the North] in providing the conditions so that women in our country can create such excellent works."[31] The beauty of such dance in its simple and natural expressions was attributed to being drawn from actual movements of labor, disciplined through long experience, while the inclusion of local customs and folk arts in the women's dances was praised as the "rightful inheritance and development of the legacies of national arts left by our ancestors."[32] Nonetheless, the review also pointed to flaws that called for improvement "in pioneering and creating mass [*kunjungsŏng*] art genres so that a wide range of women could participate en masse; there were as yet few programs with simple educational outcomes. Ignoring form and only considering its political [content], some dance works remained schematic and mechanistic, relying on individual talent, and there was a tendency to present [the works] as they are from the production process or representations of life without aestheticizing them, under the pretext that they reflect life."[33] The reviewer bemoaned the lack of diversity in the repertoire, with the mechanical emulation of the advanced arts and a retrograde tendency in inheriting the classics.

Choe's review of the festival in 1961 reiterated the relationship between everyday beauty and dance aesthetics, praising the dances founded on the truthful expression of everyday life.[34] Applying the literary principles of brevity (*kan'gyŏlsŏng*), simplicity (*p'yŏng'isŏng*), and clarity (*sŏnmyŏngsŏng*) to works of dance, Choe criticized dances that were needlessly difficult and unnatural, with superfluous movements that made the dance complex. Choe linked the creativity of labor from everyday life with artistic creativity, lauding the work of the working masses and students, who were independently creating great works of art.[35] Calling this the "age of people's creation," Choe credited the party's cultural policy for raising the people's aesthetic level and promoting the arts. She defined beauty as a life of creative work, peopled by those moving forward and upward toward things "newer, greater, and more radiant, toward true communism." Affirming this new age of "people's creation," Choe applauded the extension of the arts to the masses during her speech at the Second Supreme People's Assembly meeting in 1958, with detailed statistics that saluted the 10,057 concerts offered to 10,057,000 people at the National Theater in 1957, for a 150 percent increase over 1956; the 240,000 film screenings for 92,213,000 people, for a 162 percent increase over 1956; and the 73,000 music, dance, and drama circles formed throughout the country.[36]

Politics of Aesthetics

Even as dance became a modern art form in the early twentieth century with the avowed aim of self-expression, dancers were at the mercy of the consumer public insofar as dance productions were mediated by capital.[37] Choe had experienced this throughout her US tour in 1938 and 1940 when she was dismayed by what she perceived to be the "vices of blind faith in the audience, even by the critics."[38] In their efforts to overcome such effects of modernity, Korean intellectuals faced two choices. While conservative thinkers sought to find Korean roots in the elite literati culture of the Chosŏn dynasty, leftists were motivated to look elsewhere. As literary scholar Yi Chu-mi astutely observes, rather than defining "Koreanness" through a conservative appeal to past traditions, they sought a "Korea specific strategy" in the struggle against imperialism toward a progressive future.[39] Eschewing elite cultural forms such as *sijo* poetry as the source of Koreanness, starting in the 1930s Choe had looked for inspiration to local folk traditions such as the masked dances of the peasants, shaman dances, monk dances, and *kisaeng* dances.[40] As a result, there was already an affinity between Choe's dance form derived from folk culture and the aesthetic application of socialist realism.

With her proven ability to fuse diverse elements, Choe again excelled, this time throughout the socialist bloc with the support of the Korean government. Her dance troupe won first place at the inaugural World Festival of Youth and Students (WFYS) held in August 1947 in Prague.[41] Even in the midst of the Korean War, Choe and her dancers were able to participate in the third WFYS in 1951 in Berlin, to be followed by a three-month tour to Poland, Czechoslovakia, Hungary, Romania, and Bulgaria.[42] Throughout Choe's career, she never missed competing in these festivals, which were held every other year. By the time of the sixth WFYS in 1957, Choe's company had toured China, Mongolia, Vietnam, the Soviet Union, Bulgaria, Romania, Albania, and Czechoslovakia leading up to the festival, gaining accolades from such famed Russian artists as ballet dancer Galina Ulanova and dancer and choreographer Rostislav Vladimirovich Zakharov.[43] Choe's production of the dance suite *Song of Peace* (*P'yŏnghwa ŭi norae*) went on to win first place for the Peace Prize at the festival.[44]

Choe's centennial 2012 biography begins, like so many official publications, with a quote from Kim Il Sung. In his memoir, Kim described Choe's significance to Korean dance:

> The 1920s and 1930s were a time when there was a wellspring of fierce attempts to develop our own elements in the fields of literature and the arts, preserving our sense of *minjok* [ethnic nation][45] amid the turbulent influx of outside forces. It was at this time that Choe Seunghui succeeded in modernizing Korean dance. She contributed to laying the foundation for the development of modern Korean dance by going deeply into the dances of the people, monks, shamans, *kisaeng*, and court dances to discover one by one the elegant dance rhythms filled with our people's sentiment [*uri minjokjŏk chŏngsŏ*].[46]

Until that time, Kim noted, Korean dancers had not reached the modern theater, even though singers and instrumentalists had done so. It was only once Choe's creative dances appealed to modern sensibilities that dance was able to take to the stage along with the other arts.[47]

Despite praise, however, Choe's continued performance of solo dances came under scrutiny for lacking "mass appeal [*taejungsŏng*] and realistic content," and she was encouraged to follow the other arts in creating "spirited works singing the efforts of workers and farmers to increase production."[48] Told to create group dances rather than solos or duets because "group dances are better to watch and enable the training of many dancers to quickly develop the dance arts," political currents pushed Choe to develop song and dance "appropriate to our people's aesthetic tastes [*migam*]."[49] Collective dance portraying the realities of peasant

FIGURE 5.1. National Dance Theater member Pak Kyŏng-suk in dance costume, winner of the gold medal for her small-drum dance at the Seventh World Festival of Youth and Students. *Chosŏn Nyŏsŏng*, September 1959.

life with references to anticolonial partisan struggle took precedence over individual creative expression.

In confronting such critique, Choe faced one of the major debates to emerge with the rise of mass culture in the twentieth century: the relationship between art and popular culture, or "high" and "low" art. Her biographical narrative affirms the socialist realist principle that "artists should strive to serve the working people ... creat[ing] dances that reflect the sentiments [*chŏngsŏ*] and everyday emotions [*saenghwal kamjŏng*] of our people."[50] Dancers had to be willing to go directly to the scenes of people's lives to learn their thoughts and desires.

Choe herself had done so during the colonial era to learn about local folk culture, which she adapted in her dances. The biography points out that Choe had insisted from early in her career that dance must not be a form of entertainment (*yuhŭng*) or hobby (*hŭngmi*), and she strove to elevate the artistry of her dance toward new forms.[51]

Accepting the challenge to create group dances with mass appeal, Choe produced her first dance-drama, *Midnight Moon Elegy* (*Panya wŏlsŏnggok*), in 1948, going through several revisions before its public staging on the first anniversary of the founding of the DPRK in 1949. It was featured at the Asia Women's Conference in Beijing, going on to tour in the Soviet Union and Eastern Europe.[52] The basic plot centers on a woman warrior during the Three Kingdoms period (57 BCE—668 CE) in ancient Korea. Paekdan, the daughter of a rebel leader, emerges in male dress, training alongside other women as fiercely as the men to liberate the people oppressed by a feudal lord. A friendly competition breaks out between Paekdan and one of the young men, Yŏngnang, as they perform a sword dance duet. Her father declares her the winner of the duel, and the two vow to marry when the men have to go into battle. Yŏngnang, however, is captured, and Paekdan's father returns wounded, to die in his daughter's arms. His last words ask her to take revenge, as he passes on his dagger to her. Paekdan comes to Yŏngnang's rescue and frees him but is captured by the lord and revealed to be a woman in male disguise. Impressed by her beauty, the lord orders her to be taken to his quarters. Paekdan, reappearing onstage in beautiful noble dress, is courted by the lord, who throws a banquet with dancers in her honor to win her heart, but she is unmoved. When she sees a fire signal in the distance from the mountains, she pretends to relent and begins to dance with the lord to distract him, taking out her father's knife to kill him as Yŏngnang enters with the rebels to defeat the lord's army. In the last moment, Yŏngnang is almost hit by a stray arrow, but Paekdan puts herself in the arrow's path to save him. Dying in his arms, she passes on her father's dagger to Yŏngnang, for him to lead the rebel army. The dance-drama ends with the victorious rebel army carrying Paekdan's body in a funeral procession in honor of her sacrifice.

Composed in three acts and four scenes, the work received praise for its Korean dance elements and Paekdan's heroic fight against the feudal lord, but her "individual act of terrorism" elided the significance of mass uprising against oppression as the only viable path to defeat feudalism.[53] As a result, the original 1948 script was revised to replace the father with Yŏngnang as the leader of the rebels, with whom Paekdan attacks the lord, killing him and dancing victorious with the other rebels. She no longer dies a heroic death, but lives on for a triumphant happy ending. A similar revision was made to Choe's dance-drama *Kye Wŏlhyang*, presented in honor of Kim Il Sung's forty-ninth birthday in 1961. Based on a true story about the heroic death of a concubine during the Japanese

Hideyoshi Invasions (1592–1598), the original plot ends with Wŏlhyang helping to kill the enemy leader and then killing herself because of her shame at being raped. Kim Il Sung reportedly suggested that rather than the work ending with her death, "her patriotic fidelity should be shown to the end with her firm commitment to protect Pyongyang."[54]

While political ideology and party policies were undeniably wedded to the creative process, the party agenda often went hand in hand with Choe's own

FIGURE 5.2. Choe Seung-hui dressed in the role of Kye Wŏlhyang in the eponymous dance-drama *Kye Wŏlhyang*. *Sinsaenghwal*, May 1961.

무용극 《계 월향》을 지도하는 최 승희.

FIGURE 5.3. Choe Seung-hui preparing dancers for the dance-drama *Kye Wŏlhyang*. *Sinsaenghwal*, May 1961.

ambitions, one of which was to develop Korean ballet, combining ballet technique with narrative dance-drama. Ballet not only represented artistic superiority in the "Soviet Union's *mission civilisatrice* ... to create *k'ultura*," but it had a long history in dance as a demonstration of virtuoso bravura.[55] Choe's ambition as a dancer and choreographer to master ballet technique is therefore not surprising. Her second dance-drama reflected this convergence of ballet with folk motifs. The *Story of Sado Castle* (*Sadosŏng ŭi iyagi*) debuted in 1955 on the ten-year anniversary of Korea's liberation. Set in ancient times during the Silla dynasty (668–935 CE), the plot features another strong female character fighting the injustices of a class system oppressing the commoners, who are portrayed as the true historical subjects, embodying dignity and virtue. Featuring Choe's famous sword dance, often traced to the Three Kingdoms period by scholars of the North, the central figure as a "courageous woman warrior" (*ssikssik'an nyŏjangbu*) deftly wields double swords as she twirls and spars against her opponents.[56]

Performed in five acts with six scenes, the dance-drama opens with the lord of Sado Castle celebrating his seventieth birthday in the company of his beautiful daughter, Kŭmhŭi. Educated and trained in the martial arts of *hwarang*, she is adept at handling sword and bow on horseback and is known endearingly as the Moon of Sado Castle.[57] By contrast, the lord's second wife, who is cunning, vulgar, and deceitful, plots with Ahan, an arrogant nobleman, to take over the kingdom. Meanwhile, Kŭmhŭi has fallen for Sunji, of humble background, who displays great swordsmanship and dedication to protect the people. Refusing to dance with Ahan, Kŭmhŭi is moved to dance to Sunji's flute-playing as the two grow closer, but the lord separates them because of Sunji's low birth. Back in his fishing village, Sunji thinks of Kŭmhŭi and the injustices of the class system that divides commoners from the nobles. When there is a pirate attack, Sunji leads the people's resistance against the attackers, while Ahan leads the castle forces. But the lord has failed to prepare adequately, and there is a shortage of weapons and warriors. With Ahan on the defense, Kŭmhŭi leads the remainder of the forces with sword in hand and meets Sunji coming to her aid. The lord repents his mistake as Sunji kills the pirate leader to bring the battle to an end. The lord awards Sunji, and the two lovers are finally able to marry, as the dance-drama ends in jubilant celebration.

Thanks in part to elaborate set designs and colorful costumes, both dance-dramas were hugely successful. As already noted, *Midnight Moon Elegy* was staged internationally in Beijing for the 1949 Asia Women's Conference, while the *Story of Sado Castle* was recorded on film with newly imported Soviet technology to become the first color feature film in Korea.[58] In contrast to her earlier solos and duets, Choe had effectively incorporated group dances with folk narratives that would appeal to mass audiences.

Following Choe's return from the Asia Women's Conference—her third international tour after participating in the WFYS in Prague (1947) and Budapest (1949)—her daughter An Sŏng-hŭi wrote of her impressions.[59] The forty-two members of Choe's Dance Institute staged some of her classic early works, An recounted, including the fan dance, the drum dance, and the sword dance, to showcase some forty dances while in China, in addition to the large-scale dance-drama production of *Midnight Moon Elegy*. The ensemble went on to stage sixteen shows throughout China, including in Beijing, Shanghai, Shenyang, and Dandong. They in turn had a chance to view the Chinese classical arts, including Peking opera in Beijing, the sword dance from Mei Lanfang's *Farewell My Concubine*, and the *Yellow River Cantata*, which "showed how much the artists are trying to perfect their new national form in its excellent display of Chinese national originality and characteristics even through the vocalization and orchestral accompaniment of Western music."⁶⁰ Efforts to overcome the conventional boundaries between East and West, highbrow and lowbrow, classical and folk, were in this way a major part of creating a proletarian internationalist culture led by women artists like Choe.

Korean tours abroad were only part of the cultural exchanges across the socialist bloc, with visits from both Chinese and Soviet dance troupes to Korea.⁶¹ A Soviet art troupe's visit to Korea in June 1954 prompted Choe to editorialize in the party newspaper that the great arts of the Soviet Union must be learned in earnest, while praising the troupe's performance of the Korean fan dance.⁶² The visiting Soviet artists included an eclectic mix of classical composers, singers, actors, and dancers, alongside magicians and acrobats. Among those who probably inspired Choe were ballerina Zaituna Nasretdinova of the Bashkir State Opera and Ballet Theater, and the Uzbek choreographer and dancer Mukarram Turgunbaeva, who like Choe fused traditional folk dance with Western classical

FIGURE 5.4. Choe Seung-hui at the Asia Women's Conference. *Chosŏn Nyŏsŏng*, February 1950.

dance. Turgunbaeva performed to wildly enthusiastic audiences the Korean fan dance, possibly introduced to her by Chang Kil-ja during the Korean National Theater's visit to Uzbekistan the year before.[63]

Beyond tours and exchange visits, in a 1955 essay published in *Cho-Sso Munhwa* (Korean-Soviet culture), the official organ of the Korean-Soviet Cultural Association (Cho-Sso munhwa hyŏphoe), Choe engaged directly with ballerina Galina Ulanova's writings to affirm the hard work that went into dance as an "art that requires endless effort."[64] Reiterating Gorky's dictum that talent had to be cultivated, Choe deployed long quotes from Ulanova's dance philosophy to insist on the primacy of the dancer herself—independent of extraneous factors including "the leaders"—to freely hone her art through her own life experiences:

> In ballet dance, "study" is not only the physical study of arms, legs, and body, but it must be a study of natural psychology and emotions, and also a study of the mind. However, this study of the mind, the study of the intellect, should not begin immediately but gradually, and it should of course not only be influenced by stage design, musical score, operatic script, and the leaders; these influences are not sufficient. The dancer's intellect can gain independence, freedom, and broad amplitude as she accumulates all experiences and impressions, and as she acquires the greatest science of all sciences, the science of life.[65]

Reflecting precisely the kinds of debates about form and content that preoccupied Soviet artists, choreographer Chŏng Chi-su contributed his own views on the creation of dance in the same magazine a few months later.[66] Likely written as a form of self-critique and a response to other dancers like Choe, he provided examples of choreography combining multiple ethnic dances, as opposed to "most choreographers who created dance with a strong tendency to focus only on various combinations of dance forms because they were obsessed with the creation of art for art's sake, devoid of ideology or content, leaning toward formalism."[67] Directly challenging Choe's homage to Ulanova, Chŏng countered Choe's emphasis on the central role of the artist's independent mind to criticize "choreographers who rely solely on their ingenuity and the functioning of their brains in shaping a work, relying on spontaneous creation rather than scientific and planned creation."

Nonetheless, he continued to praise the work of the Dance Institute for creating the foundations for a Korean national ballet while developing Korean classical dances such as the monk dance, the sword dance, and the mask dance, "promoting the development of Korean national dance and diversifying the form of ballet art by ingesting the essence of Russian and Soviet dances developed over 250 years."[68] He further praised the study of dances from the "people's democracies," including China, that greatly helped to further develop Korean national dance, becoming a valuable element in the creation of ballets and operas. Interestingly, Chŏng here cited Igor Moiseyev's dance philosophy that "to create a new national dance for a new generation, it is urgent to first take in the life, customs, and character of the people," arguing that "the mission of the new generation of dancers is not to be satisfied, as if a photographer [duplicating what is there], but to match the legacy of the past to contemporary emotions by dissecting elements like an anatomist to see under what conditions people in the past were creative and what are the characteristics of the movements that people enjoyed that should be inherited today, to create a new social sensibility."[69] Despite the implicit critique of Choe, Chŏng echoed her philosophy about the importance of everyday movements in shaping aesthetic form.

Through such debates, dancers kept returning to ballet as an alluring challenge to incorporate into the development of national dance. A generation younger than Choe, Ri Sŏk-ye (1926–1998) was inspired by Choe to study traditional Korean dance in colonial Korea, performing the role of Ch'unhyang in the eponymous dance. Moving to the North after division, she joined Choe's Dance Institute, as well as the National Arts Theater. She received critical acclaim for her role as Simch'ŏng in that eponymous ballet, choreographed by her husband Chŏng Chi-su and staged in 1955. With the opportunity to study ballet in the Soviet Union, Ri, like Choe, pushed for ballet's inclusion and continued development in a 1958 commentary in *Munhak Sinmun* (Literature newspaper), stating that in her previous ballet performance of Simch'ŏng she was "immature and idle."[70] By doing away with pretenses and preoccupation with authenticity, she vowed to develop ballet as a colorful national dance form. Consequently, the National Arts Theater staged various classic ballet repertoires throughout the 1950s and 1960s. In October 1956, for example, they staged the second act of *Swan Lake* among a variety of dance pieces that included the *Moskovsky Waltz* and the *Spanish Dance*. This first staging of *Swan Lake* in Korea was choreographed by Yu Yŏng-gŭn and performed by Ri Sŏk-ye, Ryu Sŏng-hŭi, and Kim Chong-hwa, all of whom were trained in the Soviet Union. The performance was hailed for demonstrating the mastery of the advanced dance arts.[71]

Meanwhile, upon Choe Seung-hui's return from her five-month tour of the Soviet Union and Eastern Europe between 1956 and 1957, the party newspaper highlighted the experimental incorporation of ballet technique for male dancers in the *Story of Sado Castle*. Pointing to the successful tour as proof of her effective introduction of ballet into Korean dance, Choe resolved to "chew on the classic ballet elements over and over until they become part of our flesh so that our national ballet should become more beautiful and full."[72] However, the problem of fusing ballet technique with Korean dance continued to plague

Choe throughout the 1950s. During her Eastern bloc tour, Choe had viewed seventeen different ballet and opera performances, including *Swan Lake, Sleeping Beauty, The Bronze Horseman,* and *Spartacus*. Upon her return, she reported that her troupe's performance of *Story of Sado Castle* with ballet movements was well received, but that the task of "harmoniously combining Korean dance with classical ballet that is so contrary to our dance" presented a "very difficult problem."[73]

As artists debated the form best suited for the socialist age, ballet itself had been fraught with controversy in the Soviet Union.[74] When the Bolsheviks took power after the October Revolution, communist iconoclasts sided with the radical avant-garde to argue that all prerevolutionary remnants of bourgeois culture had to be destroyed to make way for new proletarian arts. But writers like Anatoly Lunacharsky, appointed as the first people's commissar of education in 1917, saw the importance of preserving the best achievements of prerevolutionary culture, which included classical ballet, in order to build *on* (rather than over) them; among his ideas was a syncretic theater combining orchestral and choral music with song, poetry, and dance.[75]

As socialist realism became dogma in the 1930s, however, classical ballet was again a source of controversy for its highly formalized movements that seemingly had nothing to do with the way people actually moved in real life. With the 1936 antiformalism campaign, ballet became an "apprentice of drama," and a new genre called *drambalet* that privileged dramatic content with attention to realistic sets and costumes over choreography dominated from the mid-1930s to the mid-1950s as the only acceptable form of socialist realist ballet.[76] In this context, *drambalet* incorporated folk dance not only to address aesthetic concerns but also the political call for *narodnost'*, the promotion of folklorism, to foster unity among the multiethnic peoples of the Soviet Union. Against the formalist art of the "decadent" West, criticized as overly stylized and pessimistic, the folk arts represented realism and optimism.[77]

In order to execute this socialist realist dictum for "positive" characters and optimistic stories, the original tragic ending to *Swan Lake* was revised in Soviet-era performances to become a happy ending, much like the revision to Choe's *Midnight Moon Elegy*.[78] Avant-garde experiments of *drambalet* incorporated pantomime and dramatic theater, blending music, song, and folk dance on contemporary themes. Choe's aesthetic preoccupations in creating her dance-dramas to combine classical ballet with folk dance show clear parallels to such movements. Ironically, her efforts to create her own kind of drambalet began just as the genre was losing favor in Soviet Russia. Owing in part to the stagnation and lack of new works, the Soviet Ministry of Culture asked in 1957 for information on the most interesting ballets staged in the socialist bloc, including the "people's democracies."[79] As a result, Soviet choreographers during the "thaw" from the mid-1950s to the mid-1960s would again call for a renewed focus on strict balletic form to recuperate the essence of ballet as a unique artistic medium.[80]

In this debate over form and content, Choe was one among six contributors to a 1956 volume *Everyday Life and the Stage*, which included contributions by leading artists in theater, music, and stage design.[81] Following the official line that was a constant refrain throughout the volume, Choe argued this time against formalism and "bourgeois cosmopolitanism," criticizing the recently censured writers such as Im Hwa and Kim Nam-ch'ŏn.[82] Negating her own attempts to adapt ballet, she now denounced it for disparaging folk dance as "unfitting for the emotions of modern people and inferior in dramatic expression."[83] Standing against aestheticism and pure art, her position amounted to self-critique as she condemned factionalism within the dance field, with dancers unable to move beyond the circle of their own theater membership to learn from dancers elsewhere and share their own creations and experiences with others.[84] In fact, she argued against the idea that ballet could constitute national dance as an "international language," rebuking the "tendency to underestimate, or even neglect, the national dance heritage of our country."[85] This closely followed arguments made by Kim Il Sung in his so-called Juche speech of 1955, in which he similarly criticized the blind adoption of foreign elements without appreciating Korea's own historical and cultural legacies.[86]

As Choe's husband and art critic An Mak came under fire during these debates and was ultimately purged in 1958, Choe's dance was increasingly embroiled in the politics of aesthetics over how to articulate national form with socialist content. For example, her 1958 work *Unrim and Okran* (*Unrim kwa Okran*), later revised as the *Legend of Okryŏn Pond* (*Okryŏnmot ŭi chŏnsŏl*), came under attack for the lack of Koreanness in the accompanying music. Choe had incorporated music as an integral part of her dance compositions, modifying Korean instruments to accommodate the stage. To reflect the hybridity of her dances, she melded traditional Korean instruments with Western orchestral music to create new sounds.[87] Decrying the "smaller number of Korean instruments and an increased proportion of loud brass instruments," however, critics complained that "the musical accompaniment consisted of thick metallic music that grated the ear, instead of the soft and gentle melodies with Korean flavor [*Chosŏn mat*]."[88]

Such criticisms came about in the context of the 1958 political crisis in which Kim Il Sung faced challenges to his rule in the aftermath of de-Stalinization.[89] But the critique was not arbitrary. The basic points of contention can be traced aesthetically. First and foremost, Choe was enmeshed in the long-standing question about the meaning of art in the "age of people's creation" as she herself had framed the issue: how to elevate artistic bravura to the highest levels even as the arts were opened to mass participation. Choe's attempt to combine the "high" art of ballet with Korean folk dance toward a new form of dance-drama was ultimately stymied by the preoccupation with national form.

From the Classical to Everyday Folk

Despite the beginning of her decline after 1958, Choe continued to publish prolifically throughout the 1960s, expanding on and perfecting her dance philosophy. She emphasized her role in crafting dance-drama as a new dance form and shaping the socialist content of contemporary Korean dance. Choe noted how many varieties of group dances were now a part of Korean dance-dramas thanks to her work, "brilliantly illustrating the power and beauty in our people's lives through the joy felt by many in the creative process of collective labor."[90] Ruminating on the challenges of writing dance-drama scripts, Choe emphasized the role of artists in "continually examining everyday life to find what is beautiful, for what is patriotic, heroic, and revolutionary, in order to turn what is beautiful in life into what is beautiful in art."[91] She concluded that the narrative conflict depicted in the script must be based on real life, or it could not embody a true sense of drama, violating the principles of socialist realism.

In line with socialist realist methods, Choe wrote extensively about the importance of observing ordinary life for artistic inspiration. She detailed this process in two insightful texts. In a 1962 magazine article in *Chosŏn Yesul* (Korean art) titled "Artistic Skill and Artistic Training" (Yesuljŏk kiryang kwa yesuljŏk yŏnma), Choe forcefully rejected arguments for autonomous art. Rather, she wrote, "artistic skill must enliven the artist's creative intention to depict truthfully, profoundly, and clearly the everyday life and human characteristics as required by the creative methods of socialist realism."[92] She went on to define true artistry as "the ability to move millions of people by wonderfully turning life truths into artistic truths, and the beauty of life into the beauty of art."[93] Choe then explained what kind of national form must be joined with such socialist content. In a 1965 article of the same magazine titled "Artistic Tradition and Artistic Creation" (Yesuljŏk chŏnt'ong kwa yesuljŏk ch'angjo), Choe clarified that looking to the past does not mean relying on it or imitating it. Rather, she argued that the past is a resource "to improve on what is weak, to shape what is rough, to revive what is lost, and to make what does not exist in order to bring artistic innovation to meet the aesthetic demands of our age."[94] Defining artistic innovation as the creation of something *new* on the basis of past artistic traditions, she insisted that the new had to be better than the old; mere novelty could not constitute true artistic innovation.

So what was the essence of modern Korean dance for Choe? Her focus on everyday movements represented both socialist content and national form to elevate folk dance as the core. But her dance philosophy and artistic oeuvre were never bound by Cold War politics, even as its impact is clearly left in her writing when toeing the official line. Paralleling dance theories beyond the socialist bloc, Choe's formulations show clear affinities with the Laban School developed by dance theorist Rudolf Laban (1879–1958), who saw dance as representative of everyday gestures and developed the Labanotation system to record bodily movements. As an older contemporary of Choe, Laban makes a brief appearance in Choe's 2012 biography, albeit in the context of underscoring the importance of political leadership; in contrast to Choe, who enjoyed state support to develop her art, Laban as an exiled Jewish artist led a difficult life, according to the text.[95] Despite the brevity, however, the reference is telling. Laban's theory was adopted by folklorist and ethnomusicologist Alan Lomax, who in the 1960s developed a method to analyze dance called *choreometrics*, claiming that "dance is composed of those gestures, postures, movements, and movement qualities most characteristic and most essential to the activity of everyday, and thus crucial to cultural continuity."[96] In line with these trends, another one of Choe's accomplishments would be her dance notation system to record Korean dance movements.

According to Choe's last major serialized treatise, in the newspaper *Munhak Sinmun* in 1966, she affirmed that dance movements reflect people's daily labor and everyday movements particular to their culture and environment.[97] As a prime example, she pointed to the traditional Korean socks (*pŏsŏn*) with their upturned front ends, which caused people to walk with their toes slightly raised; this resulted in distinctive Korean dance steps that led with the heel gliding across the stage, in contrast to the ballet pointe.[98] Prominent in her repertoire was also the skillful use of Korean clothes as costumes that shaped the dance movements themselves. Choe highlighted everyday movements such as the handling of hair ribbons (*taenggi*), the gathering and whisking of the skirt (*ch'ima*) and jacket (*turumagi*), and the tossing off of long sleeves (*hansam*) or scarves, as expressions of Koreanness in dance. She singled out her sword dance, drum dance, and fan dance as the best examples of such practices.[99] However, such everyday movements are always changing according to the times, Choe argued, so it is imperative to constantly improve upon the traditional arts to reflect current realities. Choe drew a sharp contrast between strong working women in postliberation Korea in the era of socialist revolution and women of the past, who were often depicted as frail and delicate. Pointing out that such depictions were no longer an accurate representation of women, she affirmed that "not everything from the past constitutes one's national culture," and practices demeaning to women must be cast out.[100]

Alongside such repudiation of tradition no longer reflective of current conditions, other dance specialists emphasized the need to preserve past practices in the "original form." In a 1960 essay tracing the development of dance arts in Korea since liberation, choreographers Chŏng Chi-su and Pak Chong-sŏng linked the history of Korean dance to the long tradition of collective labor, citing ancient texts that referenced the role of song and dance in collective farming, passed down through the mask dance, peasant music (*nong'ak*), the monk dance, and the sword dance.[101] Although the essay referred to works created by Choe, neither she nor any individual artist was mentioned by name in their dance history. Indeed, in highlighting the "preservation of the original form" (*wŏnhyŏng ŭl kŭdaero pojon hanŭn panghyang*) to express national characteristics, the essay parted ways with Choe, who sought to create modern dance by adapting rather than imitating traditional elements. Nonetheless, Choe herself had highlighted the importance of studying everyday movements in the creation of new dance movements, and dances in the postwar reconstruction period often thematized various occupations, such as fishers, textile workers, ceramic workers, train operators, and metalworkers, depicting their heroic efforts in building socialism.[102]

During these debates on how best to balance the old and new, *Chosŏn Nyŏsŏng* serialized, from August to December 1960, a column on "reviving the beautiful tradition of Korean clothes." Written by Kim Mu-sam on behalf of the National Central Folk Museum, the column highlighted the beauty of the traditional Korean dress for women, starting with the pairing of the short jacket top with the long skirt, appropriate for Korean women's longer torso and shorter legs compared to the Europeans'.[103] In the following issue, Kim argued that Korean language included many subtle ways to differentiate colors, suggesting appropriate colors and patterns for different age groups, with bright colors recommended for younger people and more subdued tones for those older.[104] The next two issues underscored the beautiful lines of the Korean dress and the different seasonal styles, before the final installment that advised against combining the traditional dress with more modern clothes, such as sweaters over the top and leggings falling below the skirt.[105] By January 1961, a textile researcher weighed in by suggesting that even with advancements in fashion trends in the "civilized era," these should not be followed blindly: "Of course, we should model advanced experiences and dress appropriately for the civilized era. However, wearing suits so narrow that flesh protrudes or clothes exposing too much shoulders and arms following trends in other countries are offensive, unfit for our national characteristic. Living in the Chollima era [of rapid economic development], we should be frugal and active, wearing elegant and beautiful modern clothes that fit the body and sentiments of the Korean people."[106] Referencing the form-fitting suits and the more revealing forms of dress in the increasingly globalized fashion industry, this turn toward the "original form" and "national characteristic" was likely a guarded reaction to the potential infiltration of the 1960s counterculture in the midst of the cultural thaw in the socialist bloc.

In the search for nationalist origins, the principal tenets of Korean dance have come to be attributed to the political leaders, but Choe's own writings between the 1950s and 1960s show that she set the standard. As confirmed by trained dancers and dance scholars, instead of Choe following instructions, her aesthetic philosophy was appropriated by the political leadership as the authoritative model for the development of Korean dance after her death in 1969.[107] As evidenced by Choe's continued engagement in aesthetic debates well into the 1960s, her contributions and legacy would ultimately outlive her individual fame.

The idea to fuse different genres of dance began early in her career, reinforced by her 1930s world tour when she came directly into contact with folk dances in Latin America and Europe. Choe continued such forays with her founding of the Oriental Dance Institute in Beijing in the 1940s, and again devoted time to it in China during the Korean War. In a lecture delivered to Chinese dancers in 1951 and published in 1954 under the title "Discussion of Problems in the Creation of Dance" (Muyong ch'angjak ŭi che munje rŭl ronham), Choe argued that "not only do we need to know about Oriental dance, but we must be familiar with Chinese traditional dance, dance of the Soviet Union, and Western dance (for example ballet). Only after knowing and mastering such dances and gaining the knowledge and training on the basics can one expect one's body to move freely and intentionally, and be able to express complex and varied emotions through the body's rhythms."[108] Defying conventional boundaries between tradition and modern, or East and West, against critics who dismissed her work as mere adaptation at best or decoration at worst, Choe's dance philosophy stressed the *transnational* body and mastery over it in order to properly capture human emotion through bodily rhythms and movements. The dilemma between national form and socialist content was ultimately settled by Choe's renewed commitment to folk dance in the 1960s, as shown in her writings. Choe's dance theory claimed folk culture as the most fitting art form of the everyday, aligning with socialist realism that treated art as originating from and appealing to the popular masses.

With the consolidation of power around Kim Il Sung, his 1930s partisan history began to take precedence over folk aesthetics. This new outlook clashed with Choe's views, which she maintained in her publications throughout the 1960s. Until then, politically themed works were joined by those related to the folk arts, at which Choe excelled. But at the Central Committee meeting of the Korean Dancers Union in December 1964, such folk motifs were replaced by an increasing emphasis on political themes, thereby sidelining Choe with her continued insistence on folk dance in her writings.¹⁰⁹ In effect, her ideas about Korean tradition rooted in the folk arts clashed with the new sense of tradition rooted in Kim Il Sung's anticolonial struggle, and the halo around Choe's reputation was denounced as elitist, to be replaced by a more collectivist creative process.¹¹⁰

With the rise of the 1967 Monolithic Ideological System, Kim's rivals were removed from power under allegations of "bourgeois thought, revisionism, feudal Confucianism, dogmatism, toadyism, factionalism, regionalism, and other such antirevolutionary tendencies."¹¹¹ Choe was criticized under similar charges, as dance became a group activity (*sojo hwaldong*) under the amateur art system rather than a form of "high" art. With Choe gone from the scene and Kim Jong Il's emergence as the primary figure in the arts in his bid to succeed his father, dance-dramas were now considered a form borrowed from classical ballet, to be replaced by *"Sea of Blood*-style revolutionary opera" (*P'ibadasik hyŏngmyŏng kagŭk*), a genre attributed to Kim Jong Il (see chapter 6). In its November 1969 issue, *Chosŏn Yesul* editorialized that "without songs to clearly deliver the ideological content, dance-dramas were unable to fully and powerfully depict the enormity of real life," since past dance-dramas were based on legends, myths, and fables dealing with feudalistic ethics and morals.¹¹² Instead, the editorial continued, the newly created revolutionary operas would overcome the weaknesses of the past and illustrate the revolutionary reality in the present.

However, even under criticism, Choe's influence in the creation of basic Korean dance movements was to have a lasting place. While her name was left out of official discourse until the 1990s, Kim Jong Il's writings on the art of dance continued to emphasize the importance of basic dance movement training, which was largely based on the system Choe created. A 1992 treatise attributed to Kim Jong Il essentially followed the basic principles of dance laid out by Choe more than three decades earlier. Like Choe, the treatise emphasized the importance of creating dance movements out of people's everyday lives, highlighting folk dance movements as a way to cultivate national dance.¹¹³ Indeed, the use of folk songs and fables to create folk dances was again encouraged, as "the varied movements and postures in everyday life including work life have their own national characteristics that can most clearly be demonstrated through dance."¹¹⁴ At the same time, adaptations of traditional dances should satisfy people's aesthetic expectations and not be "excessively modernized," the treatise warned. Indirectly referring to Choe's incorporation of classical ballet in the creation of Korean dance-dramas, Kim Jong Il disparaged past dance-dramas as copies of Western dance-drama "without adapting it in our style [*urisik ŭro mandŭlji mot'ago*]."¹¹⁵ Instead of such "blind" following of Western genres, he advocated the creation of "new dance-dramas in our style" (*urisik ŭi saeroun muyonggŭk*) such as *Sea of Blood*, incorporating aesthetic trends from other countries in accordance with "our own ideological and modern sentiments" to match the people's aesthetic tastes.[116] Regardless of attempts to sideline Choe, the stress on the importance of folk dances, dance scripts, and collaboration between set design, music, props, and costume to create a comprehensive dance form was a reiteration of Choe's own career and writings.[117]

With the revitalization of folk dances to diversify the creation of new dance forms, the 1990s saw a concerted attempt to catalog and systematize newly discovered folk dances, and some of Choe's dances reemerged. The *Story of Sado Castle* (1954) was reportedly remade as the *People of Pyongyang Castle* (1997) and restaged under its original title in 2011 during the centennial celebration of Choe's birth.[118] The return to folk arts as Choe had advocated also coincided with the crisis of socialism that ultimately led to the dissolution of the socialist bloc, fostering a far more inward view, as embodied in the slogan "Our Style Socialism" (*urisik sahoejuŭi*).[119] While renewed nationalism may be expected with the waning of international socialism, this chapter has underscored the role of "socialist content" with its emphasis on everyday practices wedded to "national form" in establishing folk as a definitive aesthetic practice, led by women.

Just as Choe was part of the transnational development of folk aesthetics, the next chapter continues to explore circulations of communist women in other cultural forms. Although Choe's attempt to fuse ballet with folk dance was relatively short-lived, a similar hybrid dance form was revived in China during the Cultural Revolution with the emergence of the "revolutionary model ballet" *The White-Haired Girl*. Choe's famed fan dance would also be posthumously adapted in the Korean revolutionary operas *The Flower Girl* and *A True Daughter of the Party*.[120] Despite its vicissitudes, ballet may have proved durable in revolutionary cultures from Korea to China because it broke with traditional decorum that emphasized stillness and harmony embodied in the "slow, orderly, restrained movements" of elite ceremonial culture.[121] Indeed, despite the shared legacy of the sword dance in both Koreas, the northern version reportedly uses sharper movements, with firm upright postures, whereas the southern counterpart centers the principles of "movement even in stillness" (*chŏngjungdong*) and "external flexibility even in internal strength" (*oeyunaegang*).[122] This contrast, however, should not be overstated. Choreographers Chŏng Chi-su and Pak Chong-sŏng also mention these principles among the distinctive features of Korean dance in the North.[123] This chapter ends here, but Choe's legacies continue into the next chapter with the return of the woman warrior.

6

COMMUNIST WOMEN AROUND THE WORLD

> Comrade Kim Jong Suk vigilantly surveyed the surroundings and found five or six enemies lined up crawling toward them with guns aimed through the reed field. It was truly a moment of grave danger. At that moment, she swiftly pushed the commander away, blocking his body, and shot the first one, who had his gun pointed at them from the ground.
>
> Kim Myŏng-hwa, 1967

A statue and a museum in honor of Kim Jong Suk have stood in her hometown of Hoeryŏng since the late 1970s. Born to a poor peasant family in 1917, she is said to have joined Kim Il Sung's guerrilla forces in 1935. She married him in 1940 and gave birth to their son Kim Jong Il in 1942. She died in 1949, just a year after the establishment of the Democratic People's Republic of Korea. According to historian Dae-sook Suh, tributes to her commemorate her contribution to Korean history as a "revolutionary warrior" rather than as wife and mother to the previous leaders.[1] One of the most iconic paintings of Kim Jong Suk shows her in a skirted uniform, with pistol in hand, standing in front of Kim Il Sung to protect him (see figure 6.1). Attributed to the collective work of Chŏng Yŏng-man, Ch'oe Kye-gŭn, and Kim Tong-yong and completed in 1974, the painting is officially titled *Anti-Japanese Woman Hero Comrade Kim Jong Suk Protecting with Her Life the Great Leader*.[2] True to this description, Kim Jong Suk is at the center of the painting that lionizes her actions for guarding the leader, who is thereby rendered a passive subject behind her. Lest there be any ambiguity about their identities amid their shared martial surroundings, the two figures are visually distinguished through her skirt, which makes the image all the more striking. An authoritarian leader of mythic proportions worshipped for liberating the Korean nation is, in this case, a flaccid figure protected by a woman. Her published biographies therefore include elaborate descriptions of her martial skills, especially her accurate marksmanship that was reportedly used to guard the leader, even as she takes care of the youth and supports the partisan forces with provisions of food and clothes.[3]

FIGURE 6.1. Painting of Kim Jong Suk defending Kim Il Sung, 1974. Photo credit: Roman Harak, Flickr Creative Commons.

Despite these multiple roles ascribed to Kim Jong Suk, scholars have focused on her maternal image to criticize such representation for its preservation of gendered roles. They argue that the consolidation of power by Kim Il Sung became the impetus for his position as the patriarch of a paternalistic state to "effeminize" its people.[4] Rather than equating femininity with disempowerment (and masculinity with power), I use "masculinities" and "femininities" in this chapter as gendered expressions in the plural to denote multiple possibilities *across* genders, distinct from categories of "male" and "female" that are conventionally associated with sexualized bodies. This is not to deny that gendered expressions are also embodied, but to point out that gendered expressions need not inhere in "biological sex" the way "male" and "female" do by social convention.

By focusing on masculinities and femininities, this chapter also takes a different approach from the rest of the book. It deals with *representations of* women, in most cases created by men, rather than women's lived experiences, although the two realms are dialectically related, as women interpret and adapt their lives according to representations around them, and women's experiences inform and shape those very representations. The shift in approach also reflects the increasingly limited primary sources by the mid-1960s, when Korean publications became much less diverse and no longer covered sustained connections to the socialist bloc.[5] Publications after 1967 began to include quotes from Kim Il Sung as irrefutable policy prescriptions without dissenting views, and magazines and newspapers became uniform, with little variation. Confirming this trend, the 1965 edition of the DPRK annual yearbook, *Chosŏn chung'ang nyŏn'gam*, was the last to include detailed economic indicators.[6] Likewise, *Chosŏn Nyŏsŏng* rarely carried international news to the extent that it had in the past, and the main history journal founded in 1955, *Ryŏksa Kwahak* (History science), stopped publication altogether in 1968, not to be reinstated until 1977, by which time the state ideology of Juche had been firmly institutionalized.[7] Therefore, the chapter title takes inspiration from the circulation of "modern girls" around the world with the rise of consumer culture in the 1920s and 1930s, applied to the parallel global circulation of "communist women" as ideal archetypes in the socialist world.[8] Korean participation in these global circuits once again underscores the significance of women and multiple femininities in the formation of modern subjects.

While the biologized division of sex between male and female has been used to normalize gender inequalities as the "natural" effect of sex difference, ironically feminism itself has relied on a "particular romance with the binary and the universal category of 'woman'" to critique gender discrimination.[9] What about examples of sex difference that come from outside the West? As the historian Anna Krylova meaningfully asks, "Do all binaries have to be invariably opposition-bound in order to be socially productive and operational?"[10] Offering examples of nonoppositional gender identities, Krylova shows how Soviet women joined men in combat without being seen as compromising women's sense of themselves as women. Women could be both "womanly" and "soldierly" without contradiction. Rather than eradicating gendered differences, references that prioritized other traits such as "revolutionary youth," "new Soviet people," and "October generation" challenged the hierarchies between men and women by positioning them on par.[11] Krylova concludes, "Soviet women combatants' project of creating the identity of a woman soldier was not a degendering but a *regendering* undertaking that relied on nonoppositional conceptions of gender differences."[12] While "communist feminism" may be a debatable combination of ideas that were rarely tied together historically, I use it in this chapter to refer to the communist woman archetype that appealed to nonoppositional gendered subjects adopted in state socialist countries.[13]

Building on the Soviet experience, Korea and China developed their own versions of communist feminisms that would contribute to their global circulation. As historian Tina Mai Chen has shown, the international circulation of socialist aesthetics was a critical feature of gendered subjectivities, in which the portrayal of sexuality by Soviet women film stars informed the development of communist feminism in China.[14] The common theme in the films centered on female protagonists left alone after the death or arrest of their partners, who then take up the socialist or nationalist cause, finding fulfillment in this effort rather than romantic pursuits. This is precisely what happened in Korea too. Positioning communist women among global feminisms and femininities, I compare Korea, China, and Soviet Russia through four enduring cultural works: *Sea of Blood* (*P'ibada*) and *The Flower Girl* (*Kkotp'anŭn chŏnyŏ*) from Korea, *The White-Haired Girl* (*Baimao nü*) from China, and *Mother* (*Mat'*) from Russia.

Serving as a prototype for later works, *Mother*, by the founder of socialist realism Maxim Gorky, was published as a novel in 1906, made into a silent film by Vsevolod Pudovkin in 1926, and adapted into a play by Bertolt Brecht in 1932. *The White-Haired Girl* was first staged as an opera in the 1940s under the direction of He Jingzhi and Ding Yi during the Chinese civil war, released as a black-and-white feature film in 1950 directed by Wang Bin and Shui Hua, and later revived as one of the "revolutionary model ballets" during the Cultural Revolution (1966–1976). In Korea, *Sea of Blood*, directed by Ch'oe Ik-gyu, was released as a four-hour-long black-and-white feature film in 1969, staged as an opera in 1971, and published as an epic novel in 1973. Released as a color feature film in 1972, *The Flower Girl*, again directed by Ch'oe Ik-gyu, with Pak Hak, was concurrently produced as a stage opera and later published as a novel in 1977. Underscoring these works' significance, the Shanghai Ballet continues to regularly stage *The White-Haired Girl*, and the Sea of the Blood Opera Troupe staged a revival of *The Flower Girl* in China in 2012.[15]

In the rest of the chapter, I begin by providing the backdrop to the creation of the two Korean works and then compare *Sea of Blood* with *Mother*, before examining connections between *The Flower Girl* and *The White-Haired Girl*. Through a comparative reading of the four works, I trace communist feminisms transnationally across the state socialist world, to show alternative forms of feminisms and their limits. One of the most visible strategies developed by communist feminisms was the *desexualization* of women to combat their representation as sex objects in order to *regender* the trope of the violated girl into a revolutionary woman. I begin with the two Korean works as important examples of revolutionary melodrama before introducing all four works and their alluring connections.

Revolutionary Melodrama

Sea of Blood and *The Flower Girl* are two of the three so-called great classics of anti-Japanese revolutionary works in Korea. Along with *The Fate of One Member of a Self-Defense Unit* (*Han chawidaewŏn ŭi unmyŏng*), the three works are said to have originated as stage plays during the period of anticolonial armed struggle near the Manchurian border in the 1930s as a way to galvanize the troops and local residents against Japanese rule.¹⁶ The dramatic reversals and the excesses of emotion and pathos make them perfect examples of melodrama. While the genre is often dismissed for its caricatured protagonists and predictable plot lines, it offers an ideal framework through which to understand socialist realist aesthetics, and one that brings together the North and South in a shared affective regime.

Divergent from Hollywood adaptations of novels, Korean film adaptations discussed in this chapter came before all subsequent reproductions into other media.¹⁷ This entailed privileging the visual over textual representations, and the collective exposure to the films and performances in theaters and concert halls overruled individual reading experiences. Moreover, while Hollywood depoliticized social issues by transforming conflicts of race and class into individualized narratives, in both Koreas melodrama became "the most efficacious mode of realism" precisely because personal narratives were so intertwined with national history; there was no need to "dramatize" private life, because history itself was so dramatic.¹⁸ In that sense, Korean melodrama inadvertently enacted the feminist dictum that the personal is political, while Hollywood films used personalized stories to sublimate the political.¹⁹ Melodrama offered the possibility to construct a more militant femininity in Korean filmic culture through the relationships depicted among women and their active roles as protagonists.

As shown in the last chapter through Choe Seung-hui's oeuvre, cultural productions often centered women as women warriors. They urged viewers to take charge of their own destiny rather than resigning themselves to their situation as fate, depicting revolution as the people's struggle to take back their right to self-determination.²⁰ Reviews of the revolutionary works considered the main characters to be models for a "new type of human being" (*saeroun ingan chŏnghyŏng*) who is "autonomous" (*chajujŏk*), with the power to shape one's fate as the very embodiment of Juche ideology.²¹ This kind of ethos is, of course, not unique to Korea but can be found in much of the Third World. As Frantz Fanon notably argued, armed struggle against colonial oppression and the overthrow of the colonizers herald more than destruction, transforming the formerly colonized into makers of their own history and culture.²² However, just as Choe's folk aesthetics was displaced by an increasing focus on Kim Il Sung's anticolonial struggle, this official narrative took center stage at the expense of others.²³ The three "great classics of anti-Japanese revolutionary works" came to represent *the* authentic legacy of the first truly socialist realist works in Korea, but their origins reveal a more complicated story.

Soon after the Korean War drew to a close, between August and December 1953, historians, writers, painters, photographers, and filmmakers collected testimonies from residents near the Manchurian border about their experiences of anticolonial struggle.²⁴ Their findings were published in 1956 under the title *Paektu Mountain Can Be Seen from Anywhere* (*Paektusan ŭn ŏdisŏna poinda*), which included short descriptions about the plays and the lyrics of songs performed by the partisan units.²⁵ Based on these findings, *The General History of Korean Literature* (*Chosŏn munhak t'ongsa*), published in 1959, introduced these partisan works as collective creations, with variations according to different regions.²⁶ However, by the 1970s, the publication of *The History of Korean Literature* (*Chosŏn munhaksa*) coalesced on the official line that Kim Il Sung was the sole creator.²⁷

This shift in the 1970s was the result of the May 1967 Politburo meeting that instituted the Monolithic Ideological System.²⁸ The two Korean works *Sea of Blood* (1969 film, 1971 opera) and *The Flower Girl* (1972 film and opera) appeared soon thereafter in multiple visual forms in the lead-up to 1972, the year of Kim Il Sung's sixtieth birthday. The foundational impact of these two works cannot be overstated. The first stage performances of *Sea of Blood* resulted in the creation of a genre referred to as the "*Sea of Blood*–style revolutionary opera" (*P'ibadasik hyŏngmyŏng kagŭk*) that has become the standard for all subsequent operatic performances. *The Flower Girl* and *Sea of Blood* have been seen by millions of viewers, domestically and abroad, through the international distribution of the films as well as through live tours of performances around the world, in parts of Africa (Algeria, Angola, Somalia, Nigeria, Guinea, Madagascar, Mozambique, the People's Republic of Congo), the Americas (Panama, Colombia), Europe (Russia, Czechoslovakia, Romania, Hungary, Germany, Spain), and Asia (China, Laos, Cambodia). *The Flower Girl* has reportedly been performed fifteen hundred times over the course of forty years between 1972 and 2012, and *Sea of Blood* celebrated its fifteen hundredth performance in 2001.²⁹

Beyond entertainment, these works have become subjects of study and political education through which workers and youth have learned to devote themselves to the revolutionary cause. Sea of Blood Worker Guards (*P'ibada kŭnwidae*) were formed in factories and mines throughout the 1970s, where workers vowed to adopt the classic as their "revolutionary textbook," struggling like the protagonists of *Sea of Blood* to "express an unconditional spirit and create new miracles and innovation every day at every moment."³⁰ *The Flower Girl* was widely studied in workplaces and mass organizations as part of "the struggle for the effective implementation of *The Flower Girl*" (*Kkotp'anŭn ch'ŏnyŏ sirhyo t'ujaeng*) to enable the next generation to understand the hardships of colonial rule and the importance of maintaining autonomy as an independent nation.³¹ While the works may seem limited to the Korean context as examples of a postcolonial nationalist canon, they are part of a transnational communist archetype when compared to Chinese and Russian works.

Mothers and Maidens

The 1906 *Mother* predates socialist realism by almost thirty years, and yet it is considered the original exemplar of it.[32] Coined as a term in 1932, socialist realism became Soviet cultural policy in 1934 during the First Writers' Union Congress, although there were earlier trends, such as "proletarian realism" and "revolutionary romanticism," that would provide the components for it.[33] In her pioneering cultural history of the Soviet novel as the privileged genre in the Soviet cultural sphere, literary scholar Katerina Clark distinguishes the genre from its Western counterpart for serving a social function as a forum for intellectual and political debates, rather than solely as an artistic medium as literature.[34] I borrow her method to approach socialist realist works as a kind of cultural text that includes multiple iterations as films and stage performances resting on formulaic structural conventions. Carrying the intellectual debates of the time, *Mother* was the first among a core group of canonical novels that provided the master plot for all subsequent socialist realist works. Gorky offered a ritualized parable of a "positive hero" whose life trajectory traces the historical stages of Marxist-Leninist theory, moving from oppression to rebellion and hope of communist futures.[35] In the marriage of socialism with realism, socialist realism was supposed to combine everyday reality with the promise of socialism by portraying the main protagonists heroically in anticipation of the future, even if this meant romanticizing and at times exaggerating certain elements.[36] Before socialist realism was codified, shifting the emphasis from realism to optimism, earlier works such as *Mother* reflected the conditions under which it was written. It incorporated themes found in prerevolutionary fiction, drawing on folktales and popular stories. These elements included the family as a metaphor for a movement or a new collective; a conversion or awakening of the previously unenlightened by a mentor figure; and finally, some form of martyrdom that inspires others to continue the struggle.[37] All three of these elements are found in the four works discussed in this chapter.

However, as scholars have repeatedly pointed out, the Marxist utopian project devoted little attention to theorizing sex. The Russian revolutionary and communist feminist Alexandra Kollontai (1872–1952) was the exception when she advocated sexual equality through reproductive freedom, combining *eros* (sex) and *agape* (love) toward a "comradely solidarity."[38] The contradictory appeals to demolish the bourgeois institution of family even while elevating the proletarian family as the cornerstone of a socialist society found resolution through the "cult of maternity" that gave motherhood a social role. Rather than biological kinship, motherhood became an integral part of the "great family" of the national and international collective, in which women were caretakers as both producer-worker and reproducer-mother. Socialist realism affirmed "the new Soviet woman as worker *and* mother—a new human being in which the biological and social, creative and procreative, individual and collective are synthesized, thus signifying the full attainment of human creative potential, a realization of the ultimate dream of the revolutionary utopia."[39]

Between the 1906 novel and the 1926 film of *Mother*, the 1917 October Revolution dramatically changed the political context for the two versions. Delving more deeply into the class tensions between peasants, workers, and aristocrats in prerevolutionary Russia, Gorky's novel ends tragically, much like the 1905 Revolution itself, as the mother is convicted, exiled, and killed at the hands of the gendarmes.[40] Pudovkin's film, however, hints at a brighter future. Initially, the film similarly follows the tragic life of the working class. The father dies early in the story as a result of a factory accident, and the mother, Nilovna, as an uneducated peasant woman, caves to police pressure and reveals the weapons hidden in the house by her son Pavel, leading to his arrest for fomenting worker unrest at the factory. However, the mother awakens into revolutionary consciousness, and in the celebrated concluding montage, the mother leads the revolutionary crowd with flag in hand, freeing her son from jail. Even as the mother and her accompanying protesters are gunned down, these scenes are interspersed with ice breaking up in the river, symbolic of the coming spring and ultimate revolutionary triumph.

In Korea, readers of *Chosŏn Nyŏsŏng* were introduced to an abridged version of the story in 1948.[41] The basic plot covered the abusive father's early death, with the son Pavel seeming to follow in his father's footsteps until he sees his mother crying and changes his ways. Pavel begins to read banned books and politically awakens to the exploitation of workers. Fearful of the consequences at first, the mother slowly opens her eyes to the significance of his work. When their house is searched and Pavel is arrested, he asks his mother to go to the factory on his behalf disguised as a street vendor to distribute leaflets calling for a strike. Mother sees her son rallying the workers and is both proud and inspired to join the movement, as mother and son become comrades. As winter turns into spring, with depictions of ice breaking up in the river, they prepare for May Day protests, where the mother picks up the flag from her son after he is arrested, and she takes his place.

Like *Mother*, which centers the transformation of an ignorant peasant woman into a labor organizer and eventual leader of the revolution, *Sea of Blood* begins by depicting the conditions of Korean peasant women under Japanese colonialism.[42] The protagonist is Sunnyŏ, a young mother raising three children, sons Wŏnnam and Ŭlnam and daughter Kapsun. When the Japanese raze the family's village in an attempt to root out communists and their sympathizers, Sunnyŏ's husband, Yunsŏp, is killed. Sunnyŏ is left hopeless and destitute, taking refuge in a village near the northern border, fearful of what might happen to her children. Her children grow into young adults and join the underground anticolonial movement. Watching her children, she politically awakens as she realizes that revolution is the only way to safeguard her children in the long term. Much like Nilovna, the Korean mother Sunnyŏ emerges in the second half of the story as a calm, courageous, and resolute figure, entirely different from the anxious and fearful character at the beginning of the story. Sunnyŏ is steadfast even when the police torture her in an attempt to reveal her connections to the underground movement. She refuses to disclose the whereabouts of the partisan in hiding during the climax of the story, when the police kill her youngest son, Ŭlnam. Her sacrifice and that of countless other families are not in vain, however, as the villagers stage a successful uprising against the local colonial government, with the mother leading the way. In both *Sea of Blood* and *Mother*, the father dies early in the story, and while the son awakens the mother into political consciousness, she becomes his comrade as a revolutionary in her own right, disguising herself to accomplish a dangerous mission. Where the two works diverge is in the negative depiction in *Mother* of the abusive father who beats his wife—excised in the abridged Korean version to portray the oppressed in a "positive" light.

As a heroic epic that ultimately leads to triumph, *Sea of Blood* exemplifies the archetypal vision of class and women's liberation, reflected not only in the mother's personal transformation, but also in the central role played by the women's union (*punyŏ tongmaeng*) in the people's uprising that liberates the town. The initial portrayal of the mother as a wife dependent on her husband transforms by the middle of the story into that of an archetypal mother who requires no name. There are repeated references to the "power of a mother" (*ŏmŏni ŭi him*), a power that is able to endure and conquer all hardships, equivalent to the power of the revolution.[43] Ultimately, the revolution is compared to "a mother's affectionate embrace."[44] As the partisan Cho Tong-ch'un states in both the novel and the film, "I have gone to many places and worked with many people. But more than anyone else, elderly mothers understand our revolution the best and are awakened the quickest, surprising me on numerous occasions. Listening to you, I now realize that the communists wanting to save their nation and class brethren are best understood by mothers who live for the love of their children."[45] The mother's strength as a revolutionary is attributed to her role as a mother to secure a better future for all children. Such an enlarged sense of maternal responsibility as impetus for political action was an enduring trope in the organization and mobilization of women throughout the Cold War, as seen in previous chapters. But alongside revolutionary mothers stood militant maidens, who joined the partisan militias.

The Flower Girl, like *The White-Haired Girl*, was first produced during the anticolonial struggle against Japan. Official historiography traces the origin of both works to plays performed in the late 1930s. In both stories, the main protagonist is a peasant girl, whose family is ruined by the local landlord and the father is killed early in the plot. In *The Flower Girl*, Kkotbun (the name being a derivative of the Korean word for flower, *kkot*) ekes out a living by selling flowers to earn enough money to buy her ailing mother's medicine. Her elder brother Ch'ŏryong is imprisoned after setting fire to the landlord's house in revenge for what happened to their youngest sister, Suni. Little Suni had picked up a jujube next to a boiling pot of herbal tonic, eliciting a fitful rage from the landlord's wife, who knocked over the pot and its boiling contents onto Suni's face, blinding her. Despite Kkotbun's best efforts, her mother tragically dies, and Kkotbun is forced to leave behind her blind sister to find her brother and evade the landlord's schemes to sell her to a bar in payment for the family's debt. The search for her brother fails, and when she returns home, she finds her sister missing as well. She is discovered by the landlord and locked up in a shed, but her brother triumphantly returns with his partisan comrades to rally the villagers against the evil landlord and rescue his sisters. The final scene shows Kkotbun selling flowers, but this time as a cover to pass on messages for the underground movement. She sings the same tune, but with different lyrics; whereas in the opening scene she had soulfully appealed to passersby to purchase her flowers for her sick mother, she now sings of flowers that will ignite the flames of revolution.

The possibility of sexual exploitation in *The Flower Girl* is only intimated by the reference to the bar as a place that would likely require Kkotbun to sell her sexuality. In *The White-Haired Girl*, however, the protagonist Xi'er, in repayment of her father's debt, is forcibly sold to the landlord's household, where she is raped and impregnated by Landlord Huang.[46] When she finds that she will be sold to a slave trader to avoid embarrassment in the run-up to Huang's wedding, she escapes into the mountains and gives birth in a cave, barely surviving by relying on local temple offerings. Without adequate nutrition and sunlight, her skin and hair turn white, and glimpses of her white form in the temple by superstitious villagers cast her as the white-haired goddess. When partisans attempt to rally the villagers, the villagers are reluctant to attend the meeting for fear of the goddess. Trying to find the truth behind the story, partisans hide out in the temple and discover that the white-haired goddess is none other than Xi'er. They persuade her to come back to the village to exact vengeance upon the landlord, to ring in a new world free of oppression.

The major conflict in both stories is between landlords and peasants, with detailed depictions of the landlord family as heartless, cruel, and sadistic. Kkotbun's landlady shrieks over spilled tonic while lashing out at the crying little girl with burned eyes, and Xi'er's landlady beats her and stabs her with her opium pin. Landowners extract the fruits of peasant labor while fattening their storehouses with interest on grain loans through their cunning calculations, represented by their abacus and ledger. In both tales, they live in opulence and superstition, surrounded by shrines and temples in *The White-Haired Girl*, and Bibles and shamans in *The Flower Girl*. Their selfish character is explicitly tied to the nature of superstitious beliefs centered on individual salvation. By contrast, peasants exude compassion and communal solidarity as they share their meager possessions and humble desires for New Year dumplings and medicines. In both stories, the first rash attempt at revenge fails, as Kkotbun's older brother goes to jail for setting fire to the landlord's house, and Dachun, Xi'er's fiancé, is thwarted in his attempt to beat up Mu, the landlord's steward. The turning point is the arrival of partisans at the end of the stories, whose imminent presence is accompanied by foreboding earlier in the narrative. Dachun returns as a soldier of the Eighth Route Army and is able to rally and mobilize the villagers to bring justice, as does Kkotbun's older brother with the Korean People's Revolutionary Army.

On the surface, the mothers and maidens of all four works are thus couched in the likeness of traditional women devoted to their families, as in well-known Korean folktales such as *The Story of Simch'ŏng*.[47] In fact, there are references to Simch'ŏng in both *Sea of Blood* and *The Flower Girl* to describe the characters' filial nature.[48] But in the journey of self-discovery in all four works, from a narrow concern for one's family to sacrificing oneself for the revolution, the maidens portend a radical awakening through their solitary escape.[49] Kkotbun leaves her blind younger sister, and Xi'er takes refuge in the caves. The overt reason is to flee, but the lone journey offers subversive possibilities, as that of an escape not only from the landlord's plans to sell her off but also from her domestic duties. Moreover, Kkotbun's journey takes her to specific sites of class and colonial exploitation—to the mining fields and the prison—that open her eyes to the connections between her own individual suffering and the systemic structures of oppression. Her individual rage upon her return to her village is insufficient to bring about justice, as the moral of the story underscores the necessity of collective struggle by the villagers and the partisans against the landlord. It is precisely through the maidens that the stories are able to depict the connection between the individual and the collective. Individual suffering that leads to awakening undergirds the collective struggle.

These stories of mothers and maidens as ideal communist archetypes circulated to the most remote regions through the medium of roving film cars (*idong yŏnghwach'a*). As shown in figure 6.2, one such film car traveled to Chagang Province in 1954, bordering the Chinese provinces of Jilin and Liaoning to the north. While most of the villagers are peering curiously at the inner workings of the

FIGURE 6.2. Roving film car in Chagang Province, June 8, 1954. Courtesy of the Harvard-Yenching Library.

film projector, on the painted poster hung on the side of the film car in the background is the unexpected image of Xi'er from *The White-Haired Girl*. With the young Xi'er in black braided hair on the bottom, juxtaposed against the ghostly white-haired girl on the top, the Korean vernacular script *Paekmonyŏ* runs in large block letters from top to bottom, unmistakably advertising the screening of the 1950 film.[50] The January 1954 issue of *Chosŏn Nyŏsŏng* included an evocative description of such a film car and its role in the circulation of films, in this instance a Soviet film:[51]

> A truck appeared on the pass to enter Pobu Village in Kaech'ŏn County. But it was different from the usual one, with a roof and walls made of planks over the loading bed, including windows that made it look like it was carrying a small house.... "Today I brought the Soviet film 'Faraway Lover,'" said the young commentator, now familiar after several visits, as he got out of the car, putting the movie poster on the Publicity Hall. The poster depicts a young woman singing in peasant clothes embroidered in five colors, with a dignified young man on horseback behind her.... Finishing dinner early, villagers gathered at the Hall even before dark. The projector was already set up in the room, and the technician loaded the film. Next to the white screen, the commentator was

seated at the desk ready to explain the movie.... As the film progressed, the excited girls hummed to the beautiful song of the female protagonist, while admiring the splendid Moscow streets on screen. Their gaze never left the screen.

The Soviet feature film was followed by a Korean documentary *Masters of the Land* (*Ttang ŭi chuindŭl*), featuring labor heroes and model workers from across the country. As they watched the documentary, villagers spotted their very own farmer Chŏn Ch'ang-ok featured in the film as a model plower from Kaech'ŏn. Even as Chŏn blushed at the sight of herself on screen, it was a proud moment of recognition and giddy excitement for the villagers at the sight of their own village in the film.

Feminist Erasures

In discussions of Maoist feminism, perhaps no cultural work has been the source of as much contention, productive for feminist debate, as *The White-Haired Girl*.[52] Scholars have argued that the "androgynous" female character in works such as *The White-Haired Girl* symbolizes the "suppression of sex difference," whereby issues of sexuality and gendered exploitation were overshadowed and outright replaced by class struggle. *The White-Haired Girl* offers the perfect example: the early opera performances hinged on Xi'er's rape and pregnancy, which ultimately turn her hair and skin white when she is forced to flee and give birth in the caves. But the 1950 film keeps the rape, pregnancy, and childbirth outside the frame of the camera, and the later revolutionary ballet "accelerated the process of disembodiment," as rape, pregnancy, and childbirth were no longer part of the story at all.[53] Xi'er is thus rendered a "nonwoman" and turned into an allegory of class oppression. Such a reading of *The White-Haired Girl* exemplifies the dilemma within feminist theories about what to do with sex difference. While some have celebrated women's so-called difference as a form of progressive political praxis, others have challenged the reification of such gendered differences that reproduce and naturalize gender inequality. Communist and leftist women struggled with this question too, as shown in debates within the WIDF. Rather than differentiating gender as the social construction of sex difference subject to "suppression," however, communist feminism understood gender *as* sex difference to be performative and thus subject to manipulation and change. In short, gender and sex were not separate categories. The proliferation of "sexless" women heralded the emergence of a new feminine ideal that was not tied to sexuality.

This is not to deny the propagandistic role of cultural productions that states have used to claim themselves "true liberators" of women and peasants, or that their goal of women's liberation was always incomplete. Fundamentally at issue is how communist feminisms regendered the category of woman. Regardless of whether state socialism genuinely championed women's liberation or merely used it as a convenient slogan to defeat local patriarchal authority and to mobilize women's labor power, strategies of representation are often unpredictable, opening up alternative configurations of gendered identities, unintended perhaps but no less real for the women and men expected to adopt them as role models. While communist discourse never denied sex difference, ascribing women to be "natural" reproducers even as such roles were elevated to the status of "heroes," the female subject was defined *historically*. This is evident in how China and Korea transformed the trope of violated girls into revolutionary women.

Too often, scholars have read Xi'er's sexual violation allegorically as a symbol of class exploitation and imperialist aggression by which women's bodies become "battlegrounds" rather than issues in their own right.[54] There are several key changes between the original opera performed in Yan'an and the subsequent revisions that have prompted such conclusions. The first is the moment when Xi'er fools herself into believing that the landlord's wedding preparations are for her and resigns herself to marrying him because of her pregnancy, while the landlord secretly plans to sell her to a brothel. The film adapters may have been disturbed by this extreme resignation, when Xi'er is willing to marry the very person who raped her rather than seek retribution. As a result, the film "purifies" the opera and has Xi'er flee from the landlord to give birth to a child that dies immediately thereafter. Pointing to sexual violence as "an extreme form of gender oppression," critics have also indicted the camera, which "shies away from the sexual attack and only suggests the rape through three montage cuts," rendering the act "no longer a violent gender/sexual conflict between victim and attacker but a class confrontation between owner and servant."[55] Moreover, the sequence of shots in the cave of Xi'er struggling in childbirth, followed by a baby's cries off-screen, ending in the burial of the dead infant, comes under critique for getting rid of the baby as the "landlord's seed" in order to maintain Xi'er's "pure class status as an oppressed peasant woman."[56]

But such readings miss the point entirely. The landlord is able to sexually violate Xi'er by virtue of his ownership over her. The point of the story is precisely that class exploitation is part and parcel of sexual exploitation by creating the conditions for it. Rather than a conflation, the cause of sexual violence is traced to class exploitation, as women's bodies become commodified sex objects. The camera is not all that "shies" away from the scenes of rape and childbirth. The original opera concluded the scene of Landlord Huang's attack by moving it off stage as he chased after Xi'er, and the scene of childbirth is altogether left out, as different versions of the opera either jumped three months or three years between Xi'er's escape from the Huang household to the next scene, after her having already given birth. In fact, the film is explicit about the possible horrors of childbirth. Not only do we see her clutching her pregnant belly as she makes her way through the mountains to the cave, but we also see her on her back, struggling in labor. Although the sound of the baby's cries is heard off-screen, the next scene, in which Xi'er walks through the rain to bury her dead child, suggests multiple ways to interpret the baby's death. Rather than a restoration of Xi'er's class purity, the scene leaves open the most gruesome possibilities, from complications at childbirth to infanticide, furthering the dramatic tragedy of Xi'er's circumstances.

But alterations did not stop there. The "revolutionary model theater" (*geming yangbanxi*) during the Cultural Revolution revised five Peking operas, two ballets, and a symphony that included a balletic adaptation of *The White-Haired Girl*. The ballet further transformed Xi'er with an added epilogue in which she joins the partisan forces as a militant woman warrior. Moreover, her father no longer commits suicide, as in earlier productions, but is beaten to death by the landlord's bodyguard to avoid showing any "negative" actions of the characters.[57] While the original opera made no direct mention of Mao Zedong, despite the reference to his Eighth Route Army, the ballet included slogans with references to Mao as the "sun that shines far and wide," a common practice throughout the Cultural Revolution. Most importantly, Xi'er's rape and pregnancy were entirely eliminated from the story, in which the landlord only attempts to rape her, without success.[58] For later critics, the result was the complete subordination of gender and sexuality to class politics, as they interpreted the revisions as a move to "erase" gender by the "gender free ideas of social revolution."[59] But the hypervisibility of women in these works only begs the question as to why *women* took center stage as revolutionaries if the revolution was meant to be "gender free."

While mothers and maidens may take primary place in the four works, the secondary role of male characters is worth noting. In *Mother*, the abusive husband dies early in the plot, as does the father in *The White-Haired Girl*; and in the various renditions of *Sea of Blood*, Sunnyŏ's husband either leaves home years before the plot begins, to participate in the armed struggle, or the Japanese burn him alive at the beginning of the story. Not only is the father figure eliminated early, as in *Sea of Blood*, *Mother*, and *The White-Haired Girl*, or left out from the beginning as in *The Flower Girl*, but the elder brothers in both Korean works, as well as the fiancé in *The White-Haired Girl* and the son in *Mother*, also leave the main plot line to join partisans, only to return at the end of the story. As works that were created to foment revolution, it is remarkable that the main characters are all women, while men are often impotent figures, in various states of servitude or absence, jailed, imprisoned, or killed.

To be sure, Korean publications emphasize the importance of partisan leadership by pointing to, for example, the first uprising waged by Sunnyŏ's husband at the beginning of *Sea of Blood*, which "failed miserably because there was no correct leadership and they did not know the correct method of [armed] struggle. Fighting against the enemy with bare hands only produced many victims due to the barbaric killings committed by the Japanese."[60] Undoubtedly, the role of partisans is evident in all stories, whether as individual agitators such as Cho Tongch'un in *Sea of Blood* and Pavel in *Mother*, or members of partisan forces, such as Ch'ŏryong in *The Flower Girl* and Dachun in *The White-Haired Girl*. However, the main female characters are central to all works, and it is their revolutionary transformation that inspires other villagers to follow the female lead.

Xi'er's transformation from a violated girl to a "disembodied" revolutionary can be fruitfully compared to the protagonist of *The Flower Girl*, Kkotbun. While Xi'er's sexuality is apparent from the beginning, depicted through the attraction between Xi'er and Dachun, Kkotbun has no comparable love interest, and her elder brother takes the place of the male hero in *The Flower Girl*. While Kkotbun and her female companions endure many forms of abuse, none of these are specifically sexual in nature: her mother toils in hard physical labor until her death, her sister is blinded by accident, and Kkotbun is almost sold to a bar but ultimately escapes that fate. By contrast, Xi'er is raped and impregnated by the landlord, who then plots to kill her so that he may marry another without consequence. These heroines are meant to be representations of downtrodden women oppressed under feudalism; but if their stories are viewed together, what are the implications of Xi'er's experience of sexual violence and unwanted pregnancy in relation to the experiences of Kkotbun, who remains from beginning to end within familial relations as a daughter and sister? Undoubtedly, Xi'er's transformation from violated girl to revolutionary woman warrior is closely aligned with the Cultural Revolution's desexualized aesthetics in the case of China, but how do we locate this new aesthetic within the historical trajectory of communist feminism and feminisms more broadly?

Transnational Recuperations

As historian Tani Barlow demonstrates through her close reading of Maoist feminism, Chinese feminists critical of the romantic literary representations of women in the 1920s fashioned an alternative female subjectivity defined in terms of women's work and praxis. Rejecting the sexualized and eroticized *nüxing*

(女性) identity for women, Chinese feminist Ding Ling advocated the use of *funü* (婦女) as the more "economic, historical, theoretical, and overtly political" term.[61] In place of the neologism that combined the two characters for *female* (女) and *nature* (性) to refer to women as naturalized sexual subjects, communist women appropriated and combined the characters for married female or *wife* (婦) and (unmarried) *female* (女), traditionally used to refer to women as social subjects positioned within the family, to historicize and politicize women's subjectivity. Women's oppression was not attributed to sex difference, but to their nationality and class, since sexual liberation during the height of the 1920s New Woman movement failed to address issues of imperialism and poverty that affected the conditions of subaltern women.

Aware of such limitations, colonial-era socialist women writers in 1930s Korea wrote about "failed proletarian motherhood" that exposed the inability of working-class women to become sacrificial mothers as advocated by both nationalist and imperialist programs.[62] What changed in the representations of colonized Korean mothers between the 1930s and the 1970s was of course the different political conditions. The "failed proletarian mothers" preoccupied with their children, with little individual autonomy, became militant revolutionaries in charge of the collective. Rather than a wholesale rejection of domesticity, a different kind of home and women's labor became the cornerstones of building socialism, as shown in chapter 4. As female sexuality was cast aside as a bourgeois construct, in its place stood a different kind of woman, no longer beholden to romantic love or sexual attraction governed by relationships to men, whether in the form of patriarchal tyranny or physical violence.

If Xi'er's transformation was symptomatic of these lessons in China, then the changes in *The White-Haired Girl* presaged the outcome in *The Flower Girl*, in which sexuality hardly plays any part at all, and all the female characters are cast in familial relations as mothers, daughters, and sisters. The year of the cinematic release of *The Flower Girl* in 1972, timed for Kim Il Sung's sixtieth birthday celebrations, coincided with the Shanghai Dance Troupe performing *The White-Haired Girl* in Korea. The troupe toured the country to celebrate Kim's sixtieth birthday and the fortieth anniversary of his founding of the Korean People's Revolutionary Army, as well as the thirtieth anniversary of Mao's Yan'an lecture on the arts. Arriving in Pyongyang on May 7 for a monthlong tour until their departure on June 11, 1972, the troupe held their first performance on May 10 at the Pyongyang Grand Theater.[63] They went on to tour outside the capital in the cities of Hamhŭng and Wŏnsan, visiting various sites on the way, from the birthplace of the leader at Man'gyŏngdae to textile factories, cooperative farms, the children's palace, and film studios.[64] *The White-Haired Girl* was staged on fourteen occasions, with large, colorful posters advertising the upcoming performances throughout the country. National and local broadcast stations covered the tour in great detail, as did the print media. Predictably, the plot did not include the rape or pregnancy, as the ballet had already revised the original opera. Instead, the performances ended with a display of the portraits of Kim Il Sung and Mao Zedong on the backdrop of the red curtain, with the slogan "Long live the great friendship between the peoples of China and Korea!" The show concluded with the audience and performers singing in unison "The Song of General Kim Il Sung," "East Is Red," and "The People of the World Will Be Victorious."

Reviewers lauded *The White-Haired Girl* for proving that "where there is oppression, there is rebellion, and the oppressed and the exploited masses of people can find true liberation and happiness only by rising up in revolutionary struggle with weapons in hand."[65] Such reactions were strikingly similar to reviews of *The Flower Girl*, which the Chinese performers had a chance to view during their visit.[66] The parallels between the two works surely guaranteed the success and popularity of both works beyond their respective domestic audiences.[67] With the two countries' shared experiences of Japanese imperialism, the Korean War, and postwar socialist development through corresponding movements in China (the Great Leap Forward) and Korea (Chollima), Korean films proved to be a hit in China. People lined up to see *The Flower Girl*, shown 5,847 times to over six million people in Beijing alone in 1973, breaking all previous records for foreign films shown in China.[68] In fact, as the Korean film industry reached its pinnacle in the 1970s, Korean films overtook Soviet ones as the most frequently screened foreign films in China, especially after the Sino-Soviet split and Chinese withdrawal from the socialist bloc.[69] While Soviet films had made up some 90 percent of the Chinese market between 1949 and 1952, as had been the case for Korea in its early years, there was a steady decline in Soviet market share, to 30.77 percent by 1954, the year that Tina Mai Chen regards as a turning point in the geopolitical nexus of exchange, when China began to assert itself as the central hub of socialist film.[70]

Meanwhile in Korea, newspapers published workers' impressions of the Chinese performances alongside the coverage of the tour, in which they compared the story of Xi'er with their own personal experiences of exploitation and oppression during the colonial period under landlords and factory owners "without an iota of humanity." One rubber-factory worker commented that "the cruel abuse and contempt experienced by Korean workers and peasants in the past, as well as by Xi'er's family and Chinese peasants, teach the truth that the vampire nature [*hŭp'yŏlgwijŏk in ponsŏng*] of the exploitative classes can never change and the oppressed working people cannot live under the same sky as the class enemies of evil landlords and comprador capitalists who must be destroyed."[71] Another worker, from a local branch of the women's union in Pyongyang, remembered how her older sister had been dragged off at the age of sixteen by a landlord when her family could not pay its debt, after which she did not survive to see her twentieth birthday. She praised the Chinese performance for showing the "revolutionary path that must be taken by all oppressed women."[72] Despite the novelty of the ballet performance, the story of Xi'er was already well known in Korea through the script of the opera and the 1950 film. The new ballet, however, received critical acclaim because it was not "constrained" by the original opera, and Xi'er emerges with a strong will from the beginning as the "true daughter of China, actively resisting the evil landlord's beastly acts [*yasujŏk haengwi*]," as she repels and knocks down Huang upon his sexual advances (*yayok*).[73] Furthermore, the Korean critic pointed to the leading role of the Chinese Communist Party (CCP) in recruiting Dachun and other village youth into the Eighth Route Army, for whom Xi'er longingly waits.

In these readings, her white hair is no longer associated with destitution and isolation, deprivation of nutrition and human contact, but instead is the result of her strengthened resolve for justice as she endures cold and hunger, triumphantly battling beasts in the wild. In the 1950 film, it is Xi'er's exile in the cave that transforms her from a crying plaintive girl into the white-haired goddess. No longer afraid, she nimbly climbs up steep mountain cliffs, grabs a bird right out of its nest, and hunts squirrels with the precise throw of a makeshift spear. The ballet starts with this militant image from the very beginning, so that Xi'er becomes a defiant character from the outset. Korean reviewers deemed the ballet an exemplary form of revolutionary modern dance that combined Marxist-Leninist proletarian internationalism with Chinese nationalist elements in the overall aesthetics of music, costume, and stage design.[74] Despite the relatively detailed comparisons to the original opera, no direct references to rape or unwanted pregnancy were ever made in the reviews at the time. However, a 2003 issue of the literary journal *Chosŏn Munhak* carried a short introduction to *The White-Haired Girl* that provided the original plot of the opera, describing the father's suicide and Xi'er's rape (*rŭngyok*).[75]

Read linearly as a replacement of the original Xi'er by each subsequent revision, *The White-Haired Girl* appears to outline a trajectory of female disembodiment. Xi'er begins as a victim of indentured servitude, rape, and unwanted pregnancy and motherhood in the original opera, after which maternity is cut from the film, for her to finally emerge as a pure emblem of class without becoming victim to rape, pregnancy, or childbirth in the ballet. Read comparatively, however, the revisions and the conversations over the different versions of *The White-Haired Girl* across China and Korea demonstrate varied attempts to deal with the question of sex difference *historically* rather than simply "erasing" women's sexuality. Xi'er's transformation spans a period of over three decades from the 1940s to the 1970s, during which time China and Korea underwent dramatic changes in institutions of political power, economic system, and gender relations. Xi'er's sense of shame at her loss of chastity that figured so prominently in the original opera of the 1940s was one way to represent feudal patriarchy, which induces her not only to imagine wedding her rapist but also strangling her baby. The 1950 film retained this sense of shame when Xi'er attempts to hang herself after her rape, but her reincarnation as the white-haired goddess signaled a different form of embodiment, moving beyond mere victimization under feudalism. Oppressed peasant women had the power to become godlike and change the status quo. In place of the ghostly Xi'er who resonated with the social conditions of the 1940s, the 1950 film offered a new possibility for Xi'er as goddess in the immediate aftermath of the 1949 CCP victory. Xi'er's resurrection during the Cultural Revolution marked another stage in her transformation as historical subject, now able to repel her sexual attacker and forgo unwanted pregnancy altogether. At a time when young female students were some of the most militant members of the Red Guard movement and the "sent-down" youth took pride as Iron Girls, Xi'er was brought up-to-date to join the ranks of revolutionary women throughout China. Indeed, when the Shanghai Dance School first premiered an early version of the ballet in 1964, the workers themselves rejected having Xi'er's father Yang Bailao commit suicide, stating emphatically, "When I was insulted and abused by a landlord, I rebelled and killed two of those bad eggs. That was why I escaped from the countryside to Shanghai before liberation. Yang Bailao should fight back."[76]

Paradoxically, feminist theory that first gave rise to gender as a category of analysis to be distinguished from sex has led back to reifications pitting gender and sex against class and nation. Even with the acknowledgment that all categories of difference, including gender, are socially constructed, sex and sexuality continue to be naturalized as that which can be effaced. What is thereby erased are the communist women themselves in their own attempts to tackle the woman question. In China, Jiang Qing, as Mao's wife and one of the leading cultural policy makers during the Cultural Revolution, merely uses the "revolutionary model works" such as *The White-Haired Girl* to fulfill her own personal ambitions, while in Korea, works such as *The Flower Girl* and *Sea of Blood* simply serve as propaganda. Ironically, in decoding the actions of historical figures like Jiang, or the significance of novel representations of communist women, it appears that women are mere pawns.

While state socialism is thought to be too monolithic, authoritarian, and patriarchal to allow any room for a women's movement, historian Wang Zheng has illustrated the gendered process of socialist state building, applying state feminism usually associated with Scandinavian countries to state socialist countries.[77] Women challenged traditional class and gender status by actively participating in national campaigns to "increase production and defend the homeland," as the common slogan urged the Chinese people during the Korean War. They also steered and took charge of "neighborhood work," managing street sanitation, public hygiene, immunization, literacy classes, vocational training, relief for military families, child care, tax collection, recycling of resources, sale of insurance and government bonds, and repair of public utilities, among the numerous other tasks necessary to maintain civil administration and public security.[78] Responding to top-down mobilization with bottom-up initiatives, Korean women likewise addressed local women's demands, including their own need for child care, mediation in domestic disputes, and the protection of women's and children's rights, as shown throughout this book.

Attempts to eradicate gender inequalities, however, privileged social unity through familial relations. State socialism from the Soviet Union to China and Korea tried to solve the dilemma of sex difference by putting forward nonoppositional revolutionary identities such as worker, peasant, and youth. And yet, the category of woman—as sacrificing mothers, wives, daughters, and sisters—persisted. Even as women continued to be discriminated against, doubly burdened with productive and reproductive labor, and subjected to sexual harassment and violence, state socialist rhetoric proclaimed the woman question solved and women's equality achieved through state policy. Ultimately, the limits to state socialism demonstrate that the dilemma of difference cannot be overcome by appealing to unity, but rather by embracing difference. The displacement of sex with gender in feminist theorizing has muddied the target of critique by relegating the woman question to the legal realm of inadequate rights and protections rather than the political question of how women have been defined as different from men. Rather than ask whether women were allowed to be "woman," the question is what models of personhood and communality can embrace differences, to lay to rest homogeneous and essentialized categories.

At the intersection of class, gender, and nation, uneducated peasant women in colonial Korea represented the most downtrodden and oppressed subjects, and the mother and maiden best depicted the revolution as one waged not by extraordinary men but by ordinary people. Moreover, repressive colonial conditions enabled women to stand in for men, who were either imprisoned or co-opted by colonial rule. Without strong male figures, peasants initially rely on superstition and faith, searching for a goddess in *The White-Haired Girl*, an immortal (*sinsŏn*) in *Sea of Blood*, or noble (*kwiin*) in *The Flower Girl*, who might rescue them from their tragic circumstances. But they realize the futility of waiting for a savior and take charge of their own destinies, in this shift becoming revolutionaries themselves. One notable result was the reconfiguration of motherhood and mothering as identities and practices that were not limited to women but encompassed anyone working selflessly for the collective. Mothers, as transnational activists and symbols of peace, were an integral part of the international women's movement, as well as the Korean women's movement, as seen throughout this book. Cultural productions, from Gorky's 1906 *Mother* to Korean works in the 1970s, further lionized the mother as the pure embodiment of selflessness, to the point where male leaders were likened to mothers—one of the distinctive features of Korean communism.

Indeed, "mother" in Korea had in the 1950s become more than a noun, attached to other words to denote originality and authenticity, as in "mother factory" (*ŏmŏni kongjang*), and by the early 1960s, the Korean Workers Party came to be known as the "mother party" (*ŏmŏnidang*).[79] Perhaps it is no coincidence that this trend emerged shortly after the Korean War. Philosopher Jean Bethke Elshtain observes how mothering and soldiering converge on shared expectations: "The soldier is expected to sacrifice for his country as mothers are expected to sacrifice for their children."[80] With the rising tide of militant anticolonial movements in the 1960s, *Chosŏn Nyŏsŏng* noticeably shifted its rhetoric, too. Beginning with the January 1967 issue, women were called on to "revolutionize" their families by "arming every member with communist ideology to faithfully serve the revolution," militantly rejecting revisionism, sectarianism, and flunkyism. Women were to fortify the country by upholding party directives to carry "a gun in one hand, a sickle and hammer in the other," to take up combat training and "crush any enemy maneuvers," rather than taking comfort and becoming complacent in the atmosphere of peace.[81]

> All women must be prepared to support the party policy to arm the whole people and garrison the whole country.... To this end, women must acquire military knowledge and skill by actively participating in combat training of the Worker Peasant Red Guard, and acquire the necessary knowledge including medical assistance, so that they are ready to cope with emergency situations. At the same time, all women everywhere, from the front line to the rear, from cities to the countryside, from factories to offices and neighborhood units [*inminban*], must not be caught in a peaceful mood, always raising the level of alertness in preparation for enemy invasion and possible war provocation, so that not a single spy or destructive provocateur can lay their feet [on our land].

Such calls were accompanied by international coverage of women militias engaged in anticolonial struggles across Africa, Asia, and Latin America.

With the institution of the 1967 Monolithic Ideological System, the women's magazine began to devote more space to Kim Il Sung's anticolonial exploits, with

FIGURE 6.3. Women being organized into militias. *Chosŏn Nyŏsŏng*, February 1967.

hagiography that extended to his family and a new focus on his mother, Kang Pan Sok. Starting with the April 1967 issue, *Chosŏn Nyŏsŏng* devoted half or more of its pages to a recurring section "For the Party and Leader" (*Tang kwa suryŏng ŭl wihayŏ*), and the July 1967 issue officially launched the campaign to "Learn from Madame Kang Pan Sok" (*Kang Pansŏk nyŏsa ttara paeugi*), featuring her biography as the Mother of Korea (*Chosŏn ŭi ŏmŏni*). It was about this time that Kim Jong Suk was also featured in the magazine, with reminiscences by her partisan comrades, such as the scene that was to become the famous painting with which this chapter began.[82]

According to this retelling, upon joining the partisans in 1935, Kim Jong Suk received orders in early 1937 from Kim Il Sung to conduct underground political work among women in the Changbai region along the Sino-Korean border. Despite being captured and severely tortured, she refused to divulge any information and was ultimately rescued by her comrades. During the hundred-day Arduous March in the winter of 1938, she made sure her comrades were fed and properly clothed. The battle the following year would become the subject of the famed painting, as her comrade recalled:

> In the fall of 1939, Marshal Kim Il Sung led a company directly under the command of the Second Boundary Forces to the vicinity of Hanyang in Ando Province and was on the way back. At that time, Comrade Jong Suk went with him as a member of the company. When the group reached the vicinity of Taesaha, a mountain not too large stood behind them while in front across their path was the Taesaha River. After a short rest there, the crew was just about to cross the river. With a loud gunfire, bullets fell like hail on the riverbed.... When the battle was in full swing, he climbed a boulder on the hillside to command the battle. Comrade Jong Suk was guarding him by his side. Worried about his safety, Comrade Kim Jong Suk vigilantly surveyed the surroundings and found five or six enemies lined up crawling toward them with guns aimed through the reed field. It was truly a moment of grave danger. At that moment, she swiftly pushed the commander away, blocking his body, and shot the first one, who had his gun pointed at them from the ground.

This mythology of Kim Jong Suk thereby replaced living women like Pak Chŏng-ae. Nonetheless, communist women in their lived experiences and their iconic representations across Soviet Russia, China, and Korea drew on nonoppositional gendered identities in which women could be both "womanly" and "soldierly" without contradiction. Representations of Kim Jong Suk certainly fit this mold, but the more startling outcome is the dislocation of conventional masculinities and femininities, as represented in the 1974 painting.[83] The state-commissioned painters could have depicted the story in a number of ways, but they centered Kim Jong Suk as the protector and savior of Kim Il Sung, without this being seen as "emasculating" or "effeminizing" him. This is not to deny the evidence of sexism, sexual discrimination, and sexual violence against women in Korea, but to show how communist representations of women differed from the commercialized and sexualized "pin-up girls" in the West. As Wang Zheng demonstrates in her comparison of Chinese women's magazine covers from the Mao era with those after 1978, peasants and factory workers featured on the covers of *Women of China* disappeared entirely after 1998, replaced with sexualized images of entrepreneurs and celebrities.[84] Rather than the "erasure" of gendered difference as previously charged by critics of Maoist feminism, class disappeared when "market feminism" promoted the "individualistic, privatized, and sexualized bourgeois consumer" as the new pioneering women.[85]

Conclusion
TRANSNATIONAL SOLIDARITIES

The year 1967 turned out to be a pivotal one not just for the women of Korea. As the first generation of leaders like Pak Chŏng-ae faded from the scene after the institution of the Monolithic Ideology System, the WIDF also mourned the passing of its founding president Eugénie Cotton in June 1967.[1] Meanwhile, thirteen years after the WIDF was stripped of its consultative status with the UN Economic and Social Council in 1954 for its campaigns against the Korean War, it was readmitted in 1967, in large measure aided by the new member states from the Third World, comprising two-thirds of the 122 UN member states.[2] Also in 1967, the UN General Assembly adopted the Declaration on the Elimination of Discrimination against Women, which would lead to the 1979 Convention on the Elimination of All Forms of Discrimination against Women (CEDAW), largely thanks to WIDF efforts.[3] Despite the fractures that emerged at the 1963 WIDF Congress, after which Chinese women officially withdrew their membership, the prestige of the Federation grew with the restoration of its UN status and its work in the UN Commission on the Status of Women (CSW).[4]

This concluding chapter illustrates the significant contributions of communist and leftist women not only to UN efforts on behalf of women, but also to persistent calls raising sexual violence as an international issue. Here we examine a different set of conflicts from the 1963 congress that arose at the next World Congress of Women in 1969, even as the Three Worlds came together in unprecedented ways to push the UN to designate 1975 the International Year of Women. Despite the clash, with accusations that communist women were uninterested in issues of racism and sexism—"erasing" femininity and ignoring "differences"—colonial and sexual violence were central concerns to leftist women, from the 1951 fact-finding commission during the Korean War to the "comfort women" issue that would shake the world in the 1990s.

In fact, the Federation took full advantage of its restored status, organizing several gatherings the year after its UN status was restored. A WIDF delegation visited refugee camps in the United Arab Republic, Syria, and Jordan in February 1968 after the 1967 Israeli invasion, issuing a detailed report of conditions in the Middle East.[5] Another delegation from the WIDF Secretariat toured India, Nepal, Ceylon (Sri Lanka), Pakistan, and Afghanistan in April and May 1968, and WIDF representatives attended the national congresses of member organizations in Sudan, Finland, Japan, and Bulgaria.[6] Seminars on the problems of education and living conditions of women and children in Latin America were organized in Chile and Mexico in July 1968.[7] These activities were not new, as we have seen throughout the previous chapters, but the Federation was buoyed by the rise in prestige with its restored UN standing, and its activities proved particularly pressing at this time, with the US escalation of the war in Vietnam. The WIDF had set up an International Vietnam Solidarity Committee in 1964, sending a fact-finding delegation in 1966 as it had in 1951 to Korea.[8]

Consequently, member organizations throughout the world used the 1968 International Women's Day to express solidarity with Vietnamese women against the war.[9] A delegation from the Vietnam Women's Union was invited for a press conference in Algeria; public meetings were organized by the Argentine Women's Union, the Bulgarian Women's Committee, the Chilean Women's Union, and the Federation of Cuban Women; and messages of support came from the women of Czechoslovakia, Romania, Syria, the Soviet Union, and Uruguay. Women dressed in white mourning clothes demonstrated in Ceylon against the bombing of North Vietnam; the Union of French Women organized an exhibition of 736 drawings by French children for Vietnamese children; women in France, Japan, and Spain demonstrated in front of US embassies and sent petitions to President Lyndon Johnson; women in France, East and West Germany, and Israel fund-raised for the Vietnam solidarity fund; and the National Union of Mexican Women staged a play dedicated to the "heroic women of Vietnam."

From the 1969 World Congress of Women to the 1975 International Year of Women

Because of the urgency of such activities, the Federation's sixth congress, originally scheduled for November 1968, had to be postponed until the following year at requests from member organizations.[10] The schedule was difficult to accommodate, given their own national congresses and regional activities, in addition to the special activities planned in solidarity with Vietnam. Moreover, teachers and women with children could not take time away during the school year, and two-thirds of the Federation's membership resided in warm regions with no resources for travel in the colder climate. With the exception of the first two congresses, in Paris (1945) and Budapest (1948), all subsequent congresses had taken place in June, every five years.[11] As a result, the WIDF Bureau decided to reschedule the congress for June 1969, with bulletins, brochures, postcards, special stamps, and pamphlets, alongside the *Women of the Whole World*, used to publicize the upcoming assembly in Helsinki.[12] Worried that finances would impact participation, the WIDF Council in October 1967 decided to create a solidarity fund to help delegates who would otherwise be unable to attend; as of March 1969, fifteen national organizations had made donations totaling US$36,000, and twenty-eight organizations had committed financially to send delegations.[13] Others pitched in too; seven socialist countries made available 105 tickets for delegates from fifty-seven countries in Africa, Asia, and Latin America, while the East German women's group assumed the costs of the secretariat and technical staff, and the Finnish women shouldered the logistics of holding the congress in Helsinki.[14] In asking for nominations for the secretariat and the next presidency left vacant after Cotton's death in 1967, the WIDF Bureau placed primary importance on knowledge of and experience in the women's movement, striving for a balanced representation of continents and social systems in the composition of the bureau.[15]

Predating by almost three decades the maxim that "human rights are women's rights and women's rights are human rights" declared at the 1995 UN Fourth World Conference on Women in Beijing, the WIDF argued that the role of women in society is not just a "women's matter" but the responsibility of all of society, and "All of society is responsible for the future of children, the happiness and well-being of families."[16] The 1969 World Congress of Women in Helsinki, from June 14 to 17, brought 482 delegates, guests, and observers from a total of ninety-three countries, including twenty-eight from Africa, twenty from Asia, fifteen from Latin America, and twenty-six from Europe, as well as participants from Canada, the United States, Australia, and New Zealand.[17] Although in absolute numbers this was only a third of the more than fifteen hundred participants in the previous 1963 congress in Moscow, more organizations were present, with 190 groups, including sixty-seven unaffiliated women's organizations and twenty-eight international bodies. While there had been seventy member organizations in 1963, up from forty-five in 1945, there were now ninety-five organizations in the Federation, and its UN consultative status had just been elevated to status A, with even greater latitude for UN participation after restoration to B status in 1967.[18]

In the appeal for joint action for women's rights, the Helsinki Congress noted that "the conditions of women are particularly bad in those parts of the world where the peoples are still subjected to the colonial yoke or its after-effects, where they are the victims of neo-colonialism, racism, apartheid, or imperialist aggression, and where democratic liberties are violated."[19] Especially indicting the US war in Indochina and US military bases in Okinawa and South Korea as an "illegal occupation ... a constant potential for the extension of the war to this region," the Federation called for joint action "directed against US imperialism, for it is the motivating force behind all the aggressive military blocs."[20] In view of the escalation, the Federation, beginning in 1965, had begun publishing a special Vietnam Bulletin on the Vietnamese people's struggles and solidarity actions, with a detailed report on the situation for the 1969 congress, which adopted a resolution in support of the Vietnamese struggle.[21]

Among the reports was also one on the "solidarity with the Korean women," which raised concerns over the situation in Korea, as it "grows daily more tense and dangerous."[22] Describing the South as dominated by the US "in league with the reactionary forces at present in power, who themselves placed the population under complete oppression," the report warned that "their acts of provocation against the People's Democratic Republic of Korea [sic] are being intensified and constitute a grave threat to peace in South-East Asia and in the whole world."[23] Based on the affiliation of North Korean women, with no connection to women in the South, a WIDF delegation had visited the North in 1967 and again in 1968 on the twentieth anniversary of the founding of the DPRK.[24] The WIDF secretary-general Cecile Hugel praised the women and men determined to defend their achievements with "tools in one hand and a rifle in the other" because "the terrible war machinery of American imperialism is lying in wait," as confirmed by the aggression against Vietnam.[25]

Alongside the WIDF's critique of US imperialism, state socialist countries were not spared from demands to improve women's status. Hugel underscored during the congress that the "WIDF made it possible to emphasize the universal nature of the problems to be solved, and the need for a wide discussion of them."[26] Accordingly, in her report on "Women in the Family," Elsie Leyden of the Union of Australian Women placed the responsibility of maintaining the well-being of families squarely on all of society, calling for social protections such as "guaranteed employment with adequate income, stabilised prices and cost of living, proper nourishment and education for all children," without discrimination based on race, religion, or social standing.[27] While premised on a heteronormative notion of family, the report challenged traditional gender roles by noting the equal responsibility of fathers in the upbringing of the child, who "needs the love of two people who respect one another and can fulfil themselves in every way, who can serve him as an example and instil in him the love of peace and friendship and understanding among men."[28] Criticizing the practices of purdah, dowry, trafficking of women and girls, and generally the ill treatment of women, the report also urged state socialist countries to ensure equality between husband and wife because too often women's right to work "involves hardship as it imposes an additional burden if the household work is not a communal effort shared with her by husband and children instead of being the responsibility of the mother alone. The introduction of labour-saving devices in the home, laundry and drycleaning services, home-delivery of foodstuffs, hot meals at work places, schools, crèches and kindergartens and establishment of inexpensive 'family' restaurants, all help to ease the drudgery of housework, but the only real way to overcome the problem is for a world-wide change of attitude to the role of women."[29]

Despite the strong calls for an integrated approach to women's rights, it was clear that major gaps remained, including in countries where equal rights were guaranteed by law. In her report on "Women in Society," Marta López Portillo de Tamayo, president of the National Union of Mexican Women, noted the great disparity in conditions of women across different countries, rooted in entrenched traditions and remnants of feudalism such as polygamy and prostitution. Where women had won the legal battle for equal rights, these were not adequately put into practice, so that "even in the most advanced socialist countries today, the woman devotes 60% more time to domestic labours than the man does," depriving her of "time to raise her vocational and cultural level and share in the political life of her country."[30] Tamayo concluded that "it is therefore necessary, in the socialist countries, to convert housework into work of a social character if the vestiges of inequality between men and women are to be eliminated once and for all."

Finally, reporting on "Women in the Struggle to Win and Defend National Independence, Democracy and Peace," Mahasin Abd el Aal of the Union of Sudanese Women pointed out that seventy new sovereign states had been established as a result of the disintegration of the former colonial empires, liberating 1.5 billion people worldwide.[31] While less than 4 percent of the world's territories remained under colonial rule, Portuguese colonialism in Africa continued to oppose the desire for independence of eleven million Africans. Her report criticized the vestiges of colonialism in the overseas territories of France, as well as neocolonial "economic and strategic interests" such as the US in Indochina and Israel in the Middle East. Expressing solidarity with anti-imperialist struggles in Arab, Asian, and African nations, the Korean delegate reiterated the advances in her country, in contrast to the conditions in the South "seized" by US imperialists.[32] "Particularly," she continued, "war maniac Nixon, new boss of the US imperialists, is bent more frantically on manoeuvrings to ignite a new war in our country, clamouring that 'a third world war will break out not in Europe but in Asia' and 'the Korean peninsula will be the next point of explosion in the world.'"[33] Even while sounding alarm bells, Korean women categorically rejected peace at any price, concluding that "peace secured through slavish submission is not peace."[34]

Despite the successes of the 1969 congress in forging closer ties to such groups as Women Strike for Peace in the US against the war in Vietnam, criticisms also emerged from a group of US women, who felt that the problem of racism as the "main weapon of imperialism" was not sufficiently dealt with during the congress.[35] Hugel attributed such criticisms to the lack of understanding about the work of the Federation, "for we all know that the main weapon of imperialism is the exploitation of man by man, the practice of colonialism and neo-colonialism, and recourse to wars of aggression to keep the peoples under its yoke, and that racism is only one of the multiple devices of imperialism to accentuate the division in the forces for progress and to perpetuate its oppression and exploitation."[36] Such appeals for a united front notwithstanding, participants from Africa and the Middle East also felt that not enough space had been given to problems of Israeli aggression compared to US conduct in Vietnam. On the other hand, Italian women paid compliments to the work of the 1969 congress, raising hopes that the Italians would rescind the 1963 decision to leave the Federation.[37] Furthermore, plans to open a WIDF center in Sudan gained momentum, with the National Council of Polish Women providing teaching staff, the Soviet Women's Committee sending school supplies, the Union of French Women furnishing sewing machines, the National Council of Czechoslovakian Women offering child care specialists and midwives, and the Democratic League of German Women supplying household equipment.[38]

Following the 1969 congress, the WIDF Council convened in Bulgaria in 1972. There the WIDF decided to propose to the twenty-fourth session of the CSW that 1975 be designated as International Women's Year; with the backing of nine other NGOs, the CSW took up the proposal.[39] When the UN General Assembly voted on the CSW proposal and passed Resolution 3010 in December 1972, declaring 1975 the International Year of Women, the WIDF began elaborate plans to host its next congress in East Berlin.[40] Not only would this be a meaningful way to mark the thirtieth anniversary of the Federation's founding, but it was the WIDF plans for this congress that spurred the United States, not to be outdone in its Cold War rivalry, to support the first UN World Conference on Women as the capstone event to International Women's Year.[41] Held in Mexico City from June 19 to July 2, 1975, the historic UN World Conference gathered over two thousand official government representatives, of whom 73 percent were women, from 133 countries, and the parallel NGO Tribune convened over six thousand women.[42] Despite marking a seminal moment in the history of the global women's movement, the World Conference also exposed the fault lines in the different approaches to questions of gender and sexuality among the First, Second, and Third Worlds, each bloc represented respectively by the three key conference themes of equality, peace, and development.[43] With the Second and Third Worlds aligned, however tenuously, there was strong anti-US backlash at the conference, especially given the war in Vietnam, and the US State Department forbade the US delegation from speaking even informally to delegates from the socialist countries.[44]

Since detailed histories of this watershed event have been written by historian Jocelyn Olcott, I only note here the continued tensions between China and the Soviet Union that we saw in chapter 3 and the dramatically different contributions by the two Koreas at this first state-level international women's forum in which they both officially participated since the Korean War. As during the 1963 World Congress, China, with the support of Albania, tried to include language in the conference's World Plan of Action on the problem of superpower hegemony, targeted at both the United States and the Soviet Union, while criticizing imperialism, racism, and apartheid.[45] However, as in 1963, this attempt was thwarted by the Soviet bloc countries, and China would be absent from the World Congress of Women in Berlin, even as twenty-eight new national organizations had requested to join the Federation since the last congress.[46]

Meanwhile, over thirty resolutions and decisions were adopted at the World Conference, in addition to the "Declaration of Mexico on the Equality of Women and Their Contribution to Development and Peace" and the World Plan of Action calling for women's equal access to education, health care, housing, and employment. The vast majority of these resolutions pertained to the impact of colonialism on Third World development and women's lives, reflecting the changing dynamic at the UN. Although the two Koreas were not yet UN member states (only admitted in 1991), invitations to the conference had been extended to all nations, including nonmember states in disputed and divided nations such as Korea and Vietnam, adding strength to the Third World bloc. In this context, while South Korea left no record of official voting on any of the resolutions, North Korea sided with the Second and Third Worlds to vote in favor of all resolutions that emphasized the urgency of the "New International Economic Order" founded on "equity, sovereign equality, interdependence, common interest, co-operation among all States irrespective of their social and economic systems."[47] The First World countries of the West all voted against such resolutions or abstained.

Reporting on the World Conference as a diplomatic victory, *Rodong Sinmun* described the South Korean "puppet" delegation as "sitting in their seats during the roll call vote, pretending to be absent in order to get out of their predicament."⁴⁸ Leading the North Korean delegation in these efforts was Hŏ Chŏng-suk, now over seventy years of age and vice-chair of the Standing Committee of the Supreme People's Assembly (SPA), who along with Pak Chŏng-ae had been among the highest-ranking women leaders in the North. Hŏ was assisted by two other women in the delegation, Kim Jung Suk, an SPA deputy and vice-chair of the Central Committee of the General Federation of Trade Unions, and Li Soo Wul, an SPA deputy and secretary of international affairs of the Central Committee of the KDWU.⁴⁹ As discussed earlier in the book, Hŏ Chŏng-suk was a renowned figure active since the 1920s, who along with Pak had invited the WIDF fact-finding commission during the Korean War and had held numerous posts in the government since. That the two other women delegates held offices in organizations representing workers and women indicated how the DPRK wished to represent Korean women in the historic meeting.

Meanwhile, the South Korean delegation was headed by Mary S. Lee, vice president of the (South) Korean National Red Cross, accompanied by the director of the Korean Institute for Family Planning Chung Tai Kim, and sociology professor Yi Hyo-jae (1924–2020).⁵⁰ A pioneer of women's studies in South Korea, Yi introduced many of the feminist texts to southern audiences, initiating the first women's studies program in Korea at Ewha Women's University in 1977.⁵¹ While she was devoted to women's and family issues throughout her career, it was her participation in the 1975 Mexico City Conference that turned her toward feminism.⁵² Her writing in the years soon after the trip aligned with the Mexico Declaration drafted by Third World women emphasizing national liberation as the basis for women's equality. Despite her attempts to connect with the North Korean delegation of thirty women led by Hŏ, others in the South Korean delegation frowned upon such overtures. Moreover, the South Korean consulate dissuaded Yi, appointed to deliver the keynote on behalf of the South, from referring to the women's anticolonial movement so as not to upset relations with Japan. Prohibited from participating in further deliberations, the South Korean delegation was ultimately pressured by the Seoul government to abstain from the Mexico Declaration. Upon exiting the country, Yi had to confront Mexican immigration officials sarcastically asking, "From South Korea? Colony of US?"

Despite (or perhaps because of) such biting critique, Yi credited her experience at the Mexico City Conference for opening her eyes to a sense of national identity, moved to see Hŏ appear in her Korean dress to deliver her speech in Korean as the head of the North Korean delegation. "In contrast to the dignified appearance of the North Korean delegation," Yi recalled, she "felt so embittered by the situation of the South Korean delegation whose presence seemed only for appearances that [she] resolved never to attend another international conference until [Korean] unification."⁵³ While she would go on to become a feminist scholar and dissident activist, who would advocate on behalf of victims of Japanese military sexual slavery, the other two members of her delegation illustrate the way the ROK government, in contrast to the North, conceived of women's issues as largely "apolitical." After Mexico City, a North Korean delegation went on to participate in the 1975 WIDF World Congress three months later, but South Korean women would be absent.

The historic year of women and the UN Conference provided momentum, gathering over two thousand participants from 141 countries to the World Congress of Women in East Berlin between October 20 and 24, 1975, organized by a diverse International Preparatory Committee that included the WILPF along with the WIDF, the Pan-African Women's Organization, the Afro-Asian Peoples' Solidarity Organization, the World Council of Churches, the International Peace Bureau, the International Federation for Human Rights, the International Planned Parenthood Federation, the World Association of Girl Guides and Girl Scouts, and ten other organizations.[54] The bulletins issued by the International Preparatory Committee show that North Korean women participated in some capacity from the outset, starting with the inaugural meeting in Tihany, Hungary, in November 1974, but the extent of their participation throughout is difficult to assess from the existing record.[55]

What is available suggests that the largest congress to date again resulted in discord, this time with a scathing account issued by US feminists Laura McKinley and Diana Russell, who attended from the San Francisco Bay Area, among the one hundred US delegates coordinated by the US section of the WILPF to assure diversity in race, age, class, sexuality, and religion.[56] Noting the absence of Chinese women, they saw the congress "as controlled and designed by and for men, to which mostly brainwashed women were invited," scoffing at no mention of "sexism" throughout the meeting. In response to characterizations of the conflict as one between First World feminists and Third World women, they argued that "women's freedom per se—women's issues—were being lost, cast aside or seen as 'trivial'" and that "patriarchy exists all over the globe under many different economic systems," duplicating arguments from the UN Conference over how to define women's issues.[57] Showing little sensitivity to potential differences across local contexts of struggle, they associated the "formal stiff impersonal settings" to the "covert presence of the males," and dismissed discussions about development, national independence, and peace as "socialist propaganda" overshadowing "women's concerns" about work, education, and mass media.[58] They condemned the limited time given to minority opinions to voice views on gay rights, single mothers, femicide, forced sterilization and genital mutilation, domestic abuse, sexual violence, and rape.

To be sure, the delegates were under watch by both uniformed and undercover police, not only to monitor contacts between East Germans and foreign visitors, but also to protect delegates from "sensitive" political regions who could only attend anonymously.[59] Documents and perspectives at the congress mostly presented a heteronormative, family-centered, binary view of the world as both dimorphically gendered *and* divided between capitalist and socialist systems, touting achievements in the latter with criticisms reserved for the former. As at the UN Conference, the family was "an important unit of society, to develop for the wellbeing of the individual and of society."[60] Such conventional views notwithstanding, the congress did in fact duly recognize full reproductive rights and the choice not to marry. Contrary to criticisms from US feminists, the need to support single parents and to combat sexual violence in all forms, no matter the system, was strongly emphasized throughout the work of the nine commissions of the congress—equality of women in society; women and work; women and development; family and society; education of women; women and the struggle for peace; women and the struggle for national independence and international solidarity; women and mass media; and women's joint action. The congress stressed the responsibility of society to support the social function of mothers to enable women to exercise their rights as women, workers, and citizens. Women's rights, their working conditions, health, and education were all tied to structural inequalities such as colonialism and racism.[61]

Even as women celebrated the end of the war in Vietnam and the independence of several African nations, the Federation supported the continued struggle for the withdrawal of US troops from Indochina, Korea, and Japan, insisting that "the woman question is a social question" against the "apolitical" position that women's issues could be divorced from their sociopolitical context.[62] The treatment of the condition of Third World women was especially prominent in the commissions on development, peace, and national independence, as the congress expressed solidarity with women in Latin America, Africa, and Asia, including consistent calls for the withdrawal of US troops from Korea for the peaceful reunification of the country.[63] Although both the UN Conference and the World Congress became contentious sites over sexual rights caricatured as a conflict between the First World against the Second and Third Worlds, the link between sexual violence and systems of colonialism, racism, and militarism had been made already during the Korean War in the WIDF report *We Accuse!* and would be made again in reckoning with the history of "comfort women."

From "Comfort Women" to UNSCR 1325

With the Cold War division of the country, the two Koreas were only admitted into the UN as member states in 1991 after the "end" of the Cold War. That same year, Kim Hak-sun came forward in South Korea to provide the first public testimony on her ordeals as a "comfort woman," a euphemistic term used by the Japanese military to refer to the over two hundred thousand women and girls forcibly recruited during the Asia Pacific War into a system of military sexual slavery.[64] The UN Special Rapporteur on violence against women would officially recognize the system as a war crime and crime against humanity in 1996, based on historical records and testimonies provided by Korean women.[65] This is the standard genealogy of how the world came to know about the "comfort women" system.

But three decades earlier, the North Korean women's press had taken up the issue during a 1964 roundtable on women's treatment under the Japanese occupation.[66] Conducted by reporters of *Chosŏn Nyŏsŏng*, the discussions included the participation of seven women from Anju in South P'yŏng'an Province. While most of the women spoke about the material deprivation and suppression of Korean culture and identity, cooperative farm manager Kim Ok-sŏn spoke about her experience of being taken to Anju from Pusan as a fourteen-year-old girl to work at one of the brothels for which the area around Pyongyang was known.

> When I was 14 years old, I was caught in their noose and brought to Anju from Pusan. The women gathered here would be familiar with Taiwan House [*Taemangwan*]. What kind of place was this Taiwan House? With the backing of the Japanese, Ri Yŏng-sang abducted women with debt, tricking wandering girls and women who had no place to go to put them in the Taiwan House, selling them off to distant foreign lands in southern China, Hong Kong, Manila, and Singapore, where the Japanese imperialists extended their invasion. Because I was so young, I wasn't dragged off to another country, but was sold off to another entrepreneur as an errand girl. But I saw at the time how the Japanese would creep into the Taiwan House and harass the Korean women who had been dragged there from all over the place. Some of the women who were dragged there without knowing where they were going resisted and secretly ran away. I don't know how many women resented the Japanese occupation with tears and sighs in this grievous Taiwan House.[67]

Although the issue was not a recurring topic in the pages of the magazine, another woman writer reiterated the problem in a 1974 collection of essays covering women's experiences during the Japanese occupation.[68] Tracing the system of military sexual slavery to the start of World War II in 1939, Kim Pong-suk linked the conscription of students beginning in 1943 with the creation of the Women's Voluntary Service Corps (*nyŏja chŏngsindae*) that forcibly abducted women and girls. Writing in the style of reportage or an eyewitness report, Kim indicted the Japanese for separating mothers and daughters, taking women away to distant lands throughout the Asia Pacific with false promises of employment. Treated like animals and objects, she argued, the women were exploited as tools to satisfy "perverse desires" (*suyok*) in military camps, dying at the soldiers' hands or killing themselves to avoid such a fate.[69] Recounting forced blood "donations" to outright killing of the women at the war's end, rather than allowing them to return home, Kim accused the Japanese of "vampire-like beastly brutality" (*hŭp'yŏlgwijŏk in yasujŏk manhaeng*).[70] Such harrowing accounts would become more widely known in the public testimonies of the 1990s and thereafter, but problems of sexual violence under colonialism and during war had been a consistent WIDF concern, since its 1948 report on Asia and Africa and the 1951 report on the Korean War. Drawing a continuity from Japanese colonial policies to contemporary South Korea, Kim described how women in the South were once again having to leave their homeland as "export labor" (*ilyŏk such'ul*), and children were being sent away for international adoption, "sold as if live dolls," while those within the country were recruited to work in "sex tourism" (*maech'un kwan'gwang*) to secure foreign currency.[71]

Issues of sexual violence and rape were particularly dire at this juncture because of the Vietnam War. Not only was the war escalating, with President Johnson seeking congressional approval for direct US involvement, but South Korea began committing combat troops to South Vietnam in 1965. Normalization of relations between South Korea and Japan brokered by the US that same year established a tripartite alliance that signaled to the North a return of aggressive US posturing in the region, reminiscent of the Korean War. Reciprocating the solidarity shown during that war, Korean women joined the WIDF delegation to Vietnam in February 1966.[72] The Korean lead delegate in the group was Ch'oe Kŭm-ja, vice-chair of the Central Committee of the KDWU, who shared her observations upon her return, with eerie parallels between her description and observations made by the 1951 WIDF delegation in Korea.[73]

> During my stay in the Democratic Republic of Vietnam, I witnessed the brutality committed by the US imperialists and was greatly moved by the heroic struggle of the people and women there to defeat the invaders.... Among the countless cities and villages of northern Vietnam brutally bombarded by US imperialists, we visited Thanh Hoa City, Thanh Hoa Province. According to Comrade Le Thi Ni, chair of the provincial women's union, Tuberculosis Hospital No. 71 in the suburbs of Thanh Hoa was bombed three times last year on July 8, July 14, and August 25. There remained not a single intact building among the 50 wards.... The US imperialists also launched indiscriminate bombing

against residential areas of Dong Hoi City, where there were no military facilities. Dong Hoi was a peaceful and beautiful coastal city widely known throughout the country for its resorts and vacation spots. On February 7 last year, the US imperialists bombed the residents of this city with some 100 planes, and then on the twenty-first bombing, poured down as many as 60 tons of bombs.[74]

The Vietnamese chairwoman explained that red cross symbols were clearly marked on the roof of the hospital building and its front door, and there were no military facilities or buildings that could be mistaken as such anywhere near the hospital, and yet the bombings continued, with over a hundred bombs dropped in the area. The delegation met with bombing survivors in Nam Dinh, which prompted Ch'oe to draw a straight through-line in their experiences of war from Korea to Vietnam.[75]

In the last five years, the US imperialists and their lackeys have arrested and imprisoned one million people, massacring about 150,000 of them recklessly, and in 1965 alone, they reportedly killed 7,859 women. The US imperialists are strengthening their "campaign of destruction" in southern Vietnam, implementing a "scorched earth" campaign to "kill everything, burn everything, and destroy everything." People are being slaughtered indiscriminately with bombs of napalm, poisonous gas, and white phosphorous, as well as toxic chemicals.... During my stay in Vietnam, among the crashed wreckage of American planes, I saw the three letters "U.S.A." that were already familiar to my eyes from the national liberation war [Korean War]. I felt clearly once again the truth that a jackal is always a jackal and cannot change into a sheep. The US imperialists are a vicious "international gendarme," trampling upon the struggle for national liberation all over the planet and blocking the path of justice. When we crossed the Amrok [Yalu] River covered in thick ice and then arriving in Vietnam saw the rural scenery buzzing with rice planting, I was reminded of how distant Vietnam was from Korea. The iconic southern scenes with their cool shades of palm trees, lush bamboo forests, massive elephants and water buffalos—Vietnam's environment and customs were unfamiliar, but the courageous movements amid shellfire were very familiar, reminiscent of our last war for national liberation. Bridges are immediately rebuilt as soon as they are cut off, trucks run through the night without lights, and villagers guarantee air signals lighting the night. On our way from Hanoi to Thanh Hoa, I felt strongly that our last national liberation war and Vietnam today have much in common. As a result, I was more firmly convinced that the people of Vietnam would surely win just as we had won.[76]

With a protracted war, Ch'oe observed how the Vietnamese people were waging war on two fronts—against the US invasion and to increase production—and described visits to various cooperatives and factories in Thanh Hoa and Nam Dinh. Women were involved at all levels of the struggle, fighting on the front lines while providing food and medical aid, and also taking up positions in factories left empty by their male kin.[77]

Five months after the February visit to Vietnam, Ch'oe Kŭm-ja joined another international gathering, this time to Cuba for the thirteen-year anniversary of the July 26, 1953, attack on the Moncada barracks of the Batista regime that ignited the Cuban Revolution. Visiting Cuba for her second time, Ch'oe described the invitation by the Federation of Cuban Women as one filled with solidarity, just like the global movements for peace in Korea and Vietnam.[78] After twenty-six hours of travel halfway around the world, the Korean delegation was welcomed by Cuban women and led to their lodging at Hotel Libre overlooking the Atlantic Ocean. Aware that the US was a mere ninety miles away, Ch'oe and her companions felt "a great sense of satisfaction" at the thought of the US forces defeated at Playa Girón (Bay of Pigs). The delegation was most impressed with the pride and unity of the Cuban people around Fidel Castro, gathering in the tens of thousands at the Revolutionary Square with the militant slogan *Patria o Muerte* (Homeland or death).

Marked as the precursor to the emergence of the Global South, the Tricontinental Conference was held earlier that year, in January 1966.[79] A US government study called it "the most powerful gathering of pro-Communist, anti-American forces in the history of the Western Hemisphere," with 197 delegates from Asia, 150 from Africa, and 165 from Latin America, for a total of over 500 delegates, 64 observers, and 77 guests, who collectively "designate[d] United States 'imperialism' as enemy number one in every continent."[80] At the conference, July was declared Korea-Cuba Friendship Month, with a continuous series of events planned throughout the country and articles on Korea to be published in Cuban outlets; these activities were coming to a successful conclusion during the Korean women's visit.[81] At the local women's federation, Ch'oe was moved to see a note stuck next to the office phone that called for the "promotion of Korean reunification through solidarity," there to remind people any time the phone was used. The slogan was reiterated throughout Cuban broadcasts, and the final closing of the July 26 celebrations was held on July 31, with some eight thousand Cuban cadres and foreign guests attending the ceremony in the Escambray Mountains. With a moving speech by the chair of the Cuban Solidarity Committee Velva

Hernandez, the performance of the mass games by Cuban students brought tears to the Korean women's eyes, as girls in white clothes filed across the stage, against the dark backdrop of the mountains, to form the words "Long Live the People's Solidarity of Korea and Cuba."[82]

One of the outcomes of the Tricontinental Conference was the formation of the Organization of Solidarity with the People of Asia, Africa and Latin America (OSPAAL), with headquarters in Havana. Although Ernesto Che Guevara would leave Cuba by the end of 1966, he would write to the OSPAAL Secretariat in April 1967 from the partisan jungles of Bolivia, calling for "two, three or many Vietnams" in the global struggle against imperialism in order to secure a better future for the Third World.[83] While militant resistance against imperialism was the consequence of centuries of colonial exploitation and oppression, the cost proved unsustainable. With heightened global militarism, North Korean defense spending quadrupled in 1967 to make up over 30 percent (as opposed to 10 percent in 1966) of the national budget, resulting in negative economic growth for the first time since the Korean War.[84] As if to forecast tragic ends to militarized solutions, Che Guevara would be shot dead by the Bolivian authorities later that year, four months after Eugénie Cotton died a peaceful death in another part of the world.

With the "end" of the Cold War, a different international coalition was spearheaded this time by Yi Hyo-jae, who had attended the 1975 Mexico City Conference as part of the South Korean delegation. Working to bring justice to "comfort women," Yi's efforts sparked the first inter-Korean women's exchange in 1991 and 1992 on "Peace in Asia and the Role of Women" by again mobilizing the transnational women's movement.[85] Hosted by the Japan Women's Association in Tokyo, it was the first women's meeting between the two Koreas since division, and was followed by meetings in Seoul and Pyongyang. Reminiscent of debates at the 1975 UN Conference and the WIDF Congress, North Korean women prioritized anti-imperialism, demanding the withdrawal of US forces from Korea, while South Korean women preferred to focus on "women's issues." Despite the gap, the meetings allowed former "comfort women" from the two Koreas to meet and share their stories, and this issue more than any other brought women together in a coalition across the Asia Pacific to demand accountability from Japan. While the existence of "comfort women" may have been common knowledge since wartime, as suggested by the 1964 North Korean women's roundtable, this fact required women's struggle to establish its historical truth as a crime.[86] It was the continuous push to raise sexual violence as an issue of international concern, from the early work of the WIDF to the transnational campaigns on behalf of "comfort women," that led to the historic UN Security Council Resolution 1325 on Women, Peace and Security in 2000, establishing the critical importance of women's participation in conflict resolution and peace processes.

Beyond Mainstreaming Gender

State socialist women have been key players in the development of global feminisms and the international women's movement, as we have seen throughout the book, and yet this history is largely unknown. Present-day celebrations of International Women's Day is a good case in point.[87] As historian Temma Kaplan explains, while both liberal suffragists and radical socialists began celebrating a form of women's day in the United States and Europe between 1908 and 1909, it was at the gathering of international socialist women in Copenhagen in 1910 that Clara Zetkin proposed an annual celebration.[88] With the 1917 October Revolution, March 8 marked the day when Russian women led demonstrations against deteriorating living conditions, ultimately toppling the czarist regime. The date gained official recognition as International Women's Day in 1918, joining a list of revolutionary holidays including May Day and the anniversary of the October Revolution, and was celebrated throughout the communist bloc and among socialists worldwide.[89]

Despite these origins, a website that purports to commemorate the day depoliticizes its significance by diluting its Cold War history. Created in 2001, the site appears official, as a "global ... digital hub for everything IWD ... launched to re-energize the day as an important platform to celebrate the successful achievements of women and to continue calls for accelerating gender parity."[90] Although it claims that "no one government, NGO, charity, corporation, academic institution, women's network or media hub is solely responsible for International Women's Day," the site and its activities are made possible each year through support from private corporations that have included McDonald's, Caterpillar, British Petroleum, and Pepsico. As a result, despite appeals to action, the site channels its fund-raising toward philanthropy. It is yet another example of how feminist analyses and praxes have been co-opted, echoing Lin Farley's commentary that "sexual harassment," a term that she coined back in the 1970s, has been "made bloodless," "associated with H.R. training manuals," and "swallowed up as corporate-friendly legalese."[91]

More telling, however, is the historical chronology provided by the website. Even as it notes the critical role of US socialists in celebrating National Woman's Day in 1909 and the role of Russian women that ultimately sparked the October Revolution in 1917, there is a conspicuous break in the official timeline from 1917 to 1975. As we have seen in this chapter, however, the first suggestion and the subsequent work to designate 1975 as International Women's Year to launch the International Women's Decade (1975–1985) came from the WIDF, and socialist women were instrumental in the development of a women's agenda within the UN for the three decades between 1945 and 1975.[92] And yet we know relatively little about them, and this disappearance of communist women is dramatically illustrated by their invisibility made hypervisible precisely by the chronological gap between 1917 and 1975, erasing the complexities of feminisms and international women's activisms in these years.[93]

This elision is one of the glaring effects of the "end" of the Cold War. The First World "victory" in the Cold War and declarations of the "end of history" have hollowed out the rich history of transnational and international connections among women across the First, Second, and Third Worlds. The Cold War galvanized women to take action as global activists, embodying notions of transversal solidarity based on shared experiences of womanhood as mothers, workers, and citizens. One of the most paradoxical results of feminist analyses of communist women is to render them invisible by accepting at face value the official state narrative that places all power on the ruling party and the "wise" leader. While such outcomes highlight the limits of Cold War feminisms, these limits pale in comparison to the atrophy of feminist possibilities after the "end" of the Cold War. The fall of the socialist bloc and the subsequent dismantling of Cold War competition over the best way to advance women's rights have only served to expand the authority of the UN and the use of UN mechanisms and "peacekeeping" forces as yet another mode of global policing focused on violence against women that relegates women to the status of victims.[94] This is not to argue that violence against women is not a serious problem, from domestic violence in local communities to systemic rape in conflict zones globally. However, such an emphasis in framing international and national policy sidelines the continued everyday impact on women of unequal pay and the lack of economic opportunities, child care, and other social welfare that ultimately stem from structural violence. As shown by the history of the WIDF and Korean women's participation in this global movement, women intervened during and after the Korean War to call attention to violence against women, too, but did so in the context of critiquing US intervention in Korea as an example of imperialism and continued to work toward a more just distribution of power and self-determination for the Third World.

The conflicting views at the various international forums in 1975 between individual sexual rights and structural concerns over imperialism and poverty reflect the different meanings of gender and sexuality specific to each context. For Third World and minority women, sexuality could not embody individual expression because it was so often used as a weapon of abuse, the "comfort women" system itself being one egregious example. Rather than sexual liberation, "gender complementarity" gave women leverage within a conventionally structured gendered division of labor.[95] Ironically, however, the WIDF's active engagement with the UN, especially after its status was restored in 1967, contributed to the process of "gender mainstreaming." As women's liberation was couched in the UN discourse of human rights, the more radical strategies *outside* institutionalized mechanisms that defined the WIDF's earlier activities to challenge structural violence became less salient, with several milestones that coincided with the 1975 International Women's Year. The Vietnam War, which had radicalized new social movements of the 1960s, finally came to an end in 1975 as a finale to the global anti-imperialist struggle, and the Helsinki Accords signed that same year formalized the process of détente between East and West.

And yet the Korea question remained unresolved in a perennial international quagmire, despite an unprecedented UN General Assembly resolution, also in 1975. In November, the UN General Assembly passed Resolution 3390B calling for the parties to the 1953 Armistice Agreement that halted the Korean War to "replace the Korean Military Armistice Agreement with a peace agreement as a measure to ease tension and maintain and consolidate peace in Korea in the context of the dissolution of the 'United Nations Command' and the withdrawal of all the foreign troops stationed in South Korea under the flag of the United Nations."[96] It was a major coup for North Korea, thanks in large part to its Third World allies. While the Western-dominated UN in 1948 had granted official recognition to the South as the sole sovereign state on the peninsula after UN-administered elections, its application for UN membership since 1949 had stalled because of the Soviet veto in the Security Council.[97] The South nonetheless participated in the UN as an observer and advocated for its position, with US backing, but the North never received comparable recognition. This inequity was at the root of the UN intervention during the Korean War on behalf of one recognized state against the unrecognized other. The UN did not accept the DPRK or the PRC as legitimate states, thereby regarding them "unlawful aggressors," while turning a blind eye to hostile actions on the other side, exposing the Cold War divisions already embedded in the UN from its very beginning.[98] The UN had thereby become a permanent presence in the South with the stationing of the UN Command and the establishment of the UN Commission for the Unification and Rehabilitation of Korea (UNCURK) to create "a unified, independent, and democratic government of Korea."[99] Despite the lofty sounding aim, UNCURK "lacked the essential qualities of independence and impartiality" and was "a partisan instrumentality to serve the foreign policy interests of the UN's leading state"—the US—never able to serve any mediating function since it was limited to the South and unrecognized by the socialist bloc.[100] North Korea never recognized UNCURK's authority either, since it was itself not recognized by the UN.

But with the admission of the newly independent states from Africa and Asia in the 1960s, and the PRC finally admitted into the UN in 1971, tables had turned in favor of the North. With this change buttressed by the "Nixon Doctrine" that shifted US policy to hold Asian countries liable for their own defense, UNCURK was dissolved by the UN General Assembly in 1973.[101]

This was the backdrop to the 1975 UN General Assembly resolution.[102] The diplomatic victory had been several years in the making, with the DPRK establishing full diplomatic relations with several First World countries in 1973, including Denmark, Norway, Sweden, Finland, and Iceland, and also gaining membership in the World Health Organization in 1973, which finally gave it observer status at the UN.[103] Kim Il Sung also made rare state visits between April and June 1975, to China, Romania, Algeria, Mauritania, Bulgaria, and Yugoslavia, leading up to the UN resolution, which brought the North membership in the Non-Aligned Movement, while South Korea's application was rejected.[104] The resolution to dissolve the UN Command was a dramatic reversal of prior UN General Assembly voting, moving from twenty-four in favor and sixty against in 1967 to sixty-eight in favor and twenty-five against in 1971 in just four years, and this support for the North came largely from African nations, increasing from four votes in 1966 to twenty-two in 1974.[105] Despite the vindication of women's repeated calls since the 1950s for precisely the measures called for in the UN resolution to bring a permanent peace to the Korean peninsula, the 1953 Armistice remains as of this writing, as do the UN Command and US troops in South Korea.

Explaining the consequences of "gender mainstreaming," anthropologist Malathi de Alwis argues that the institutionalization and professionalization of feminism through international humanitarian and development aid has *depoliticized* it. Rather than "strategies of refusal" such as strikes, boycotts, fasts, and demonstrations, the vast majority of actions today revolve around "strategies of request" in the form of lobbying, online signature campaigns, and email petitions.[106] "It is worth considering," she suggests, "how influential the processes adopted by the United Nations have been in circumscribing feminist practices this way. Since 1975, since meetings in Mexico, Nairobi, and Beijing and those convened post-Beijing, a great deal of local feminists' energies has gone into disseminating information about these meetings nationally and petitioning governments and holding them accountable to international charters, plans of action, and so on, that are promulgated at these meetings."[107] Rather than discounting such approaches, she points to the predominance of and preference for reformist and philanthropic strategies by relying on bureaucratic UN mechanisms and other international agencies, over more radical and revolutionary politics.

At a time when so much has moved into the virtual realm, worth remembering are the risks women took in forging connections across divided worlds to put their bodies and lives on the line in the name of transnational solidarity for a better world. The women in this book embodied relational and situated forms of agency, not as autonomous individual women in opposition to men, but as complementary and integral members of a collective, explicitly connecting women's liberation to national liberation. From the 1949 Asia Women's Conference to the 1952 Asia Pacific Peace Conference and the 1958 Afro-Asian Peoples' Solidarity Conference, Asia stood at the center of demands for decolonization as the "East" became a unifying umbrella in the anti-imperialist struggle for a just peace. While the Korean War is rarely included in the histories of decolonial movements, focused as they are on struggles in Algeria, Cuba, and Vietnam that resonated with the 1960s social movements, this book opened with the Korean War as the crucible that gave rise to many of the radical politics now lost because of the war's forgottenness in the West. Sexual violence as a war crime, women's rights as human rights, peace with justice, and intersectional critique all came to the fore during the Korean War, to be carried on by later movements, thanks to the work of the women in this book. *Among Women across Worlds* tracked the transnational solidarities between women of Korea and the world, showing how maternalist strategies enabled women to appeal to their gendered role as mothers and caregivers to demand their rightful place in politics, even while insisting that these duties were not women's alone. Rather than disavowing violence, in contrast to the pacifist movements of the West, women under the umbrella of the WIDF called for the "militancy of peace" in support of anticolonial, anti-imperialist struggles.

Despite the schisms between the Second and Third Worlds over "peaceful coexistence" after Soviet détente, which ultimately led Chinese women to renounce their WIDF membership, these maternalist strategies saw parallels in Korea as women combined productive and reproductive labor as socialist builders and patriotic mothers. The hardships of the "double burden" noted in the Korean women's press, however, sharply illustrate how the conceptual division between production and reproduction fall apart when applied to the totality of women's work. Their demands that men also take up reproductive labor anticipated arguments to come from later "second wave" feminists. The push for women's ever-increasing labor was the result of increasing economic difficulties in Korea, which ultimately led to the 1967 Monolithic Ideological System, sublimating all forms of labor as sacrifice for the collective. Such an emphasis on the collective also permeated the cultural sphere. The imperative for decolonization foregrounded women's everyday labor in the creation of folk aesthetics, even as nationalist works drew upon the transnational circulation of militant women as archetypes for the ideal communist. While women behind these creations as choreographers, dancers, writers, and actors have been dismissed as manipulated by men and rendered "sexless," devoid of femininity, it is paradoxically a "feminist" lens that erases the work of figures like Pak Chŏng-ae to uncritically reproduce narratives of state beneficence.

Undoubtedly, there are gaps in the book. I can only account for records left behind and not even all of those, since I was limited by what I could find. An ongoing movement spread across the world, doubly scrutinized by the states within which it works and by critics outside, cannot afford to leave meticulous records, not only because it is verboten but because the difficulties of forging transnational solidarities are immense and the work too intense, involving political differences and personality clashes. Even as I yearned to know more about these details, I have appreciated what was left behind and respected what could not be recorded, to protect personal feelings and organizational longevity. It was a reminder that history ought to be approached with humility.

In the face of Cold War bloc politics from Stalinism to McCarthyism, women traversed the divide to call for peace and justice for the sake of humanity. Opening new terrains of political struggle, they activated a radical paradigm for women's place in politics, the economy, and the cultural sphere to redefine the meaning of peace, women's labor, and feminisms. Their goal of liberation may appear abstract and utopian, but this book has tried to bring life back to the stories of women in Korea and their international comrades to show in detail what liberation meant for them in concrete terms. They traveled across worlds to be among women in the belief that what they had in common would give them the power to change the world. While they may not have achieved everything they set out to do, the legacies they have left behind inspire continued efforts to forge transnational connections in the name of women's liberation as an integral part of liberation for all.

Acknowledgments

Mirroring the history in this book, the story of how the book came to be is a collective one. Tani Barlow hosted a workshop on "Communist Feminism(s): A Transnational Perspective" at Rice University in 2012, just as I was beginning to think about a new project. I thank her for modeling intellectual praxis and scholarly teamwork that can be both fun and fruitful. The gathering included an amazing group of women upon whose scholarship this book builds, including works by Tani herself, Maria Bucur, Michelle Chase, Francisca de Haan, Kristen Ghodsee, Anna Krylova, and Judy Wu. At this meeting, Francisca first alerted me to the Korean women's participation in the WIDF, and I have shared her quest ever since to discover the WIDF's important role in international history. Almost two decades have passed since I left Chicago, but Bruce Cumings and Kyeong-Hee Choi continue to be sources of encouragement and support, and I thank them for their friendship.

Outside the academy, I've been blessed to be among women who have inspired this book with their tireless work for peace and social justice in Korea and beyond. The beginnings of the book overlapped with the beginnings of Women Cross DMZ, a women's peace organization of which I am a founding member. The parallel universes of women seemed uncanny at times. For the friendships and collective journeys through the ups and downs, I am truly grateful; this book would not have been the same without them. Though I have not included an exhaustive list of names, for it is a growing movement, I hope this book can still convey the significance and appreciation I attach to each individual in the long shared arc of collective history.

A circle of friends, mentors, and colleagues supported the project at various stages with advice, encouragement, panel discussions, careful readings, and translations, sharing helpful sources and leads. I thank Christine Ahn, JeongAe Ahn-Kim, Kozue Akibayashi, Nadia Al-Bagdadi, Elisabeth Armstrong, Tani Barlow, Ruth Barraclough, Adam Cathcart, Michelle Chase, Hee Sun Choi, Yong Wook Chung, Koen de Ceuster, Francisca de Haan, Ewa Eriksson Fortier, Kevin Gray, Eun Heo, Keun-sik Jung, Jane Jin Kaisen, Eunkyung Kim, Flora Kim, Jinhyouk Kim, Jisoo Kim, Myung-hwan Kim, Seong-su Kim, Jessie Kindig, Ross King, Gwyn Kirk, Jooho Lee, Deann Borshay Liem, M. Brinton Lykes, Owen Miller, Peter Moody, Hwasook Nam, Margo Okazawa-Rey, Albert Park, Carey Park, Chris Hyunkyu Park, Hye-Jung Park, Sunyoung Park, James Person, Oksana

Sarkisova, Andre Schmid, Marsha Siefert, Hazel Smith, Robyn Spencer, Jae-Jung Suh, Vladimir Tikhonov, Zheng Wang, Cora Weiss, Emily Wilcox, Judy Wu, Jun Yoo, and Dafna Zur. A special thanks to Dafna for our shared research trip to Moscow and recruiting Adrien Smith. My gratitude to Adrien for her gracious assistance at Krasnogorsk.

The book also received help from archivists, librarians, and faculty who guided me to the sources. I thank Sonya Lee at the Library of Congress, Mikyung Kang at the Harvard-Yenching Library, Natasha An at the Russian State Library (Moscow), Elena Kolikova at the Russian State Documentary Film and Photo Archive (Krasnogorsk), Kim Gwang Oon at the University of North Korean Studies (Seoul), and the staff at Korea University (Tokyo), the Smith College Library (Massachusetts), the Information Center on North Korea (Seoul), and the International Institute of Social History (Amsterdam).

Support for research and writing was provided by fellowships from the Fulbright IIE, the Institute for Advanced Study at the Central European University, the National Endowment for the Humanities, and the Korea Foundation. At Rutgers, the Chancellor's Scholar Award, the Institute for Research on Women, and the Center for Cultural Analysis provided faculty fellowships and research travel funding. Additional travel funding was provided by the Rutgers University Research Council Grant and the Association for Asian Studies Northeast Asia Council Travel Grant.

At Rutgers University, the chair of my home department in Asian Languages and Cultures, Paul Schalow, has fearlessly yet with kindness steered the department through some tough times, and I thank him for his support and encouragement. Thanks also to Young-mee Yu Cho, Hee Chung Chun, Jae Won Chung, Jaehyun Jo, David Foglesong, Asher Ghertner, Chie Ikeya, Christian Lammerts, Ji Lee, Rick Lee, Preetha Mani, Haruki Eda, Jeongeun Park, and Mi Hyun Yoon for providing a sense of community.

The book benefits from earlier publications, and editorial and curatorial projects. Chapter 1 expands on "The Origins of Cold War Feminism during the Korean War," *Gender & History* 31, no. 2 (July 2019): 460–79. Chapter 5 expands on "Choe Seung-hui between Ballet and Folk: Aesthetics of National Form and Socialist Content in North Korea," in *Corporeal Politics: Dancing East Asia*, ed. Emily Wilcox and Katherine Mezur (Ann Arbor: University of Michigan Press, 2020). Chapter 6 draws on "From Violated Girl to Revolutionary Woman: The Politics of Sexual Difference from China to North Korea," *positions: asia critique* 28, no. 3 (August 2020): 631–57, and "Mothers and Maidens: Gendered Formation of Revolutionary Heroes in North Korea," *Journal of Korean Studies* 19, no. 2 (Fall 2014): 256–90. I acknowledge Wiley, the University of Michigan Press, and Duke University Press for permission to include revised versions of these works.

Parts of Pak Chŏng-ae's biography in this book are included in the 2022 edited volume by Francisca de Haan, *The Palgrave Handbook of Communist Women Activists from around the World*, and I thank her for her valuable comments and support of this project.

I learned a great deal from editing the special issue of *positions: asia critique* titled "Cold War Feminisms in East Asia" (vol. 28, no. 3, 2020), and coediting with Gwyn Kirk and M. Brinton Lykes a special issue of *Social Justice* titled "Unsettling Debates: Women and Peace Making" (vol. 46, no. 1, 2019) based on the 2017 International Women's Day roundtable at Rutgers University on "Women Organizing for Peace: Theories and Praxes." Also helpful was the opportunity to contribute to a dossier coedited by Crystal Baik and Jane Jin Kaisen for *Periscope: Social Text Online* titled "Korea and Demilitarized Peace" (2018). My thanks also to Kayo Denda and Annie Fukushima for our co-organized international symposium "Rethinking the Asia Pivot: Challenging Everyday Militarisms and Bridging Communities of Women," in 2014. Being a member of the editorial collective of *positions* has sharpened my eyes, and I thank Tani Barlow, Arnika Fuhrmann, Katsuya Hirano, Rebecca Karl, Fabio Lanza, Lan Li, Juliet Robson, Aminda Smith, Gavin Walker, and Angela Zito. Memberships in the Korean Association of Women's History, the Korean Women Peace Research Institute, and the Korean Association for Cold War Studies have enriched my journey, and the Department of Korean Language and Literature at Yonsei University provided a much needed home in the final stages of writing during a pandemic.

At Cornell University Press, I thank Emily Andrew and Sarah Grossman for being the kind of editors all authors need, and Karen Hwa, Susan Specter, and Jackie Teoh for shepherding the manuscript through production. Three anonymous reviewers gave helpful suggestions, and one of them especially saved me from myself through a meticulous reading with detailed comments and advice on almost every page of the manuscript. The book has greatly improved thanks to their unrecognized labor. Glenn Novak provided careful copyediting.

Throughout all this, my closest friends and family kept me sane. I thank Sarah Chee, Christine Hahn, Maryanne Kim, Kay Rhie, and Anna Song. Anna directs the female vocal ensemble *In Mulieribus*, a Latin phrase meaning "among women," which gave me the title for this book. In Korea, Song Soyeon and Kang-Mun Minseo make me feel at home. I am grateful to my brother Charles for holding down the fort in California, and my sister-in-law Elizabeth for doing the same in Iowa. My mother's independence and resilience are constant sources of awe, and my spouse puts up with everything I throw his way—this book owes so much to both of them. My deepest gratitude goes to the women in this book, who prompted the search to keep digging to bring their stories to light.

Notes

NOTE ON TERMS, TRANSLITERATION, AND TRANSLATION

1. For discussion on the salience of Global South as a term see Mukoma Wa Ngugi, "Rethinking the Global South," *Journal of Contemporary Thought* (2012) at http://www.globalsouthproject.cornell.edu/rethinking-the-global-south.html; Nour Dados and Raewyn Connell, "The Global South," *Context* 11, no. 1 (2012): 12–13; Anne Garland Mahler, "Global South," *Oxford Bibliographies in Literary and Critical Theory*, ed. Eugene O'Brien (New York: Oxford University Press, 2017).

2. For helpful debates on this see Barbara Ehrenreich, "What Is Socialist Feminism?," *WIN Magazine*, 1976, http://www.marxists.org/subject/women/authors/ehrenreich-barbara/socialist-feminism.htm; and "Forum: Is 'Communist Feminism' a *Contradictio in Terminis*?," *Aspasia* 1 (2007): 197–246.

3. Francisca de Haan, "Continuing Cold War Paradigms in the Western Historiography of Transnational Women's Organisations: The Case of the Women's International Democratic Federation (WIDF)," *Women's History Review*, September 2010, 547–73.

INTRODUCTION

Epigraph: Kate Fleron, *Nord-Korea: Rapporter fra et haerget land* (Copenhagen: Hoffenberg, 1951), 29. I thank Jane Jin Kaisen for sharing her translation of Fleron's text.

1. *Международная женская делегация в Корее* [International women's delegation in Korea] (Moscow: TsSDF, 1951). The Russian State Documentary Film and Photo Archive (Rossiiskii gosudarstvennyi arkhiv kinofotodokumentov, RGAKFD) documents the history of Russian filmmaking starting with the first footage of the 1896 coronation of Czar Nicholas II and includes an almost complete collection of newsreels from 1919 to 1985. See https://www.russianarchives.com/archives/the-russian-state-documentary-film-and-photo-archive/ (accessed September 22, 2021). I thank Owen Miller for directing me to this archive. Clips from this footage are included in the six-part documentary film *Choguk haebang chŏnjaeng* [The fatherland liberation war] (Pyongyang: Korea Film, 1994). Although 1994 is listed on the DVD cover, the actual production date appears closer to the 1970s. The film includes 1950s original wartime footage in black and white.

2. Saidiya Hartman powerfully explores such questions in her histories of transatlantic slavery. See especially her "Venus in Two Acts," *Small Axe* 12, no. 2 (2008): 1–14. In the East Asian context, Ueno Chizuko makes a compelling critique of positivist history in "The Politics of Memory: Nation, Individual and Self," *History and Memory* 11, no. 2 (1999): 129–52.

3. For a cogent critique of Western feminist scholarship see Chandra Mohanty, "Under Western Eyes: Feminist Scholarship and Colonial Discourses," *Feminist Review* 30, no. 1 (Autumn 1988): 61–88.

4. Yu Ho-jun, "Nyŏsŏngdŭl ŭi wanjŏnhan p'yŏngdŭng ŭl wihayŏ" [For the complete equality of women], *Chosŏn Nyŏsŏng*, February 1960, 13.

5. My biography of Pak Chŏng-ae is part of the 2022 volume *The Palgrave Handbook of Communist Women Activists from around the World*, edited by Francisca de Haan, and I thank her for her valuable suggestions and generous support of this project.

For de Haan's inclusion of Pak as part of a transnational feminist network see Francisca de Haan, "Eugénie Cotton, Pak Chong-ae, and Claudia Jones: Rethinking Transnational Feminism and International Politics," *Journal of Women's History* 25 (Winter 2013): 174–89.

6. The collection is officially known as the "Record Seized by the U.S. Military Forces in Korea" and is at the National Archives and Records Administration II. For details about this collection see Thomas Hosuck Kang, "North Korean Captured Records at the Washington National Records Center, Suitland, Maryland," *Committee on East Asian Libraries Bulletin*, no. 58 (1979): 30–37. Some of this archive has been reproduced by Kuksa P'yŏnch'an Wiwŏnhoe (National Institute of Korean History, formerly known as the National History Compilation Committee), in eighty volumes to date, as the *Pukhan kwan'gye saryojip* (Historical materials related to North Korea), published in South Korea.

7. One of the foremost scholars on the Korean communist movement, Dae-sook Suh, explains that there is very little Korean material remaining, and most available sources are from the records of the Japanese police, which must be treated with caution, since they are often the result of torture. See Dae-sook Suh, *The Korean Communist Movement, 1918–1948* (Princeton, NJ: Princeton University Press, 1967), xii–xiii.

8. For a comprehensive treatment of the women's anticolonial movement see Pak Yong-ok, *Han'guk yŏsŏng hang'il undongsa yŏn'gu* [History of the Korean women's anticolonial movement] (Seoul: Chisik sanŏpsa, 1996).

9. For example, see *Tong'a Ilbo*, dated September 23, 1935, and October 5, 1935; *Chosŏn Chung'ang Ilbo*, dated September 23, 1935, and October 5, 1935; *Maeil Sinbo*, dated September 24, 1935; October 5, 1935; and October 6, 1935.

10. "Habibin kŏyu tongp'o yŏsŏng tanch'e chojik" [Harbin resident Koreans organize women's organization], *Tong'a Ilbo*, February 18, 1936. I thank Sunyoung Park for this source and help in finding colonial-era sources on Pak.

11. "P'yŏnghwa wa minju rŭl wihan segye minju nyŏsŏngdŭl kwa ŭi kongdong chŏnsŏn esŏ: Kukje minju nyŏsŏng ryŏnmaeng kaip 3chunyŏn e chehayŏ" [United front with the world democratic women for peace and democracy: On the 3-year anniversary of joining the Women's International Democratic Federation], *Chosŏn Nyŏsŏng*, October 1949, 10–12.

12. Francisca de Haan, "The Women's International Democratic Federation (WIDF): History, Main Agenda, and Contributions, 1945–1991," in *Women and Social Movements, International 1840 to Present*, ed. Kathryn Kish Sklar and Thomas Dublin (Alexandria, VA: Alexander Street, 2012).

13. For details about *Soviet Woman* see Christine Varga-Harris, "Between National Tradition and Western Modernization: *Soviet Woman* and Representations of Socialist Gender Equality as a 'Third Way' for Developing Countries, 1956–1964," *Slavic Review* 78, no. 3 (Fall 2019): 758–81. For *Women of China* see Wang Zheng, "Creating a Socialist Feminist Cultural Front: *Women of China* (1949–1966)," *China Quarterly* 204 (December 2010): 827–49.

14. Amanda Anderson, "Mothers and Labourers: North Korea's Gendered Labour Force in *Women in Korea*," *Journal of History and Cultures* 6 (2016): 14–36.

15. For the significance of internationalism in early state formation see Adam Cathcart and Charles Kraus, "Internationalist Culture in North Korea, 1945–1950," *Review of Korean Studies* 11, no. 3 (September 2008): 123–48. They also note similar iconography of Korean women among international women (127–28).

16. For her date of birth see the September 1957 issue of *Chosŏn Nyŏsŏng*, which begins with a photo spread of Pak's fiftieth birthday celebration on August 23, 1957. There are conflicting sources of information on where she was born, with colonial-era newspapers

noting that she comes from a Soviet Korean peasant family in Vladivostok, whereas later South Korean sources give North Hamgyŏng Province. For various aspects of the northern border area see Sun Joo Kim, ed., *The Northern Region of Korea: History, Identity, and Culture* (Seattle: University of Washington Center for Korea Studies, 2010).

17. *Tong'a Ilbo*, February 11, 1933, quoted in Kang Man-gil, *Ilje sidae pinmin saenghwalsa yŏn'gu* [Study of poor people's everyday life during the colonial period] (Seoul: Ch'angjaksa, 1987), 221.

18. See *Minutes of the National Congress of People's Committee Representatives* (Seoul: Chosŏn chŏngp'ansa, 1946), in *Collection of Modern Korean History Materials*, vol. 12 (Seoul: Tolbaege, 1986), 488. See also Sŏ Tong-man, *Pukchosŏn sahoejuŭi ch'eje sŏngripsa, 1945–1961* [History of the founding of the socialist system in North Korea, 1945–1961] (Seoul: Sŏnin, 2005), 286, 505.

19. Chi Su-gŏl, *Ilje ha nongmin chohap undong yŏn'gu* [Study of the peasant union movement under Japanese colonial rule] (Seoul: Yŏksa pip'yŏngsa, 1993), 118–19. For a full treatment of colonial conditions that would lead to social revolution in Korea see Suzy Kim, *Everyday Life in the North Korean Revolution, 1945–1950* (Ithaca, NY: Cornell University Press, 2013), chap. 2.

20. Andrei Lankov, *From Stalin to Kim Il Sung: The Formation of North Korea 1945–1960* (New Brunswick, NJ: Rutgers University Press, 2002), 114.

21. This information comes from Kim Yong-bŏm's Comintern file available at the Russian State Archive of Socio-political History, RGASPI f. 495, op. 228, d. 418, l. 009. Vladimir Tikhonov kindly shared a copy with an explanation of its contents, as I do not read Russian. I thank him for his generosity.

22. Sŏ Tong-man, *Pukchosŏn sahoejuŭi ch'eje sŏngripsa*, 250. Sŏ distinguishes between factions (*p'a*) and sects (*gye*) to differentiate factions that had a strong sense of cohesion with a clear leadership from the more fluid sects without a leader. For a helpful review of Sŏ's work in English see Kim Seongbo, "The History of the State Socialist System of North Korea Brought to Light through a Wealth of Sources," *Korea Journal* 46, no. 3 (2006): 260–74.

23. For a compelling argument against viewing state socialist women as mere mouthpieces of the party state in the Eastern European context see Kristen Ghodsee, *Second World, Second Sex: Socialist Women's Activism and Global Solidarity during the Cold War* (Durham, NC: Duke University Press, 2019). For my critique of the contemporary Korean context see Suzy Kim, "Women as 'Dupes,' 'Stooges,' and 'Armies of Beauties,'" Periscope: Social Text Online (December 2018), https://socialtextjournal.org/periscope_article/women-as-dupes-stooges-and-armies-of-beauties/.

24. For a comparable socialist feminist who studied at the KUTV between 1925 and 1929 see Lee Sung-woo, "Sahoejuŭi yŏsŏng undongga Ko Myŏng-ja ŭi saeng'ae wa hwaldong" [Socialist woman activist Ko Myungja's life and activity], *Inmunhak yŏn'gu* [Humanities research] 84 (2011): 247–74. Despite similar commitments to communism, Ko Myŏng-ja (1904–?) resurfaced by 1939 in pro-Japanese publications, advocating allegiance to the Japanese Empire in support of *naisen ittai* (Japan and Korea as one body), whereas Pak disappears from public record by 1937. Both Ko and Pak would end up in North Korea after Korean liberation in 1945. For a good overview of Korean socialist women during the Japanese colonial period see Sunyoung Park, "Rethinking Feminism in Colonial Korea: Kang Kyŏngae's Portraits of Proletarian Women," *positions: asia critique* 21, no. 4 (2013): 947–85.

25. Masha Kirasirova, "The 'East' as a Category of Bolshevik Ideology and Comintern Administration: The Arab Section of the Communist University of the Toilers of the East," *Kritika* 18, no. 1 (Winter 2017): 7–34.

26. Kirasirova, 18. As she explains, this ambiguity of the "East" as an ideological category also "allowed KUTV students to position themselves as insiders or outsiders in ways that were unavailable to Soviet and other Western foreign Communists" (33).

27. Courtney Sato, "'A Picture of Peace': Friendship in Interwar Pacific Women's Internationalism," *Qui Parle: Critical Humanities and Social Sciences* 27, no. 2 (2018): 480. See also Rumi Yasutake, *Transnational Women's Activism: The United States, Japan, and Japanese Immigrant Communities in California, 1859–1920* (New York: NYU Press, 2004).

28. Joyce Goodman, "International Women's Organizations, Peace and Peacebuilding," in *The Palgrave Handbook of Global Approaches to Peace*, ed. Aigul Kulnazarova and Vesselin Popovski (Cham, Switzerland: Palgrave Macmillan, 2019), 445. One of the first Korean women to receive a doctorate, Kim Hwal-lan (Helen Kim), was active in the IFUW (see chapter 2).

29. Woodford McClellan, "Africans and Black Americans in the Comintern Schools, 1925–1934," *International Journal of African Historical Studies* 26, no. 2 (1993): 377. As McClellan explains, the Soviet leadership had no clear program for eradicating discrimination, whether for its own minorities or for the Black students at the Comintern schools, but "so far as the Comintern schools were concerned, the atmosphere for blacks, if far from ideal, ranked as the best anywhere in the world from both the educational and the personal standpoint. No other country then offered blacks such opportunities" (387). See also Heather Ashby, "Third World Activists and the Communist University of the Toilers of the East" (PhD diss., University of Southern California, 2014).

30. Robeson Taj Frazier, *The East Is Black: Cold War China in the Black Radical Imagination* (Durham, NC: Duke University Press, 2014), 48–49.

31. On the shifting Soviet perspectives on Korea see Vladimir Tikhonov, "Korea in the Russian and Soviet Imagination, 1850s–1945: Between Orientalism and Revolutionary Solidarity," *Journal of Korean Studies* 21, no. 2 (2016): 385–421. For a critical study showing continuities in czarist racial legacies that carried into the Soviet nationalities policy, resulting in the Korean deportation, see Jon K. Chang, *Burnt by the Sun: The Koreans of the Russian Far East* (Honolulu: University of Hawai'i Press, 2016).

32. Francine Hirsch, *Empire of Nations: Ethnographic Knowledge and the Making of the Soviet Union* (Ithaca, NY: Cornell University Press, 2005), 7–9.

33. Vladimir Tikhonov, "Demystifying the Nation: The Communist Concept of Ethno-nation in 1920s–1930s Korea," *Cross-Currents: East Asian History and Culture Review* (e-journal) 28 (2018): 69–92.

34. Kim Kuk-hwa, "Tongbang noryŏkja kongsan taehak Chosŏn hakpu yŏn'gu (1924–25-nyŏn)" [A study on the Korean group of KUTV, 1924–25], *Inmun kwahak* [Humanities science] 57 (2015): 176–206. This study is based on the Comintern archives, looking specifically at the large cohort of Koreans at the KUTV in 1924–25, to show the expulsion of a number of Korean students as a result of factionalism and disagreements in the process of organizing the KCP. As a result, over twenty students were expelled from some one hundred Korean students at the KUTV in this period (185, 195). For information on the formation of the first KCP within Korea and the role of the KUTV graduates see Suh, *Korean Communist Movement*, esp. 68–72, 102–8. For earlier attempts to form the KCP by Korean émigrés in the Russian Far East with rival factions in Shanghai and Irkutsk see Suh, chapters 1 and 2.

35. Suh, *Korean Communist Movement*, 103.

36. Suh, 111. For more on the challenges of finding sources on the Korean communist movement and an assessment of Suh's use of sources see Kentarō Yamabe, "A Note on the Korean Communist Movement by Dae-sook Suh: With Special Reference to Source Materials Used," *Developing Economies* 5, no. 2 (June 1967): 405–12. Yamabe's discussion

of the various Comintern directives that resulted in the December Theses can be found on page 409. For the important role that factional debates played in defining communist tactics such as the role of the vanguard, united front, and agents of revolution under Korean conditions see Vladimir Tikhonov, "The Issue of Factionalism in the Korean Communist Movement of the 1920s–early 1930s," *Marŭk'ŭsŭjuŭi yŏn'gu* [Marxism 21] 15, no. 2 (2018): 152–83.

37. Suh, *Korean Communist Movement*, 193–99.

38. Suh, 196.

39. Kim Kyŏng-il, *Iljeha nodong undongsa* [History of labor movements under Japanese imperialism] (Seoul: Ch'angjak kwa pip'yŏngsa, 1992), 26, 124–26. As Kim makes clear, as a result of severe colonial oppression that shifted open and legal labor organizing in the 1920s to the underground in the 1930s, the red labor unions and other revolutionary labor unions that made up the bulk of labor organizing in the 1930s left very few records, except for the occasional news article or police and court records (29fn2). By the late 1930s, many of the recognized organizers and activists from the earlier period had been imprisoned or co-opted by colonial authorities (31).

40. Kim Kyŏng-il, *Iljeha nodong undongsa*, 124–26.

41. Yŏsŏngsa yŏn'gu moim Kilbak sesang, "Ŭlmildae wiŭi t'usa, Kang Chu-ryong: 1931-nyŏn P'yŏngwŏn komu kongjang p'aŏp" [Warrior atop the Ŭlmil Pavilion, Kang Chu-ryong], in *20-segi yŏsŏng sagŏnsa* [Twentieth-century women's history] (Seoul: Yŏsŏng sinmunsa, 2001), 90–99. For more on Kang and the lasting significance of her high-altitude protest see Hwasook Nam, *Women in the Sky: Gender and Labor in the Making of Modern Korea* (Ithaca, NY: Cornell University Press, 2021).

42. Ri Tong-hŭi, "Pyongyang ŭi ttal Kang Chu-ryong" [Daughter of Pyongyang Kang Chu-ryong], *Chosŏn Nyŏsŏng*, August 1964, 14–15; Kim Yŏng-gŭn, "Rodong kyegŭp ŭi ttal Kang Chu-ryong nyŏsŏng" [Daughter of the working class Kang Chu-ryong], *Chosŏn Nyŏsŏng*, August 1959, 26–28.

43. This brief résumé was compiled from multiple sources, including announcements in *Chosŏn Nyŏsŏng* and *Rodong Sinmun*, along with information from secondary sources using Soviet documents: Lankov, *From Stalin to Kim Il Sung*, and Sŏ Tong-man, *Pukchosŏn sahoejuŭi ch'eje sŏngripsa*.

44. For a biography of Hŏ Chŏng-suk see Ruth Barraclough, "Red Love and Betrayal in the Making of North Korea: Comrade Hŏ Jŏng-suk," *History Workshop Journal* 77 (Spring 2014): 86–102.

45. Sŏ Tong-man, *Pukchosŏn sahoejuŭi ch'eje sŏngripsa*, 114–15.

46. For details of this bottom-up process of social revolution see Suzy Kim, *Everyday Life in the North Korean Revolution*.

47. Kim, *Everyday Life in the North Korean Revolution*, 116–17. In this previous work I translated the name as the Korean Democratic Women's League but have opted to use in this book the Korean Democratic Women's Union, as this is its own English rendition.

48. Yi Im-ha, *Haebang konggan, ilsang ŭl pakkun yŏsŏngdŭl ŭi yŏksa* [Liberated space: Women's history of changes in everyday life] (Seoul: Ch'ŏlsu wa yŏnghŭi, 2015), 322.

49. Yi Im-ha, 321–22.

50. For a biography of Yu Yŏng-jun see Kim Sŏng-dong, "Yŏmaeng wiwŏnjang Yu Yŏng-jun" [Chair of women's union Yu Yŏng-jun], *Chugan Kyŏnghyang* [Weekly Kyunghyang], February 10, 2009, at http://weekly.khan.co.kr/khnm.html?mode=view&art_id=19264. Sources from South Korea do not provide the year of her death, but her obituary was published in North Korea in 1972. See "Ryu Yŏng-jun tongji ŭi sŏgŏ e taehan pugo" [Obituary on the death of Comrade Yu Yŏng-jun], *Rodong Sinmun*, September 19, 1972, 3. For a biography of Chŏng Ch'il-sŏng see Roh Jiseung, "Chendŏ, nodong, kamjŏng kŭrigo chŏngch'ijŏk kaksŏng ŭi sun'gan—yŏsŏng sahoejuŭija Chŏng Ch'il-sŏng

ŭi sam kwa hwaldong e taehan yŏn'gu" [Gender, labor, emotion, and moment of political awakening—a study on life and activities of female socialist Chung Chil-sung], *Pigyo munhwa yŏn'gu* [Comparative cultural studies] 43 (2016): 7–50.

51. Yi Sŭng-hŭi, *Han'guk hyŏndae yŏsŏng undongsa* [History of the women's movement in modern Korea] (Seoul: Paeksan sŏdang, 1994), 65–75.

52. Suzy Kim, "Revolutionary Mothers: Women in the North Korean Revolution, 1945–1950," *Comparative Studies in Society and History* 52, no. 4 (October 2010): 751–52.

53. Monica Felton, *That's Why I Went* (London: Lawrence & Wishart, 1953), 105.

54. A 2019 electronic search of Pak through the digital database of North Korean publications dating back to 1950 at the Information Center on North Korea in Seoul led to 259 results between March 1950 and August 1965, more than half of them, or 153 articles, dated between 1950 and 1953. Half of these pertained to the Stalin Peace Prize awarded to Pak in 1951 (see chapter 2). According to the database, there were no further published references to Pak after 1965.

55. On the politics of 1967 see James F. Person, "The 1967 Purge of the Gapsan Faction and Establishment of the Monolithic Ideological System," North Korea International Documentation Project E-Dossier No. 15, at https://www.wilsoncenter.org/publication/the-1967-purge-the-gapsan-faction-and-establishment-the-monolithic-ideological-system.

56. Andrei Lankov, *Crisis in North Korea: The Failure of De-Stalinization, 1956* (Honolulu: University of Hawai'i Press, 2005); Balázs Szalontai, *Kim Il Sung in the Khrushchev Era: Soviet-DPRK Relations and the Roots of North Korean Despotism, 1953–1964* (Palo Alto, CA: Stanford University Press, 2005). James Person argues that the 1956 challenge was not a real threat but provided the pretext to purge from the party ranks over three thousand people with Soviet or Chinese ties. See James F. Person, "North Korea in 1956: Reconsidering the August Plenum and the Sino-Soviet Joint Intervention," *Cold War History* 19, no. 2 (2019): 271.

57. For a biography of Im Sun-dŭk and the significance of her work see Yi Sang-gyŏng, *Im Sun-dŭk, taeanjŏk yŏsŏng chuch'e rŭl hyanghayŏ* [Im Sun-dŭk, toward an alternative women's subjectivity] (Seoul: Somyŏng, 2009).

58. "Ch'oego inmin hoeŭi sŏn'gŏ esŏ sŭngrihan kiserŭl sahoejuŭi kŏnsŏl ero! Choguk ŭi p'yŏnghwajŏk t'ong'il talsŏng ero!" [Put the successful momentum from the Supreme People's Assembly elections to socialist construction! To achieve the peaceful unification of the homeland!], *Chosŏn Nyŏsŏng*, September 1957, 2–4.

59. "Kŭnŭn taeŭiwŏn i toeŏtta" [They became Supreme People's Assembly representatives], *Chosŏn Nyŏsŏng*, October 1962, 2.

60. Sŏng Hye-rang, *Tŭngnamujip* [Wisteria tree house] (Seoul: Chisik nara, 2001), 323. Written by the personal tutor to Kim Jong Il's first son, the memoir provides useful insights into Korean society, and especially the intimate life of the Kim family in the years between 1976 and 1996, but is less reliable for the earlier years regarding facts to which the author did not have direct access and is therefore based on conjecture. The author attributes the lack of a second generation of women leaders to Pak's "jealousy" of other women that prevented her from sharing the spotlight, pointing to the author's own mother Kim Wŏn-ju, who as a journalist by training was one of the early female writers in colonial Korea and yet was overlooked from leadership positions. The author argues that Pak's downfall was due to Kim Sŏng-ae, the second wife of Kim Il Sung, who became the most prominent female figure beginning in the early 1970s. Originally from Seoul, the author's family moved to the North during the Korean War.

61. This is included in a video biography of Pak produced by historian German Nikolaevich Kim, available at https://www.youtube.com/watch?v=p-yqFdvYPl4. I thank Vladimir Tikhonov for this reference. A 1994 KBS News broadcast mentions that Pak died at

the age of eighty in 1987, but no evidence is given. See http://mn.kbs.co.kr/news/view.do?ncd=3742750. I thank Sunyoung Park for this reference.

62. Pak Yŏng-ja, *Pukhan nyŏja: T'ansaeng kwa kuljŏl ŭi 70-nyŏnsa* [North Korean women: 70-year history of birth and refraction] (Seoul: Aelp'i, 2017), 6.

63. Pak Yŏng-ja's *Pukhan nyŏja* is an example, but there are many others.

64. Donna Harsch, *Revenge of the Domestic: Women, the Family, and Communism in the German Democratic Republic* (Princeton, NJ: Princeton University Press, 2007), 11.

65. Harsch, 312–13.

66. Wang Zheng, *Finding Women in the State: A Socialist Feminist Revolution in the People's Republic of China, 1949–1964* (Oakland: University of California Press, 2017), 17–18.

67. For challenges in this kind of research, with the scattered archives requiring multilingual skills, see Kristen Ghodsee, "Research Note: The Historiographical Challenges of Exploring Second World–Third World Alliances in the International Women's Movement," *Global Social Policy* 14, no. 2 (2014): 244–64.

68. Jay Song and Steven Denney, "Studying North Korea through North Korean Migrants: Lessons from the Field," *Critical Asian Studies* 51, no. 3 (2019): 451–66. Nonetheless, for examples of what oral history can offer see Pak Yŏng-ja's *Pukhan nyŏja*; Cho Young-Ju, "Pukhan yŏsŏng ŭi silch'ŏn kwa chendŏ rejim ŭi tonghak" [The practice of women and dynamics of gender regime in North Korea] (PhD diss., Ewha Women's University, 2012); and An T'ae-yun, "Pukhan yŏsŏngdŭri kyŏkkŭn Han'guk chŏnjaeng" [North Korean women's wartime experiences during the Korean War], *Yŏsŏng kwa yŏksa* [Women and history] 20 (2014): 178–213.

69. *International Women's Delegation in Korea* (see note 1 above). The film of the commission's visit covers the official receptions, including speeches and exchanges of gifts in the extensive underground bunkers used as North Korean military headquarters during the war.

70. Maria Bucur, "Women and State Socialism: Failed Promises and Radical Changes Revisited," *Nationalities Papers* 44, no. 5 (2016): 855.

71. Amy Borovoy and Kristen Ghodsee, "Decentering Agency in Feminist Theory: Recuperating the Family as a Social Project," *Women's Studies International Forum* 35 (2012): 153–65. The authors examine examples of women's social advancement achieved through their membership in family and community as mothers, wives, and caregivers, referred to in US feminist debates as "social feminism" or "difference feminism" (156). Korean emphasis on the family as the "cell" of society is therefore not a Confucian legacy, but rather a global phenomenon (a point I return to in the concluding chapter).

72. *Women of the Whole World*, May 1958, n.p. Although the Federation's efforts to publish in Arabic had limited success initially, order forms for the magazine available in the WIDF collection at the International Institute of Social History indicate that by 1969, when the Federation's UN consultative status with ECOSOC was upgraded to *A*, there was an Arabic edition of the magazine.

73. The three other major international women's organizations were "bourgeois and dominated by women of European origin," according to Leila Rupp. The International Woman Suffrage Alliance, formed in 1904, launched *Jus Suffragii* in 1906, which became the *International Women's News* in 1930. The International Council of Women, founded in 1881, began publishing its *Bulletin* in 1922, and the Women's International League for Peace and Freedom, formed in 1915, issued *Pax* in 1925. But concerns about circulation figures and publishing costs plagued all three, especially during the Depression. At its height, *Pax* was published in English, German, and French, with a circulation of approximately three thousand. See Leila J. Rupp, *Worlds of Women: The Making of an International Women's Movement* (Princeton, NJ: Princeton University Press, 1997), 5, 175–77.

74. Barbara Wiseman, "The Women's Press of Great Britain," *Women of the Whole World*, April 1954, 20.

75. "Our Press," *Women of the Whole World*, May 1954, 7.

76. Eugénie Cotton, "The Leading Educational Role of Our Press," *Women of the Whole World*, May 1954, 8.

77. "The Editors Speak," *Women of the Whole World*, May 1954, 9.

78. "Editors Speak," 10.

79. Marie-Claude Vaillant-Couturier, "The Task of Our Publications," *Women of the Whole World*, May 1954, 11.

80. "For a Women's Press Worthy of Its Readers," *Women of the Whole World*, March 1954, 15.

81. Grazia Cesarini, "Italy: The Meeting of Canvassers," *Women of the Whole World*, March 1956, 20–21.

82. "Women Write to Us," *Women of the Whole World*, June 1956, 23 (emphasis in original).

83. "Women Write to Us," *Women of the Whole World*, October 1956, 23.

84. "Women Write to Us," *Women of the Whole World*, February 1957, 23.

85. "Women Write to Us," *Women of the Whole World*, January 1957, 23.

86. Most WIDF and its affiliate organizational documents used in the book come from the Women's International Democratic Federation Sophia Smith Collection, Smith College, Northampton, Massachusetts, and the *Women and Social Movements, International—1840 to Present*, ed. Kathryn Kish Sklar and Thomas Dublin, also known as the WASI digital database of primary materials related to the international women's movements. For details about this collection see Kathryn Kish Sklar and Thomas Dublin, "About Women and Social Movements, International," http://search.alexanderstreet.com/wasi/about. These are supplemented by the WIDF Collection at the International Institute of Social History, especially documents related to the 1969 and the 1975 congresses discussed in the conclusion. On the difficulties, as well as unexpected surprises, in finding WIDF-related archives see Francisca de Haan, "Research Experiences," United Nations History Project, at http://unhistoryproject.org/research/research_experiences-haan.html.

87. I have opted to use the revised South Korean romanization of her name in the rest of the book in order to reduce diacritical marks and to follow the convention of the majority of recent publications on her.

88. Anthropologist Lisa Yoneyama has used the term "Cold War feminism" to refer to liberal feminist understandings of "gender justice," a concept that was used to justify US occupation and intervention after World War II; from the 1945–1952 occupation of Japan to the 2003 Operation Iraqi Freedom, these actions were framed as "liberating" oppressed women. See Lisa Yoneyama, *Cold War Ruins: Transpacific Critique of American Justice and Japanese War Crimes* (Durham, NC: Duke University Press, 2016), chap. 2, 81–110. In this regard, sociologist Mire Koikari specifically refers to Cold War imperial feminism. See Mire Koikari, *Pedagogy of Democracy: Feminism and the Cold War in the U.S. Occupation of Japan* (Philadelphia: Temple University Press, 2008), 5.

1. WOMEN AGAINST THE KOREAN WAR

1. *As One! For Equality, for Happiness, for Peace: World Congress of Women, Copenhagen, June 5–10, 1953* (Berlin: WIDF, 1953), 35.

2. *As One!*, 252–53.

3. Instead of a comprehensive list, because of the limitations of space I cite the main representative scholarship to depict the 1950s in the United States as largely a period of

retrenchment. See Elaine Tyler May, *Homeward Bound: American Families in the Cold War Era* (1988; repr. New York: Basic Books, 2008), and Lawrence S. Wittner, *Rebels against War: The American Peace Movement, 1933–1983* (Philadelphia: Temple University Press, 1984), who concludes that the outbreak of the Korean War in June 1950 "dealt the final hammerblow [sic] to the fragile postwar peace movement," 201.

4. Wittner, *Rebels against War*, 203.

5. Kate Weigand, Erik McDuffie, Dayo Gore, and Jacqueline Castledine are among those who have previously challenged the "containment" thesis, but Castledine places peace at the center of progressive activism in addition to racial and gender issues. See Jacqueline Castledine, *Cold War Progressives: Women's Interracial Organizing for Peace and Freedom* (Champaign: University of Illinois Press, 2012), 4. For emphasis on Asian actors neither as victims nor puppets but as having "critical *reverse* impact on the Cold War" see Tuong Vu and Wasana Wongsurawat, eds., *Dynamics of the Cold War in Asia: Ideology, Identity, and Culture* (New York: Palgrave Macmillan, 2009).

6. For an account emphasizing the civil origins of the war see Bruce Cumings, *Origins of the Korean War*, vol. 1, *Liberation and the Emergence of Separate Regimes, 1945–1947* (Princeton, NJ: Princeton University Press, 1981), and vol. 2, *The Roaring of the Cataract, 1947–1950* (Princeton, NJ: Princeton University Press, 1990), and for a focus on international relations see William Stueck, *The Korean War: An International History* (Princeton, NJ: Princeton University Press, 1995). For a North Korea focus see Avram Agov, "North Korea's Alliances and the Unfinished Korean War," *Journal of Korean Studies* 18, no. 2 (2013): 225–62. For the South Korean situation see Su-kyoung Hwang, *Korea's Grievous War* (Philadelphia: University of Pennsylvania Press, 2016), and Heonik Kwon, *After the Korean War: An Intimate History* (New York: Cambridge University Press, 2020). For the Chinese perspective see Chen Jian, *China's Road to the Korean War: The Making of the Sino-American Confrontation* (New York: Columbia University Press, 1996), and Shen Zhihua, *Mao, Stalin and the Korean War: Trilateral Communist Relations in the 1950s*, trans. Neil Silver (New York: Routledge, 2012). For multiple transnational dimensions of the Korean War see Tessa Morris-Suzuki, ed., *The Korean War in Asia: A Hidden History* (New York: Rowman & Littlefield, 2018). For treatment of the stakes of the prisoner-of-war question that dragged on the armistice negotiations for two years see Monica Kim, *The Interrogation Rooms of the Korean War: The Untold History* (Princeton, NJ: Princeton University Press, 2019), and David Cheng Chang, *The Hijacked War: The Story of Chinese POWs in the Korean War* (Palo Alto, CA: Stanford University Press, 2020).

7. For social histories of the Korean War and its aftermath produced by South Korean scholars in English see Dong-choon Kim, *The Unending Korean War: A Social History* (Larkspur, CA: Tamal Vista, 2009); Lee Im Ha, "The Korean War and the Role of Women," *Review of Korean Studies* 9 (June 2006): 89–110; Kim Seong-nae, "Lamentations of the Dead: The Historical Imagery of Violence on Cheju Island, South Korea," *Journal of Ritual Studies* 3, no. 2 (1989): 251–85. Additional sources in Korean on the war's impact on women include Kim Kwi-ok, "Han'guk chŏnjaenggi Han'guk-gun e ŭihan sŏngp'okryŏk ŭi yuhyŏng kwa hamŭi" [Patterns and implications of sexual violence by the Korean military during the Korean War], *Kusulsa yŏn'gu* [Oral history studies] 3, no. 2 (2012): 7–37; and Park Jeong-Mi, "Han'guk chŏnjaenggi sŏngmaemae chŏngch'aek e kwanhan yŏn'gu: Wianso wa wianbu rŭl chungsim ŭro" [A study on prostitution policies during the Korean War: Focusing on comfort stations and comfort women], *Han'guk yŏsŏnghak* [Journal of Korean Women's Studies] 27, no. 2 (2011): 35–72.

8. Hajimu Masuda, *Cold War Crucible: The Korean Conflict and the Postwar World* (Cambridge, MA: Harvard University Press, 2015).

9. Masuda, 1.

10. Kim Tong-ch'un, *Chŏnjaeng kwa sahoe* [War and society] (P'aju, South Korea: Dolbegae, 2016).

11. Marjorie Lansing, "Women's Power," *New York Times*, September 25, 1980, A27. Perhaps not coincidentally, Lansing was active in the Progressive Party in the 1940s and '50s as noted by Castledine, *Cold War Progressives*, 142.

12. Castledine, *Cold War Progressives*, 1.

13. Francisca de Haan, "Continuing Cold War Paradigms in the Western Historiography of Transnational Women's Organisations: The Case of the Women's International Democratic Federation (WIDF)," *Women's History Review* 19, no. 4 (September 2010): 547–73; Erik S. McDuffie, *Sojourning for Freedom: Black Women, American Communism, and the Making of Black Left Feminism* (Durham, NC: Duke University Press, 2011); Castledine, *Cold War Progressives*; Celia Donert, "From Communist Internationalism to Human Rights: Gender, Violence and International Law in the Women's International Democratic Federation Mission to North Korea, 1951," *Contemporary European History* 25 (2016): 313–33. While Donert emphasizes the importance of communist internationalism in the development of human rights, I use the example of women's solidarity during the Korean War to show how communist internationalism recognized *difference* rather than appealing to universalized notions of human rights.

14. This debate has a long history, but for a helpful introduction see Anne C. Herrmann and Abigail J. Stewart, eds., *Theorizing Feminism: Parallel Trends in the Humanities and Social Sciences* (Boulder, CO: Westview, 2001). For a history of how vernacular sociology and commercial advertising in the age of industrial capitalism led to the "event of women" as a sexually differentiated being see Tani Barlow, *In the Event of Women* (Durham, NC: Duke University Press, 2022).

15. Kate Weigand, *Red Feminism: American Communism and the Making of Women's Liberation* (Baltimore: Johns Hopkins University Press, 2001), 24. Weigand's history of American feminism shows the extent to which socialist feminism and its critique of race, gender, and class in the 1940s and 1950s laid the foundation for the 1960s. This continuity has been erased both by feminists who wanted nothing to do with the history of communism, as well as by communism that officially denounced feminism as a "bourgeois degeneracy."

16. Castledine, *Cold War Progressives*, 44.

17. For example, see Leila J. Rupp, *Worlds of Women: The Making of an International Women's Movement* (Princeton, NJ: Princeton University Press, 1997); Amy Swerdlow, *Women Strike for Peace: Traditional Motherhood and Radical Politics in the 1960s* (Chicago: University of Chicago Press, 1993); Harriet Hyman Alonso, *Peace as a Women's Issue: A History of the U.S. Movement for World Peace and Women's Rights* (Syracuse, NY: Syracuse University Press, 1993); Wendy Pojmann, "For Mothers, Peace and Family: International (Non)-Cooperation among Italian Catholic and Communist Women's Organisations during the Early Cold War," *Gender & History* 23, no. 2 (August 2011): 415–29; Catia Cecilia Confortini, *Intelligent Compassion: Feminist Critical Methodology in the Women's International League for Peace and Freedom* (New York: Oxford University Press, 2012). For an alternative account of the hollowness of claims to global maternalism and international solidarity among "free" and "independent" voluntary associations during the Cold War, as shown by the collusion between US women's organizations and the CIA, see Helen Laville, *Cold War Women: The International Activities of American Women's Organisations* (Manchester: Manchester University Press, 2002). For theorization of maternalism as transcending biological motherhood see Sara Ruddick, *Maternal Thinking: Toward a Politics of Peace* (Boston: Beacon, 1989). As a feminist philosopher, Ruddick refers to "maternal

thinking" to describe the kind of praxis that arises from caring labor, a human activity that transcends gender but has come to be associated with femininity and motherhood owing to historical developments.

18. Bruce Cumings, *Parallax Visions: Making Sense of American–East Asian Relations* (Durham, NC: Duke University Press, 1999), 51.

19. Francisca de Haan, "The Women's International Democratic Federation (WIDF): History, Main Agenda, and Contributions, 1945–1991," in *Women and Social Movements, International 1840 to Present*, ed. Kathryn Kish Sklar and Thomas Dublin (Alexandria, VA: Alexander Street, 2012), http://wasi.alexanderstreet.com.proxy.libraries.rutgers.edu/help/view/the_womens_international_democratic_federation_widf_history_main_agenda_and_contributions_19451991.

20. Melanie Ilic, "Soviet Women, Cultural Exchange and the Women's International Democratic Federation," in *Reassessing Cold War Europe*, ed. Sari Autio-Sarasmo and Katalin Miklóssy (New York: Routledge, 2010), 157–74; Jadwiga E. Pieper Mooney, "Fighting Fascism and Forging New Political Activism: The Women's International Democratic Federation (WIDF) in the Cold War," in *De-centering Cold War History: Local and Global Change*, ed. Jadwiga E. Pieper Mooney and Fabio Lanza (New York: Routledge, 2013), 52–72; Katharine E. McGregor, "The Cold War, Indonesian Women and the Global Anti-imperialist Movement, 1946–65," in Pieper Mooney and Lanza, *De-centering Cold War History*, 31–51; Elisabeth Armstrong, "Before Bandung: The Anti-imperialist Women's Movement in Asia and the Women's International Democratic Federation," *Signs: Journal of Women in Culture and Society* 41 (2016): 305–31; Donert, "From Communist Internationalism to Human Rights"; Katharine McGregor, "Opposing Colonialism: The Women's International Democratic Federation and Decolonisation Struggles in Vietnam and Algeria 1945–1965," *Women's History Review* 25, no. 6 (2016): 925–44; and Yulia Gradskova, *The Women's International Democratic Federation, the Global South, and the Cold War: Defending the Rights of Women of the "Whole World"?* (New York: Routledge, 2021).

21. Fédération Démocratique Internationale des Femmes, *Congrès International des Femmes, compte rendu des travaux du congrès qui s'est tenu à Paris du 26 Novembre au 1ᵉʳ Décembre 1945* (Paris, 1946). For an abridged Korean edition see *Kukje minju yŏsŏng yŏnmaeng taehoe munhŏnjip* [Documents of the Women's International Democratic Federation Congress] (Pyongyang: Chosŏn yŏsŏngsa, 1947).

22. Eugénie Cotton, "I Work at the WIDF Just as I Did at the Sèvres Institute, for the Complete Emancipation of Women," *Women of the Whole World*, June 1958, 17.

23. Armstrong, "Before Bandung," 320.

24. Confortini, *Intelligent Compassion*, 30, 37–38, 125.

25. Armstrong, "Before Bandung," 322–23.

26. Committee on Un-American Activities, US House of Representatives, *Report on the Congress of American Women* (October 23, 1949; repr., Washington, DC: Government Printing Office, 1950), 1.

27. Castledine, *Cold War Progressives*, 45.

28. "Report by Muriel Draper," Information Bulletin on the 2nd International Congress of Women, no. 3 (WIDF, 1948), 5. For more on Black women's leadership in CAW see Dayo F. Gore, *Radicalism at the Crossroads: African American Women Activists in the Cold War* (New York: NYU Press, 2011), chapter 2.

29. *What Is the Congress of American Women*, pamphlet, n.d.

30. *Bulletin of the Congress of American Women*, October 1946, 2.

31. "Congress of American Women," Information Bulletin no. 37 (June 1949), 14.

32. *Information Bulletin on the 2nd International Congress of Women*, no. 3 (WIDF, 1948), 3.

33. *Information Bulletin on the 2nd International Congress of Women*, no. 3 (WIDF, 1948), 3.

34. M. Makarova, "Kukje minju nyŏsŏng tongmaeng taehoe esŏ" [At the Congress of the Women's International Democratic Federation], *Chosŏn Nyŏsŏng*, January 1949, 26.

35. Pieper Mooney, "Fighting Fascism," 55–56. Pieper Mooney explains that some of the bias against the WIDF was the result of conflations with the Soviet "peace offensive." For the variety of women's organizations that took part in the WIDF see 60–61. For an example of scholarship based on Soviet sources that criticizes the WIDF for the superficiality of its anticolonial position that did not translate to actual decision-making power for Third World women in the organization see Yulia Gradskova, "Women's International Democratic Federation, the 'Third World' and the Global Cold War from the Late-1950s to the Mid-1960s," *Women's History Review* 29, no. 2 (2020): 270–88. Like any record, archival sources privilege their authors, and Soviet sources are bound to ascribe greater weight and power to their own agents and institutions. A more nuanced approach is taken in her monograph, where she argues that despite the lack of commitment to Third World independence in its early years and attempts by the Soviet Ministry of Foreign Affairs and the Communist Party to exert control through the Soviet Women's Committee representative at the WIDF Secretariat, the diversity in membership and increasing power of Third World women gave the Federation autonomy, with a level of independence in its work. See Gradskova, *Women's International Democratic Federation*.

36. De Haan, "Women's International Democratic Federation (WIDF)," 1. For a good overview of the Federation's work between 1945 and 1985 see *Women's International Democratic Federation: Published for the 40th Anniversary of the Founding of the WIDF* (Berlin: WIDF, n.d.). According to the latter anniversary publication, World Congresses were distinct from WIDF congresses, although the two were often organized together. With the exception of the 1945 founding congress and the congresses in 1948 and 1958, all other congresses were held together.

37. For 1945, see Fédération Démocratique Internationale des Femmes, *Congrès International des Femmes*, 403–8; for 1948, see Women's International Democratic Federation, *Second Women's International Congress in Budapest (Hungary) from 1st to the 6th of December 1948* (Paris, 1949). The election of Pak and Yu to the executive committee can be found on page 555. Representing the North was Cho Yŏng (identified as Tcho En). Her speech highlighted progress made in North Korea with Soviet support (166–72), while Yu (identified as Yu Yen-dun or You Yen Dun), representing the South Korea League of Democratic Women (that is, the KDWU southern branch), detailed oppressive conditions in South Korea under the US occupation forces, requesting the WIDF to send a fact-finding mission to call for the withdrawal of US forces from Korea (512–16).

38. Ilic, "Soviet Women, Cultural Exchange," 160.

39. The Federation was governed by a triennial (later, every five to six years) international congress. The size and voting power of each national delegation was based on proportional representation of its national population. The antifascist principle was dropped during the 1958 congress. See De Haan, "Women's International Democratic Federation (WIDF)," endnote 44.

40. Lothar Roher, Rolf Jubisch, and Werner Gerwinski, eds., *10th Anniversary of the Women's International Democratic Federation* (Berlin: WIDF, 1955), 10.

41. *For Their Rights as Mothers, Workers, Citizens* (Berlin: WIDF, 1952), 3. The publication is a good example of Cold War feminism from the other side, in which the "liberated" women of the Second World are contrasted against the "oppressed" women of the West, especially highlighting the oppression of African American women.

42. Roher, Jubisch, and Gerwinski, *10th Anniversary*, 8.

43. In 2002, the WIDF relocated to São Paolo, headed by Brazilian president Marcia Campos. See De Haan, "Women's International Democratic Federation," endnote 75.

44. *We Accuse! Report of the Commission of the Women's International Democratic Federation in Korea, May 16 to 27, 1951* (Berlin: WIDF, 1951).

45. Dora Russell Grace, "At the UNO Economic and Social Council," *Women of the Whole World*, May 1954, 12, emphasis in original.

46. Grace, 13.

47. WIDF Bureau Meeting, Berlin, June 14–17, 1968, *Documents and Information* 9 (Berlin: WIDF, 1968), appendix 1–2.

48. *As One!*, 257.

49. *Women of the Whole World*, February 1951, 50–65.

50. Marie-Claude Vaillant-Couturier, "Democratic Federation in Realising the World Peace Congress," *Women of the Whole World*, February 1951, 5.

51. Gowgiel and other members of Save Our Sons Committee came under investigation by the HUAC in 1956, falsely accused of being a Communist "front" by an FBI informant. See "Investigation of Communist Propaganda among Prisoners of War in Korea (Save Our Sons Committee)," *Hearings before the Committee on Un-American Activities, House of Representatives, 84th Congress, Second Session, June 18 and 19, 1956* (Washington, DC: Government Printing Office, 1956), 5087–91, 5111–47.

52. *Special Information Bulletin Preparing for the World Congress of Women*, no. 4 (April 8, 1953), 4.

53. Betty Millard, "On the Edge of the Precipice, the American People Awake," *Women of the Whole World*, February 1951, 26.

54. Betty Millard, *Women on Guard: How the Women of the World Fight for Peace* (New York: New Century, 1952), 29; Committee on Un-American Activities, US House of Representatives, *Report on the Communist "Peace" Offensive: A Campaign to Disarm and Defeat the United States* (Washington, DC: Government Printing Office, April 1, 1951), 75.

55. Alonso, *Peace as a Women's Issue*, 190–91.

56. *Special Information Bulletin Preparing for the World Congress of Women*, no. 7 (May 8, 1953), 1.

57. Millard, *Women on Guard*, 30.

58. Castledine, *Cold War Progressives*, 78. Robeson Taj Frazier, *The East Is Black: Cold War China in the Black Radical Imagination* (Durham, NC: Duke University Press, 2014), 78–80.

59. Gore, *Radicalism at the Crossroads*; McDuffie, *Sojourning for Freedom*, 22. For earlier works showing how anticolonial critique linking racism at home with imperialism abroad was domesticated by US government prosecution of African Americans while advancing civil rights reforms see Penny M. Von Eschen, *Race against Empire: Black Americans and Anticolonialism, 1937–1957* (Ithaca, NY: Cornell University Press, 1997), and Mary L. Dudziak, *Cold War Civil Rights: Race and the Image of American Democracy* (Princeton, NJ: Princeton University Press, 2000).

60. McDuffie, *Sojourning for Freedom*, 173.

61. Committee on Un-American Activities, US House of Representatives, *Report on the Communist "Peace" Offensive*, 51–53.

62. Herbert Goldhamer, *The 1951 Korean Armistice Conference: A Personal Memoir* (Santa Monica, CA: RAND, 1994), 159. This publication is based on a transcription of Goldhamer's observations with the US/UN armistice negotiation team in 1951, classified until 1971.

63. Goldhamer, 161.

64. Rosemary Foot, *A Substitute for Victory: The Politics of Peacemaking at the Korean Armistice Talks* (Ithaca, NY: Cornell University Press, 1990), 14.
65. Roher, Jubisch and Gerwinski, *10th Anniversary*, 32.
66. *The Children of Korea Call to the Women of the World* (Berlin: WIDF, n.d.), 3.
67. *Children of Korea*, 3.
68. *Children of Korea*, 10.
69. *Children of Korea*, 9. For the first communiqué, dated July 1, 1950, by the KDWU to the WIDF in response to the outbreak of war, requesting their help toward all possible measures against the US imperialist intervention in the Korean civil war, see "Kukje minju nyŏsŏng ryŏnmaeng sŏgiguk kwijung" [To the Secretariat of the Women's International Democratic Federation]," *Chosŏn Nyŏsŏng*, July 1950, 12–13.
70. The list of members comes from *We Accuse!*, 4, and where available their occupations and ages are drawn from Felton, *That's Why I Went*, and Kate Fleron, *Nord-Korea: Rapporter fra et haerget land* (Copenhagen: Hoffenberg, 1951). For additional details about the commission members see Kim Tae-woo, *Naengjŏn ŭi manyŏdŭl: Han'guk chŏnjaeng kwa yŏsŏngjuŭi p'yŏnghwa undong* [Witches of the Cold War: The Korean War and the feminist peace movement] (P'aju, South Korea: Ch'angbi, 2021), 78–98.
71. See Fleron's biography at KVINFO, at https://www.kvinfo.dk/side/170/bio/668/.
72. Kim Tae-woo, *Naengjŏn ŭi manyŏdŭl*, 89–90.
73. For Abassia Fodil see Pierre-Jean Le Foll-Luciani, "'If Only I Could Have Been a Bomb, I Would Have Exploded': Algerian Women Communist Militants, between Assignation and Subversion of Gender Roles (1944–1962)," *Le Mouvement Social* 255, no. 2 (2016): 35–55; and for Trees Soenito-Heyligers see Katharine McGregor, "The Cold War, Indonesian Women and the Global Anti-imperialist Movement, 1946–65," in *De-centering Cold War History*, 31–51.
74. Felton, *That's Why I Went*, 27, 40.
75. *We Accuse!*, 2. For reference to the report being compiled in five languages see page 46, but by 1955 it had been published in twenty-three languages. See Roher, Jubisch, and Gerwinski, *10th Anniversary*, 11.
76. *We Accuse!*, 6.
77. *Military Situation in the Far East: Hearings before the Committee on Armed Services and the Committee on Foreign Relations, United States Senate, 82nd Congress* (Washington, DC: Government Printing Office, 1951), 82. The hearing was held in the process of evaluating MacArthur's dismissal.
78. *We Accuse!*, 14–15.
79. *We Accuse!*, 16.
80. *We Accuse!*, 19.
81. *We Accuse!*, 48.
82. Felton, *That's Why I Went*, 36. Felton had been one of the vocal members who insisted on visiting the South, but ultimately support for this position waned within the delegation and Felton herself had to give up on the idea when the trip took longer than expected and she had to hurry home (49, 103). Felton's memoir is an important resource that complements the official report of the commission with greater nuance as she reflects on the internal disagreements and personal impressions of the delegation, including Cold War suspicions evident within the group itself. See especially pp. 35–36, 41–49, 66–71. On Felton see also Fujime Yuki, "Monik'a P'elt'ŭn kwa kukje yŏsŏng minju yŏnmaeng (WIDF) Han'guk chŏnjaeng chinsang chosadan" [Monica Felton and the WIDF fact-finding mission to the Korea War], *Sahoe wa yŏksa* [Society and history] 100 (2013): 279–324.
83. Monica Felton, *What I Saw in Korea* (London: Farleigh, 1951), 3. I thank Gwyn Kirk for a copy of this pamphlet and the one below.

84. Monica Felton, *Korea! How to Bring the Boys Home* (London: Britain China Friendship Association, 1953).

85. Laville, *Cold War Women*, 135.

86. Commission of International Association of Democratic Lawyers, *Report on U.S. Crimes in Korea, 31 March 1952* (Pyongyang: International Association of Democratic Lawyers, 1952). This commission was made up of legal professionals from Austria (Heinrich Brandweiner), Italy (Luigi Cavalieri), the UK (Jack Gaster), France (Marc Jacquier), China (Ko Po-nien), Belgium (Marie-Louise Moerens), Brazil (Letelba Rodrigues de Britto), and Poland (Zofia Wasilkowska), visiting Korea from March 3 to 19, 1952.

87. Laville, *Cold War Women*, 171.

88. Jennifer De Forest, "Women United for the United Nations: US Women Advocating for Collective Security in the Cold War," *Women's History Review* 14, no. 1 (2005): 70.

89. Francisca de Haan, "The WIDF, the NVB and the Korean War: Women Traversing the Local and the Global," unpublished paper presented at the Swiss Historical Conference, University of Fribourg, February 2013, 10.

90. Eugénie Cotton, "To the Women of Korea," *Information Bulletin* 45 (June 1950), 1–3.

91. See, for example, Fleron, *Nord-Korea*, 7, and "The Borderline of Treason," *Economist*, August 11, 1951, 324–26.

92. Felton, *That's Why I Went*, 116–17.

93. Dora Russell, *The Tamarisk Tree 3: Challenge to the Cold War* (London: Virago, 1985), 145–46; Donert, "From Communist Internationalism to Human Rights," 325; Michelle Chase, "'Hands Off Korea!': Women's Internationalist Solidarity and Peace Activism in Early Cold War Cuba," *Journal of Women's History* 32, no. 3 (Fall 2020): 64–88.

94. Geoffrey Wakeford, "Mrs Felton: Government Act," *Daily Mail*, June 15, 1951, 1; "Mrs Felton 'Over-Tired,'" *Daily Mail*, June 19, 1951, 1; "A Visitor to Korea," *Daily Mail*, June 12, 1951, 2; "Stevenage to Korea," *Daily Mail*, June 9, 1951, 1. I thank Adam Cathcart for the collection of British news reporting on Monica Felton throughout this chapter.

95. Fleron, *Nord-Korea*, 34.

96. Anthony Brown, "A Peculiarly Vile Form of Red Propaganda," *Daily Mail*, December 2, 1952, 1. According to the latter, Monica Felton delivered 157 letters from British POWs in Korea from her meeting with Korean women at the Asia Pacific Peace Conference in Beijing (see chapter 2). Previously from her 1951 trip, she carried twenty-six letters back from British POWs. See "British Woman in Red Korea," *Daily Mail*, June 9, 1951, 3.

97. "Through the Years with NAW—History Repeating Itself," *Sisters: Journal of the NAW*, Special Souvenir Issue, 1983: 5, https://www.sisters.org.uk/wp-content/uploads/2020/04/1963-souvenir_compressed.pdf.

98. Jeannette Vermeersch, "The People of Korea Fight for Happiness," *Information Bulletin* 45 (June 1950), 15.

99. "This Is the 'Democracy' That the U.S. Government Wants to Export!," *Information Bulletin* 45 (June 1950), 7.

100. "This Is the 'Democracy,'" 7.

101. "Women Leaders among Thirteen Convicted for Peace Activities in U.S.A.," *News in Brief* 3 (February 11, 1953).

102. Jones was a leading theoretician on issues of race and gender, elected to the Communist Party USA National Committee in 1945 as the only Black woman to sit on its executive board. Jones was first arrested in 1948 for violating the 1918 Immigration Act and threatened with deportation; arrested again in 1950 for violation of the Internal Security Act (McCarran Act), which authorized deportation of the foreign-born deemed subversive; and finally arrested in 1951 for violating the Smith Act and jailed for nine months before being deported to Great Britain in 1955. See McDuffie, *Sojourning for Freedom*,

167–71. For a full biography of Jones see Carole Boyce Davies, *Left of Karl Marx: The Political Life of Black Communist Claudia Jones* (Durham, NC: Duke University Press, 2007).

103. Claudia Jones, "Half the World," *Daily Worker*, November 25, 1951, cited in Cristina Mislán, "Claudia Jones Speaks to 'Half the World': Gendering Cold War Politics in the *Daily Worker*, 1950–1953," *Feminist Media Studies* 17, no. 2 (2017): 291. Mislán notes how Jones's column was already infused with the idea that "the personal is political" two decades before the publication of Carol Hanisch's "The Personal Is Political" in 1970 (283).

104. "Miguk ŭi ŏmŏnidŭl ŭn adŭl i toraol kŏsŭl yogu hago itta" [American mothers are demanding the return of their sons], *Chosŏn Nyŏsŏng*, February 1953, 58–60.

105. Ri Hye-yŏng, "P'yŏnghwa t'usa: Rilli Pehŭch'erŭ 'Chosŏn ŭi unmyŏng ŭrobut'ŏ Togil ŭl panghwi hara'" [Peace Fighter: Lilly Waechter "Protect Germany from the Fate of Korea"], *Chosŏn Nyŏsŏng*, August 1952, 42–43.

106. "Pelgi ŭi 'P'yŏnghwa wa haengbok ŭl wihan nyŏsŏnghoe' eso Pak Chŏng-ae wiwŏnjang ege ch'insŏn ŭi sŏhan" [Letter of friendship to Chair Pak Chŏng-ae from the "Women's Association for Peace and Happiness" of Belgium], *Chosŏn Nyŏsŏng*, September 1952, 34.

107. Ko Hyŏn-bok, "Monik'a P'elt'on: Nyŏsa wa ŭi chwadamhoe esŏ" [Monica Felton: At the roundtable with the madam], *Chosŏn Nyŏsŏng*, September 1952, 26.

108. Paek Rang (trans. Pak Hŭng-byŏng), "Nanŭn kŭdŭrŭl norae haryŏnda" [I shall sing for them], *Chosŏn Nyŏsŏng*, September 1952, 41.

109. "Solidarity with the Korean Women," *Documents and Information* 4 (Berlin: WIDF, 1969), 2.

110. Kim Tong-ch'un, *Chŏnjaeng kwa sahoe*; Cumings, *Origins of the Korean War*.

111. *Documents and Information* 9 (Berlin: WIDF, 1970), 25.

112. *We Accuse!*, 2–3.

113. *Special Information Bulletin* 1 (7 March 1953), 5–8.

114. *Women of the Whole World*, June 1953, 17, 19.

115. *Special Information Bulletin after the World Congress of Women* 1 (August 8, 1953), 5.

116. *Special Information Bulletin after the World Congress of Women*, 7.

117. Mooney, "Fighting Fascism," 63.

118. Judy Tzu-Chun Wu, *Radicals on the Road: Internationalism, Orientalism, and Feminism during the Vietnam Era* (Ithaca, NY: Cornell University Press, 2013), 197.

119. Suzy Kim, "Mothers and Maidens: Gendered Formation of Revolutionary Heroes in North Korea," *Journal of Korean Studies* 19 (Fall 2014): 257–89.

120. Che Den Suk, "We Give Our Blood and Our Lives for Our People, for All People. Whatever the Price, We Will Win," *Women of the Whole World*, February 1951, 24. Hŏ Chŏng-suk was transliterated to English in WIDF publications as Che Den Suk.

121. Ilic, "Soviet Women," 162.

122. Ilic, 164.

123. "Speech of the Korean Women's Delegation at the World Women's Congress" (Helsinki: WIDF, June 1969), 18. For more on UNCURK as a one-sided geopolitical tool of the US see Kwang Ho Lee, "A Study of the United Nations Commission for the Unification and Rehabilitation of Korea (UNCURK)—the Cold War and a United Nations Subsidiary Organ" (PhD diss., University of Pittsburgh, 1974).

124. *We Accuse!*, 25.

125. Jean Bethke Elshtain, *Women and War* (New York: Basic Books, 1987), 253–55.

126. "The Women of the Whole World Support Their Sisters in Korea," *Women of the Whole World*, August–September 1953, 6.

127. *14th Session of the Executive Committee Meeting* (Geneva, January 16–19, 1954), 3.

128. *14th Session*, 45.
129. *14th Session*, 11.
130. Mark Clapson, "The Rise and Fall of Monica Felton, British Town Planner and Peace Activist, 1930s to 1950s," *Planning Perspective* 30, no. 2 (2015): 211–29. Appreciating her pioneering feminist role in the history of urban planning, Clapson laments Felton's career cut short by her peace activism.
131. Felton's Speech, April 8, 1952, Summary of World Broadcasts: BBC Written Archives Centre, quoted in Clapson, 225.
132. Ri Yong-ak, "Monik'a P'elt'on nyŏsa ege: Kukje nyŏmaeng chosadan Yŏngguk taep'yo Monik'a P'elt'on nyŏsa e taehan Aet'ŭri chŏngbu ŭi pakhaerŭl tŭkko" [To Ms. Monica Felton: Upon hearing of Attlee government's persecution of Ms. Monica Felton, British member of the WIDF fact-finding commission], in *Sijip: Nyŏsŏngdŭl ege* [Anthology of poems: For women] (Pyongyang: Chosŏn nyŏsŏngsa, 1952), 102–8.
133. That the WIDF and other left feminists had pioneered the intersectional approach has been long argued by Francisca de Haan, and more recently Jacqueline Castledine and Erik McDuffie, among others. See Francisca de Haan, "Eugénie Cotton, Pak Chong-ae, and Claudia Jones: Rethinking Transnational Feminism and International Politics," *Journal of Women's History* 25 (Winter 2013): 174–89, and "La Federación Democrática Internacional de Mujeres (FDIM) y América Latina, de 1945 a los años 70," in *Queridas Camaradas. Historias iberoamericanas de mujeres comunistas*, ed. Adriana Maria Valobra and Mercedes Yusta Rodrigo (Buenos Aires: Miño y Dávila, 2017), 17–44; Castledine, *Cold War Progressives*; and McDuffie, *Sojourning for Freedom*.
134. Geoff Eley, "From Welfare Politics to Welfare States: Women and the Socialist Question," in *Women and Socialism, Socialism and Women: Europe between the Two World Wars*, ed. Helmut Gruber and Pamela Graves (New York: Berghahn Books, 1998), 516–46.

2. ANTI-IMPERIALIST STRUGGLE FOR A JUST PEACE

First epigraph: Chang Sun-il, "Mossŭk'ŭba wa Reningŭradŭ rŭl pogo" [Upon seeing Moscow and Leningrad], *Chosŏn Nyŏsŏng*, January 1953, 55. Second epigraph: From Lothar Roher, Rolf Jubisch, and Werner Gerwinski, eds., *10th Anniversary of the Women's International Democratic Federation* (Berlin: WIDF, 1955), 22.

1. Simone Bertrand, "The Women of Asia and Africa Fight for Their Emancipation and for Peace," *Women of the Whole World*, September 1954, 3–4.
2. Raicho Hiratsuka, "Ten Years of the Japanese Women's Movement," *Women of the Whole World*, February 1956, 10–11.
3. Hiratsuka, 11.
4. "Chaeil Chosŏn minju nyŏsŏng tongmaeng che-9-ch'a chŏnch'e taehoe kŏnŭian: Chaeil Chosŏn minju nyŏsŏng tongmaeng ch'angrip 10-chunyŏn" [KDWU of Japan 9th Congress proposal on the ten-year anniversary of foundation], (n.d. but likely 1956), A10–02212.
5. With Japan's defeat in the Asia Pacific War, Koreans in Japan formed the communist-aligned League of Koreans in October 1945 with support from as much as two-thirds of all Korean residents. Although considered the precursor to Ch'ongryŏn (aligned with the North), the League of Koreans predated the foundation of two separate states in Korea and had branch offices throughout the peninsula. It was expressly founded as an interim organization to facilitate the repatriation of Koreans, especially through Korean-language instruction in which women played a key part as teachers; by October 1946, a year after the league's formation, there were 539 schools. See Sonia Ryang, *North Koreans in Japan: Language, Ideology, and Identity* (Boulder, CO: Westview, 1997), 79–85.

6. "Chaeilbon Chosŏn minju nyŏsŏng tongmaeng che-3-hoe chŏnch'e taehoe unyŏng wiwŏnhoe pogosŏ mit ŭian" [KDWU of Japan 3rd Congress Executive Committee report and agenda], September 1951, 14, A10–02207.

7. "Chaeil Chosŏn minju nyŏsŏng tongmaeng chung'ang wiwŏnhoe che-6-hoe chŏn'guk taehoe pogo pangch'imsŏ (ch'oan)" [KDWU of Japan Central Committee 6th national conference report and policy (draft)], November 4–5, 1954, 28–30, A10–02208.

8. Erez Manela, *The Wilsonian Moment: Self-Determination and the International Origins of Anticolonial Nationalism* (New York: Oxford University Press, 2007).

9. Rachel Leow, "A Missing Peace: The Asia-Pacific Peace Conference in Beijing, 1952 and the Emotional Making of Third World Internationalism," *Journal of World History* 30, no. 1–2 (June 2019): 26.

10. John Sexton, ed., *Alliance of Adversaries: The Congress of the Toilers of the Far East* (Leiden: Brill, 2019), 1. This is an adapted and annotated publication of the 1970 Hammersmith reprint of the 1922 English edition of the congress minutes, printed in Petrograd. Sexton corrected mistakes, especially in the transliteration of Asian names, by consulting contemporary sources and making comparisons to the Russian, Chinese, and German versions of the minutes in the Comintern archive. The information on the congress in this chapter comes from Sexton's helpful introduction.

11. The US occupation refused to recognize the KPR as representative of the Korean people, and the center-left coalition collapsed when Yŏ was assassinated by a rightist in July 1947.

12. Alyssa M. Park, *Sovereignty Experiments: Korean Migrants and the Building of Borders in Northeast Asia, 1860–1945* (Ithaca, NY: Cornell University Press, 2019).

13. Sexton, *Alliance of Adversaries*, 31.

14. Ernestine Evans, "Looking East from Moscow," *Asia*, December 1922, 976.

15. The delegate questionnaire forms and congress credentials committee did not record the gender of the delegates, but the congress did set up a women's caucus (Sexton, *Alliance of Adversaries*, 24fn60). Three of the seven women spoke at the congress, as indicated by the minutes, two from Korea (Kwŏn Ae-ra and Kim Wŏn-gyŏng) and one from China (Huang Bihun). Other women from Korea at the congress were Chŏng Su-jŏng, with the Women's Patriotic Assembly, and Kim Tŏk-yong, a member of the Korean Communist Party. See Sexton, *Alliance of Adversaries*, 331–34.

16. Sexton, 211.

17. Sexton, 243–44.

18. Sexton, 245.

19. Chŏng Ch'il-sŏng, "3-wŏl ŭi hoesang" [Reminiscences of March], *Chosŏn Nyŏsŏng*, February 1957, 2–3.

20. Roh Jiseung, "Chendŏ, nodong, kamjŏng kŭrigo chŏngch'ijŏk kaksŏng ŭi sun'gan—yŏsŏng sahoejuŭija Chŏng Ch'il-sŏng ŭi sam kwa hwaldong e taehan yŏn'gu" [Gender, labor, emotion and moment of political awakening—a study on life and activities of female socialist Chung Chil-sung], *Pigyo munhwa yŏn'gu* [Comparative cultural studies] 43 (2016): 7–50. The March First Movement was the first mass nationalist uprising, through which people came to identify as "Korean" rather than their respective social status, and Chŏng chose at this time to leave her profession after having been entered into the *kisaeng* register at the age of eight (17–19).

21. Despite her feminist politics, Kim's legacy is mixed with charges of colonial collaboration during the Japanese occupation. She was also a founding member of the Asian People's Anti-Communist League in South Korea in support of authoritarian leader Syngman Rhee. See Haeseong Park, "Christian Feminist Helen Kim and Her Compromise in Service to Syngman Rhee," *Korea Journal* 60, no. 4 (2020): 169–93; and Joyce Goodman, "International Women's Organizations, Peace and Peacebuilding," in *The Palgrave*

Handbook of Global Approaches to Peace, ed. Aigul Kulnazarova and Vesselin Popovski (Cham, Switzerland: Palgrave Macmillan, 2019), 441–60.

22. Modern Girl Around the World Research Group (Alys Eve Weinbaum, Lynn M. Thomas, Priti Ramamurthy, Uta G. Poiger, Madeleine Yue Dong, and Tani E. Barlow, eds.), *The Modern Girl Around the World* (Durham, NC: Duke University Press, 2008); Theodore Jun Yoo, *The Politics of Gender in Colonial Korea: Education, Labor, and Health, 1910–1945* (Berkeley: University of California Press, 2008); Hyaeweol Choi, *Gender and Mission Encounters in Korea: New Women, Old Ways* (Berkeley: University of California Press, 2009).

23. Yi Im-ha, *Haebang konggan, ilsang ŭl pakkun yŏsŏngdŭl ŭi yŏksa* [Liberated space: Women's history of changes in everyday life] (Seoul: Ch'ŏlsu wa yŏnghŭi, 2015), 23, from "Namnyŏ t'oron: Yŏja tanbal i kahan'ga pulhan'ga" [Pros and cons of women's bob], *Pyŏlgon'gŏn*, no. 18 (1929): 128–30.

24. For more on the emergence of feminisms in colonial Korea and differences between New Women and socialist women see Sunyoung Park, "Rethinking Feminism in Colonial Korea: Kang Kyŏngae's Portraits of Proletarian Women," *positions: asia critique* 21, no. 4 (2013): 947–85. For brief biographies, for Kim Hwal-lan see https://www.c250.columbia.edu/c250_celebrates/remarkable_columbians/helen_kim.html, and for Chŏng Chong-myŏng see https://terms.naver.com/entry.nhn?docId=1232315&cid=40942&categoryId=33384.

25. Manu Goswami, "Imaginary Futures and Colonial Internationalisms," *American Historical Review* 117, no. 5 (2012): 1461–85. Demonstrating the extent to which antiimperial internationalisms gained unprecedented global prominence in the 1920s and 1930s, Goswami rightly points out that the hegemony of the nation-state form since the end of World War II has relegated internationalism to "a minor key of anti-colonialism or a 'futile holding operation' against the inevitable consolidation of the nation form," thereby "flattening" anti-imperialism to nationalism in a linear trajectory of decolonization from empire to nation-states that erases alternative futures imagined by antiimperialist movements (1462).

26. Vladimir Tikhonov, "Worldwide 'Red Age' and Colonial-Era Korea: An Attempt at Meta-historical Analysis," *Marŭk'ŭsŭjuŭi yŏn'gu* [Marxism 21] 17, no. 2 (2020): 146–82. For another helpful study that traces the idea of the Third World and the development of a radical anticolonial left to the interwar years at the Communist University of the Toilers of the East (KUTV) see Heather Ashby, "Third World Activists and the Communist University of the Toilers of the East" (PhD diss., University of Southern California, 2014).

27. Scholarship on this is vast, but for representative examples see Antoinette Burton, *Burdens of History: British Feminists, Indian Women, and Imperial Culture, 1865–1915* (Chapel Hill: University of North Carolina Press, 1994), and Mire Koikari, *Pedagogy of Democracy: Feminism and the Cold War in the U.S. Occupation of Japan* (Philadelphia: Temple University Press, 2008).

28. Sophie Skelton, "From Peace to Development: A Re-Constitution of British Women's International Politics, c. 1945–1975" (PhD diss., University of Birmingham, 2014), 4.

29. Young-sun Hong, *Cold War Germany, the Third World, and the Global Humanitarian Regime* (Cambridge: Cambridge University Press, 2015), 24.

30. Hong, 38–41.

31. For reference to the origin of the "three worlds" see https://www.history.com/news/why-are-countries-classified-as-first-second-or-third-world. For a concise discussion of the relationship between decolonization and the emergence of the Cold War see Mark Philip Bradley, "Docolonization, the Global South, and the Cold War, 1919–1962," in *The Cambridge History of the Cold War*, vol. 1, ed. Melvyn P. Leffler and Odd Arne Westad (Cambridge: Cambridge University Press, 2010), 464–86. Even while noting that

the "outbreak of the Korean War in 1950 brought the dynamics of the Cold War more fully into the processes of decolonization" (474), however, Bradley does not include Korea among the decolonizing nations after 1945 because Japanese imperialism in Asia is left out (478).

32. Vijay Prashad, *The Darker Nations: A People's History of the Third World* (New York: New Press, 2007), xv. While Prashad traces the beginning of the Third World project to the 1955 Bandung Conference as somewhat distinct from the Second World, this chapter advances a different genealogy led by women, in which the Third and Second Worlds were more closely intertwined. In a later book, Prashad also makes connections between the Third World and the inspiration left by the October Revolution. See his *Red Star over the Third World* (New Delhi: LeftWord Books, 2017).

33. Elisabeth Armstrong, "Before Bandung: The Anti-imperialist Women's Movement in Asia and the Women's International Democratic Federation," *Signs: Journal of Women in Culture and Society* 41 (2016): 305–31.

34. *Second Women's International Congress*, December 1–6, 1948 (Paris: WIDF, 1948), 20. For *Chosŏn Nyŏsŏng*'s coverage of the Budapest Congress by an unnamed participant see "Uridŭl ŭn tan'gyŏl toeŏtta: Che-2-ch'a kukje minju nyŏsŏng taehoe e ch'amgahan han taep'yo ŭi sugi esŏ" [We are united: Notes from a representative attending the Second World Congress of Women], *Chosŏn Nyŏsŏng*, July 1949, 68–73.

35. *The Women of Asia and Africa: Documents* (Budapest: WIDF, December 1948), 7.

36. *Women of Asia and Africa*, 3. Korean names in WIDF publications were often based on Cyrillized transliterations, which make them difficult to identify. Here the four Korean women were identified as Tscho Ene (Cho Yŏng) and Kim Hon-ek (Kim Hong-ok) from the North, and Sene Vone Ip (Sŏng Wŏn-il?) and You Ene Dune (Yu Yŏng-jun) from the South. A Korean news article lists Cho, Yu, and Kim as delegates to the Budapest meeting but does not name the fourth individual. See "Che-2-ch'a kukje nyŏsŏng taehoe e ch'amgahayŏttŏn Chosŏn nyŏsŏng taep'yo kwiguk" [Return of the Korean women delegates participating in the second World Congress of Women]," *Rodong Sinmun*, January 8, 1949, 1. Although representing the South, Yu had by this time settled in the North, after attending the North-South Leadership Conference in April 1948. Vladimir Tikhonov generously helped identify the women, with the exception of Sene Vone Ip, whom I have not been able to identify. Cho Yŏng was wife of Yun Kong-hŭm, aligned with the China faction. According to Soviet documents, she was a KWP Central Committee member in 1953 but may have been purged after Yun's flight to China in 1956. For excerpts from reports by Yu and Cho at the February 6, 1949, All Korean Women Enthusiasts Congress that summarizes the WIDF congress proceedings see "Che-2-ch'a kukje nyŏsŏng taehoe ch'onggyŏl kwa Chosŏn nyŏsŏng ŭi immu e taehayŏ" [Summary of the Second World Congress of Women and on the duties of Korean women]," *Chosŏn Nyŏsŏng*, February 1949, 28–41.

37. *Women of Asia and Africa*, 169 (emphasis added).

38. Simone Bertrand, "The Asian Women's Conference," *Information Bulletin* no. 31 (September–October 1948), 4. For details about how India was first proposed as an important site of anticolonial struggle but ultimately failed to host the conference see Armstrong, "Before Bandung."

39. *Information Bulletin* no. 32 (November 1948), 6.

40. *Information Bulletin* no. 37 (June 1949), 1–2. There is now a large body of scholarship to show how such stunning organization of women was possible, but for a sample of foundational works in English see the works by Tani Barlow, Christina Gilmartin, Gail Hershatter, and Wang Zheng, among others.

41. "All over the world, women are preparing for the conference," *Information Bulletin* no. 38 (July–August 1949), 10.

42. *Information Bulletin* no. 39 (September 1949), 10.

43. WIDF British Committee, *British Woman in New China: Marian Ramelson's Report on the Asian Women's Conference, Peking, 1949* (London: Farleigh, 1949). See also Elisabeth Armstrong, "Peace and the Barrel of the Gun in the International Women's Movement, 1945–49," *Meridians: Feminism, Race, Transnationalism* 18, no. 2 (October 2019): 261–77.

44. "Documents of the Conference of the Women of the Countries of Asia, Peking, December 10–15, 1949," *Information Bulletin*, Special Issue, April 1950, 8.

45. "Documents of the Conference of the Women of the Countries of Asia," 13.

46. Ko Yŏng-ja, "Asea nyŏsŏng taep'yo taehoe sojip e taehayŏ" [On the gathering of the Asia Women's Conference], *Chosŏn Nyŏsŏng*, July 1949, 24. For an introduction to women's organizations in Asia in the lead-up to the conference see "Asea chegukka esŏ ŭi minju nyŏsŏng tanch'edŭl ŭi kaegwan" [Survey of democratic women's organizations in Asia], *Chosŏn Nyŏsŏng*, August 1949, 58–61. For communications and calls related to the conference see *Chosŏn Nyŏsŏng*, September 1949, 22–25. For coverage of Asian women's continued struggle against imperialism after the conference see "Chegukjuŭi rŭl pandae hayŏ ssaunŭn Asea cheguk nyŏsŏngdŭl" [Women of Asia fighting against imperialism], *Chosŏn Nyŏsŏng*, March 1950, 16–19.

47. *Chosŏn Nyŏsŏng*, January 1950, back cover.

48. "Asea cheguk nyŏsŏng taehoe kyŏljŏngsŏ rŭl chiji hanŭn chŏn Chosŏn nyŏsŏng yŏlsŏngja taehoe" [All Korean Women Enthusiasts Congress in support of the Asia Women's Conference resolution], *Chosŏn Nyŏsŏng*, February 1950, 4.

49. "Kyŏljŏngsŏ: Asea cheguk nyŏsŏng taehoe ch'onggyŏl kwa nyŏsŏngdŭl ŭi tangmyŏn kwaŏp e taehayŏ" [Resolution: Summary of the Asia Women's Conference and on the women's task at hand], *Chosŏn Nyŏsŏng*, February 1950, 6.

50. Kim Im-sŏng, "Asea cheguk nyŏsŏng taehoe ch'amgwangi" [Observations from the Asia Women's Conference], *Chosŏn Nyŏsŏng*, February 1950, 8–16. For a summary pamphlet on the Asia Women's Conference published by the KDWU see KDWU Central Committee Cultural Education Department, "Asea nyŏsŏngdŭl ŭn p'yŏnghwa wa minju rŭl wihan t'ujaeng esŏ kutge tan'gyŏl toeŏtta" [Women of Asia are firmly united in the struggle for peace and democracy], December 1949.

51. Kim Im-sŏng, "Asea cheguk nyŏsŏng taehoe ch'amgwangi," 8.

52. Kim Kwi-sŏn, "Asea cheguk nyŏsŏng taehoe ŭi kŏdaehan sŏnggwa" [Great results of the Asia Women's Conference], *Chosŏn Nyŏsŏng*, January 1950, 8–11. There were a total of twenty formal representatives and seventeen candidate representatives from Korea. See KDWU Central Committee Cultural Education Department, "Asea nyŏsŏngdŭl ŭn p'yŏnghwa wa minju rŭl wihan t'ujaeng esŏ kutge tan'gyŏl toeŏtta."

53. Kim Im-sŏng, "Asea cheguk nyŏsŏng taehoe ch'amgwangi," 10.

54. Kim Im-sŏng, 13.

55. Jeannette Vermeersch, "The People of Korea Fight for Happiness," *Information Bulletin* no. 45 (June 1950), 15.

56. Kim Im-sŏng, "Asea cheguk nyŏsŏng taehoe ch'amgwangi," 16.

57. Pak Chŏng-ae, "Chosŏn inmin ŭi choguk haebang t'ujaeng ŭn segye p'yŏnghwa rŭl wihan t'ujaeng ida" [The Korean people's struggle for national liberation is a struggle for world peace], *Rodong Sinmun*, April 18, 1951, 2.

58. There is as yet no comprehensive study on the World Peace Council, but for a succinct summary of its beginnings see its seventieth anniversary statement, at https://www.wpc-in.org/statements/70-years-ago-first-world-congress-peace-partisans-0. For scholarship on its role in specific regions see Patrick Iber, *Neither Peace nor Freedom: The Cultural Cold War in Latin America* (Cambridge, MA: Harvard University Press, 2015); Günter Wernicke, "The Communist-Led World Peace Council and the Western Peace Movements: The Fetters of Bipolarity and Some Attempts to Break Them in the Fifties

and Early Sixties," *Peace & Change* 23, no. 3 (July 1998): 265–311; Günter Wernicke, "The Unity of Peace and Socialism? The World Peace Council on a Cold War Tightrope between the Peace Struggle and Intrasystemic Communist Conflicts," *Peace & Change* 26, no. 3 (July 2001): 332–51; and Chŏng Yong-uk, "Naengjŏn ŭi p'yŏnghwa, pundan ŭi p'yŏnghwa: 6.25 chŏnjaeng chŏnhu Pukhan ŭi p'yŏnghwa undong e nat'anan p'yŏnghwaron" [Cold War peace, division peace: Debates in the North Korean peace movement before and after the Korean War], in *Sŏul taehakkyo yŏksa yŏn'guso 10-chunyŏn kinyŏm haksul taehoe: 'P'yŏnghwa' ŭi yŏksa, yŏksa sok ŭi p'yŏnghwa* [Ten-year anniversary conference of the Institute of Historical Research at Seoul National University: History of "peace," peace in history] (Seoul: Institute of Historical Research, 2013), 85–111. See also Kim Tae-woo, "Naengjŏn p'yŏnghwaron ŭi sasaeng'a: Ssoryŏn kwa Pukhan ŭi Han'guk chŏnjaeng pukch'im sinario chojak ŭi chŏngch'ijŏk paegyŏng kwa kwajŏng" [Bastard child of Cold War peace: Political background to the Soviet and North Korean fabrication on the northern attack of the Korean War], *T'ong'il inmunhak* [Journal of the humanities for unification] 64 (2015): 263–304, and "1948–50-nyŏn sahoejuŭi chinyŏng ŭi p'yŏnghwaron kwa p'yŏnghwa undong ŭi Tong'asiajŏk suyong kwa pyŏnyong" [East Asian reception and transformation of socialist camp ideas of peace and the peace movement in 1948–50], *Tongbuga munhwa yŏn'gu* [Research on the cultures of Northeast Asia] 58 (2019): 83–101. Kim conflates peace activism with pacifism, thereby arguing that socialist peace initiatives were ultimately hypocritical and duplicitous, as evidenced by preparations for war. However, civil war was imminent throughout the Korean peninsula to varying degrees since 1947, and North Korean conceptions of anti-imperialist peace were always contingent on a *just* peace, explicitly in opposition to pacifism.

59. "P'yŏnghwa ongho chŏn'guk ryŏnhap taehoe sŏnŏnsŏ" [Declaration of the National Peace Committee], *Chosŏn Nyŏsŏng*, April 1949, 9–11.

60. "P'yŏnghwa ongho chŏn'guk ryŏnhap taehoe sŏnŏnsŏ."

61. Kim Im-sŏng, "P'yonghwa ongho segye taehoe ch'amga taep'yo kwihwan pogo taehoe esŏ" [At the report back of participation at the World Congress of Peace]," *Chosŏn Nyŏsŏng*, July 1949, 33. For film footage of the 1949 congress that includes Paul Robeson's speech and singing see "Congrès Mondial des Partisans de la Paix," at https://www.cinearchives.org/Films-447-533-0-0.html.

62. Kim, "P'yonghwa ongho segye taehoe ch'amga taep'yo kwihwan pogo taehoe esŏ," 34.

63. Chŏng Yong-uk, "Naengjŏn ŭi p'yŏnghwa, pundan ŭi p'yŏnghwa," 89; Pak Chŏng-ae, "Chosŏn inmin ŭi choguk haebang t'ujaeng ŭn segye p'yŏnghwa rŭl wihan t'ujaeng ida."

64. The March 4 through 6, 1950, issues of *Rodong Sinmun* covered the launch of the Stockholm Peace Appeal across most of its pages with the support of the appeal at the meeting of the SPA that included speeches by the chair of the KNPC Han Sŏl-ya and other leaders, including Pak Chŏng-ae. For coverage of the signature campaign during the war see "Segye p'yŏnghwa risahoe hosomun chijihayŏ sŏmyŏng e ch'amgahalgŏsŭl hoso" [Appeal to participate in the signature campaign in support of the World Peace Council appeal]," *Rodong Sinmun*, April 14, 1951, 1.

65. "Urinŭn chŏnjaeng ŭl pandae hamyŏ p'yŏnghwa rŭl yoguhanda," *Chosŏn Nyŏsŏng*, June 1950, 18–19.

66. Ri T'ae-jun, "Che-2-ch'a p'yŏnghwa ongho segye taehoe esŏ ŭi Pak Chŏng-ae nyŏsa" [Ms. Pak Chŏng-ae at the Second World Peace Congress], *Rodong Sinmun*, April 23, 1951, 2.

67. Nikkolai JJihonop'ŭ, trans. Chŏn Ch'i-bong, "Pak Chŏng-ae: Che-2-ch'a segye p'yŏnghwa onghoja taehoe esŏ" [Pak Chŏng-ae: At the Second World Peace Congress],

in *Sijip: Nyŏsŏng dŭl ege* [Anthology of poems: For women] (Pyongyang: Chosŏn nyŏsŏngsa, 1952), 6–11.

68. Chosŏn chung'ang t'ongsin [Korean Central News Agency], "Kakgukgan p'yŏnghwa ŭi konggohwa rŭl wihan kukje SSŭttalinsang susangja kyŏljŏng: Pak Chŏng-ae tongji tŭng kakguk p'yŏnghwa t'usa 7-ssi ege" [Announcement of winners of the International Stalin Peace Prize for the consolidation of peace among nations], *Rodong Sinmun*, April 9, 1951, 1.

69. "P'yŏng'an namdo Kangsŏgun nongmindŭl ŭi hwanyŏng ch'ukhahoe esŏ chinsulhan kukje SSŭttalin p'yŏnghwasang susangja, Pak Chŏng-ae tongji ŭi yŏnsŏl" [Winner of the Stalin Peace Prize, Comrade Pak Chŏng-ae's speech at the welcome celebration of the farmers of the South P'yŏng'an Province, Kangsŏ County], *Rodong Sinmun*, April 21, 1951, 2.

70. Sŏ Tong-man, *Pukchosŏn sahoejuŭi ch'eje sŏngripsa, 1945–1961* [History of the founding of the socialist system in North Korea, 1945–1961] (Seoul: Sŏnin, 2005), 457. If the average increase in population during peacetime is taken into account, Sŏ estimates that population loss due to migration and death in North Korea amounted to almost 30 percent of prewar levels over the course of the war.

71. Leow, "Missing Peace," 28–29. While Leow rightly points to the significance of the peace movements in Asia as a decolonial antecedent to Bandung, their legacy was more militant than simply a precursor to Bandung. As shown by the Sino-Soviet split (see chapter 3) and other parallel reactions in Vietnam and Korea, "peaceful coexistence" was not a viable option for those violently impacted by the Cold War.

72. Kim Yŏng, "Asea mit t'aep'yŏngyang chiyŏk p'yŏnghwa ongho taehoe chunbi hoeŭi" [Preparatory meeting for the Asia Pacific Peace Conference], *Chosŏn Nyŏsŏng*, July 1952, 39–41.

73. Kim, 40.

74. Chosŏn chung'ang t'ongsin [Korean Central News Agency], "Asea mit t'aep'yŏngyang chiyŏk p'yŏnghwa ongho taehoe chunbi hoeŭi esŏ chinsulhan Pak Chŏng-ae tongji ŭi yŏnsŏl (yoji)" [Speech of Comrade Pak Chŏng-ae at the preparatory meeting for the Asia Pacific Peace Conference (main points)], *Rodong Sinmun*, June 8, 1952, 1.

75. Leow, "Missing Peace," 32.

76. *Asea mit t'aep'yŏngyang chiyŏk p'yŏnghwa ongho taehoe munhŏnjip* [Asia Pacific Peace Conference document collection] (Pyongyang: Kungrip ch'ulp'ansa, 1953), 18.

77. *Asea mit t'aep'yŏngyang chiyŏk p'yŏnghwa ongho taehoe munhŏnjip*, 34.

78. Kim Yŏng-su, "Pukkyŏng esŏ" [In Beijing], *Chosŏn Nyŏsŏng*, October–November 1952, 17–21.

79. Kim, 17.

80. Kim, 17–18.

81. *Asea mit t'aep'yŏngyang chiyŏk p'yŏnghwa ongho taehoe munhŏnjip*, 21–23. For more on the Anti-imperialist League as an earlier coalition of anti-imperialist movements between Latin America and Asia see Ricardo Melgar Bao and Mariana Ortega-Breña, "The Anti-imperialist League of the Americas between the East and Latin America," *Latin American Perspectives* 35, no. 2 (2008): 9–24.

82. *Asea mit t'aep'yŏngyang*, 29–30.
83. *Asea mit t'aep'yŏngyang*, 32–33.
84. *Asea mit t'aep'yŏngyang*, 40–41.
85. *Asea mit t'aep'yŏngyang*, 43–44.
86. *Asea mit t'aep'yŏngyang*, 49–51.
87. *Asea mit t'aep'yŏngyang*, 76–85.
88. *Asea mit t'aep'yŏngyang*, 84–85.
89. *Asea mit t'aep'yŏngyang*, 224–28.

90. *Asea mit t'aep'yŏngyang*, 230.
91. *Asea mit t'aep'yŏngyang*, 86–95.
92. *What We Saw in China by 15 Americans* (New York: Weekly Guardian Associates, 1952). The US delegation toured China before the conference and noted the impressions made by *The White-Haired Girl*, which made them weep as a "tragic, magnificent opera" that revealed "the depths of suffering of the Chinese woman" (20). See chapter 6 for more on this opera. In addition, the *Song of Peace* performed by Choe Seunghui's ballet troupe garnered "a prolonged ovation" (53). See chapter 5 for more on Choe.
93. *Asea mit t'aep'yŏngyang*, 239–46.
94. *Asea mit t'aep'yŏngyang*, 322–28.
95. Kim, "Pukkyŏng esŏ," 20
96. *Asea mit t'aep'yŏngyang*, 256–64.
97. *Asea mit t'aep'yŏngyang*, 258–61.
98. Kim, "Pukkyŏng esŏ," 20.
99. Margaret Garland, *Journey to New China* (Christchurch: Caxton, 1954), 118. Invited to the 1952 conference through the New Zealand Federation of Women, Garland left a fascinating memoir that includes extensive details about her trip. Although mostly focused on observations about developments in new Communist China, The chapter on the conference details how it worked in eight commissions to arrive at the consensus resolutions through long debates, sometimes lasting all night.
100. *Asea mit t'aep'yŏngyang*, 51–53.
101. Oscar Sanchez-Sibony, *Red Globalization: The Political Economy of the Soviet Cold War from Stalin to Khrushchev* (Cambridge: Cambridge University Press, 2014), 4–7.
102. *Asea mit t'aep'yŏngyang*, 418–23. The text mistakenly attributes *On Guard for Peace* to Shostakovich, rather than Prokofiev.
103. *Asea mit t'aep'yŏngyang*, 424–28.
104. *Asea mit t'aep'yŏngyang*, 446–47.
105. Kim Kwi-ryŏn, "Winna p'yŏnghwa ongho inmin taehoe" [Vienna Peace Conference], *Chosŏn Nyŏsŏng*, February 1953, 32–38.
106. Kim, "Winna p'yŏnghwa," 37.
107. Kim, 38.
108. Chang Sun-il, "Mossŭk'ŭba wa Reningŭradŭ rŭl pogo" [Upon seeing Moscow and Leningrad], *Chosŏn Nyŏsŏng*, January 1953, 55.
109. Quinn Slobodian, "Socialist Chromatism: Race, Racism, and the Racial Rainbow in East Germany," in *Comrades of Color: East Germany in the Cold War World*, ed. Quinn Slododian (New York: Berghahn Books, 2015), 23–39.
110. Glenda Sluga, *Internationalism in the Age of Nationalism* (Philadelphia: University of Pennsylvania Press, 2013), 113.
111. Hong, *Cold War Germany*, chap. 2, esp. 18–19.
112. Hong, chap. 3, esp. 83–86.
113. "Che-3-ch'a kukje nyŏsŏng taehoe sŏnggwa" [Results of the Third World Congress of Women], *Chosŏn Nyŏsŏng*, June 1953, 15–18; "World Congress of Women Held in Copenhagen (June 5–10, 1953)," *Women of the Whole World*, June 1953, 5. According to the latter, there were five delegates from Korea and ten from Vietnam. For footage of the 1953 World Congress see *As One for Equality, Happiness and Peace* (Berlin: DEFA, n.d.) available at the British Film Institute in the Socialism on Film collection.
114. "We Shall Fight Unceasingly to End the Wars in Progress!," *Women of the Whole World*, June 1953, 31.
115. "We Shall Fight," 31.
116. Maria Opsyannikkoba, "K'op'enhagen esŏ ŭi sangbong" [Reunion in Copenhagen], *Chosŏn Nyŏsŏng*, March 1954, 63–80.

117. Opsyannikkoba, 65.
118. Opsyannikkoba, 66–67.
119. Opsyannikkoba, 67.
120. Opsyannikkoba, 71.
121. Opsyannikkoba, 72.
122. Opsyannikkoba, 77. The rose of Sharon was said to have been unofficially regarded the national flower of Korea since the early twentieth century owing to its prevalence in Korea, and is still regarded as such in the South. Although the date is unclear, North Korea adopted the magnolia as the national flower sometime after the Korean War. See its official website: https://www.korea-dpr.com/flower.html.
123. Opsyannikkoba, "K'op'enhagen esŏ ŭi sangbong," 77.
124. Opsyannikkoba, 78.
125. Opsyannikkoba, 80.
126. Monica Felton, *That's Why I Went* (London: Lawrence & Wishart, 1953), 49.
127. Felton, 66–70.
128. Felton, 71.
129. Felton, 131, 163.
130. Im Sun-dŭk, "Chungguk chamaedŭl ŭn uridŭl ŭl komu handa: Chungguk kukkyŏngjŏl kwallesik e ch'amga hagosŏ" [Chinese sisters inspire us: After participating in the Chinese national foundation day ceremony], *Chosŏn Nyŏsŏng*, December 1954, 20–24. Representatives from some fifty countries had attended, including Korea, Mongolia, and Vietnam from among the fraternal Asian countries.
131. Nora Rodŭ, "K'anada esŏ ponae on p'yŏnji" [Letter from Canada], *Chosŏn Nyŏsŏng*, July 1956, 16–17.
132. Rodŭ, "K'anada," 16
133. "K'anada esŏ on p'yŏnji" [Letter from Canada], *Chosŏn Nyŏsŏng*, August 1958, 23.
134. "K'anada," 23.

3. STRUGGLE BETWEEN TWO LINES

1. Ruth Distler, "The Women's Peace Caravan in Berlin," *Women of the Whole World*, October 1958, 5–6.
2. Eugenia Kiranova, "For You, Mothers, the First Flowers of Spring," *Women of the Whole World*, April 1958, 11.
3. *Women's Caravan of Peace* (Concord Media, 1958) provides excellent details about the trip, and is available at https://www.concordmedia.org.uk/products/womens-caravan-of-peace-2788/. For further details about the trip, including internal dynamics between the women and the conflict between Russell and Julia James over the film rights, see Michaela Maria Magdalena Schwarz-Santos Gonçalves Henriques, "Minding His-Story: Dora Russell's Voice on the Side of Life against the Backdrop of Her Peace Mission in the 1950s" (PhD diss., University of Lisbon, 2015), 138–44, and part 3. Henriques's work on Russell is an important contribution, but her characterization of the Cold War as a "war without bloodshed," or organizations such as the WIDF as a "Communist front organization," is misleading.
4. Gisella Floreanini, "Men Will Follow Women's Example," *Women of the Whole World*, October 1958, 17.
5. Dora Russell, *The Tamarisk Tree 3: Challenge to the Cold War* (London: Virago, 1985), 246–47.
6. A large body of scholarship treats the Sino-Soviet split, but for an overview see Lorenz M. Lüthi, *The Sino-Soviet Split: Cold War in the Communist World* (Princeton, NJ: Princeton University Press, 2008). Lüthi argues that principled differences over

socialist socioeconomic development and peaceful coexistence were at the root of the conflict.

7. "Appeal for the World Congress of Mothers," *Women of the Whole World*, March 1955, 5.

8. For one of the few English-language publications on the World Congress of Mothers and its lasting impact on the movement in Japan with the formation of the Japan Mothers' Congress held annually since 1955 see Vera Mackie, "From Hiroshima to Lausanne: The World Congress of Mothers and the Hahaoya Taikai in the 1950s," *Women's History Review* 25, no. 4 (2016): 671–95.

9. *Special Information Bulletin*, no. 25 (May 1955), 3.

10. "Lausanne—Meeting Place of Peace and Affection," *Women of the Whole World*, August/September 1955, 3.

11. "Lausanne—Meeting Place of Peace and Affection," 3.

12. *Documents of World Congress of Mothers* (WIDF, 1955), 3–5.

13. *Documents of World Congress of Mothers* (WIDF, 1955), 10–11.

14. "Manifesto of the World Congress of Mothers," *Women of the Whole World*, August/September 1955, 40–41.

15. "United States' Mothers Express Friendship with All Mothers," *Women of the Whole World*, August/September 1955, 28.

16. Ko Hyŏn-bok, "Ilyu ŭi chŏlbanin nyŏsŏngdŭl ŭn tan'gyŏl hago itta: Segye mosŏng taehoe kwihan pogo taehoe" [Women who make up half of humanity are united: Report on the World Congress of Mothers], *Chosŏn Nyŏsŏng*, September 1955, 9.

17. Lothar Roher, Rolf Jubisch, and Werner Gerwinski, eds., *10th Anniversary of the Women's International Democratic Federation* (Berlin: WIDF, 1955), 22.

18. Ko Hyŏn-bok, "Ilyu ŭi chŏlbanin nyŏsŏngdŭl ŭn tan'gyŏl hago itta," 8.

19. Vera Mackie also noted this trend, as did Quinn Slobodian in the gatherings of the World Festival of Youth and Students. See Mackie, "From Hiroshima to Lausanne," 680–81, and Quinn Slobodian, "Socialist Chromatism: Race, Racism, and the Racial Rainbow in East Germany," in *Comrades of Color: East Germany in the Cold War World*, ed. Quinn Slododian (New York: Berghahn Books, 2015), 23–39.

20. "Segye mosŏng taehoe" [World Congress of Mothers], *Chosŏn Nyŏsŏng*, August 1955, 9.

21. M. M. Brumagne, "Points of View on the World Congress of Mothers," *Women of the Whole World*, November 1955, 17.

22. "Meeting of the Permanent International Committee of Mothers," *Women of the Whole World*, March 1956, 3.

23. "Meeting," 4–5.

24. Maxim Gorky, "I Address Myself to the Women, to the Mothers . . . ," *Women of the Whole World*, June 1955, 8–9.

25. Clara-Maria Fassbinder, "The Things Dividing Us Are Trifling," *Women of the Whole World*, August/September 1955, 20 (emphasis added).

26. Nancy Cott, *The Grounding of Modern Feminism* (New Haven, CT: Yale University Press, 1989).

27. Kikue Ihara, "I Want You to Remember Them," *Women of the Whole World*, June 1955, 20–21.

28. Nazim Hikmet, "The Little Dead Girl," *Women of the Whole World*, June 1955, 23.

29. Russell, *Tamarisk Tree 3*, 221.

30. Russell, 227.

31. Russell, 248.

32. "A Great Council Meeting," *Women of the Whole World*, June 1956, 3–4. The World Peace Council would also meet for the first time in an Asian country the following year in June 1957 in Colombo, capital of Ceylon (Sri Lanka). See Umi Sardjono, "Meeting of

the World Council of Peace at Colombo," *Women of the Whole World*, August/September 1957, 21.

33. Safia Begum, "The Women of Asia and Africa Advance," *Women of the Whole World*, June 1956, 7.

34. Kim Chŏng-sin, "Chungguk ŭl tanyŏ wasŏ" [After visiting China], *Chosŏn Nyŏsŏng*, June 1956, 24–25.

35. "Kukje minju nyŏsŏng ryŏnmaeng sŏgiguk ŭrobutŏŭi Chosŏn nyŏsŏng taep'yo ch'och'ŏng kwa kwalyŏnhayŏ Ryu Yŏng-jun nyŏsa nambanbu nyŏsŏngdŭl ege pangsong" [Ms. Yu Yŏng-jun broadcasts to the women of the South regarding the invitation of Korean women delegates from the Secretariat of the Women's International Democratic Federation], *Rodong Sinmun*, April 9, 1956, 1.

36. Kim Chŏng-sin, "Chungguk ŭl tanyŏ wasŏ," 24.

37. For recent literature on the significance of the Bandung Conference see Luis Eslava, Michael Fakhri, and Vasuki Nesiah, eds., *Bandung, Global History, and International Law: Critical Pasts and Pending Futures* (Cambridge: Cambridge University Press, 2017); Quỳnh N. Phạm and Robbie Shilliam, eds., *Meanings of Bandung: Postcolonial Orders and Decolonial Visions* (New York: Rowman & Littlefield, 2016); Christopher J. Lee, ed., *Making a World after Empire: The Bandung Moment and Its Political Afterlives* (Athens: Ohio University Press, 2010). Phạm and Shilliam rightly note that a global fora of women's internationalism existed both before and after Bandung, such as the 1928 Pan-Pacific Women's Association's conference in Honolulu, the 1931 All-Asian Women's Conference in Lahore, the 1944 Pan-Arab Feminist Conference in Cairo, the 1949 Conference of the Women of Asia in Beijing, the 1958 Asian-African Conference of Women in Colombo, and the 1961 Afro-Asian Women's Conference in Cairo (12–13).

38. For a helpful collection that shows how "Bandung was built on much older traditions of anti-imperialist struggle" by "largely forgotten actors" see the special journal issue, Su Lin Lewis and Carolien Stolte, eds., "Other Bandungs: Afro-Asian Internationalisms in the Early Cold War," *Journal of World History* 30, no. 1–2 (June 2019): 1–246.

39. For a cogent argument on the Bolshevik Revolution as the antecedent to Bandung in its emphasis on anti-imperialist struggle see Boris N. Mamlyuk, "Decolonization as a Cold War Imperative: Bandung and the Soviets," in Eslava, Fakhri, and Nesiah, *Bandung, Global History, and International Law*, 196–214. Despite this early commitment to anti-imperialism, Soviet domestic policies prioritized state security and internal forms of colonialism, ultimately leading to a split between the Second and Third Worlds.

40. Katharine McGregor and Vannessa Hearman, "Challenging the Lifeline of Imperialism: Reassessing Afro-Asian Solidarity and Related Activism in the Decade 1955–1965," in Eslava, Fakhri, and Nesiah, *Bandung, Global History, and International Law*, 161–76; and Carolien Stolte, "'The People's Bandung': Local Anti-imperialists on an Afro-Asian Stage," *Journal of World History* 30, no. 1–2 (June 2019): 142–43.

41. Stolte, "'People's Bandung,'" 142. Stolte incorrectly states that this was the first major international Global South conference the North Koreans attended (139).

42. Stolte, "'People's Bandung,'" 144.

43. Hong Chong-uk, "1950-nyŏndae ŭi Bandung hoeŭi wa pidongmaeng undong insik—chapji 'Kukje Saenghwal' kisa rŭl chungsim ŭro" [North Korea's recognition of the Bandung Conference and the Non-Aligned Movement in the 1950s: Focusing on the magazine *International Life*], *Tongbuga yŏksa nonch'ong* [Northeast Asian History Journal] 61 (2018): 387.

44. Mao's ideas were canonized as "Mao Zedong Thought" at the Seventh Congress of the Chinese Communist Party in 1945. Mao eschewed "ism" as too formal, but "Maoism" as a theory of revolution was globalized by Western left intellectuals. See Liu Kang, "Maoism: Revolutionary Globalism for the Third World Revisited," *Comparative Literature*

Studies 52, no. 1 (2015): 12–28; and Arif Dirlik, "Mao Zedong Thought and the Third World/Global South," *interventions* 16, no. 2 (2014): 223–56.

45. For a cogent intellectual history of the emergence of Third Worldism and its Eurocentric limits see Andrew Nash, "Third Worldism," *African Sociological Review / Revue Africaine de Sociologie* 7, no. 1 (2003): 95–97, 112–13.

46. Kang, "Maoism," 19–20; Dirlik, "Mao Zedong Thought," 249–50; Paek Wŏn-dam, "Asia esŏ 1960–70 nyŏndae Pidongmaeng / Che-3-segye undong kwa minjok minjung kaenyŏm ŭi ch'angsin" [Non-Aligned / Third World Movement in Asia during the 1960–'70s and the creation of the concept of nation and people], *Chungguk hyŏndae munhak* [Modern Chinese literature] 29 (2009): 161–62.

47. Christina Van Houten, "Simone de Beauvoir Abroad: Historicizing Maoism and the Women's Liberation Movement," *Comparative Literature Studies* 52, no. 1 (2015): 121–25.

48. Hong Chong-uk, "1950-nyŏndae ŭi Bandung," 397.

49. For a full treatment of the women of Yugoslavia see Chiara Bonfiglioli, "Revolutionary Networks: Women's Political and Social Activism in Cold War Italy and Yugoslavia (1945–1957)" (PhD diss., University of Utrecht, 2012).

50. "Decision of the Secretariat," *Information Bulletin* no. 39 (September 1949), 4.

51. Jeannette Vermeersch, "On Yugoslavia," *Information Bulletin* no. 31 (September–October, 1948), 10–11.

52. "Resolution Passed by the Plenum of the Central Committee of the WAF," *Information Bulletin of the Central Committee of the Women's Anti-Fascist Front of Yugoslavia*, February 1950, 3.

53. Eugénie Cotton "The Most Noble of Our Ambitions," *Women of the Whole World*, June 1956, 18.

54. "Let Us Respect All Opinions," *Women of the Whole World*, June 1956, 8.

55. "Stop Press," *Women of the Whole World*, November 1956, 4.

56. Yulia Gradskova, *The Women's International Democratic Federation, the Global South, and the Cold War: Defending the Rights of Women of "Whole World"?* (New York: Routledge, 2021), 48.

57. "Supplement of the Draft Constitution of WIDF Adopted at WIDF Council Meeting, Helsinki, June 22–27, 1957," *Women of the Whole World*, December 1957, 1–14.

58. "A Great Step Forward," *Women of the Whole World*, November 1956, 3.

59. "The Growing Family of the WIDF," *Women of the Whole World*, May 1958, 15.

60. Gradskova, *Women's International Democratic Federation*, chap. 6. For example, a 1957 letter from the Soviet representative at the WIDF Secretariat informed the Soviet Women's Committee that of the nine countries represented at the secretariat, seven of the representatives were from Europe, one from the US, and another from China (119). As a result of such internal critique, two Argentinian women came to occupy the position of secretary-general in the 1960s and 1970s, and a majority of subsequent leadership positions went to Third World women (133).

61. "We Saw and Heard at the Council Meeting," *Women of the Whole World*, August/September 1957, 19.

62. Kim Yŏng-su, "Helsingk'i esŏ sojiptoen kukje nyŏmaeng risahoe e ch'amga hagosŏ" [After attending the WIDF Council meeting in Helsinki], *Chosŏn Nyŏsŏng*, August 1957, 18.

63. "Kukje minju nyŏsŏng ryŏnmaeng che-4-ch'a taehoerŭl apdugo" [Ahead of the fourth congress of the Women's International Democratic Federation], *Chosŏn Nyŏsŏng*, April 1958, 23.

64. "Kukje minju nyŏsŏng," 22.

65. "P'yŏnghwa rŭl sarang hanŭn ŏmŏnidŭl ŭi ilch'ihan nyŏmwŏn" [The united wish of peace-loving mothers], *Chosŏn Nyŏsŏng*, May 1958, 1.

66. The chronology toward the 1958 nuclear test ban petition in this paragraph comes from the Arms Control Association, "Nuclear Testing and Comprehensive Test Ban Treaty (CTBT) Timeline," at https://www.armscontrol.org/factsheets/NuclearTestingTimeline (accessed December 22, 2020). The Soviet Union heeded the call for a test ban as the first superpower to propose it in 1954, leading to a unilateral suspension of testing in March 1958 and a Soviet-US moratorium on nuclear testing from November 1958 until 1960.

67. "Linus Pauling and the International Peace Movement," Special Collections and Archives Research Center, Oregon State University, http://scarc.library.oregonstate.edu/coll/pauling/peace/narrative/page27.html.

68. "P'yŏnghwa rŭl sarang hanŭn ŏmŏnidŭl ŭi ilch'ihan nyŏmwŏn," 1.

69. Lee Jae-Bong, "U.S. Deployment of Nuclear Weapons in 1950s South Korea and North Korea's Nuclear Development: Toward the Denuclearization of the Korean Peninsula," *Asia-Pacific Journal* 7, no. 8 (2009), Steven Hugh Lee, "The Korean Armistice and the End of Peace: The US-UN Coalition and the Dynamics of War-Making in Korea, 1953–76," *Journal of Korean Studies* 18, no. 2 (2013): 183–224.

70. "The Cairo Conference for Solidarity between the People of Africa and Asia," *Women of the Whole World*, February 1958, 6. Despite hopes, AAPSO became the arena for some of the sharpest Sino-Soviet clash and China left the group in 1967. See Jeremy Friedman, *Shadow Cold War: The Sino-Soviet Competition for the Third World* (Chapel Hill: University of North Carolina Press, 2015), 196.

71. Carmen Zanti, "Two Continents in Cairo," *Women of the Whole World*, March 1958, 6.

72. Eslanda Goode Robeson, "Paul Robeson Jitterbugs in Middle Asia," *Women of the Whole World*, no. 1 (1959), 14.

73. "They Called It the Writers' Bandung," *Women of the Whole World*, no. 1 (1959), 11. See also Shirley Graham, "African Women Take Their Rightful Place!," *Women of the Whole World*, no. 1 (1959), 12–13.

74. "They Called It the Writers' Bandung," 11.

75. Although the Afro-Asian Writers' Bureau as a permanent committee formed in Colombo, Sri Lanka, as suggested at the Writers' Bandung, this also splintered in 1966 between a Beijing-based bureau and a Cairo-based Permanent Bureau of Afro-Asian Writers. Before this split, however, the bureau published an anthology of translated poems from Asia and Africa, *Afro-Asian Poems: Anthology*, vol. 1, 2 parts (Colombo: Afro-Asian Writers' Bureau, 1963). Korean poets featured in the anthology include Paik In Joon, Jo Ki Chon, Jung Joon Ki, Lee Maik, Jung Ha Chon, Choi Yong Hwa, Jung Dong Woo, Kim Cho Kyew, and An Sung Soo. For more on this see Duncan McEachern Yoon, "Cold War Africa-China: The Afro-Asian Writers' Bureau and the Rise of Postcolonial Literature" (PhD diss., University of California Los Angeles, 2014). After the split, the Cairo-based bureau published a trilingual quarterly journal, *Lotus*, from 1968 until the early 1990s, through which many important works from Asia and Africa continued to be translated. See Zeyad el Nabolsy, "*Lotus* and the Self-Representation of Afro-Asian Writers as the Vanguard of Modernity," *Interventions*, 2020; Hala Halim, "Afro-Asian Third-Worldism into Global South: The Case of *Lotus* Journal," *Global South Studies: A Collective Publication with the Global South*, November 22, 2017.

76. Eslanda Goode Robeson, "Africa for the Africans," *Women of the Whole World*, no. 3 (1959), 11.

77. Gabriela Mistral, "The Accursed Word," *Women of the Whole World*, no. 3 (1959), 32.

78. For similar debates in the context of the women's peace movement in the United States see Amy Swerdlow, *Women Strike for Peace: Traditional Motherhood and Radical Politics in the 1960s* (Chicago: University of Chicago Press, 1993).

79. *Special Information Bulletin after the World Congress of Women*, no. 6 (December 1, 1953), 2.

80. Ina Möller, "Women Are Adult Persons—They Have the Right to Equality," *Women of the Whole World*, June 1958, 11–12.

81. Russell, *Tamarisk Tree 3*, 220 (emphasis in original).

82. *Protection of Motherhood: As a Right of Women and a Responsibility of Society* (Berlin: WIDF, 1958), 3.

83. Maria-Teresa Gallo, "The Study Days in Potsdam," *Women of the Whole World*, November 1957, 5.

84. Gallo, 5–6.

85. Gallo, 6.

86. *Protection of Motherhood*, 83–84.

87. Dora Russell, "What Is Political?," *Women of the Whole World*, no. 1 (1959), 16.

88. "Peace, National Independence, Women's Rights," *Women of the Whole World*, July/August 1958, 5.

89. "The Role and Responsibility of Women in the World Today and the Tasks of the WIDF," *Women of the Whole World*, July/August 1958, 6–12, 29.

90. Kim Yŏng-su, "Han'gaji nyŏmwŏn ŭro tanhap toeyŏtta: Kukje nyŏmaeng che-4-ch'a taehoe e ch'amga hago" [United in one wish: Upon attending the WIDF fourth congress], *Chosŏn Nyŏsŏng*, July 1958, 14.

91. "Kukje minju nyŏsŏng ryŏnmaeng che-4-ch'a taehoe ŭi sŏnŏn ŭl chiji handa: Pyongyang nyŏsŏng yŏlsŏngja hoeŭi esŏ" [We support the declaration of the WIDF fourth congress: At the Pyongyang women enthusiast meeting], *Chosŏn Nyŏsŏng*, July 1958, 18.

92. "Che-1-ch'a Asea Ap'ŭrik'a nyŏsŏng taehoe" [The first Asian-African Women's Conference], *Chosŏn Nyŏsŏng*, February 1961, 19.

93. Armstrong, "Before Bandung," 316–17.

94. Kim Se-gyŏng, "Sujŏngjuŭi nŭn chegukjuŭijadŭl ege pokmu hanŭn sasang ida" [Reformism is an ideology that serves imperialists], *Chosŏn Nyŏsŏng*, August 1958, 28–29. The editorial attacks reformism as a form of bourgeois ideology that neutralizes the power of class revolution under the pretext that Marxism-Leninism is dogmatic and outdated. The critique was made in the context of purging domestic challengers such as Ch'oe Ch'ang-ik, Kim Tu-bong, and Sŏ Hwi against Kim Il Sung's hegemony amid de-Stalinization campaigns within the socialist bloc. While the editorial took indirect aim at Soviet reformism, it nonetheless concluded by hailing the Soviet Union as liberator of Korea, indicative of Korean dependence on Soviet support during the Cold War.

95. I have not found archival evidence on precisely when membership was withdrawn. However, the China National Museum of Women and Children in Beijing (visited May 24, 2018) included a display indicating the withdrawal in 1969. Not surprisingly, there was no mention in the museum of the impact of the Cultural Revolution on the cessation of ACWF activities between 1966 and 1978, but given this and the geopolitical impact of the Sino-Soviet split, I found no indication of Chinese women's involvement in the WIDF after 1963. The ACWF sent a telegram to the WIDF refusing to participate in the 1966 World Conference for Children, expressing disagreement with the agenda; the WIDF in turn rejected the telegram as "unacceptable." See "World Conference for Children: Four Well-Spent Days," *Women of the Whole World*, no. 4 (1966), 38.

96. Soviet Women's Committee documents seem to highlight the positives, especially Soviet achievements on women's rights as exemplified by Tereshkova herself, with little detail about conflicts at the congress. See Anna Kadnikova, "The Women's International Democratic Federation World Congress of Women, Moscow, 1963: Women's Rights and World Politics during the Cold War" (MA thesis, Central European University, 2011). For readings of greater dissent from the same archive see Gradskova, *Women's International Democratic Federation*, 127–31.

97. *World Congress of Women, Moscow, June 1963* (Berlin: WIDF, 1963), 3.

98. *World Congress of Women*, 83.
99. *World Congress of Women*, 84.
100. *World Congress of Women*, 84.
101. *World Congress of Women*, 3.
102. *World Congress of Women*, 15.
103. *World Congress of Women*, 17–18.
104. *World Congress of Women*, 11–12.
105. *World Congress of Women*, 9.
106. *The Struggle between Two Lines at the Moscow World Congress of Women* (Peking: Foreign Languages Press, 1963).
107. *Struggle between Two Lines*, 2.
108. *Struggle between Two Lines*, 4.
109. *Struggle between Two Lines*, 5.
110. *Struggle between Two Lines*, 6.
111. *Struggle between Two Lines*, 12–15.
112. *Struggle between Two Lines*, 39–40.
113. *Struggle between Two Lines*, 23.
114. *Struggle between Two Lines*, 25–30.
115. *Struggle between Two Lines*, 29–30.
116. *Struggle between Two Lines*, 33. Quotes in the rest of the paragraph come from pages 33–34.
117. *Struggle between Two Lines*, 42. Information in the rest of this paragraph can be found on pages 42–44.
118. Kadnikova, "Women's International Democratic Federation," 34.
119. The Group of 77, or G-77, was formed on June 15, 1964, by the signatory countries to the "Joint Declaration of the Seventy-Seven Developing Countries" at the end of the first session of the UN Conference on Trade and Development (UNCTAD), to "promote their collective economic interests and enhance their joint negotiating capacity." Although the original name has been retained for its historical significance, there are currently 134 member states, including North Korea. See https://www.g77.org/doc/index.html.
120. *Struggle between Two Lines*, 45. Information in the rest of this paragraph can be found on pages 45–50.
121. *World Congress of Women*, 93–94.
122. Katharine McGregor, "The Cold War, Indonesian Women and the Global Anti-imperialist Movement, 1946–65," in *De-centering Cold War History: Local and Global Change*, ed. Jadwiga E. Pieper Mooney and Fabio Lanza (New York: Routledge, 2013), 31–51.
123. Katharine McGregor, "The World Was Silent? Global Communities of Resistance to the 1965 Repression in the Cold War Era," in *Truth, Silence and Violence in Emerging State Histories of the Unspoken*, ed. Aidan Russell (New York: Routledge, 2019), 149.
124. McGregor, "World Was Silent?," 157. For more on Soenito-Heyligers and her Indonesian husband see the biographical entry for Raden Mas Djojowirono Sunito (also spelled Soenito) at https://socialhistory.org/bwsa/biografie/sunito.
125. Nina Popova, "Cement the Unity of the Women in the Struggle for Peace and Progress," Soviet Women's Committee (Moscow, 1963), 22.
126. Popova, "Cement the Unity," 24 (emphasis in original).
127. "Segye nyŏsŏng taehoe p'emak" [Closing of the World Congress of Women], *Rodong Sinmun*, July 2, 1963, 3.
128. "Segye nyŏsŏng taehoe e ch'amgahan Chosŏn nyŏsŏng taep'yodan sŏngmyŏng palp'yo" [Korean women's delegation to the World Congress of Women releases statement], *Rodong Sinmun*, July 2, 1963, 3.

129. See full-page spread under the heading "P'yŏnghwa wa chayu wa haebang ŭl wihayŏ segye nyŏsŏng tŭrŭn chegukjuŭi rŭl pandae hayŏ kyŏn'gyŏrhi t'ujaeng haja!" [For peace, freedom, and liberation, let us women around the world fight steadfastly against imperialism!], *Rodong Sinmun*, July 24, 1963, 3–4.

130. "Let's Defend the Socialist Camp" [Sahoejuŭi chinyŏng ŭl ongho haja], *Rodong Sinmun*, October 28, 1963, cited in Kevin Gray and Jong-Woon Lee, *North Korea and the Geopolitics of Development* (Cambridge: Cambridge University Press, 2021), 94. Despite the strong rhetoric, relations with the Soviet Union would improve after Khrushchev's fall in 1964, while those with China would worsen, especially after the Red Guards criticized Kim Il Sung as revisionist in 1967 (94–95).

131. Odd Arne Westad, *The Global Cold War: Third World Interventions and the Making of Our Times* (Cambridge: Cambridge University Press, 2005), 107; Gradskova, *Women's International Democratic Federation*, 35.

132. Kay Ann Johnson, *Women, the Family and Peasant Revolution in China* (Chicago: University of Chicago Press, 1983), 180–81.

133. Reem Abou-El-Fadl, "Building Egypt's Afro-Asian Hub: Infrastructures of Solidarity and the 1957 Cairo Conference," *Journal of World History* 30, no. 1–2 (June 2019): 191. As Abou-El-Fadl shows, even throughout Nasser's reign, popular solidarity was limited by state control of political expression, Sino-Soviet conflict, and competing regional loyalties between Arab, Muslim, and African identities in the Middle East, as well as tensions caused by different positions toward Israel.

134. Mark T. Berger, "After the Third World? History, Destiny and the Fate of Third Worldism," *Third World Quarterly* 25, no. 1 (2004): 27.

4. WOMEN'S WORK IS NEVER DONE

1. "Who Says Women's Work Is Never Done?," *Women of the Whole World*, no. 2 (1959), 23–26.

2. "Who Says," 23.

3. "Who Says," 26.

4. "Uri ŭi charang uri ŭi him" [Our pride our strength], *Chosŏn Nyŏsŏng*, March 1953, 60–64.

5. Hyŏn Yonggyun, "Nyŏsŏnjang" [Female captain], in *Nyŏsŏng tŭl ŭi iyagi* [Women's stories] (Pyongyang: Chosŏn nyŏsŏngsa, 1957), 3, 17.

6. Hyŏn, 18, 20.

7. *Chŏn'guk nyŏsŏng sahoejuŭi kŏnsŏlja hoeŭi munhŏnjip* [Documents of the national meeting of women socialist builders] (Pyongyang: Chosŏn nyŏsŏngsa, 1959), 100–102.

8. Kim T'ae-sŏng, "Nae kohyang" [My hometown], *Chosŏn Nyŏsŏng*, March 1954, 37.

9. For a discussion of how Soviet Stakhanovism was adapted in China to launch the model laborer campaign beginning already in 1942 see Miin-ling Yu, "'Labor Is Glorious': Model Laborers in the People's Republic of China," in *China Learns from the Soviet Union, 1949–Present*, ed. Thomas P. Bernstein and Hua-Yu Li (Lanham, MD: Lexington Books, 2010), 231–58. Yu distinguishes the Chinese from the Soviet campaign in valorizing the peasantry and focusing on cost-saving measures rather than record-breaking productivity because of material constraints, sharing similarities to North Korea. For additional sources on Chinese women's experiences of work with parallels to Korea see Gail Hershatter, "Local Meanings of Gender and Work in Rural Shaanxi in the 1950s," 79–96, and Emily Honig, "Iron Girls Revisited: Gender and the Politics of Work in the Cultural Revolution, 1966–76," 97–110, in *Re-drawing Boundaries: Work, Households, and Gender in China*, ed. Barbara Entwisle and Gail E. Henderson (Berkeley: University of California Press, 2000).

10. "Ttŭrakttorŭrŭl unjŏn hanŭn nyŏsŏngdŭl" [Tractor-driving women], *Chosŏn Nyŏsŏng*, March 1954, 39–40. On Pasha Praskovya see Angelina Praskovya, *My Answer to an American Questionnaire* (Moscow: Foreign Language Publishing House, 1951), Marxists Internet Achive, https://www.marxists.org/archive/praskovya/1947/my-answer/text.htm. For a discussion of "tractor girls" in China see Daisy Yan Du, "Socialist Modernity in the Wasteland: Changing Representations of the Female Tractor Driver in China, 1949–1964," *Modern Chinese Literature and Culture* 29, no. 1 (2017): 55–94.

11. "Ch'ŏnyŏ ttŭrakttorŭ unjŏnsu: Pyongyang nonggigye chagŏpso ttŭrakttorŭ unjŏnsu Kim Yŏng-ja tongmu" [Tractor-driving maiden: Tractor Comrade Kim Yŏng-ja], *Chosŏn Nyŏsŏng*, January 1964, 48–49.

12. For a recent introduction to the main arguments see the dossier on social reproduction theory in *Radical Philosophy* 2, no. 4 (Spring 2019), https://www.radicalphilosophy.com/issues/204, and Susan Ferguson, *Women and Work: Feminism, Labour, and Social Reproduction* (London: Pluto, 2019).

13. Pointing to the vast majority of the world in which informal rather than waged labor makes up most work, Alessandra Mezzadri shows how reproductive work contributes to value generation by expanding the rate of exploitation in the process of externalizing and subsidizing the reproductive costs of capital. In doing so, Mezzadri indicts the whole corpus of classical political economy from Adam Smith and David Ricardo to Marx for the "reification and fetishisation of the wage as the value rather than the cost of labour that provides the premises for productivist understandings of value generation." See Alessandra Mezzadri, "On the Value of Social Reproduction: Informal Labour, the Majority World and the Need for Inclusive Theories and Politics," *Radical Philosophy* 2, no. 04 (Spring 2019): 36.

14. Maria Mies, *Patriarchy and Accumulation on a World Scale: Women in the International Division of Labour* (1986; London: Zed Books, 2014), 110.

15. Mies examines the Soviet Union, China, and Vietnam to argue that state attempts to liberate women by enabling their entry into "socially productive" labor failed to do so because women were still in charge of "unproductive" housework. Provision of public services remained concentrated in cities and inadequate to meet all needs, she argues, and labor was still segregated along gendered lines, while women were unable to compete in the labor market or in political positions because of their household responsibilities. Still, Mies's examination of China shows how women became worse off in the post-Mao era, as they were no longer considered workers, but housewives and breeders under the one-child policy. However limited, Mies's discussion of China therefore challenges her own argument by showing the potential for state intervention and mass revolutionary campaigns to upend gender roles.

16. Mies, *Patriarchy and Accumulation*, 108–9.

17. Marsha Siefert, introduction to *Labor in State-Socialist Europe, 1945–1989: Contributions to a History of Work*, edited by Marsha Siefert (Budapest: Central European University Press, 2020), 14. See also Chiara Bonfiglioli, "Discussing Women's Double and Triple Burden in Socialist Yugoslavia: Women Working in the Garment Industry," 195–218, in the same volume.

18. An Yŏng-suk, "Chasaeng chagyŏl ŭi maŭl" [Village of self-production, self-determination], *Chosŏn Nyŏsŏng*, December 1953, 26–28.

19. Yi Im-ha, *Haebang konggan, ilsang ŭl pakkun yŏsŏngdŭl ŭi yŏksa* [Liberated space: Women's history of changes in everyday life] (Seoul: Ch'ŏlsu wa yŏnghŭi, 2015), 50.

20. Editorial team, "Saenghwal munhwarŭl malhanŭn chwadamhoe" [Roundtable on everyday life culture], *Saenghwal munhwa* [Everyday life culture] 1, no. 2 (1946): 23–32, quoted in Yi, *Haebang konggan*, 51.

21. For a helpful introduction to the development of SRT from which much of this paragraph's discussion is based see Zöe Sutherland and Marina Vishmidt, "The Soft Disappointment of Prefiguration," lecture at the Centre for Social and Political Thought, University of Sussex, June 2015. The authors warn that Silvia Federici (2018), in her recent expanded notion of reproductive commons from an eco-feminist position advocating "egalitarian subsistence" through self-organized care in the face of disasters, risks conflating what is necessary for survival (means) with what is actually the solution (end), "renaturalising" gendered and racialized labor as inherently resistant. For other helpful discussions on the topic see also Cinzia Arruzza, "Functionalist, Determinist, Reductionist: Social Reproduction Feminism and Its Critics," *Science & Society* 80, no. 1 (January 2016): 9–30; and Amy De'Ath, "Gender and Social Reproduction," in *The SAGE Handbook of Frankfurt School Critical Theory*, ed. Beverley Best, Werner Bonefeld, and Chris O'Kane (London: SAGE, 2018), 1534–50.

22. Lise Vogel, *Marxism and the Oppression of Women* (1983; Boston: Brill, 2013). A version of this crisis was seen during the COVID-19 pandemic as waged care work, already woefully underpaid, could no longer be relied on by families dependent on outsourcing domestic labor to sustain their "minimized" social reproduction.

23. Lise Vogel, foreword to *Social Reproduction Theory: Remapping Class, Recentering Oppression*, edited by Tithi Bhattacharya (London: Pluto, 2017), x.

24. Arruzza, "Functionalist, Determinist, Reductionist," 21–22.

25. Im Sun-dŭk, "Nyŏsŏng kwa kŭllo" [Women and labor], *Chosŏn Nyŏsŏng*, April 1950, 43.

26. Im, 44.

27. Susan Ferguson, "Intersectionality and Social-Reproduction Feminisms: Toward an Integrative Ontology," *Historical Materialism* 24, no. 2 (2016): 48. Tithi Bhattacharya likewise defines labor broadly: "The fundamental insight of SRT is, simply put, that human labor is at the heart of creating or reproducing society as a whole." See Tithi Bhattacharya, Introduction to *Social Reproduction Theory*, 2.

28. "The Logic of Gender: On the Separation of Spheres and the Process of Abjection," Endnotes 3—Gender, Race, Class, and Other Misfortunes, September 2013, https://endnotes.org.uk/issues/3/en/endnotes-the-logic-of-gender. All quotes and discussion in this paragraph come from this helpful essay. The piece was later republished under Maya Gonzalez and Jeanne Neton, "The Logic of Gender: On the Separation of Spheres and the Process of Abjection," in *Contemporary Marxist Theory: A Reader*, ed. Andrew Pendakis, Jeff Diamanti, Nicholas Brown, Josh Robinson, and Imre Szeman (London: Bloomsbury, 2014), 149–74. Criticizing the ahistorical and imprecise binary terms such as productive-reproductive, paid-unpaid, and public-private that undergird biologized accounts of gender inequality, Gonzalez and Neton conceptualize gender as two separated spheres that take on different values in the economy, with one *structurally made non-labor*. To call this sphere "private" or "reproductive" or "unwaged" is inaccurate, they argue, since what renders it separate is not its location or its function, but rather the level at which labor is mediated by the market.

29. For a helpful conceptual differentiation between capitalist and socialist accumulation, as explained by a 1974 socialist political economy primer, see Klaus Hagendorf, "On Socially Necessary Labour," December 3, 2013, at https://ssrn.com/abstract=2362858. This is an English translation of a section from *Introduction to the Political Economy of Socialism*, chap. 8: "The Planned Use of Commodity Money Relations in Socialism," produced by the Institute of Social Sciences of the Central Committee of the Socialist Party in the former German Democratic Republic. A chart on page 12 differentiates between socialist accumulation of "funds" aimed to provide for the reproduction of the population by planned use of surplus to increase welfare, whereas the accumulation of capital

provides capitalists with private profits through the exploitation of the population, leading to class polarization.

30. Kim Kang-sik, "Pukhan ŭi rodong chedo wa Pukhan ilyŏk kwalli" [Labor system and human resource management in North Korea], *Chilsŏ kyŏngje chŏnŏl* [Journal of economic order] 4, no. 2 (2001): 9.

31. Yun Ŭi-sŏp and Ch'a Sun-hŏn, *Konghwaguk esŏŭi imgŭm chojik hwa rodong ŭi kijunhwa* [The organization of wages and labor standardization in the republic] (Pyongyang: Kungrip ch'ulp'ansa, 1955), 13, 17–18.

32. Yun and Ch'a, 41.

33. Yun and Ch'a, 41, 155–56.

34. Joseph Sang-hoon Chung, *The North Korean Economy: Structure and Development* (Stanford, CA: Hoover Institution, 1974), 144.

35. Min Sŏn-bi, "Nong'ŏp hyŏpdong chohap esŏ ŭi na ŭi nyŏmaengban saŏp" [My women's union work in the agricultural cooperative], *Chosŏn Nyŏsŏng*, July 1954, 20–24.

36. O Yi-suk, "Chikjang, kajŏng, chanyŏ kyoyuk" [Work, family, children's education], *Chosŏn Nyŏsŏng*, October 1954, 34–38.

37. O, "Chikjang," 37.

38. Hwang Kŭm-ja, "Uri tong ŭi yesul ssŏk'ŭl kyŏnghŏm" [Experience in our county arts circle], *Chosŏn Nyŏsŏng*, May 1966, 72.

39. Ko Wŏn-ja, "Nanŭn tto tasi kyodan e sŏtta" [I stand again at the podium], *Chosŏn Nyŏsŏng*, March 1955, 53.

40. Carter Eckert, *Offspring of Empire: The Koch'ang Kims and the Colonial Origins of Korean Capitalism, 1876–1945* (Seattle: University of Washington Press, 1991); Ken Kawashima, *The Proletarian Gamble: Korean Workers in Interwar Japan* (Durham, NC: Duke University Press, 2009).

41. Martina Deuchler, *The Confucian Transformation of Korea: A Study of Society and Ideology* (Cambridge, MA: Harvard University Press, 1995).

42. An Kŭm-sŏn, "Uri ŭi rodong ŭn 'p'ump'ari' ka animnida" [Our labor is not for wages], *Chosŏn Nyŏsŏng*, June 1955, 48–49.

43. Kang Kŭm-nan, "Roryŏk e taehayŏ sŏngsilhan t'aedorŭl kajipsida" [Let's have a sincere attitude toward labor], *Chosŏn Nyŏsŏng*, September 1955, 30–31.

44. Kim Chŏng-hye, "Saenghwal ŭi saegyosil: Chikjang e chinch'ulhan puyang kajokdŭl ŭi chwadamhoe" [New classroom of life: Roundtable of dependent families of working women], *Chosŏn Nyŏsŏng*, March 1956, 12–14.

45. "Kajŏng puindŭl ŭn ŏttŏk'e sahoejuŭi kŏnsŏl e ch'amgahal kŏsin'ga" [How will housewives participate in building socialism], *Chosŏn Nyŏsŏng*, July 1957, 4–5.

46. Kevin Gray and Jong-Woon Lee, *North Korea and the Geopolitics of Development* (Cambridge: Cambridge University Press, 2021), 72.

47. Gray and Lee, 62. Although foreign aid focused on rebuilding the industrial base by providing machinery and technical assistance to various existing factories and power plants, aid also went to addressing consumer needs by building new meat-processing, fish-canning, and textile factories (64). Nonetheless, during the Three-Year Plan, as much as 80 percent of investments in the industrial sector went to heavy industry, resulting in especially negative impacts on the agricultural sector, with reports of food shortages in the mid-1950s (66–68). See also Rüdiger Frank, "Lessons from the Past: The First Wave of Development Assistance to North Korea and the German Reconstruction of Hamhung," *Pacific Focus* 23, no 1 (2008): 46–74.

48. Gray and Lee, *North Korea and the Geopolitics of Development*, 65, 78–79.

49. "Chŏn'guk nyŏsŏng sahoejuŭi kŏnsŏlja hoeŭi" [National conference of women socialist builders], *Chosŏn Nyŏsŏng*, April 1959, 2–3.

50. *Chŏn'guk nyŏsŏng sahoejuŭi kŏnsŏlja hoeŭi munhŏnjip*, 15.

278   NOTES TO PAGES 147–153

51. In North Korean usage, a "trust" refers to the pooling of investments in a particular industry into a monopoly to avoid competition and foster cooperation. See http://krdic.naver.com/detail.nhn?docid=39859000.
52. *Chŏn'guk nyŏsŏng sahoejuŭi kŏnsŏlja hoeŭi munhŏnjip*, 19.
53. *Chŏn'guk nyŏsŏng sahoejuŭi*, 33.
54. *Chŏn'guk nyŏsŏng sahoejuŭi*, 38–39.
55. *Chŏn'guk nyŏsŏng sahoejuŭi*, 27.
56. "Nyŏsŏng tŭrŭl wihayŏ" [For women], *Chosŏn Nyŏsŏng*, November 1958, 29.
57. Chu Hyŏng-do, "Puŏk esŏ haebang toeyŏtta" [Liberated from the kitchen], *Chosŏn Nyŏsŏng*, April 1959, 20–21.
58. "Saehoejuŭi kŏnsŏl esŏ nyŏsŏngdŭl ŭi yŏk'al ŭl chegohalde taehayŏ" [On uplifting women's role in building socialism], *Rodong Sinmun*, March 29, 1959, 2.
59. "Saehoejuŭi kŏnsŏl esŏ," 2.
60. *Chŏn'guk nyŏsŏng sahoejuŭi*, 109–12.
61. "Kisul hyŏksin kwa nyŏsŏng" [Technological innovation and women], *Chosŏn Nyŏsŏng*, May 1965, 14–19. For an analysis of the Seven-Year Plan and the difficulties in meeting its goals that coincided with a slowdown in the rest of the centrally planned economies see Gray and Lee, *North Korea and the Geopolitics of Development*, 91.
62. Kim Chŏng-sun, "Ssŭlde ŏpsi namjadŭl ŭi himman paraji malja" [Let's not rely on men's strength needlessly], *Chosŏn Nyŏsŏng*, May 1965, 14.
63. Kim Ok-sun, "Han'gaji il ŭl orae haeya handa" [One must commit to one type of work for a long time], *Chosŏn Nyŏsŏng*, May 1965, 15.
64. Pak Sun-ja, "Na ŭi ch'ehŏm" [My experience], *Chosŏn Nyŏsŏng*, May 1965, 17.
65. "Sangdamsil" [Consultation room], *Chosŏn Nyŏsŏng*, May 1965, 46.
66. Chŏn Kŭm-ok, "Taedamsŏng i issŏya handa" [Be bold], *Chosŏn Nyŏsŏng*, May 1965, 18.
67. Ri Yŏng-suk, "Sinbisŏng ŭi wŏninŭn" [Reason for mysticism], *Chosŏn Nyŏsŏng*, May 1965, 19.
68. "Rodong e taehan chinsilhan t'aedo" [Sincere attitude toward labor], *Chosŏn Nyŏsŏng*, October 1959, 14–16.
69. "Manhwa: % pyŏng e kŏllin kyŏlgwa" [Comic: As a result of percentage illness], *Chosŏn Nyŏsŏng*, March 1959, 40.
70. Ryuk Man-su, "Sahoejuŭijŏk punbae wŏnch'ik ŭl ch'ŏljŏhi chik'ija" [Let's strictly keep to the principle of socialist distribution], *Chosŏn Nyŏsŏng*, November 1959, 6–7.
71. "Sahoejuŭi punbae wŏnch'ik ŭl ch'ŏljŏhi kwanch'ŏl sik'ija!" [Let's strictly carry out the principle of socialist distribution], *Chosŏn Nyŏsŏng*, October 1960, 26–27.
72. Cho Young-Ju, "Pukhan ŭi inmin mandŭlgi wa chendŏ chŏngch'i: Paegŭp kwa sŏngbun-tang'wŏn chedo rŭl chungsim ŭro" [Making the people and gender politics in North Korea: Distribution and partisan system], *Han'guk yŏsŏnghak* [Journal of Korean women's studies] 29, no. 2 (2013): 129–30. Resources, whether in the form of better-paid jobs or PDS benefits, were allocated according to social hierarchy dependent on party membership, which could only be attained by proving one's commitment and loyalty to the state through one's personal and family history, whether as colonial-era revolutionaries, Korean War veterans, or productive workers (121–23).
73. Lee Seung-Yoon, Hwang Eun-Joo, and Kim Yuhwi, "Pukhan kongsik-pigongsik nodong sijang ŭi hyŏngsŏng kwa yŏsŏng" [Formal-informal labor market and women in North Korea], *Pip'an sahoe chŏngch'aek* [Journal of critical social policy] 48 (2015): 299. For a compilation of economic statistics published in North Korea for the 1946–1960 period without gender-disaggregated data see *Chosŏn minjujuŭi inmin konghwaguk inmin kyŏngje paljŏn t'onggyejip (1946–1960)* [Statistics on the people's economic development in the

Democratic People's Republic of Korea (1946–1960)] (Pyongyang: Kungrip ch'ulp'ansa, 1961).

74. Cho Young-Ju, "Pukhan yŏsŏng ŭi silch'ŏn kwa chendŏ rejim ŭi tonghak" [The practice of women and dynamics of gender regime in North Korea] (PhD diss., Ewha Women's University, 2012), 74.

75. Donna Harsch, *Revenge of the Domestic: Women, the Family, and Communism in the German Democratic Republic* (Princeton, NJ: Princeton University Press, 2007), 93–94. As Harsch shows in the case of East Germany, with parallels to North Korea, women themselves often did not want to go into manual labor, and women often moved jobs after marriage, depressing their wages. Nonetheless, women were overrepresented in poorly paid sectors and often took up the worse-paid positions even in the higher-paid sectors, with structural disadvantages in which women were arbitrarily ranked lower in skill level, leading to lower pay, and were not awarded bonuses at the same rate as men (96–99).

76. "Yi mobŏm ŭl ttarŭpsida" [Let's follow this model], *Chosŏn Nyŏsŏng*, September 1960, 36–37.

77. "Aegukjuŭi wa nara sallim sari" [Patriotism and the country's housekeeping], *Chosŏn Nyŏsŏng*, April 1966, 9.

78. "Chagŭn kŏsedo" [Even on small things], *Chosŏn Nyŏsŏng*, April 1966, 11.

79. Kong Kŭm-sŏn, "Saemmul i moyŏ pada ka toegŏnŭl" [As the spring water gathers to become the sea], *Chosŏn Nyŏsŏng*, April 1966, 13.

80. "Ajik tŏ chŏlyak halsu itta: Namp'osi kajŏng puindŭl kwa ŭi chwadamhoe" [One can still save more: Roundtable with housewives of Nampo City], *Chosŏn Nyŏsŏng*, June 1966, 39–41.

81. "Musimhi poji annŭn maŭm: Hwanghae pukdo Songrimsi yŏnyu chaesaeng kongjang p'eyu chaesaeng chagŏpban Kim Hyo-suk tongmu" [Heart that doesn't look carelessly: Comrade Kim Hyo-suk], *Chosŏn Nyŏsŏng*, June 1966, 42.

82. Ch'oe Hak-sin, "Pŏril kŏsiran ŏpsŭmnida" [There is nothing to throw away], *Chosŏn Nyŏsŏng*, June 1966, 42.

83. Andre Schmid argues, by contrast, that the state perceived domestic spaces as unproductive, with only rare references to domestic labor, using instead domestic affairs (*kasa*) as the naturalized work of women. See Andre Schmid, "The Gendered Anxieties of Apartment Living in North Korea, 1953–65," in *Postsocialist Landscapes: Real and Imaginary Spaces from Stalinstadt to Pyongyang*, ed. Thomas Lahusen and Schamma Schahadat (Bielefeld, Germany: transcript Verlag, 2020), 281–303. He notes, however, that women pushed back against the idea of "unproductive" domestic spaces, and the state compromised to promote "household labour" (*kanae nodong*) to mobilize women outside the workforce. See Andre Schmid, "Comrade Min, Women's Paid Labour, and the Centralising Party-State: Postwar Reconstruction in North Korea," in *Everyday Life in Mass Dictatorship: Collusion and Evasion*, ed. Alf Lüdtke (London: Palgrave Macmillan, 2015), 197–198.

84. "Chŏn'guk ŏmŏni taehoe" [National Mothers Congress], *Chosŏn Nyŏsŏng*, November 1961, 8.

85. Cheehyung Harrison Kim, *Heroes and Toilers: Work as Life in Postwar North Korea, 1953–1961* (New York: Columbia University Press, 2018).

86. Pak Yŏng-ja, *Pukhan nyŏja: T'ansaeng kwa kuljŏl ŭi 70-nyŏnsa* [North Korean Women: 70-year history of birth and refraction] (Seoul: Aelp'i, 2017).

87. *Chŏn'guk ŏmŏni taehoe munhŏnjip* [Documents of the National Mothers Congress] (Pyongyang: Chosŏn nyŏsŏngsa, 1961).

88. *Chŏn'guk ŏmŏni*, 49.

89. *Chŏn'guk ŏmŏni*, 76.

90. "Chikjang kwa nyŏsŏng: Chikjang e taninŭn aegi ŏmŏnidŭl kwa ŭi chwadamhoe esŏ" [Workplace and women: At a roundtable of working mothers with babies], *Chosŏn Nyŏsŏng*, August 1962, 18–21.

91. "Ronsŏl: Ŏmŏni taehoe kyosi kwanch'ŏl ŭl wihan saŏp ŭl tŏuk simhwa sik'ikja" [Editorial: Let's deepen the work to carry out the lessons of the Mothers Congress], *Chosŏn Nyŏsŏng*, November 1964, 11–12.

92. "Mosŏng rodongjadŭl e taehan tang kwa chŏngbu ŭi ttohana ŭi paeryŏ" [Another consideration by the party and government for mother workers], *Chosŏn Nyŏsŏng*, November 1966, 20.

93. "Tang kwa suryŏng e taehan muhanhan ch'ungsŏng ŭi chŏng i hŭllŏ nŏmch'in chŏn'guk poyugwŏn kyoyangwŏn taehoe" [The National Congress of Childcare Workers full of unlimited loyalty to the party and the leader], *Chosŏn Nyŏsŏng*, December 1966, 25–26.

94. Kim Ok-sun, "Chŏn'guk poyugwŏn kyoyangwŏn taehoe esŏ han pogo" [Report at the National Congress of Childcare Workers], *Chosŏn Nyŏsŏng*, December 1966, 5–6.

95. Gray and Lee, *North Korea and the Geopolitics of Development*, 82–83.

96. Kim Ok-sun, "Chŏn'guk poyugwŏn kyoyangwŏn taehoe esŏ han pogo," 7.

97. Kim, 9.

98. Kim, 11.

99. Kim, 10.

100. Joungwon Alexander Kim, "The 'Peak of Socialism' in North Korea: The Five and Seven Year Plans," *Asian Survey* 5, no. 5 (1965): 265. Although primary investment still went into heavy industry, the first half of the Seven-Year Plan stressed light over heavy industry so that "the percentage of investment in light industry increased from 18.4% of total investment in industry in 1959 to 36.3% in 1962, whereas heavy industrial investment decreased correspondingly from 81.6% to 63.7%" (262).

101. Chung, *North Korean Economy*, 159.

102. Joseph Sang-hoon Chung, "North Korea's 'Seven Year Plan' (1961–70): Economic Performance and Reforms," *Asian Survey* 12, no. 6 (1972): 529. Chung attributes North Korea's poor economic performance in the 1960s to the declining efficiency of central planning, planning errors from statistical inflation and unrealistic targets, and increasing defense burdens, in the context of general slowdowns throughout Eastern Europe and the Soviet Union that led those regions to adopt reforms. While its reforms were more limited, North Korea also adopted incentive systems, with a work-team bonus system at collective farms and decentralized decision-making in the use of resources at the consumption level by abolishing the national agricultural tax-in-kind and expanding local state enterprises managed at the county and municipal levels (rather than by provincial authorities) through an independent economic accounting system (*tongrip ch'aesanje*) rather than a budget allocation system (540–42). Nonetheless, Chung argues that countermovements by the State Planning Commission and non-material campaigns offset any of these tendencies toward liberalization and decentralization (543–45). For fuller treatment see Chung, *North Korean Economy*. For the impact of international geopolitics on economic policy see Gray and Lee, *North Korea and the Geopolitics of Development*, and on the impact of catch-up industrialization on the development of the political system see Kim Yŏn-ch'ŏl, *Pukhan ŭi sanŏphwa wa kyŏngje chŏngch'aek* (Seoul: Yŏksa Pip'yŏngsa, 2001).

103. Yun Se-p'yŏng, "Kojŏn munhak e panyŏngdoen Chosŏn nyŏsŏng ŭi todŏkjŏk p'umsŏng" [The moral character of Korean women reflected in classical literature], *Chosŏn Nyŏsŏng*, March 1955, 40. Yun Se-p'yŏng (known as Yun Kyu-sŏp before moving to the North) settled in the North in 1946 to become a member of the Central Executive Committee of the North Korean Literature and Arts League (Pukchosŏn munhak yesul ch'ong tongmaeng). Throughout the 1950s into the early 1960s, he actively published on

topics related to the construction of a new national literature, with a particular interest in Korean literary classics. See the biographical entry in Kwŏn Yŏng-min, *Han'guk hyŏndae munhak sajŏn* [Modern Korean literature dictionary] (Seoul: Seoul National University Press, 2004), at https://terms.naver.com/entry.nhn?docId=1832563&cid=41708&categoryId=41737.

104. Yun, "Kojŏn munhak e panyŏngdoen Chosŏn nyŏsŏng ŭi todŏkjŏk p'umsŏng," 41.
105. Yun, 41.
106. Yun, 42.
107. Yun, 42.
108. Yun Se-p'yŏng, "Ryŏksasang e nat'anan Chosŏn nyŏsŏngdŭl ŭi todŏkjŏk p'umsŏng" [The moral character of Korean women in history], *Chosŏn Nyŏsŏng*, April 1955, 38.
109. Yun, "Ryŏksasang e nat'anan Chosŏn," 40.
110. Cho Pyŏng-ryun, "Rijo sigi ŭi nyŏsŏngdŭl ŭi saenghwal" [Life of women during the Yi dynasty], *Chosŏn Nyŏsŏng*, June 1955, 60.
111. Cho, 63.
112. "Kŭnŭn taeŭiwŏni toeyŏtta" [She became a Supreme People's Assembly representative], *Chosŏn Nyŏsŏng*, October 1962, 2–8.
113. "Chosŏn minju nyŏsŏng tongmaeng che-3-ch'a tahoe chinhaeng" [Third Congress of the Korean Democratic Women's Union], *Chosŏn Nyŏsŏng*, September 1965, 55–56.
114. *Chosŏn minju nyŏsŏng tongmaeng che-3-ch'a taehoe munhŏnjip* [Documents of the Korean Democratic Women's Union Third Congress] (Pyongyang: Kŭllo tanch'ae ch'ulp'ansa, 1965), 112–13.
115. *Chosŏn minju nyŏsŏng*, 11.
116. *Chosŏn minju nyŏsŏng*, 34.
117. *Chosŏn minju nyŏsŏng*, 35, 44.
118. *Chosŏn minju nyŏsŏng*, 241.
119. *Chosŏn minju nyŏsŏng*, 367.
120. Kim Ok-sun, "Namnyŏ p'yŏngdŭnggwŏn pŏmryŏng palp'o 20 chunyŏn" [Twenty-year anniversary of the promulgation of the Equal Rights Law], *Chosŏn Nyŏsŏng*, July 1966, 2–3.
121. Chang Ŭn-dŏk, "Kŭnal ŭi kamgyŏk" [The thrill of that day], *Chosŏn Nyŏsŏng*, July 1966, 5–7.
122. Chang, 5.
123. Chang, 6.
124. Chang, 6.
125. Chang, 7.
126. A poem dedicated to Kang Pan-sŏk was published in the April 1960 issue of *Chosŏn Nyŏsŏng*, as well as a short biography in the July 1961 issue. See Min Pyŏng-gyun, "Si: Chosŏn ŭi ŏmŏni—Kang Pan-sŏk ŏmŏnirŭl ch'umo hayŏ" [Poem: Mother of Korea—remembering Mother Kang Pan-sŏk], *Chosŏn Nyŏsŏng*, April 1960, 16–17; Pak Ryŏng-bo, "Chosŏn ŭi ŏmŏni" [Mother of Korea], *Chosŏn Nyŏsŏng*, July 1961, 6–9.
127. James F. Person, "The 1967 Purge of the Gapsan Faction and Establishment of the Monolithic Ideological System," North Korea International Documentation Project E-Dossier No. 15, https://www.wilsoncenter.org/publication/the-1967-purge-the-gapsan-faction-and-establishment-the-monolithic-ideological-system (accessed August 31, 2020).
128. For brief biographies of Kim Sŏng-ae see Fyodor Tertiskiy, "The Ebbs and Flows of Former N. Korean First Lady Kim Song Ae," Daily NK, November 20, 2019, at https://www.dailynk.com/english/the-ebbs-and-flows-of-former-n-korean-first-lady-kim-song-ae/,

and the entry for Kim Song Ae at the North Korea Leadership Watch, at https://nkleadershipwatch.wordpress.com/kim-family/kim-song-ae-kim-song-ae/.

129. Hwang Eun-ju, "Pukhan sŏng'in yŏsŏng ŭi chongch'i sahoehwa e kwanhan yŏn'gu: Chosŏn minju nyŏsŏng tongmaeng kwa 'Chosŏn Nyŏsŏng' punsŏk ŭl chungsim ŭro" [A study of women's political socialization in North Korea: Focusing on the Korean Democratic Women's Union and *Chosŏn Nyŏsŏng*] (MA thesis, Hanyang University, 1994).

5. AESTHETICS OF EVERYDAY FOLK

1. Young-Hoon Kim, "Border Crossing: Choe Seung-hui's Life and the Modern Experience," *Korea Journal* 46 (Spring 2006): 170–97.

2. While this list is not meant to be exhaustive, in addition to the materials cited in the rest of the chapter, publications in Korean include Chŏng Pyŏng-ho, *Ch'umch'unŭn Ch'oe Sŭnghŭi—segye rŭl huiŏjabŭn Chosŏn yŏja* [Dancing Choe Seung-hui—Korean woman who ruled the world] (Seoul: Ppuri kip'ŭn namu, 1995); Yu Mi-hŭi, "Pukhan muyong yesul kwa yŏsŏng haebang" [North Korean dance arts and women's liberation], *Han'guk muyong kyoyuk hakhoeji* [Journal of Korean dance education] 9, no. 1 (1998): 153–71; Ch'oe Sŏng-ok, "Haewoe kong'yŏn i Ch'oe Sŭnghŭi ŭi yesul segye e mich'in yŏnghyang" [Influence of tours abroad on Choe Seung-hui's artistic world], *Han'guk muyong kirok hakhoe* [Association of Korean dance documentation] 20 (2010): 107–33; Tong Kyŏng-wŏn, "Ch'oe Sŭng-hŭi muyong yŏn'gu: Chakp'um punsŏk mit kong'yŏn yesulsajŏk iŭi rŭl chungsim ŭro" [A study of Choe Seung-hui's dance: focusing on the artistic significance of her performance and analysis of her work], *Han'guk yesul yŏn'gu* [Korean arts studies] 9 (June 2014): 151–205, and in English, Young-Hoon Kim, "Border Crossing"; Sang Mi Park, "The Making of a Cultural Icon for the Japanese Empire: Choe Seung-hui's U.S. Dance Tours and 'New Asian Culture' in the 1930s and 1940s," *positions* 14, no. 3 (Winter 2006): 585–626; Judy Van Zile, *Perspectives on Korean Dance* (Middletown, CT: Wesleyan University Press, 2001) and "Performing Modernity in Korea: The Dance of Ch'oe Sŭng-hŭi," *Korean Studies* 37 (2013): 124–49; Faye Yuan Kleeman, *In Transit: The Formation of the Colonial East Asian Cultural Sphere* (Honolulu: University of Hawai'i Press, 2014); Emily Wilcox, "Crossing Over: Choe Seung-hui's Pan-Asianism in Revolutionary Time," *Muyong yŏksa kirokhak* [Journal of Society for Dance Documentation and History] 51 (December 2018): 65–97.

3. This is a reference to the concept "national in form and socialist in content" first articulated in a speech by Stalin. See J. V. Stalin, "The Political Tasks of the University of the Peoples of the East," speech delivered at a meeting of students of the Communist University of the Toilers of the East, May 18, 1925, at https://www.marxists.org/reference/archive/stalin/works/1925/05/18.htm. For Choe's influence in China see Wilcox, "Crossing Over."

4. Suk-Young Kim, *Illusive Utopia: Theater, Film, and Everyday Performance in North Korea* (Ann Arbor: University of Michigan Press, 2010), 11–16, 264, 277.

5. See, for example, Park, "Making of a Cultural Icon"; Van Zile, *Perspectives on Korean Dance*; and Kleeman, *In Transit*.

6. Okju Son, "Korean Dance beyond Koreanness," in *Corporeal Politics: Dancing East Asia*, ed. Emily Wilcox and Katherine Mezur (Ann Arbor: University of Michigan Press, 2020), 98–114.

7. For discussion of Choe's influence in the creation of a new Chinese dance vocabulary based on Peking opera and Kunqu, which led to the dance style known as Chinese classical dance, see Emily Wilcox, *Revolutionary Bodies: Chinese Dance and the Socialist Legacy* (Oakland: University of California Press, 2019).

8. For a definition of folk see https://www.merriam-webster.com/dictionary/folk, and for the use of the term over time see https://books.google.com/ngrams/graph?content=folk&year_start=1800&year_end=2008&case_insensitive=on&corpus=15.

9. For a helpful study tracing the colonial roots of the Chosŏn studies movement to the decolonizing Marxist ethnography in post-liberation North Korea of *Minsokhak* see Elli Sua Kim, "Rituals of Decolonization: The Role of Inner-Migrant Intellectuals in North Korea, 1948–1967" (PhD diss., University of California Los Angeles, 2014), chap. 1. On the indigenization of socialist realism in Korea, see Kim Tae-kyung, "Pukhan 'sahoejuŭi riŏlijŭm ŭi Chosŏnhwa': munhak esŏ ŭi tang ŭi yuilsasang ch'egye ŭi yŏksajŏk hyŏngsŏng" (PhD diss., Seoul National University, 2018).

10. Wilcox, *Revolutionary Bodies*, chap. 2.

11. For a fuller treatment of the emergence of the "everyday" as a novel experiential and temporal category in the age of industrial capital see Suzy Kim, *Everyday Life in the North Korean Revolution, 1945–1950* (Ithaca, NY: Cornell University Press, 2013).

12. Irina Gutkin, *The Cultural Origins of the Socialist Realist Aesthetic, 1890–1934* (Evanston, IL: Northwestern University Press, 1999), chap. 3. For a helpful history of the ways in which the arts came to serve everyday life as "industrial arts" in North Korea see Ch'oe Hŭi-sŏn, *Pukhan edo tijain i issŭlkka: Pukhan sanŏp misul 70-nyŏn* [Industrial art as design in North Korea] (Seoul: Damdi, 2020).

13. Francine Hirsch, *Empire of Nations: Ethnographic Knowledge and the Making of the Soviet Union* (Ithaca, NY: Cornell University Press, 2005).

14. Steven S. Lee, *The Ethnic Avant-Garde: Minority Cultures and World Revolution* (New York: Columbia University Press, 2015).

15. Sunyoung Park, *The Proletarian Wave: Literature and Leftist Culture in Colonial Korea, 1910–1945* (Cambridge, MA: Harvard University Asia Center, 2015), 112–13.

16. Park, 137, 155.

17. Anthony Shay, "Parallel Traditions: State Folk Dance Ensembles and Folk Dance in 'The Field,'" *Dance Research Journal* 31, no. 1 (Spring 1999): 29–56. See also David Caute, *The Dancer Defects: The Struggle for Cultural Supremacy during the Cold War* (New York: Oxford University Press, 2003), 478–80. Igor Moiseyev criticized the stagnation in the Bolshoi and focused on incorporating folk dance into ballet, becoming a fan of Broadway shows such as *West Side Story* and *My Fair Lady* after his first visit to the US in 1958.

18. *Ocherk* originated in Russia as a hallmark of a socialist realist literary genre, usually published in newspapers and magazines, that aimed to describe everyday people's lives, to educate and mobilize readers. For more on *ocherk*, especially as it developed in Korea, see Elli Sua Kim, "Rituals of Decolonization," chap. 2. For more on the wall novel see Sunyoung Park, *Proletarian Wave*, 115.

19. Philipp Herzog, "'National in Form and Socialist in Content' or Rather 'Socialist in Form and National in Content'? The 'Amateur Art System' and the Cultivation of 'Folk Art' in Soviet Estonia," *Nar. umjet* 47, no. 1 (2010): 125.

20. Chŏng Chi-su and Pak Chong-sŏng, "Haebang hu muyong yesul ŭi paljŏn" [Development of dance art after liberation], in *Pitnanŭn uri yesul* [Our brilliant arts] (Pyongyang: Chosŏn yesulsa, 1960), 286.

21. Yi Yŏng-ran, *Ch'oe Sŭng-hŭi muyong yesul sasang* [Choe Seung-hui on the dance arts] (Seoul: Minsogwŏn, 2014), 74.

22. Pae Yunhŭi, *T'aeyang ŭi p'um esŏ yŏngsaeng hanŭn muyongga* [Everlasting dancer in the bosom of the sun] (Pyongyang: Munhak yesul ch'ulp'ansa, 2012), 12.

23. Charles Armstrong, "The Cultural Cold War in Korea, 1945–1950," *Journal of Asian Studies* 62, no. 1 (February 2003): 77.

24. Yi Yŏng-ran, *Ch'oe Sŭng-hŭi muyong*, 74.

25. Pae, *T'aeyang ŭi p'um*, 43.

26. On the election see Kim, *Everyday Life in the North Korean Revolution*, chap. 3.

27. Pae, *T'aeyang ŭi p'um*, 127.

28. Ri Ran-sun, "Inmin paeu Ch'oe Sŭng-hŭi" [People's artist Choe Seung-hui], *Chosŏn Nyŏsŏng*, September 1957, 20–21.

29. Choe Seung-hui, *Chosŏn minjok muyong kibon* [Basics of Korean national dance] (Pyongyang: Chosŏn yesul ch'ulp'ansa, 1958); Choe Seung-hui, *Muyonggŭk taebonjip* [Collection of dance-drama scripts] (Pyongyang: Chosŏn yesul ch'ulp'ansa, 1958); Choe Seung-hui, *Chosŏn adong muyong kibon* [Basics of Korean children's dance] (Pyongyang: Chosŏn munhak yesul ch'ongtongmaeng ch'ulp'ansa, 1964).

30. Ra Sŭng-p'yo, "Rodong nyŏsŏngdŭl sogesŏ charanŭn yesul: Chŏn'guk ch'ukjŏn ŭl pogo" [Arts developing among working women: After watching the National Arts Festival], *Chosŏn Nyŏsŏng*, September 1954, 48–52.

31. Ra, 49.

32. Ra, 50–51.

33. Ra, 52.

34. Choe Seung-hui, "Hwanggŭm taeji ue p'in minjok muyong yesul ŭi saeroun chŏnghwa: Chŏn'guk yesul ch'ukjŏn nongch'on pumun ssŏk'ŭl kyŏngyŏn e ch'amgahan muyong chakp'umdŭl e taehayŏ" [New national dance blossoms on golden earth: On the dance works presented to the farmers circles competition of the National Arts Festival], *Munhak Sinmun*, February 17, 1961, 3.

35. Choe Seung-hui, "Inmin ch'angjak ŭi sidae" [Age of people's creation], *Munhak Sinmun*, October 27, 1961, 3.

36. Choe Seung-hui, "Ch'oego inmin hoeŭi che-2-gi che-2-ch'a hoeŭi esŏ t'oron (yoji)" [Discussion at the Second Supreme People's Assembly second meeting (key points)], *Rodong Sinmun*, February 19, 1958, 3.

37. Yi Chu-mi, "Ch'oe Sŭng-hŭi ŭi 'Chosŏnjŏk in kŏt' kwa 'Tongyangjŏk in kŏt'" [Choe Seung-hui's "Koreanness" and "Asianness"], *Hanminjok munhwa yŏn'gu* [Korean culture studies] 23 (November 2007): 336.

38. Sŏng Hyŏn-kyŏng, ed., *Kyŏngsŏng elittŭ ŭi man'guk yuramgi* [Travelogues of the Seoul elite] (Seoul: Hyŏnsil munhwa yŏn'gu, 2015), 86.

39. Yi, "Ch'oe Sŭng-hŭi ŭi 'Chosŏnjŏk in kŏt,'" 340.

40. Yi, 341.

41. Pae, *T'aeyang ŭi p'um*, 155.

42. Pae, 158.

43. Pae, 160.

44. Pae, 120.

45. *Minjok* has been variously translated as "people" or "nation." A neologism imported through China and Japan at the turn of the century similar to the German *Volk*, the concept coincides with the rise of the modern nation-state and nationalism in East Asia. Depending on the context, I have also used "our" or "Korean" in addition to "people" and "nation."

46. Pae, *T'aeyang ŭi p'um*, 1.

47. Pae, 164.

48. Pae, 59.

49. Pae, 46.

50. Pae, 55.

51. Pae, 57.

52. Pae, 68–71.

53. Pae, 70.

54. Pae, 118.

55. Kristen Elizabeth Hamm, "'The Friendship of Peoples': Soviet Ballet, Nationalities Policy, and the Artistic Media, 1953–1968" (MA thesis, University of Illinois, Urbana-Champaign, 2009), 3.

56. Choe, *Muyonggŭk taebonjip*, 53. For Silla roots of the sword dance see Van Zile, *Perspectives on Korean Dance*, 129. For dating it to the Three Kingdoms period based on

murals found in the Anak tombs see Pak Chong-sŏng, *Chosŏn minsok muyong* [Korean folk dance] (Pyongyang: Munye ch'ulp'ansa, 1991), 10–13. For comparisons of the sword dance between the North and South see Keith Howard, *Songs for "Great Leaders": Ideology and Creativity in North Korean Music and Dance* (Oxford: Oxford University Press, 2021), 210.

57. Choe, *Muyonggŭk taebonjip*, 53.

58. Pae, *T'aeyang ŭi p'um*, 68–71, 109.

59. An Sŏng-hŭi, "Asea cheguk nyŏsŏng taehoe kyŏngch'uk kong'yŏn ŭl mach'igo" [After the celebration performance at the Asia Women's Conference], *Chosŏn Nyŏsŏng*, February 1950, 22–24.

60. An, 23–24.

61. For example see "Yŏngwŏnhan ch'insŏn ŭi norae: Chungguk inmin munye kongjakdan kong'yŏn" [Song of eternal friendship: Chinese people's arts troupe performance], *Rodong Sinmun*, June 2, 1953, 3; "Uri nara rŭl pangmunhal paeu tŭl" [Artists to visit our country], *Rodong Sinmun*, May 27, 1954, 3. According to the latter article, the first visit by Soviet artists to the North was made in 1949, and the first Korean tour, including Choe, to the Soviet Union occurred in the spring of 1950.

62. "Chŏlch'an patnŭn palle" [Highly acclaimed ballet], *Rodong Sinmun*, June 8, 1954, 4. Choe Seung-hui, "Widaehan Ssoryŏn yesul ŭl chinjihage paeuja" [Let's earnestly learn the great arts of the Soviet Union], *Rodong Sinmun*, June 12, 1954, 3.

63. Song Hŭi-sun, "Ch'insŏn kwa wimun ŭi sajŏldŭl ŭl majihago" [Meeting with the envoy of friendship and goodwill], *Chosŏn Nyŏsŏng*, July 1954, 40–42.

64. Choe Seung-hui, "Ssobet'ŭ palle yesul kwa Ullanoba" [Soviet ballet art and Ulanova], *Cho-Sso Munhwa*, February 1955, 43.

65. Choe, 43–44.

66. Chŏng Chi-su, "Muyong ch'angjak ŭi kil esŏ" [On the path of dance creation], *Cho-Sso Munhwa*, July 1955, 49–54.

67. Chŏng, 49.

68. Chŏng, 50.

69. Chŏng, 50–51.

70. Ri Sŏk-ye, "Minjok pallet'ŭ ŭi paljŏn ŭl wihayŏ" [For the development of national ballet], *Munhak Sinmun*, February 13, 1958, 3. By 1966, Ri and her husband had successfully staged *La Esmeralda*, a ballet inspired by the 1831 Victor Hugo novel *Notre-Dame de Paris*. See Yu Yŏng-gŭn, "'Esŭmeraldŭ' ga kŏdun yesuljŏk sŏnggwa" [Artistic achievements of *Esmeralda*], *Munhak Sinmun*, April 19, 1966, 3.

71. "Palletŭ 'Paekjo ŭi hosu' chung ŭi che-2-pu rŭl kong'yŏn" [Performance of act 2 of ballet *Swan Lake*], *Rodong Sinmun*, October 12, 1956, 3.

72. "Ch'oe Sŭng-hŭi muyong yŏn'guso ŭi kwihwan kong'yŏn sŏnghwang" [Successful return concert of the Choe Seung-hui Dance Institute], *Rodong Sinmin*, February 4, 1957, 3.

73. Yi Ae-sun, *Ch'oe Sŭng-hŭi muyong yesul munjip* [Choe Seung-hui on the dance arts] (Seoul: Kukhak charyowŏn, 2002), 190. See also "Choe Seung-hui muyong yŏn'guso ŭi kwihwan kong'yŏn sŏnghwang," 3.

74. For the history of the ways ballet navigated its aristocratic roots to become part of the revolutionary tradition in Soviet Russia see Christina Ezrahi, *Swans of the Kremlin: Ballet and Power in Soviet Russia* (Pittsburgh: University of Pittsburgh Press, 2012). Ezrahi notes that the 1950s and 1960s represented the "golden age" of Soviet ballet, and advocates for a broader framing of creative autonomy in state socialist countries. She argues that professional values maintained a degree of continuity in aesthetic debates and artistic goals to navigate around the institutional and ideological constraints that became "enabling factors, inspiring extraordinary creativity to overcome the constraining pressure of circumstance" (7).

75. Ezrahi, 22–27.
76. Ezrahi, 32.
77. Ezrahi, 60.
78. Ezrahi, 48.
79. Ezrahi, 71, 103.
80. Hamm, "'Friendship of Peoples,'" 11–20.
81. *Saenghwal kwa mudae* [Everyday life and the stage] (Pyongyang: Kungnip ch'ulp'ansa, 1956). The volume was based on discussions at the Artist Enthusiasts Meeting (Yesurin yŏlsŏngja hoeŭi) of February 27, 1956, and includes a translated piece by seminal Russian theater artist Konstantin Stanislavski on his method of acting.
82. Choe Seung-hui, "Muyong yesul ŭi kailch'ŭng ŭi paljŏn ŭl wihayŏ" [For the further development of dance art], in *Saenghwal kwa mudae*, 31–42.
83. Choe, 35.
84. Choe, 39–40.
85. Choe, 38.
86. Kim Il Sung, "On Eliminating Dogmatism and Formalism and Establishing Juche in Ideological Work," speech to party propagandists and agitators, December 28, 1955, https://www.marxists.org/archive/kim-il-sung/1955/12/28.htm. While Juche is often translated as self-reliance by those inside and outside Korea, it is *not* a neologism unique to the North, but has been in usage since the early twentieth century to denote subjectivity, or in literal translation, "master of self."
87. The practice of modifying and improving traditional instruments, which Choe began in the 1950s, became part of state policy in November 1964, eventually becoming a key part in the production of the revolutionary operas *Sea of Blood* (1971) and *The Flower Girl* (1972). See Kim Ch'ae-wŏn, *Ch'oe Sŭng-hŭi ch'um: Kyesŭng kwa pyŏnyong* [Choe Seung-hui dance: Legacies and transformations] (Seoul: Minsogwŏn, 2008), 170.
88. Pae, *T'aeyang ŭi p'um*, 125.
89. Andrei Lankov, *Crisis in North Korea: The Failure of De-Stalinization, 1956* (Honolulu: University of Hawai'i Press, 2005).
90. Choe Seung-hui, "Muyongguk yesul kwa muyongguk wŏnbon" [Art and origin of dance-drama], *Munhak Sinmun*, March 16, 1965, 3.
91. Choe Seung-hui, "Muyongguk wŏnbon changjak eso ŭi kibon munje" [Basic questions in the creation of dance-drama], *Munhak Sinmun*, April 23, 1965, 3.
92. Yi, *Ch'oe Sŭng-hŭi muyong yesul munjip*, 78.
93. Yi, 79.
94. Yi, 72.
95. Pae, *T'aeyang ŭi p'um*, 64–65.
96. Alan Lomax, Irmgard Bartenieff, and Forrestine Paulay, "Dance Style and Culture," in *Folk Song Style and Culture* (Washington, DC: American Association for the Advancement of Science, 1968), 224.
97. Choe Seung-hui, "Chosŏn muyong tongjak kwa kŭ kibŏp ŭi ususŏng mit minjokjŏk t'ŭksŏng" [Korean dance movements, its superior technique and national characteristics], *Munhak Sinmun*, March 25, 1966, 4. The article was published serially across four issues, from March 22 to April 1, 1966.
98. Choe Seung-hui, "Chosŏn muyong tongjak kwa kŭ kibŏp ŭi ususŏng mit minjokjŏk t'ŭksŏng," *Munhak Sinmun*, March 29, 1966, 4.
99. Choe Seung-hui, "Chosŏn muyong tongjak kwa kŭ kibŏp ŭi ususŏng mit minjokjŏk t'ŭksŏng," *Munhak Sinmun*, April 1, 1966, 3.
100. Choe, 3.
101. Chŏng and Pak, "Haebang hu muyong yesul ŭi paljŏn," 281–82. Keith Howard explains that Choe fused the monk dance (*sŭngmu*) with the shaman dance (*munyŏ ch'um*) to create the sleeve dance (*sugŏn ch'um*), which can also include dances by the

kisaeng. This had the effect of replacing the religious and spiritual overtones with a focus on the element of costume. See Howard, *Songs for "Great Leaders,"* 206.

102. Chŏng and Pak, "Haebang hu muyong yesul ŭi paljŏn," 313–14.

103. Kim Mu-sam, "Chosŏnot ŭi arŭmdaun chŏnt'ong ŭl sallija (1)" [Let's preserve the beautiful tradition of Korean clothes (1)], *Chosŏn Nyŏsŏng*, August 1960, 39–40.

104. Kim Mu-sam, "Chosŏnot ŭi arŭmdaun chŏnt'ong ŭl sallija (2)," *Chosŏn Nyŏsŏng*, September 1960, 39.

105. Kim Mu-sam, "Chosŏnot ŭi arŭmdaun chŏnt'ong ŭl sallija (3)," *Chosŏn Nyŏsŏng*, October 1960, 35; Kim Mu-sam, "Chosŏnot ŭi arŭmdaun chŏnt'ong ŭl sallija (4)," *Chosŏn Nyŏsŏng*, November 1960, 39; Kim Mu-sam, "Chosŏnot ŭi arŭmdaun chŏnt'ong ŭl sallija (5)," *Chosŏn Nyŏsŏng*, December 1960, 39.

106. Sŏnu Imja, "Otch'arim ŭl arŭmdapgo kŏmbak hage" [Beautiful and frugal clothes], *Chosŏn Nyŏsŏng*, January 1961, 39.

107. Kim Ch'ae-wŏn, *Ch'oe Sŭng-hŭi ch'um*, 61; Paek Hyang-ju, "Ch'oe Sŭng-hŭi 'Chosŏn minjok muyong kibon' ŭi hyŏngsŏng kwa pyŏnhwa" [Formation and change of Choe Seung-hui's "Basics of Korean National Dance"] (MA thesis, Korean National University of Arts, 2006); Howard, *Songs for "Great Leaders,"* 206–7. Choe's 2012 biography gives August 8, 1969, as the date of her death and makes no mention of any purges; her husband An Mak does not appear in her biography at all. See Pae, *T'aeyang ŭi p'um*, 163.

108. Yi, *Ch'oe Sŭng-hŭi muyong yesul munjip*, 123.

109. Paek, "Ch'oe Sŭng-hŭi," 51.

110. Paek, 52–53.

111. Paek, 54.

112. Paek, 87.

113. Kim Jong Il, *Muyong yesullon* [Theory on dance art] (Pyongyang: Chosŏn rodongdang ch'ulp'ansa, 1992), 6.

114. Kim, 32, 35.

115. Kim, 46.

116. Kim, 50.

117. Kim, 8.

118. For reference to the 1997 production see Paek, "Ch'oe Sŭng-hŭi," 111, and for footage of the 2011 production see the DVD *T'aeyang ŭi p'um esŏ yŏngsaeng hanŭn muyongga* [Everlasting dancer in the bosom of the sun] (Pyongyang: Mokran Video, 2012).

119. Paek, "Ch'oe Sŭng-hŭi," 113.

120. Howard, *Songs for "Great Leaders,"* 206.

121. Gloria B. Strauss, "Dance and Ideology in China, Past and Present: A Study of Ballet in the People's Republic," *Asian and Pacific Dance: Selected Papers from the 1974 CORD-SEM Conference*, ed. Adrienne L. Kaeppler, Judy Van Zile, and Carl Wolz (New York: Committee on Research in Dance, 1977), 26. Strauss notes that the jumps and leaps in ballet could be seen as a metaphor for the Great Leap Forward itself, drawing on Chinese acrobatic and martial arts traditions (28–33). The same could be said of Korea.

122. Howard, *Songs for "Great Leaders,"* 210.

123. Chŏng and Pak, "Haebang hu muyong yesul ŭi paljŏn," 283.

6. COMMUNIST WOMEN AROUND THE WORLD

1. Dae-sook Suh, *Kim Il Sung: The North Korean Leader* (New York: Columbia University Press, 1988), 52.

2. Chŏn Ch'ang-mo, *Minjok ŭi charang Chosŏnhwa: Chŏnt'ongjŏgin Chosŏnhwa hwabŏp yŏn'gu* [The nation's pride Chosŏnhwa paintings: On the traditional painting technique of Chosŏnhwa] (Pyongyang: 2.16 Yesul kyoyuk ch'ulp'ansa, 2002).

3. Hwang Sun-hŭi, *Widaehan chŏnsa ŭi saeng'ae chung'esŏ* [From the life of a great warrior] (Pyongyang: Kŭllo tanch'ae ch'ulp'ansa, 1988).

4. Sonia Ryang, "Gender in Oblivion: Women in the Democratic People's Republic of Korea," *Journal of Asian and African Studies* 35, no. 3 (2000): 323–49. Ryang argues that it is not the legacy of Confucianism that is at the heart of gender construction in Korea, but rather the distinct cult of leadership and its patriarchal discourses that replace the category of "woman" with "motherhood," in which femininity is equated with maternity. There are many South Korean analyses of the North as a "paternalistic patriarchy," but for examples see Pak Hyŏnsŏn, *Hyŏndae Pukhan sahoe wa kajok* [Contemporary North Korean society and family] (Seoul: Hanul, 2003) and Pak Yŏng-ja, *Pukhan nyŏja: T'ansaeng kwa kuljŏl ŭi 70-nyŏnsa* [North Korean women: 70-year history of birth and refraction] (Seoul: Aelp'i, 2017). My point is not to argue against this body of important scholarship, but to suggest that the problem of gender inequality cannot be narrowly confined to national policy and must take into account women's own strategic use of maternal feminism.

5. Kyŏngnam taehakkyo Pukhan taehagwŏn, *Pukhan yŏn'gu pangbŏpron* [Methodology of North Korean studies] (Seoul: Hanul, 2003).

6. Ryu Kil-jae, "Kim Il Sung, Kim Jong Il ŭi munhŏn ŭl ŏttŏk'e ilgŭl kosin'ga" [How to read the works of Kim Il Sung and Kim Jong Il], in *Pukhan yŏn'gu pangbŏpron*, 63–65; Yi Chu-ch'ŏl, "Pukhan yŏn'gurŭl wihan munhŏn charyo hwaryong" [Use of documents in North Korean research], in *Pukhan yŏn'gu pangbŏpron*, 120–23; Yang Mun-su, "Pukhan kyŏngje yŏn'gu pangbŏpron: Sigak, charyo, punsŏkt'ŭrŭl chungsim ŭro" [Methodology in North Korean economy research], in *Pukhan yŏn'gu pangbŏpron*, 215–16.

7. Hong Chong-uk, "Pukhan yŏksahak hyŏngsŏng e Ssoryŏn yŏksahak i mich'in yŏnghyang" [The influence of Soviet historiography on the formation of North Korean historiography], *Inmun nonch'ong* [Journal of humanities] 77, no. 3 (2020): 53.

8. Modern Girl Around the World Research Group (Alys Eve Weinbaum, Lynn M. Thomas, Priti Ramamurthy, Uta G. Poiger, Madeleine Yue Dong, and Tani E. Barlow, eds.), *The Modern Girl Around the World* (Durham, NC: Duke University Press, 2008).

9. Veronica Sanz, "No Way out of the Binary: A Critical History of the Scientific Production of Sex," *Signs: Journal of Women in Culture and Society* 43, no. 1 (2017): 1. The binary model of sex and gender has been effectively challenged by important scholarship in trans studies in the last two decades, drawing upon Third World, women of color, and queer feminisms. For a concise overview see Kritika Agarwal, "What Is Trans History?," *Perspectives on History* (2018), at https://www.historians.org/publications-and-directories/perspectives-on-history/may-2018/what-is-trans-history-from-activist-and-academic-roots-a-field-takes-shape.

10. Anna Krylova, *Soviet Women in Combat* (New York: Cambridge University Press, 2010), 19.

11. Krylova, 48–49.

12. Krylova, 269 (emphasis added).

13. For a spirited debate about the viability and the usefulness of the term *communist feminism* see the inaugural issue of *Aspasia*, ed. Francisca de Haan, "Forum: Is 'Communist Feminism' a *Contradictio in Terminis*?," *Aspasia* 1 (2007): 197–246.

14. Tina Mai Chen, "Socialism, Aestheticized Bodies, and International Circuits of Gender: Soviet Female Film Stars in the People's Republic of China, 1949–1969," *Journal of the Canadian Historical Association* 18, no. 2 (2007): 53–80.

15. For Shanghai Ballet repertoires see http://www.shanghaiballet.com/shblwt/n49/index.html. See also Xiaomei Chen, *Acting the Right Part: Political Theater and Popular Drama in Contemporary China* (Honolulu: University of Hawai'i Press, 2002). For the 2012 staging of *The Flower Girl* see https://www.globaltimes.cn/content/718231.shtml.

16. Kyung Hyun Kim, "The Fractured Cinema of North Korea: The Discourse of the Nation in *Sea of Blood*," in *In Pursuit of Contemporary East Asian Culture*, ed. Xiaobing Tang and Stephen Snyder (Boulder, CO: Westview, 1996), 85–106. In his discussion of *Sea of Blood*, Kim also notes parallels with *The White-Haired Girl* and Gorky's *Mother*, although left underexplored (105).

17. As Im Hŏn-yŏng points out, this sort of development was not uncommon in the artistic works traditionally produced in Korea. Well-known folktales such as the "Story of Ch'unhyang" and the "Story of Hŭngbu" were passed down orally by storytelling in the form of a traditional Korean operatic genre called *p'ansori*, and only codified into textual form in modern times. Im Hŏn-yŏng, "Pukhan ŭi hang'il hyŏngmyŏng munhak" [Anti-Japanese revolutionary literature of North Korea], in *Pukhan ŭi munhak* [North Korean literature], ed. Kwŏn Yŏng-min (Seoul: Ŭryu munhawsa, 1989), 155.

18. Kathleen McHugh and Nancy Abelmann, eds., *South Korean Golden Age Melodrama: Gender, Genre, and National Cinema* (Detroit: Wayne State University Press, 2005), 4.

19. Kathleen McHugh, "South Korean Film Melodrama: State, Nation, Woman, and the Transnational Familiar," in McHugh and Abelmann, *South Korean Golden Age Melodrama*, 19. Like North Korean narratives discussed in this chapter, South Korean films produced in the postwar period between the 1950s and 1960s show a lack of strong male protagonists, dominated instead by female characters, often with children but without a husband, operating as "a structuring absence" that allows women to emerge as agents (22). On the revolutionary significance of melodrama and the socialist family in the Chinese context as critiques against essentialized gender roles and the public-private, production-reproduction divisions see Xiao Liu, "*Red Detachment of Women*: Revolutionary Melodrama and Alternative Socialist Imaginations," *differences* 26, no. 3 (2015): 116–41.

20. Yi Sang-t'ae, "Hang'il mujang t'ujaeng kwajŏng esŏ ch'angjodoen hyŏngmyŏngjŏk yŏn'gŭk" [Revolutionary plays created in the process of anti-Japanese armed struggle], in *Hang'il mujang t'ujaeng kwajŏng esŏ ch'angjodoen hyŏngmyŏngjŏk munhak yesul* [Revolutionary literature and art created in the process of anti-Japanese armed struggle] (Pyongyang: Kwahagwŏn ch'ulp'ansa, 1960), 62–96.

21. "In'gan ŭi chonŏm kwa chajusŏng e taehan pulmyŏl ŭi hyŏngsang: Purhu ŭi kojŏnjŏk myŏngjak *Kkotp'anŭn chŏnyŏ* ch'angjak kong'yŏn 50-dol e chŏŭmhayŏ" [Editorial: Immortal form on human dignity and autonomy: On the fiftieth anniversary of the immortal classic masterpiece *The Flower Girl*], *Rodong Sinmun*, November 7, 1980.

22. Frantz Fanon, *The Wretched of the Earth* (New York: Grove, 1963).

23. Minjok Munhaksa Yŏn'guso, *Pukhan ŭi uri munhaksa insik* [Understanding of the history of our literature in North Korea] (Seoul: Ch'angjak kwa pip'yŏngsa, 1991), 392.

24. Kim Chae-yong, *Pukhan munhak ŭi yŏksajŏk ihae* [Historical understanding of North Korean literature] (Seoul: Munhak kwa chisŏngsa, 1994), 200–201.

25. Kim Chae-yong, "Hang'il hyŏngmyŏng munhak ŭi wŏnhyŏng kwa kŭ pyŏnyong" [The origin and changes in anti-Japanese revolutionary literature], *Yŏksa pip'yŏng* [History criticism] 25 (November 1993): 382–84.

26. Minjok Munhaksa Yŏn'guso, *Pukhan ŭi uri munhaksa insik*, 395; and Im Hyŏng-t'aek, Ch'oe Wŏn-sik, Kim Myŏng-hwan, and Kim Hyŏng-su, "T'ong'il ŭl saenggak hamyŏ Pukhan munhak ŭl ingnŭnda" [Reading North Korean literature with reunification in mind], *Ch'angjak kwa pip'yŏng* [Creation and criticism] 17, no. 3 (Winter 1989): 21. For research by Korean-Chinese scholars in Yanbian on the local Kando origins of *Sea of Blood* and other colonial-era works see Kim Chŏng-ŭn, "Chosŏn ŭi 'pulhu ŭi kojŏnjŏk myŏngjak' 'P'ibada' ŭi ppurirŭl tŏdŭmŏ" [Tracing the roots of the "immortal classic masterpiece" of Korea *Sea of Blood*], *Chunghwa ŏnŏ munhwa yŏn'gu* [Chinese language and culture studies] 9 (2015): 57–77.

27. Minjok Munhaksa Yŏn'guso, *Pukhan ŭi uri munhaksa insik*, 395.

28. James F. Person, "The 1967 Purge of the Gapsan Faction and Establishment of the Monolithic Ideological System," North Korea International Documentation Project E-Dossier No. 15, https://www.wilsoncenter.org/publication/the-1967-purge-the-gapsan-faction-and-establishment-the-monolithic-ideological-system.

29. Chosŏn chung'ang t'ongsin, "Ŏbŏi suryŏngnim ŭl mosigo widaehan changgunnim kkesŏ" [The great general with the parent leader], *Rodong Sinmun*, December 1, 2012; and Chŏng Yŏng-hwa, "Sunan ŭi p'ibada rŭl t'ujaeng ŭi p'ibadaro, onŭl ŭn sahoejuŭi suhojŏn ŭro!" [From the suffering sea of blood to the fighting sea of blood, to the war to defend socialism today!], *Rodong Sinmun*, April 3, 2001.

30. For examples of Sea of Blood Worker Guards see Chŏng To-gyŏng, "Ŏnjena himdŭn il ŭi apjang esŏ" [Always on the forefront of difficult tasks], *Rodong Sinmun*, August 28, 1973; and Im Tŏ-gyŏng, "Koji e p'o rŭl kkŭrŏ ollidŏn kŭ kibaek ŭro" [In the same spirit that lifted the cannon to the highlands], *Rodong Sinmun*, August 25, 1974.

31. For examples of *The Flower Girl* used in education and production see Yi Chi-yŏng, "Hyŏngmyŏng kagŭk *Kkot p'anŭn ch'ŏnyŏ* e taehan sirhyo t'ujaeng ŭl hwalbarhi pŏryŏ" [Active struggle for the effective implementation of the revolutionary opera *Flower Girl*], *Rodong Sinmun*, November 3, 1988; Kim Sŏng-ch'ŏl, "T'ujaeng kwa saenghwal ŭi ch'amdoen kyokwasŏ ro samgo" [Taken as a true textbook in the struggle and life], *Rodong Sinmun*, December 16, 1988; and Ham Wŏn-sik, "Hyŏnsil kwa kyŏlbu hayŏ kip'i ikke" [In depth in accordance with reality], *Rodong Sinmun*, February 28, 1989.

32. Katerina Clark, *The Soviet Novel: History as Ritual* (Chicago: University of Chicago Press, 1981), 4–5, 52.

33. Clark, 27, 33.

34. Clark, xi–xii

35. Clark, 9–15.

36. Clark, 34.

37. Clark, 48–49.

38. Alexandra Kollontai, "Make Way for Winged Eros: A Letter to Working Youth," *Molodoya Gvardiya* [Young Guard] 3 (1923), https://www.marxists.org/archive/kollonta/1923/winged-eros.htm.

39. Irina Gutkin, *Cultural Origins of the Socialist Realist Aesthetic, 1890–1934* (Evanston, IL: Northwestern University Press, 1999), 143.

40. For a translation of the novel, I have relied on Maxim Gorky, *Mother*, trans. Margaret Wettlin (Honolulu: University Press of the Pacific, 2000).

41. Original by Gorky and translated by Ku Po-he, "Myŏngjak sogae: Ŏmŏni" [Introduction of masterpiece: *Mother*], *Chosŏn Nyŏsŏng*, September 1948, 53–60. For a full translation and publication of *Mother* see Makssim Korikki, *Ŏmŏni* [Mother], trans. Ch'oe Ho (Pyongyang: Kungrip ch'ulp'ansa, 1957).

42. *Sea of Blood* was also published under a revised title in South Korea in 1988 among a series of publications of North Korean literary works after the 1987 democratic opening. All textual citations of *Sea of Blood* are drawn from *Minjung ŭi pada* [Sea of the masses], 2 vols. (Seoul: Hanmadang, 1988). For a musicological comparison between Gorky's *Mother* and the *Sea of Blood* opera see Yi Hyŏn-ju, "Pukhan P'ibadasik hyŏngmyŏng kagŭk ŭi yŏksasŏng" [The historicity of the North Korean *Sea of Blood*–style revolutionary opera], *Chosŏndae tongbuga yŏn'guso* [Chosŏn University Northeast Asia Research Institute] 21, no. 1 (2006): 87–107. Yi traces the creation of *Sea of Blood* to a confluence of multiple influences, including Gorky's *Mother*, the traditional Korean musical storytelling genre called *p'ansori*, socialist realism, and Juche ideology, arguing that *Sea of Blood* gave rise to a brand-new genre as the first "revolutionary opera."

43. *Minjung ŭi pada*, 1:227.

44. *Minjung ŭi pada*, 1:328.

45. *Minjung ŭi pada*, 2:42.

46. For a translation of *The White-Haired Girl*, I have relied on Ho Ching-chi and Ting Yi, *The White-Haired Girl: An Opera in Five Acts*, trans. Yang Hsien-yi and Gladys Yang (Peking: Foreign Languages Press, 1954). Ho Ching-chi and Ting Yi in pinyin is He Jingzhi and Ding Yi.

47. For a translation of the story see Chong-wha Chung, *Korean Classical Literature: An Anthology* (London: Kegan Paul International, 1989).

48. *Minjung ŭi pada*, 1:162; and *Kkot p'anŭn ch'ŏnyŏ* [The flower girl] (Pyongyang: Munye ch'ulp'ansa, 1977), 397.

49. I thank Kim Myŏng-hwan for this reading of *The Flower Girl*.

50. Confirming the extent to which popular works circulated internationally across East Asia, *The White-Haired Girl* was also staged as a ballet by the Matsuyama Ballet in Japan in 1955, decades before the Chinese "revolutionary model ballet" and the Matsuyama Ballet toured China in 1958. See Emily Wilcox, *Revolutionary Bodies: Chinese Dance and the Socialist Legacy* (Oakland: University of California Press, 2019), 140.

51. Ko In-myŏng, "Idong yŏngsadae" [Mobile projector], *Chosŏn Nyŏsŏng*, January 1954, 73–75.

52. For arguments that CCP policy on women effectively "erased" gender and disempowered women in favor of class struggle see Meng Yue, "Female Images and National Myth," in *Gender Politics in Modern China: Writing and Feminism*, ed. Tani E. Barlow (Durham, NC: Duke University Press, 2003), 118–36; Harriet Evans, "The Language of Liberation: Gender and *Jiefang* in Early Chinese Communist Party Discourse," *Intersections: Gender, History and Culture in the Asian Context* 1 (1998): 1–19, and Harriet Evans, "Sexed Bodies, Sexualized Identities, and the Limits of Gender," *China Information* 22, no. 2 (2008): 361–86; Harry H. Kuoshu, *Lightness of Being in China: Adaptation and Discursive Figuration in Cinema and Theater* (New York: Peter Lang, 1999); Xiaomei Chen, *Acting the Right Part: Political Theater and Popular Drama in Contemporary China* (Honolulu: University of Hawai'i Press, 2002); Shuqin Cui, *Women through the Lens: Gender and Nation in a Century of Chinese Cinema* (Honolulu: University of Hawai'i Press, 2003); and Xiaofei Kang, "Revisiting *White-Haired Girl*: Women, Gender, and Religion in Communist Revolutionary Propaganda," in *Gendering Chinese Religion: Subject, Identity, and Body*, ed. Jinhua Jia, Xiaofei Kang, and Ping Yao (New York: SUNY Press, 2014), 133–56. To be fair, Evans highlights the "limits of gender" both in terms of its conventional binary framework and its affinity with identity politics, in which "sex and sexuality become components of individual exploration, dissociated from the broader issues of power and injustice" (2008, 378). Despite her critique of the sexualized body in consumerist market-driven contemporary China, Evans still attributes the source of gender inequality to the sexed body, criticizing Chinese communist discourse for conflating gender with class. For scholarship that challenges the "erasure" thesis by arguing that traditional femininity continued into the Cultural Revolution see Rosemary Roberts, "Positive Women Characters in the Revolutionary Model Works of the Chinese Cultural Revolution: An Argument against the Theory of Erasure of Gender and Sexuality," *Asian Studies Review* 28, no. 4 (2004): 407–22, and Rosemary Roberts, "Gendering the Revolutionary Body: Theatrical Costume in Cultural Revolution China," *Asian Studies Review* 30, no. 2 (2006): 141–59.

53. Meng Yue, "Female Images and National Myth," 121.

54. Kuoshu, *Lightness of Being in China*, 78. For additional examples of allegorical readings see Thomas Elsaesser, "Tales of Sound and Fury: Observations on the Family Melodrama," in *Movies and Methods*, ed. Bill Nicols (Berkeley: University of California Press, 1985), 165–89, and Ma Ning, "The Textual and Critical Difference of Being Radical: Reconstructing Chinese Leftist Films of the 1930s," *Wide Angle* 11, no. 2 (1989): 22–31.

55. Cui, *Women through the Lens*, 59.
56. Cui, 59.
57. Walter J. Meserve and Ruth I. Meserve, eds., *Modern Drama from Communist China* (New York: New York University Press, 1970).
58. According to Martin Ebon, this result was the consequence of clashes between Jiang Qing and Liu Shaoqi when the latter lost the "political-cultural tug-of-war" to resist the revisions in favor of characters with internal struggles and subtlety without blatant propaganda. See his *Five Chinese Communist Plays* (New York: John Day, 1975), 32.
59. Kuoshu, *Lightness of Being in China*, 82. Kuoshu claims that Xi'er no longer has reason to hide in the mountains without a baby except to wait for the return of her fiancé Dachun, arguing that this is why the film elaborates on their romantic love more than the opera. But the film makes it clear why Xi'er had to hide in the mountains with or without the baby, since Huang commands his steward Mu to find her dead or alive after her escape.
60. *Widaehan suryŏng Kim Ilsŏng tongji munhak yŏngdosa* [History of the great leader comrade Kim Il Sung's guidance in literature] (Pyongyang: Munye ch'ulp'ansa, 1992), 360.
61. Tani E. Barlow, *The Question of Women in Chinese Feminism* (Durham, NC: Duke University Press, 2004), 152.
62. Sunyoung Park, *The Proletarian Wave: Literature and Leftist Culture in Colonial Korea, 1910–1945* (Cambridge, MA: Harvard University Asia Center, 2015), 200. Park argues that the feminist message embedded in many of the works of socialist women writers can be overlooked when the text is read on its own, abstracted from its discursive context. My argument about the need to read Korean works within the larger socialist canon parallels Park's point.
63. Chosŏn chung'ang t'ongsin [Korean Central News Agency], "Ch'insŏn ŭi kkot manbal hago tan'gyŏl ŭi norae nop'i ullinda" [Flowers of friendship bloom and songs of solidarity ring high], *Rodong Sinmun*, June 9, 1972, 5.
64. Chosŏn chung'ang t'ongsin [Korean Central News Agency], "Chungguk Sanghae muyonggŭkdan i Hamhŭngsi pangmun iljŏng ŭl sŏnggwajŏk ŭro mach'igo P'yŏngyang ŭro ch'ulbal" [Chinese Shanghai Dance Troupe leaves for Pyongyang after a successful visit of Hamhŭng City], *Rodong Sinmun*, May 22, 1972, 4.
65. Sŏ Ki-sang, "Sudo kŭllojadŭl ŭi yŏlyŏrhan hwanyŏng soge Chosŏn pangmun Chungguk Sanghae muyonggŭkdan ŭi ch'ŏt kong'yŏn i issŏtta" [First performance by Chinese Shanghai Dance Troupe during Korea visit amid avid welcome by workers in the capital], *Rodong Sinmun*, May 11, 1972, 3.
66. Chosŏn chung'ang t'ongsin [Korean Central News Agency], "Chungguk Sanghae muyonggŭkdan i Mansudae ŭi tae'ginyŏmbi rŭl ch'amgwan, P'yŏngyang pangjik kongjangdo pangmun hayŏtta" [Chinese Shanghai Dance Troupe visits Grand Mansudae Monument and Pyongyang textile factory], *Rodong Sinmun*, May 15, 1972, 4.
67. Only a few feature films were made in China between 1967 and 1972, limited to a dozen of the filmed performances of the "revolutionary model theater": five in 1970, two in 1971, and five in 1972, which included *The White-Haired Girl*. See Kuoshu, *Lightness of Being in China*, 157n12. *The Flower Girl* became popular in China in the 1970s owing in part to the shortage of domestic films, but *The White-Haired Girl* was also seen by over twenty-two million people outside China between 1949 and 1957, according to official Chinese figures. See Chen, "Socialism, Aestheticized Bodies, and International Circuits of Gender," 70n45.
68. Huang Yongyuan, "Kaehyŏk kaebang ijŏn Chungguk e taehan Pukhan munhwa ŭi yŏnghyangryŏk: 1950–70 nyŏndae Chungguk ŭi Pukhan yŏnghwa suip ŭl chungsim ŭro" [The impact of North Korean culture on China before China's reform and opening-up

policy: Focusing on China's North Korean film imports in the 1950s–70s]," *Tongbang hakji* [Journal of Asian studies] 177 (December 2016): 355.

69. Huang, 346–47.

70. Tina Mai Chen, "Film and Gender in Sino-Soviet Cultural Exchange, 1949–1969," in *China Learns from the Soviet Union, 1949–Present*, ed. Thomas P. Bernstein and Hua-Yu Li (Lanham, MD: Lexington Books, 2010), 424. For distribution of Soviet films in Korea during its Soviet occupation (1945–1948) see Yi Myŏng-ja, "Haebang konggan esŏ Pukhan ŭi kŭndae kyŏnghŏm ŭi maegaech'erosŏ Soryŏn yŏnghwa ŭi suyong yŏn'gu" [The post-liberation reception of Soviet films as experience of modernity in North Korea], *T'ong'il munje yŏn'gu* [Unification studies] 54 (2010): 243–74.

71. Cho Yŏng-gil, "Kyegŭpjŏk wŏnsu wanŭn han hanŭl ŭl igo salsu ŏpda" [Can't live under the same sky with a class enemy], *Rodong Sinmun*, May 22, 1972, 4.

72. Sŏ Chae-ryŏl, "Uri nyŏsŏngdŭl ŭl t'ujaeng ero komu hanŭn pitnanŭn hyŏngsang" [Brilliant form that inspires us women to struggle], *Rodong Sinmun*, June 5, 1972, 5.

73. Yu Yŏng-gŭn, "Chungguk inmin ŭi nop'ŭn hyŏngmyŏng chŏngsin ŭl noraehan hyŏngmyŏngjŏk imyŏ chŏnt'ujŏgin yesul" [Revolutionary militant art that sings the Chinese people's high revolutionary spirit], *Rodong Sinmun*, May 26 1972, 4.

74. For Chinese receptions of *The White-Haired Girl* and "revolutionary model ballets" see Wilcox, *Revolutionary Bodies*, chap. 4. According to Wilcox, the Shanghai Dance School staged *The White-Haired Girl* as a ballet performance in 1965, before it was designated as one of two "model ballets" during the Cultural Revolution and made into a film in 1971 (150).

75. Kim Wang-sŏp, "Paekmonyŏ" [*The White-Haired Girl*], *Chosŏn Munhak* [Korean literature] 10 (2003): 63.

76. Chen, *Acting the Right Part*, 87.

77. Wang Zheng, *Finding Women in the State: A Socialist Feminist Revolution in the People's Republic of China, 1949–1964* (Oakland: University of California Press, 2017).

78. Wang Zheng, "'State Feminism'? Gender and Socialist State Formation in Maoist China," *Feminist Studies* 31, no. 3 (2005): 525–29.

79. Sŏng Mal-hŭi, "Pyŏkdol kongjang" [Brick factory], *Chosŏn Nyŏsŏng*, December 1953, 25. On more recent examples of militarized maternalism since the 1990s see Suzy Kim, "Mothers and Maidens."

80. Jean Bethke Elshtain, *Women and War* (New York: Basic Books, 1987), 222.

81. Kim Ok-sun, "Nyŏmaeng chojikdŭl ŭi saehae chŏnt'ujŏk kwaŏp" [The new year militant task of the women's union groups], *Chosŏn Nyŏsŏng*, January 1967, 3.

82. Kim Myŏng-hwa, "Hang'il ppaljjisan ch'amgajadŭl ŭi hoesanggi: Kim Jong Suk tongjirŭl hoesang hamyŏ" [Reminiscences of the participants of the anti-Japanese partisan struggle: Remembering Comrade Kim Jong Suk], *Chosŏn Nyŏsŏng*, May–June 1967, 29; for an English-language version of the same article see Kim Myung Hwa, "In Memory of Comrade Kim Jong Suk," *Women of Korea* 63 (March 1974): 15–19.

83. Pak Kye-ri, "Pukhan ŭi misul chŏngch'aek pyŏnhwa e ttarŭn misul chakp'um ŭi tosang kwa hyŏngsik ŭi pyŏnhwa yŏn'gu" [A study on changes in the iconography and form of artworks in response to changes in North Korea's art policy], in *Pukhan misul ŏje wa onŭl* [Art in North Korea, its past and present] (Daejeon, South Korea: National Research Institute of Cultural Heritage, 2016), 93–115. Pak notes the disappearance of the gun from Kim Il Sung's hand in a 1997 poster of the same scene to heighten Kim Jong Suk's protective role, as Kim Jong Il took the reins after his father's death in 1994.

84. Wang, *Finding Women in the State*, 250–51.

85. Wang, 252–53.

CONCLUSION

1. *Eugénie Cotton: The Full Life of a Woman of This Century* (Berlin: WIDF, 1970).
2. "WIDF Bureau Meeting (Berlin, June 14–17, 1968)," Documents and Information No. 9 (Berlin: WIDF, 1968), appendix, 1–2.
3. For background and text to CEDAW see https://www.un.org/womenwatch/daw/cedaw/cedaw.htm. For the WIDF role in these efforts see Francisca de Haan, "Continuing Cold War Paradigms in the Western Historiography of Transnational Women's Organisations: The Case of the Women's International Democratic Federation (WIDF)," *Women's History Review* 19, no. 4 (September 2010): 547–73.
4. "WIDF Bureau Meeting (Berlin, June 14–17, 1968)," 3–4.
5. *We Have Seen . . .* (Berlin: WIDF, 1968).
6. Documents and Information No. 10 (Berlin: WIDF, 1968). The national congresses raised similar concerns regarding women's equal access to work and equal pay for equal work; improved working conditions, including a minimum wage; school reform and vocational training; social security, including maternity leave and child care; and peace and disarmament.
7. "Seminars in Latin America," Documents and Information No. 1 (WIDF, 1969).
8. Francisca de Haan, "The Vietnam Activities of the Women's International Democratic Federation (WIDF)," in *Protest in the Vietnam Era*, ed. Alexander Sedlmaier (London: Palgrave Macmillan, 2022).
9. "March 8 International Women's Day," Documents and Information No. 8 (Berlin: WIDF, 1968). Information in the rest of the paragraph comes from this document.
10. "Bureau Meeting (Berlin, June 14–17, 1968)," 11. The Soviet invasion of Czechoslovakia in 1968 may have been another factor, although not mentioned in the records.
11. *Women's International Democratic Federation: Published for the 40th Anniversary of the Founding of the WIDF* (Berlin: WIDF, n.d.).
12. "Plan of Work for Publicising the World Congress of Women," Documents and Information No. 9 (Berlin: WIDF, 1968), appendix, 1–2.
13. "Bureau Meeting (Berlin, March 21–25, 1969)," Documents and Information No. 3 (Berlin: WIDF, 1969), 10.
14. "Bureau Meeting," 10.
15. "Bureau Meeting," 5.
16. "The Role of Women in the Economic and Social Development in their Countries," Documents and Information No. 12 (Berlin: WIDF, 1968), 15. This report was part of the WIDF response to the UN questionnaire on the role of women in the economic and social development of their countries per Resolution 1133 of UN ECOSOC, including extracts from the activities of the WIDF and resolutions made at its council meeting in Budapest (October 4–8, 1961).
17. "Congress Special I," Documents and Information No. 5 (Berlin: WIDF 1969), 7.
18. "Sixth Congress of the WIDF, Helsinki, June 18, 1969," Documents and Information No. 6 (Berlin: WIDF, 1969), 2. For a history of the different categories for NGO participation at the UN and the impact of the Cold War see Peter Willetts, ed., *"The Conscience of the World": The Influence of Non-governmental Organisations in the UN System* (Washington, DC: Brookings Institution, 1996), chap. 2.
19. "Congress Special I," 12.
20. "Congress Special I," 16–18.
21. For the resolution see "Congress Special I," 8–10. For the list of publications see "Sixth Congress of the WIDF, Helsinki, June 18, 1969," 35. For the report on Vietnam see "Congress Special II," Documents and Information No. 7 (Berlin: WIDF 1969).
22. "Solidarity with the Korean Women," Documents and Information No. 4 (Berlin: WIDF, 1969), 2.

23. "Solidarity with the Korean Women," 2.

24. I found few details about the 1967 trip, but for records of it see *Women's International Democratic Federation: Published for the 40th Anniversary of the Founding of the WIDF*, 26, and "Chosŏn nyŏsŏng kwa ŭi sangbong" [Meeting with Korean women], *Chosŏn Nyŏsŏng*, September 1967, 43.

25. "Solidarity with the Korean Women," 11–12.

26. "Sixth Congress of the WIDF, Helsinki, June 18, 1969," 10. In addition to the report on Vietnam, there were four additional reports, "Women in the Family," "Women at Work," "Women in Society," and "Women in the Struggle to Win and Defend National Independence, Democracy and Peace." For the full texts of these reports see "Congress Special III," Documents and Information No. 8 (Berlin: WIDF, 1969).

27. Elsie Leyden, "Women in the Family," report at the World Congress of Women, Helsinki, June 14–17, 1969, 2. For a compilation of discussions on this report at the congress see "Congress Special VI," Documents and Information No. 9C (Berlin: WIDF, 1969).

28. Leyden, "Women in the Family," 3.

29. Leyden, 6.

30. Marta López Portillo de Tamayo, report on "Women in Society" at the World Congress of Women, Helsinki, June 14–17, 1969, 4–5. For contributions to discussion on this report at the congress see "Congress Special IV," Documents and Information No. 9A (Berlin: WIDF, 1969). For the report on "Women and Work" see "Congress Special V," Documents and Information No. 9B (Berlin: WIDF, 1969).

31. Mahasin Abd el Aal, report on "Women in the Struggle to Win and Defend National Independence, Democracy and Peace" at the World Congress of Women, Helsinki, June 14–17, 1969, 5. For contributions to discussion on this report at the congress see "Congress Special VII," Documents and Information No. 10 (Berlin: WIDF, 1969).

32. Speech of the Korean Women's Delegation at the World Women's Congress, Helsinki, June 1969, 5. There was no name given in the copy of the speech, and I have been unable to confirm the names of the Korean women who participated in this congress.

33. Speech of the Korean Women's Delegation, 14.

34. Speech of the Korean Women's Delegation, 18.

35. "Bureau Meeting, Berlin, January 21–24, 1970," Documents and Information No. 1 (Berlin: WIDF, 1970), 3.

36. "Bureau Meeting, Berlin, January 21–24, 1970," 4.

37. "Bureau Meeting, Berlin, January 21–24, 1970," 5.

38. "Bureau Meeting, Berlin, January 21–24, 1970," 13.

39. "WIDF Council Meeting, Varna, Bulgaria, 30 April–5 May, 1972," Documents and Information No. 1 (Berlin: WIDF, 1972), III:2; "WIDF Council Meeting, Varna, Bulgaria, 30 April–5 May, 1972," Documents and Information No. 2 (Berlin: WIDF, 1972), I:6. On the impact of the WIDF proposal and subsequent role of the international women's movement at the UN see Martha Alter Chen, "Engendering World Conferences: The International Women's Movement and the United Nations," *Third World Quarterly* 16, no. 3 (1995): 477–93.

40. "1975 International Women's Year," *Women of the Whole World*, no. 2 (1973), 4–5; Kristen Ghodsee, *Second World, Second Sex: Socialist Women's Activism and Global Solidarity during the Cold War* (Durham, NC: Duke University Press, 2019), 6.

41. Ghodsee, 139.

42. Ghodsee, 146; Jocelyn Olcott, "Cold War Conflicts and Cheap Cabaret: Sexual Politics at the 1975 United Nations International Women's Year Conference," *Gender & History* 22, no. 3 (2010): 733–54; E/CONF.66/34, *Report of the World Conference of the International Women's Year: Mexico City, 19 June–2 July 1975* (New York: United Nations, 1976), 120.

43. Jocelyn Olcott, *International Women's Year: The Greatest Consciousness-Raising Event in History* (New York: Oxford University Press, 2017).
44. Ghodsee, *Second World*, 147.
45. Ghodsee, 151–52.
46. *7th WIDF Congress* (Berlin: WIDF, 1975), 9. For details on the World Congress for International Women's Year (October 20–24, 1975) see the collection of WIDF documents at the International Institute of Social History in Amsterdam.
47. E/CONF.66/34, *Report of the World Conference of the International Women's Year*, 5.
48. Korean Central News Agency, "Mehikko esŏ 'Kukje nyŏsŏng ŭi hae segye taehoe' chinhaeng" [The World Conference on the International Year of Women held in Mexico], *Rodong Sinmun*, July 26, 1975, 3. While half of the full-page article is devoted to praise of Kim Il Sung, allegedly by Third World leaders, the article mentions Hŏ Chŏng-suk as the lead delegate.
49. E/CONF.66/INF.2, List of Participants of the World Conference of the International Women's Year (New York: United Nations, 1976), 20. With the exception of Hŏ and Yi, I have followed the spelling of names as provided in the UN document and have been unable to confirm the correct Korean spelling.
50. E/CONF.66/INF.2, List of Participants, 77.
51. Yi's edited volume *Yŏsŏng haebang ŭi iron kwa hyŏnsil* [Theory and reality of women's liberation] (Seoul: Ch'angjak hwa pip'yŏngsa, 1979) includes a translated copy of the Declaration of Mexico on the Equality of Women and Their Contribution to Development and Peace, 1975, and *Yŏsŏng kwa sahoe* [Women and society] (Seoul: Chŏng'usa, 1979) includes a chapter on global developments of the women's rights movement that references the 1975 UN Year of Women and the Mexico City Conference, although Yi makes no mention of her own participation. By the end of the UN Decade of Women in 1985, Yi published a landmark, award-winning study of the effects of the Korean division on Korean society, family, and women, *Pundan sidae ŭi sahoehak* [Sociology of the division era] (Seoul: Han'gilsa, 1985), republished in 2021. She studied sociology at the University of Alabama (BA, 1952), Columbia University (MA, 1957), UC Berkeley (visiting scholar, 1962), and Fisk University (Fulbright visiting professor, 1974). For an obituary of Yi Hyo-jae see https://www.nytimes.com/2020/11/14/world/asia/lee-hyo-jae-dead.html.
52. Pak Chŏng-hŭi, *YiYi Hyo-jae: Taehanminguk yŏsŏng undong ŭi sara itnŭn yŏksa* [YiYi Hyo-jae: Living history of the women's movement in the Republic of Korea] (P'aju, South Korea: Dasan Books, 2019), 115–20. This is a biography of Yi based on conversations between Yi and the author. Information about South Korean participation at the Mexico Conference in the rest of this paragraph comes from these pages.
53. Yi Ch'un-a, "Kŭ maŭm i yŏsŏngdŭrŭl umjigyŏtta" [Her heart moved women], in *Yŏsŏng, sam ŭi iyagi 10-injŏn* [Women, ten life stories] (Seoul: Pukbu yŏsŏng paljŏn sent'ŏ, 2001), https://m.blog.daum.net/choonahlee/559. I thank KangMun Minseo for this reference.
54. World Congress for International Women's Year Bulletin No. 3 (Berlin, 1975), 3.
55. World Congress for International Women's Year Bulletin No. 1 through 4 (Berlin, 1974, 1975). The first bulletin identifies Ho Ryon Suk and Yang Ki Souk representing the National Preparatory Committee of Korea for International Women's Year (12), and the fourth identifies Li Hen Suk and Choz Kyong Suk of the Korean Women's Organization (12), but I have not been able to trace them beyond this reference.
56. Laura McKinley and Diana Russell, "World Congress of Women: The 'Old Left' Divided in Berlin over the 'Woman Question,'" *Majority Report*, March 6–20, 1976, 10–12.
57. McKinley and Russell, 11.
58. McKinley and Russell, 10.

59. For a good overview of the 1975 congress based on East German archives see Celia Donert, "Whose Utopia? Gender, Ideology, and Human Rights at the 1975 World Congress of Women in East Berlin," in *The Breakthrough: Human Rights in the 1970s*, ed. Jan Eckel and Samuel Moyn (Philadelphia: University of Pennsylvania Press, 2013), 68–87.

60. "Working Paper for Commission No. 4," Source Materials for the Participants (Berlin: World Congress for International Women's Year, 1975), 1, 3–6. The UN Conference also considered the family as "the primary and fundamental nucleus of society" and "the fundamental institution of natural origin . . . as the first school of social relations," in which "man and woman form two aspects of the same vital essence and, united, make human life possible." See E/CONF.66/34, *Report of the World Conference of the International Women's Year*, 90.

61. *7th WIDF Congress*, 17.

62. *7th WIDF Congress*, 11–14, 23.

63. "Working Paper for Commission No. 3," Source Materials for the Participants (Berlin: World Congress for International Women's Year, 1975), 7; "Working Paper for Commission No. 6," Source Materials for the Participants (Berlin: World Congress for International Women's Year, 1975), 10; "Working Paper for Commission No. 7," Source Materials for the Participants (Berlin: World Congress for International Women's Year, 1975), 6, 11.

64. Yoshiaki Yoshimi, *Comfort Women: Sexual Slavery in the Japanese Military during World War II* (1995; New York: Columbia University Press, 2000).

65. *Report of the Special Rapporteur on Violence against Women, Its Causes and Consequences, Ms. Radhika Coomaraswamy, in Accordance with Commission on Human Rights Resolution 1994/45*, Commission on Human Rights, E/CN.4/1996/53/Add.1, January 4, 1996. The report cites the principles from the Geneva Conventions and the charters of the International Military Tribunal and the Tokyo Tribunal to conclude that the military sexual slavery system constituted a war crime and crime against humanity (para. 98, 99, 113).

66. "Chwadamhoe: Ilje ŭi chwehaeng ŭl ijji malja" [Roundtable: Let's not forget the crimes of Japanese imperialism], *Chosŏn Nyŏsŏng*, August 1964, 16–20.

67. "Chwadamhoe," 19–20.

68. Kim Pong-suk, "Iyŏkttang e sŏrin wŏnhan" [Bitter resentment in an alien land], in *Chosŏn nyŏsŏng dŭri kŏrŏ on sunan ŭi ryŏksa nŭn toep'uri toelsu ŏpta* [The history of the sufferings of Korean women cannot be repeated] (Pyongyang: Kŭllo nyŏsŏng sinmunsa, 1974), 20.

69. Kim, 21.

70. Kim, 25.

71. Kim, 29–31. For a scholarly treatment of the use of sex as part of diplomacy and geopolitics in US–South Korea relations see Katharine Moon, *Sex among Allies: Military Prostitution in U.S.-Korea Relations* (New York: Columbia University Press, 1997).

72. *Une délégation de la Fédération Démocratique Internationale des Femmes en République Démocratique du Vietnam, 14–25 février 1966* (Berlin: WIDF, 1966). The WIDF report identifies the North Korean delegate as Choi Gum Ja (8) or Choi Keum Za (36). I thank Francisca de Haan for sharing this source.

73. Ch'oe Kŭm-ja, "Yŏng'ung ŭi nara yonggamhan inmin" [Heroic country courageous people], *Chosŏn Nyŏsŏng*, June 1966, 23–26.

74. Ch'oe, 23.

75. Ch'oe, 23.

76. Ch'oe, 24.

77. Ch'oe, 25.

78. Ch'oe Kŭm-ja, "Kkuba rŭl pangmun hago" [After visiting Cuba], *Chosŏn Nyŏsŏng*, October 1966, 59–61.

79. Manuel Barcia, "'Locking Horns with the Northern Empire': Anti-American Imperialism at the Tricontinental Conference of 1966 in Havana," *Journal of Transatlantic Studies* 7, no. 3 (2009): 208–17.

80. *The Tricontinental Conference of African, Asian, and Latin American Peoples: A Staff Study* (Washington, DC: Government Printing Office, 1966), 1–2.

81. Ch'oe, "Kkuba rŭl pangmun hago," 59.

82. Ch'oe, 60.

83. Ernesto Che Guevara, "Message to the Tricontinental," Secretariat of the Organization of the Solidarity of the Peoples of Africa, Asia, and Latin America (OSPAAL) (Havana, April 16, 1967), https://www.marxists.org/archive/guevara/1967/04/16.htm.

84. Kevin Gray and Jong-Woon Lee, *North Korea and the Geopolitics of Development* (Cambridge: Cambridge University Press, 2021), 99–100. Despite a drop in defense spending as a proportion of the national budget by 1972, North Korean military expenditures relative to the overall budget have remained high in a failing attempt to keep up with the South, at enormous economic cost. North Korea averaged around US$3.06 billion in annual military spending between 2005 and 2015, which amounted to 23.3 percent of its estimated GDP, whereas South Korea averaged US$32.3 billion, ten times North Korean spending, at only 2.6 percent of its GDP (101). Regarding shifts in North Korea's militant strategy vis-à-vis the Vietnam War see Balázs Szalontai, "In the Shadow of Vietnam: A New Look at North Korea's Militant Strategy, 1962–1970," *Journal of Cold War Studies* 14, no. 4 (2012): 122–66.

85. Pak, *YiYi Hyo-jae*, 209–16. On the first public "comfort woman" testimony in the North in 1992 by Ri Kyŏng-saeng and the formation of the Committee on the Measures for Compensation to the Former Korean Comfort Women for the Japanese Army and the Pacific War Victims (Chonggun wianbu mit T'aep'yŏngyang chŏnjaeng p'ihaeja posang taech'aek wiwŏnhoe) in the North see Kim Tang, "Pukhan ŭi chonggun wianbu silt'ae mit t'ŭksŏng e kwanhan yŏn'gu" [A study on the situation and characteristics of military comfort women in North Korea], *Yŏsŏng kwa p'yŏnghwa* [Women and peace] 2 (2002): 41–94.

86. Ueno Chizuko, "The Politics of Memory: Nation, Individual and Self," *History and Memory* 11, no. 2 (1999): 129–52.

87. This example is drawn from Suzy Kim, "Cold War Feminisms in East Asia: Introduction," *positions: asia critique* 28, no. 3 (2020): 501–16.

88. Temma Kaplan, "On the Socialist Origins of International Women's Day," *Feminist Studies* 11, no. 1 (Spring 1985): 163–71.

89. Choi Chatterjee, *Celebrating Women: Gender, Festival Culture, and Bolshevik Ideology, 1910–1939* (Pittsburgh: University of Pittsburgh Press, 2002).

90. "About International Women's Day," n.d., International Women's Day, www.internationalwomensday.com/About.

91. Lin Farley, "I Coined the Term 'Sexual Harassment.' Corporations Stole It," *New York Times*, October 18, 2017, www.nytimes.com/2017/10/18/opinion/sexual-harassment-corporations-steal.html.

92. Raluca Maria Popa, "Translating Equality between Women and Men across Cold War Divides: Women Activists from Hungary and Romania and the Creation of International Women's Year," in *Gender Politics and Everyday Life in State Socialist Eastern and Central Europe*, ed. Shana Penn and Jill Massino (London: Palgrave Macmillan, 2010); Kristen Ghodsee, "Rethinking State Socialist Mass Women's Organizations: The Committee of the Bulgarian Women's Movement and the United Nations Decade for Women, 1975–1985," *Journal of Women's History* 24, no. 4 (2012): 50–51; and Olcott, *International Women's Year*, 19.

93. For more on Cold War feminisms and an introduction to women's active international engagement in these years see the special issue "Cold War Feminisms in East Asia," *positions: asia critique* 28, no. 3 (2020).

94. Carol Harrington, "Resolution 1325 and Post–Cold War Feminist Politics," *International Feminist Journal of Politics* 13 (December 2011): 557–75.

95. Olcott, "Cold War Conflicts and Cheap Cabaret," 745–47.

96. "United Nations General Assembly Resolution 3390A/3390B, 'Question of Korea,'" November 18, 1975, History and Public Policy Program Digital Archive, United Nations Office of Public Information, *Yearbook of the United Nations 1975* (New York: United Nations, Office of Public Information, 1978), 203–4.

97. Chong-Ki Choi, "The Korean Question in the United Nations," *Verfassung und Recht in Übersee / Law and Politics in Africa, Asia and Latin America* 8, no. 3/4 (1975): 395–96.

98. For more on the Cold War roots of the UN and its human rights mechanisms see Suzy Kim, "After Human Rights and the Liberal Order: Toward a New Theory and Praxis of Personhood," *Journal of Human Rights Studies* 1, no. 2 (December 2018): 65–106.

99. Choi, "Korean Question in the United Nations," 397.

100. Kwang Ho Lee, "A Study of the United Nations Commission for the Unification and Rehabilitation of Korea (UNCURK)—the Cold War and a United Nations Subsidiary Organ" (PhD diss., University of Pittsburgh, 1974), 2, 195–96.

101. Lee, 198.

102. Barry Gills argues that this "victory," while historic, was "far from clear-cut" because a competing resolution also passed in favor of South Korea as Resolution 3390A. While this demonstrates the Cold War impasse as Gills argues, the two resolutions are not quite as "contradictory" as he interprets, because Resolution 3390A also called for "new arrangements designed to replace the Armistice Agreement . . . so that the United Nations Command may be dissolved . . . so that by that date no armed forces under the United Nations flag will remain in the South of Korea." See B. K. Gills, *Korea versus Korea: A Case of Contested Legitimacy* (London: Routledge, 1996), 137–43, and "United Nations General Assembly Resolution 3390A, 'Question of Korea.'"

103. Choi, "Korean Question in the United Nations," 399.

104. Young C. Kim, "The Democratic People's Republic of Korea in 1975," *Asian Survey* 16, no. 1 (1976): 86.

105. Choi, "Korean Question in the United Nations," 401.

106. Malathi de Alwis, "Feminist Politics and Maternalist Agonism," in *South Asian Feminisms*, ed. Ania Loomba and Ritty A. Lukose (Durham, NC: Duke University Press, 2012), 169–70.

107. de Alwis, 171.

Bibliography

ARCHIVES AND LIBRARIES

Harvard-Yenching Library (Cambridge, MA)
Information Center on North Korea (Seoul)
International Institute of Social History (Amsterdam)
Korea University Library and Center for Korean Studies (Tokyo)
Library of Congress (Washington, DC)
National Archives and Records Administration II (College Park, MD)
Russian State Documentary Film and Photo Archive (Krasnogorsk)
Russian State Library (Moscow)
Sophia Smith Collection, Smith College Library (Northampton, MA)

NEWSPAPERS, MAGAZINES, AND SERIALS

Chosŏn Nyŏsŏng [Korean women]
Cho-Sso Munhwa [Korean-Soviet culture]
Munhak Sinmun [Literature newspaper]
Rodong Sinmun [Workers newspaper]
Sinsaenghwal [New everyday life]
Ssoryŏn Nyŏsŏng [Soviet women]
WIDF Documents and Information
WIDF Information Bulletin
Women of the Whole World

FILMS

As One for Equality, Happiness and Peace. Berlin: DEFA, n.d.
Baimao nü [The white-haired girl]. Dir. Wang Bin and Shui Hua, 1950.
Choguk haebang chŏnjaeng [The fatherland liberation war]. Pyongyang: Korea Film, 1994.
"Congrès Mondial des Partisans de la Paix." Dir. Louis Daquin, 1949.
Kkotp'anŭn ch'ŏnyŏ [The flower girl]. Dir. Pak Hak and Ch'oe Ik-gyu, 1972.
Mat' [Mother]. Dir. Vsevolod Pudovkin, 1926.
Международная женская делегация в Корее [International women's delegation in Korea]. Moscow: TsSDF, 1951.
P'ibada [Sea of blood]. Dir. Ch'oe Ik-gyu, 1969.
T'aeyang ŭi p'um esŏ yŏngsaeng hanŭn muyongga [Everlasting dancer in the bosom of the sun]. Pyongyang: Mokran Video, 2012.
Women's Caravan of Peace. Concord Media, 1958.

SELECTED PRIMARY SOURCES IN KOREAN

Asea mit t'aep'yŏngyang chiyŏk p'yŏnghwa ongho taehoe munhŏnjip [Asia Pacific Peace Conference document collection]. Pyongyang: Kungrip ch'ulp'ansa, 1953.
Choe, Seung-hui. *Chosŏn adong muyong kibon* [Basics of Korean children's dance]. Pyongyang: Chosŏn munhak yesul ch'ongtongmaeng ch'ulp'ansa, 1964.

Choe, Seung-hui. *Chosŏn minjok muyong kibon* [Basics of Korean national dance]. Pyongyang: Chosŏn yesul ch'ulp'ansa, 1958.
Choe, Seung-hui. *Muyonggŭk taebonjip* [Collection of dance-drama scripts]. Pyongyang: Chosŏn yesul ch'ulp'ansa, 1958.
Chŏn, Ch'ang-mo. *Minjok ŭi charang Chosŏnhwa: Chŏnt'ongjŏgin Chosŏnhwa hwabŏp yŏn'gu* [The nation's pride Chosŏnhwa paintings: On the traditional painting technique of Chosŏnhwa]. Pyongyang: 2.16 Yesul kyoyuk ch'ulp'ansa, 2002.
Chŏn'guk nyŏsŏng sahoejuŭi kŏnsŏlja hoeŭi munhŏnjip [Documents of the National Conference of Women Socialist Builders]. Pyongyang: Chosŏn nyŏsŏngsa, 1959.
Chŏn'guk ŏmŏni taehoe munhŏnjip [Documents of the National Mothers Congress]. Pyongyang: Chosŏn nyŏsŏngsa, 1961.
Chosŏn minju nyŏsŏng tongmaeng che-3-ch'a taehoe munhŏnjip [Documents of the Korean Democratic Women's Union Third Congress]. Pyongyang: Kŭllo tanch'ae ch'ulp'ansa, 1965.
Chosŏn minjujuŭi inmin konghwaguk inmin kyŏngje paljŏn t'onggyejip (1946–1960) [Statistics on the people's economic development in the Democratic People's Republic of Korea (1946–1960)]. Pyongyang: Kungrip ch'ulp'ansa, 1961.
Chosŏn nyŏsŏng dŭri kŏrŏ on sunan ŭi ryŏksa nŭn toep'uri toelsu ŏpta [The history of the sufferings of Korean women cannot be repeated]. Pyongyang: Kŭllo nyŏsŏng sinmunsa, 1974.
Hang'il mujang t'ujaeng kwajŏng esŏ ch'angjodoen hyŏngmyŏngjŏk munhak yesul [Revolutionary literature and art created in the process of anti-Japanese armed struggle]. Pyongyang: Kwahagwŏn ch'ulp'ansa, 1960.
Hwang, Sun-hŭi. *Widaehan chŏnsa ŭi saeng'ae chung'esŏ* [From the life of a great warrior]. Pyongyang: Kŭllo tanch'ae ch'ulp'ansa, 1988.
Kim, Jong Il. *Muyong yesullon* [Theory on dance art]. Pyongyang: Chosŏn rodongdang ch'ulp'ansa, 1992.
Kkot p'anŭn ch'ŏnyŏ [The flower girl]. Pyongyang: Munye ch'ulp'ansa, 1977.
Korikki, Makssim. *Ŏmŏni* [Mother]. Translated by Ch'oe Ho. Pyongyang: Kungrip ch'ulp'ansa, 1957.
Kukje minju yŏsŏng yŏnmaeng taehoe munhŏnjip [Documents of the Women's International Democratic Federation Congress]. Pyongyang: Chosŏn yŏsŏngsa, 1947.
Minjung ŭi pada [Sea of the masses]. 2 vols. Seoul: Hanmadang, 1988.
Minutes of the National Congress of People's Committee Representatives. Seoul: Chosŏn chŏngp'ansa, 1946. In *Collection of Modern Korean History Materials*, vol. 12. Seoul: Dolbegae, 1986.
Nyŏsŏng tŭl ŭi iyagi [Women's stories]. Pyongyang: Chosŏn nyŏsŏngsa, 1957.
Pae, Yunhŭi. *T'aeyang ŭi p'um esŏ yŏngsaeng hanŭn muyongga* [Everlasting dancer in the bosom of the sun]. Pyongyang: Munhak yesul ch'ulp'ansa, 2012.
Pak, Chong-sŏng. *Chosŏn minsok muyong* [Korean folk dance]. Pyongyang: Munye ch'ulp'ansa, 1991.
Pitnanŭn uri yesul [Our radiant arts]. Pyongyang: Chosŏn yesulsa, 1960.
Sijip: Nyŏsŏng dŭl ege [Anthology of poems: For women]. Pyongyang: Chosŏn nyŏsŏngsa, 1952.
Saenghwal kwa mudae [Everyday life and the stage]. Pyongyang: Kungnip ch'ulp'ansa, 1956.
Yi, Ae-sun. *Ch'oe Sŭng-hŭi muyong yesul munjip* [Choe Seung-hui on the dance arts]. Seoul: Kukhak charyowŏn, 2002.
Yun, Ŭi-sŏp and Ch'a Sun-hŏn. *Konghwaguk esŏŭi imgŭm chojik hwa rodong ŭi kijunhwa* [The organization of wages and labor standardization in the republic]. Pyongyang: Kungrip ch'ulp'ansa, 1955.

SELECTED PRIMARY SOURCES IN ENGLISH AND OTHER WESTERN LANGUAGES

Afro-Asian Poems: Anthology. Vol. 1, 2 parts. Colombo: Afro-Asian Writers' Bureau, 1963.
As One! For Equality, for Happiness, for Peace: World Congress of Women, Copenhagen, June 5–10, 1953. Berlin: Women's International Democratic Federation, 1953.
The Children of Korea Call to the Women of the World. Berlin: WIDF, n.d.
Commission of International Association of Democratic Lawyers. *Report on U.S. Crimes in Korea, 31 March 1952*. Pyongyang: International Association of Democratic Lawyers, 1952.
Committee on Un-American Activities, US House of Representatives. *Report on the Communist "Peace" Offensive: A Campaign to Disarm and Defeat the United States*. April 1, 1951. Washington, DC: Government Printing Office.
Committee on Un-American Activities, US House of Representatives. *Report on the Congress of American Women*. October 23, 1949. Repr., Washington, DC: Government Printing Office, 1950.
Documents of World Congress of Mothers. WIDF, 1955.
Eugénie Cotton: The Full Life of a Woman of This Century. Berlin: WIDF, 1970.
Fédération Démocratique Internationale des Femmes. *Congrès International des Femmes, compte rendu des travaux du congrès qui s'est tenu à Paris du 26 Novembre au 1er Décembre 1945*. Paris, 1946.
Felton, Monica. *That's Why I Went*. London: Lawrence & Wishart, 1953.
Fleron, Kate. *Nord-Korea: Rapporter fra et haerget land*. Copenhagen: Hoffenberg, 1951.
For Their Rights as Mothers, Workers, Citizens. Berlin: WIDF, 1952.
Garland, Margaret. *Journey to New China*. Christchurch: Caxton, 1954.
Goldhamer, Herbert. *The 1951 Korean Armistice Conference: A Personal Memoir*. Santa Monica, CA: RAND, 1994.
Hearings before the Committee on Un-American Activities, House of Representatives, 84th Congress, Second Session, June 18 and 19, 1956. Washington, DC: Government Printing Office, 1956.
Ho, Ching-chi, and Yi Ting. *The White-Haired Girl: An Opera in Five Acts*. Translated by Yang Hsien-yi and Gladys Yang. Peking: Foreign Languages Press, 1954.
Military Situation in the Far East: Hearings Before the Committee on Armed Services and the Committee on Foreign Relations, United States Senate, 82nd Congress. Washington, DC: Government Printing Office, 1951.
Millard, Betty. *Women on Guard: How the Women of the World Fight for Peace*. New York: New Century, 1952.
Protection of Motherhood: As a Right of Women and a Responsibility of Society. Berlin: WIDF, 1958.
Report of the World Conference of the International Women's Year, Mexico City, 19 June—2 July 1975. New York: United Nations, 1976.
Roher, Lothar, Rolf Jubisch, and Werner Gerwinski, eds. *10th Anniversary of the Women's International Democratic Federation*. Berlin: WIDF, 1955.
Russell, Dora. *The Tamarisk Tree 3: Challenge to the Cold War*. London: Virago, 1985.
Second Women's International Congress in Budapest (Hungary) from 1st to the 6th of December 1948. Paris, 1949.
Sexton, John, ed. *Alliance of Adversaries: The Congress of the Toilers of the Far East*. Leiden: Brill, 2019.
The Struggle between Two Lines at the Moscow World Congress of Women. Beijing: Foreign Languages Press, 1963.

Une délégation de la Fédération Démocratique Internationale des Femmes en République Démocratique du Vietnam, 14–25 février 1966. Berlin: WIDF, 1966.
We Accuse! Report of the Commission of the Women's International Democratic Federation in Korea, May 16 to 27, 1951. Berlin: WIDF, 1951.
We Have Seen . . . Berlin: WIDF, 1968.
What We Saw in China by 15 Americans. New York: Weekly Guardian Associates, 1952.
WIDF British Committee. British Woman in New China: Marian Ramelson's Report on the Asian Women's Conference, Peking, 1949. London: Farleigh, 1949.
The Women of Asia and Africa: Documents. Budapest: WIDF, December 1948.
Women's International Democratic Federation: Published for the 40th Anniversary of the Founding of the WIDF. Berlin: WIDF, n.d.
World Congress of Women, Moscow, June 1963. Berlin: WIDF, 1963.

SECONDARY SOURCES IN KOREAN

An, T'ae-yun. "Pukhan yŏsŏngdŭri kyŏkkŭn Han'guk chŏnjaeng" [North Korean women's wartime experiences during the Korean War]. Yŏsŏng kwa yŏksa [Women and history] 20 (2014): 178–213.
Cho, Young-Ju. "Pukhan ŭi inmin mandŭlgi wa chendŏ chŏngch'i: Paegŭp kwa sŏngbun-tangwŏn chedo rŭl chungsim ŭro" [Making the people and gender politics in North Korea: Distribution and partisan system]. Hanguk yŏsŏnghak [Journal of Korean women's studies] 29, no. 2 (2013): 111–42.
Cho, Young-Ju. "Pukhan yŏsŏng ŭi silch'ŏn kwa chendŏ rejim ŭi tonghak" [The practice of women and dynamics of gender regime in North Korea]. PhD diss., Ewha Women's University, 2012.
Ch'oe, Hŭi-sŏn. Pukhan edo tijain i issŭlkka: Pukhan sanŏp misul 70-nyŏn [Industrial art as design in North Korea]. Seoul: Damdi, 2020.
Ch'oe, Sŏng-ok. "Haewoe kongyŏn i Ch'oe Sŭnghŭi ŭi yesul segye e mich'in yŏnghyang" [Influence of tours abroad on Choe Seung-hui's artistic world]. Han'guk muyong kirok hakhoe [Association of Korean dance documentation] 20 (2010): 107–33.
Chŏng, Pyŏng-ho. Ch'umch'unŭn Ch'oe Sŭnghŭi—segye rŭl huiŏjabŭn Chosŏn yŏja [Dancing Choe Seung-hui—Korean woman who ruled the world]. Seoul: Ppuri kip'ŭn namu, 1995.
Chŏng, Yong-uk. "Naengjŏn ŭi p'yŏnghwa, pundan ŭi p'yŏnghwa: 6.25 chŏnjaeng chŏnhu Pukhan ŭi p'yŏnghwa undong e nat'anan p'yŏnghwaron" [Cold War peace, division peace: Debates in the North Korean peace movement before and after the Korean War]. In Sŏul taehakkyo yŏksa yŏn'guso 10-chunyŏn kinyŏm haksul taehoe: 'P'yŏnghwa' ŭi yŏksa, yŏksa sok ŭi p'yŏnghwa [Ten-year anniversary conference of the Institute of Historical Research at Seoul National University: History of "peace," peace in history], 85–111. Seoul: Institute of Historical Research, 2013.
Hong, Chong-uk. "1950-nyŏndae ŭi Bandung hoeŭi wa pidongmaeng undong insik—chapji 'Kukje Saenghwal' kisa rŭl chungsim ŭro" [North Korea's recognition of the Bandung Conference and the Non-aligned Movement in the 1950s: Focusing on the magazine International Life]. Tongbuga yŏksa nonch'ong [Northeast Asian history journal] 61 (2018): 374–406.
Hong, Chong-uk. "Pukhan yŏksahak hyŏngsŏng e Ssoryŏn yŏksahak i mich'in yŏnghyang" [The influence of Soviet historiography on the formation of North Korean historiography]. Inmun nonch'ong [Journal of humanities] 77, no. 3 (2020): 13–58.

Huang, Yongyuan. "Kaehyŏk kaebang ijŏn Chungguk e taehan Pukhan munhwa ŭi yŏnghyangryŏk: 1950–70 nyŏndae Chungguk ŭi Pukhan yŏnghwa suip ŭl chungsim ŭro" [The impact of North Korean culture on China before China's reform and opening-up policy: Focusing on China's North Korean film imports in the 1950s–70s]." *Tongbang hakji* [Journal of Asian studies] 177 (December 2016): 335–66.

Hwang, Eun-ju. "Pukhan sŏng'in yŏsŏng ŭi chongch'i sahoehwa e kwanhan yŏn'gu: Chosŏn minju nyŏsŏng tongmaeng kwa 'Chosŏn Nyŏsŏng' punsŏk ŭl chungsim ŭro" [A study of women's political socialization in North Korea: Focusing on the Korean Democratic Women's Union and *Chosŏn Nyŏsŏng*]." MA thesis, Hanyang University, 1994.

Im, Hŏn-yŏng. "Pukhan ŭi hang'il hyŏngmyŏng munhak" [Anti-Japanese revolutionary literature of North Korea]. In *Pukhan ŭi munhak* [North Korean literature], edited by Kwŏn Yŏngmin. Seoul: Ŭryu munhwasa, 1989.

Im, Hyŏng-t'aek, Ch'oe Wŏn-sik, Kim Myŏng-hwan, and Kim Hyŏng-su. "T'ong'il ŭl saenggak hamyŏ Pukhan munhak ŭl ingnŭnda" [Reading North Korean literature with reunification in mind]. *Ch'angjak kwa pip'yŏng* [Creation and criticism] 17, no. 3 (Winter 1989): 8–56.

Kim, Ch'ae-wŏn. *Ch'oe Sŭng-hŭi ch'um: Kyesŭng kwa pyŏnyong* [Choe Seung-hui dance: Legacies and transformations]. Seoul: Minsogwŏn, 2008.

Kim, Chae-yong. "Hang'il hyŏngmyŏng munhak ŭi wŏnhyŏng kwa kŭ pyŏnyong" [The origin and changes in anti-Japanese revolutionary literature]. *Yŏksa pip'yŏng* [History criticism] 25 (November 1993): 382–84.

Kim, Chae-yong. *Pukhan munhak ŭi yŏksajŏk ihae* [Historical understanding of North Korean literature]. Seoul: Munhak kwa chisŏngsa, 1994.

Kim, Chŏng-ŭn. "Chosŏn ŭi 'pulhu ŭi kojŏnjŏk myŏngjak' 'P'ibada' ŭi ppurirŭl tŏdŭmŏ" [Tracing the roots of the "immortal classic masterpiece" of Korea *Sea of Blood*]. *Chunghwa ŏnŏ munhwa yŏn'gu* [Chinese language and culture studies] 9 (2015): 57–77.

Kim, Kang-sik. "Pukhan ŭi rodong chedo wa Pukhan illyŏk kwalli" [Labor system and human resource management in North Korea]. *Chilsŏ kyŏngje chŏnŏl* [Journal of economic order] 4, no. 2 (2001): 3–32.

Kim, Kuk-hwa. "Tongbang noryŏkja kongsan taehak Chosŏn hakpu yŏn'gu (1924–25-nyŏn)" [A study on the Korean Group of KUTV, 1924–25]. *Inmun kwahak* [Humanities science] 57 (2015): 176–206.

Kim, Kwi-ok. "Han'guk chŏnjaenggi Han'guk-gun e ŭihan sŏngp'okryŏk ŭi yuhyŏng kwa hamŭi" [Patterns and implications of sexual violence by the Korean military during the Korean War]. *Kusulsa yŏn'gu* [Oral history studies] 3, no. 2 (2012): 7–37.

Kim, Kyŏng-il. *Iljeha nodong undongsa* [History of labor movements under Japanese imperialism]. Seoul: Ch'angjak kwa pip'yŏngsa, 1992.

Kim, Tae-woo. "Naengjŏn p'yŏnghwaron ŭi sasaeng'a: Ssoryŏn kwa Pukhan ŭi Han'guk chŏnjaeng pukch'im sinario chojak ŭi chŏngch'ijŏk paegyŏng kwa kwajŏng [Bastard child of Cold War peace: Political background to the Soviet and North Korean fabrication on the northern attack of the Korean War]." *T'ong'il inmunhak* [Journal of the humanities for unification] 64 (2015): 263–304.

Kim, Tae-woo. *Naengjŏn ŭi manyŏdŭl: Han'guk chŏnjaeng kwa yŏsŏngjuŭi p'yŏnghwa undong* [Witches of the Cold War: The Korean War and the feminist peace movement]. P'aju, South Korea: Ch'angbi, 2021.

Kim, Tae-woo. "1948–50-nyŏn sahoejuŭi chinyŏng ŭi p'yŏnghwaron kwa p'yŏnghwa undong ŭi Tong'asiajŏk suyong kwa pyŏnyong" [East Asian reception and transformation of socialist camp ideas of peace and the peace movement in 1948–50]. *Tongbuga munhwa yŏn'gu* [Research on the cultures of Northeast Asia] 58 (2019): 83–101.

Kim, Tang. "Pukhan ŭi chonggun wianbu silt'ae mit t'ŭksŏng e kwanhan yŏn'gu" [A study on the situation and characteristics of military comfort women in North Korea]. *Yŏsŏng kwa p'yŏnghwa* [Women and peace] 2 (2002): 41–94.

Kim, Tong-ch'un. *Chŏnjaeng kwa sahoe* [War and society]. P'aju, South Korea: Dolbegae, 2016.

Kim, Yŏn-ch'ŏl. *Pukhan ŭi sanŏphwa wa kyŏngje chŏngch'aek* [Industrialization and economic policy in North Korea]. Seoul: Yŏksa pip'yŏngsa, 2001.

Kyŏngnam taehakkyo Pukhan taehagwŏn. *Pukhan yŏn'gu pangbŏpron* [Methodology of North Korean studies]. Seoul: Hanul, 2003.

Lee, Seung-Yoon, Hwang Eun-Joo, and Kim Yuhwi. "Pukhan kongsik-pigongsik nodong sijang ŭi hyŏngsŏng kwa yŏsŏng" [Formal-informal labor market and women in North Korea]. *Pip'an sahoe chŏngch'aek* [Journal of critical social policy] 48 (2015): 285–328.

Lee, Sung-woo. "Sahoejuŭi yŏsŏng undongga Ko Myŏng-ja ŭi saeng'ae wa hwaldong" [Socialist woman activist Ko Myungja's life and activity]. *Inmunhak yŏn'gu* [Humanities research] 84 (2011): 247–74.

Minjok Munhaksa Yŏn'guso. *Pukhan ŭi uri munhaksa insik* [Understanding of the history of our literature in North Korea]. Seoul: Ch'angjak kwa pip'yŏngsa, 1991.

Paek, Hyang-ju. "Ch'oe Sŭng-hŭi 'Chosŏn minjŏk muyong kibon' ŭi hyŏngsŏng kwa pyŏnhwa" [Formation and change of Choe Seung-hui's "Basics of Korean National Dance"]. MA thesis, Korean National University of Arts, 2006.

Paek, Wŏn-dam. "Asia esŏ 1960–70 nyŏndae Pidongmaeng/Che-3-segye undong kwa minjok minjung kaenyŏm ŭi ch'angsin" [Non-aligned / Third World movement in Asia during the 1960–'70s and the creation of the concept of nation and people]. *Chungguk hyŏndae munhak* [Modern Chinese literature] 29 (2009): 127–90.

Pak, Chŏng-hŭi. *YiYi Hyo-jae: Taehanmin'guk yŏsŏng undong ŭi sara itnŭn yŏksa* [YiYi Hyo-jae: Living history of the women's movement in the Republic of Korea]. P'aju, South Korea: Dasan Books, 2019.

Pak, Hyŏnsŏn. *Hyŏndae Pukhan sahoe wa kajok* [Contemporary North Korean society and family]. Seoul: Hanul, 2003.

Pak, Kye-ri. "Pukhan ŭi misul chŏngch'aek pyŏnhwa e ttarŭn misul chakp'um ŭi tosang kwa hyŏngsik ŭi pyŏnhwa yŏn'gu" [A study on changes in the iconography and form of artworks in response to changes in North Korea's art policy]. In *Pukhan misul ŏje wa onŭl* [Art in North Korea, its past and present]. Daejeon, South Korea: National Research Institute of Cultural Heritage, 2016.

Pak, Yŏng-ja. *Pukhan nyŏja: T'ansaeng kwa kuljŏl ŭi 70-nyŏnsa* [North Korean women: 70-year history of birth and refraction]. Seoul: Aelp'i, 2017.

Pak, Yong-ok. *Han'guk yŏsŏng hang'il undongsa yŏn'gu* [History of the Korean women's anticolonial movement]. Seoul: Chisik sanŏpsa, 1996.

Park, Jeong-Mi. "Han'guk chŏnjaenggi sŏngmaemae chŏngch'aek e kwanhan yŏn'gu: Wianso wa wianbu rŭl chungsim ŭro" [A study on prostitution policies during the Korean War: Focusing on comfort stations and comfort women]. *Han'guk yŏsŏnghak* [Journal of Korean Women's Studies] 27, no. 2 (2011): 35–72.

Roh, Jiseung. "Chendŏ, nodong, kamjŏng kŭrigo chŏngch'ijŏk kaksŏng ŭi sun'gan—yŏsŏng sahoejuŭija Chŏng Ch'il-sŏng ŭi sam kwa hwaldong e taehan yŏn'gu" [Gender, labor, emotion, and moment of political awakening—a study on life and activities of female socialist Chung Chil-sung]. *Pigyo munhwa yŏn'gu* [Comparative cultural studies] 43 (2016): 7–50.

Sŏ, Tong-man. *Pukchosŏn sahoejuŭi ch'eje sŏngripsa, 1945–1961* [History of the founding of the socialist system in North Korea, 1945–1961]. Seoul: Sŏnin, 2005.

Sŏng, Hye-rang. *Tŭngnamujip* [Wisteria tree house]. Seoul: Chisik nara, 2001.

Sŏng, Hyŏn-kyŏng, ed. *Kyŏngsŏng elittŭ ŭi man'guk yuramgi* [Travelogues of the Seoul elite]. Seoul: Hyŏnsil munhwa yŏn'gu, 2015.

Tong, Kyŏng-wŏn. "Ch'oe Sŭng-hŭi muyong yŏn'gu: Chakp'um punsŏk mit kong'yŏn yesulsajŏk iŭi rŭl chungsim ŭro" [A study of Choe Seung-hui's dance: Focusing on the artistic significance of her performance and analysis of her work]. *Han'guk yesul yŏn'gu* [Korean arts studies] 9 (2014): 151–205.

Yi, Chu-mi. "Ch'oe Sŭng-hŭi ŭi 'Chosŏnjŏk in kŏt' kwa 'Tongyangjŏk in kŏt'" [Choe Seung-hui's "Koreanness" and "Asianness"]. *Hanminjok munhwa yŏn'gu* [Korean culture studies] 23 (2007): 335–59.

Yi, Hyo-jae. *Pundan sidae ŭi sahoehak* [Sociology of the division era]. Seoul: Han'gilsa, 1985.

Yi, Hyŏn-ju. "Pukhan P'ibadasik hyŏngmyŏng kagŭk ŭi yŏksasŏng" [The historicity of the North Korean *Sea of Blood*–style revolutionary opera]. *Chosŏndae tongbuga yŏn'guso* [Chosŏn University Northeast Asia Research Institute] 21, no. 1 (2006): 87–107.

Yi, Im-ha. *Haebang konggan, ilsang ŭl pakkun yŏsŏngdŭl ŭi yŏksa* [Liberated space: Women's history of changes in everyday life]. Seoul: Ch'ŏlsu wa yŏnghŭi, 2015.

Yi, Sang-gyŏng. *Im Sun-dŭk, taeanjŏk yŏsŏng chuch'e rŭl hyanghayŏ* [Im Sun-dŭk, toward an alternative women's subjectivity]. Seoul: Somyŏng, 2009.

Yi, Sŭng-hŭi. *Han'guk hyŏndae yŏsŏng undongsa* [History of the women's movement in modern Korea]. Seoul: Paeksan sŏdang, 1994.

Yi, Yŏng-ran. *Ch'oe Sŭng-hŭi muyong yesul sasang* [Choe Seung-hui on the dance arts]. Seoul: Minsogwŏn, 2014.

Yŏsŏngsa yŏn'gu moim Kilbak sesang. *20-segi yŏsŏng sagŏnsa* [Twentieth-century women's history]. Seoul: Yŏsŏng sinmunsa, 2001.

Yu, Mi-hŭi. "Pukhan muyong yesul kwa yŏsŏng haebang" [North Korean dance arts and women's liberation]. *Han'guk muyong kyoyuk hakhoeji* [Journal of Korean dance education] 9, no. 1 (1998): 153–71.

Yuki, Fujime. "Monik'a P'elt'ŭn kwa kukje yŏsŏng minju yŏnmaeng (WIDF) Han'guk chŏnjaeng chinsang chosadan" [Monica Felton and the WIDF fact-finding mission to the Korea War]. *Sahoe wa yŏksa* [Society and history] 100 (2013): 279–324.

SECONDARY SOURCES IN ENGLISH

Abou-El-Fadl, Reem. "Building Egypt's Afro-Asian Hub: Infrastructures of Solidarity and the 1957 Cairo Conference." *Journal of World History* 30, no. 1–2 (June 2019): 157–92.

Agov, Avram. "North Korea's Alliances and the Unfinished Korean War." *Journal of Korean Studies* 18, no. 2 (2013): 225–62.

Alonso, Harriet Hyman. *Peace as a Women's Issue: A History of the U.S. Movement for World Peace and Women's Rights*. Syracuse, NY: Syracuse University Press, 1993.

Anderson, Amanda. "Mothers and Labourers: North Korea's Gendered Labour Force in Women in Korea." *Journal of History and Cultures* 6 (2016): 14–36.

Armstrong, Elisabeth. "Before Bandung: The Anti-imperialist Women's Movement in Asia and the Women's International Democratic Federation." *Signs: Journal of Women in Culture and Society* 41 (2016): 305–31.

Armstrong, Elisabeth. "Peace and the Barrel of the Gun in the International Women's Movement, 1945–49." *Meridians: Feminism, Race, Transnationalism* 18, no. 2 (2019): 261–77.

Arruzza, Cinzia. "Functionalist, Determinist, Reductionist: Social Reproduction Feminism and Its Critics." *Science & Society* 80, no. 1 (2016): 9–30.

Ashby, Heather. "Third World Activists and the Communist University of the Toilers of the East." PhD diss., University of Southern California, 2014.

Bao, Ricardo Melgar, and Mariana Ortega-Breña. "The Anti-imperialist League of the Americas between the East and Latin America." *Latin American Perspectives* 35, no. 2 (2008): 9–24.

Barcia, Manuel. "'Locking Horns with the Northern Empire': Anti-American Imperialism at the Tricontinental Conference of 1966 in Havana." *Journal of Transatlantic Studies* 7, no. 3 (2009): 208–17.

Barlow, Tani. *In the Event of Women*. Durham, NC: Duke University Press, 2022.

Barlow, Tani. *The Question of Women in Chinese Feminism*. Durham, NC: Duke University Press, 2004.

Barraclough, Ruth. "Red Love and Betrayal in the Making of North Korea: Comrade Hŏ Jŏng-suk." *History Workshop Journal* 77 (Spring 2014): 86–102.

Berger, Mark T. "After the Third World? History, Destiny and the Fate of Third Worldism." *Third World Quarterly* 25, no. 1 (2004): 9–39.

Bhattacharya, Tithi, ed. *Social Reproduction Theory: Remapping Class, Recentering Oppression*. London: Pluto, 2017.

Bonfiglioli, Chiara. "Revolutionary Networks: Women's Political and Social Activism in Cold War Italy and Yugoslavia (1945–1957)." PhD diss., University of Utrecht, 2012.

Borovoy, Amy, and Kristen Ghodsee. "Decentering Agency in Feminist Theory: Recuperating the Family as a Social Project." *Women's Studies International Forum* 35 (2012): 153–65.

Bradley, Mark Philip. "Decolonization, the Global South, and the Cold War, 1919–1962." In *The Cambridge History of the Cold War*, vol. 1, edited by Melvyn P. Leffler and Odd Arne Westad, 464–86. Cambridge: Cambridge University Press, 2010.

Bucur, Maria. "Women and State Socialism: Failed Promises and Radical Changes Revisited." *Nationalities Papers* 44, no. 5 (2016): 847–55.

Castledine, Jacqueline. *Cold War Progressives: Women's Interracial Organizing for Peace and Freedom*. Champaign: University of Illinois Press, 2012.

Cathcart, Adam, and Charles Kraus. "Internationalist Culture in North Korea, 1945–1950." *Review of Korean Studies* 11, no. 3 (2008): 123–48.

Caute, David. *The Dancer Defects: The Struggle for Cultural Supremacy during the Cold War*. New York: Oxford University Press, 2003.

Chang, David Cheng. *The Hijacked War: The Story of Chinese POWs in the Korean War*. Palo Alto, CA: Stanford University Press, 2020.

Chang, Jon K. *Burnt by the Sun: The Koreans of the Russian Far East*. Honolulu: University of Hawai'i Press, 2016.

Chase, Michelle. "'Hands Off Korea!': Women's Internationalist Solidarity and Peace Activism in Early Cold War Cuba." *Journal of Women's History* 32, no. 3 (2020): 64–88.

Chatterjee, Choi. *Celebrating Women: Gender, Festival Culture, and Bolshevik Ideology, 1910-1939*. Pittsburgh: University of Pittsburgh Press, 2002.
Chen, Jian. *China's Road to the Korean War: The Making of the Sino-American Confrontation*. New York: Columbia University Press, 1996.
Chen, Martha Alter. "Engendering World Conferences: The International Women's Movement and the United Nations." *Third World Quarterly* 16, no. 3 (1995): 477–93.
Chen, Tina Mai. "Socialism, Aestheticized Bodies, and International Circuits of Gender: Soviet Female Film Stars in the People's Republic of China, 1949–1969." *Journal of the Canadian Historical Association* 18, no. 2 (2007): 53–80.
Chen, Xiaomei. *Acting the Right Part: Political Theater and Popular Drama in Contemporary China*. Honolulu: University of Hawai'i Press, 2002.
Choi, Chong-Ki. "The Korean Question in the United Nations." *Verfassung Und Recht in Übersee / Law and Politics in Africa, Asia and Latin America* 8, no. 3/4 (1975): 395–406.
Choi, Hyaeweol. *Gender and Mission Encounters in Korea: New Women, Old Ways*. Berkeley: University of California Press, 2009.
Chung, Joseph Sang-hoon. *The North Korean Economy: Structure and Development*. Stanford, CA: Hoover Institution, 1974.
Chung, Joseph Sang-hoon. "North Korea's 'Seven Year Plan' (1961–70): Economic Performance and Reforms." *Asian Survey* 12, no. 6 (1972): 527–45.
Clapson, Mark. "The Rise and Fall of Monica Felton, British Town Planner and Peace Activist, 1930s to 1950s." *Planning Perspective* 30, no. 2 (2015): 211–29.
Clark, Katerina. *The Soviet Novel: History as Ritual*. Chicago: University of Chicago Press, 1981.
Confortini, Catia Cecilia. *Intelligent Compassion: Feminist Critical Methodology in the Women's International League for Peace and Freedom*. New York: Oxford University Press, 2012.
Cott, Nancy. *The Grounding of Modern Feminism*. New Haven, CT: Yale University Press, 1989.
Cui, Shuqin. *Women through the Lens: Gender and Nation in a Century of Chinese Cinema*. Honolulu: University of Hawai'i Press, 2003.
Cumings, Bruce. *Origins of the Korean War*. 2 vols. Princeton, NJ: Princeton University Press, 1981, 1990.
Cumings, Bruce. *Parallax Visions: Making Sense of American–East Asian Relations*. Durham, NC: Duke University Press, 1999.
Davies, Carole Boyce. *Left of Karl Marx: The Political Life of Black Communist Claudia Jones*. Durham, NC: Duke University Press, 2007.
de Alwis, Malathi. "Feminist Politics and Maternalist Agonism." In *South Asian Feminisms*, edited by Ania Loomba and Ritty A. Lukose, 162–80. Durham, NC: Duke University Press, 2012.
De'Ath, Amy. "Gender and Social Reproduction." In *The SAGE Handbook of Frankfurt School Critical Theory*, edited by Beverley Best, Werner Bonefeld, and Chris O'Kane, 1534–50. London: SAGE, 2018.
De Forest, Jennifer. "Women United for the United Nations: US Women Advocating for Collective Security in the Cold War." *Women's History Review* 14, no. 1 (2005): 61–74.
de Haan, Francisca. "Continuing Cold War Paradigms in the Western Historiography of Transnational Women's Organisations: The Case of the Women's

International Democratic Federation (WIDF)." *Women's History Review* 19, no. 4 (September 2010): 547–73.
de Haan, Francisca. "Eugénie Cotton, Pak Chong-ae, and Claudia Jones: Rethinking Transnational Feminism and International Politics." *Journal of Women's History* 25 (Winter 2013): 174–89.
de Haan, Francisca, ed. "Forum: Is 'Communist Feminism' a *Contradictio in Terminis?*" *Aspasia* 1 (2007): 197–246.
de Haan, Francisca. "The Vietnam Activities of the Women's International Democratic Federation (WIDF)." In *Protest in the Vietnam Era*, edited by Alexander Sedlmaier, 51–82. London: Palgrave Macmillan, 2022.
de Haan, Francisca. "The WIDF, the NVB and the Korean War: Women Traversing the Local and the Global." Unpublished paper presented at the Swiss Historical Conference, University of Fribourg, February 2013.
de Haan, Francisca. "The Women's International Democratic Federation (WIDF): History, Main Agenda, and Contributions, 1945–1991." In *Women and Social Movements, International 1840 to Present*, edited by Kathryn Kish Sklar and Thomas Dublin. Alexandria, VA: Alexander Street, 2012. https://alexanderstreet.com/products/women-and-social-movements-international-1840-present.
Deuchler, Martina. *The Confucian Transformation of Korea: A Study of Society and Ideology*. Cambridge, MA: Harvard University Press, 1995.
Dirlik, Arif. "Mao Zedong Thought and the Third World / Global South." *interventions* 16, no. 2 (2014): 223–56.
Donert, Celia. "From Communist Internationalism to Human Rights: Gender, Violence and International Law in the Women's International Democratic Federation Mission to North Korea, 1951." *Contemporary European History* 25 (2016): 313–33.
Donert, Celia. "Whose Utopia? Gender, Ideology, and Human Rights at the 1975 World Congress of Women in East Berlin." In *The Breakthrough: Human Rights in the 1970s*, edited by Jan Eckel and Samuel Moyn, 68–87. Philadelphia: University of Pennsylvania Press, 2013.
Du, Daisy Yan. "Socialist Modernity in the Wasteland: Changing Representations of the Female Tractor Driver in China, 1949–1964." *Modern Chinese Literature and Culture* 29, no. 1 (2017): 55–94.
Dudziak, Mary L. *Cold War Civil Rights: Race and the Image of American Democracy*. Princeton, NJ: Princeton University Press, 2000.
Ebon, Martin, ed. *Five Chinese Communist Plays*. New York: John Day, 1975.
Eckert, Carter. *Offspring of Empire: The Koch'ang Kims and the Colonial Origins of Korean Capitalism, 1876–1945*. Seattle: University of Washington Press, 1991.
Ehrenreich, Barbara. "What Is Socialist Feminism?" *WIN Magazine*, 1976.
Eley, Geoff. "From Welfare Politics to Welfare States: Women and the Socialist Question." In *Women and Socialism, Socialism and Women: Europe between the Two World Wars*, edited by Helmut Gruber and Pamela Graves, 516–46. New York: Berghahn Books, 1998.
el Nabolsy, Zeyad. "*Lotus* and the Self-Representation of Afro-Asian Writers as the Vanguard of Modernity." *Interventions*, 2020.
Elsaesser, Thomas. "Tales of Sound and Fury: Observations on the Family Melodrama." In *Movies and Methods*, vol. 2, edited by Bill Nichols, 165–89. Berkeley: University of California Press, 1985.
Elshtain, Jean Bethke. *Women and War*. New York: Basic Books, 1987.

Eslava, Luis, Michael Fakhri, and Vasuki Nesiah, eds. *Bandung, Global History, and International Law: Critical Pasts and Pending Futures*. Cambridge: Cambridge University Press, 2017.

Evans, Harriet. "The Language of Liberation: Gender and *Jiefang* in Early Chinese Communist Party Discourse." *Intersections: Gender, History and Culture in the Asian Context* 1 (1998): 1–19.

Evans, Harriet. "Sexed Bodies, Sexualized Identities, and the Limits of Gender." *China Information* 22, no. 2 (2008): 361–86.

Ezrahi, Christina. *Swans of the Kremlin: Ballet and Power in Soviet Russia*. Pittsburgh: University of Pittsburgh Press, 2012.

Fanon, Frantz. *The Wretched of the Earth*. New York: Grove, 1963.

Federici, Silvia. *Re-enchanting the World: Feminism and the Politics of the Commons*. Oakland, CA: PM, 2018.

Ferguson, Susan. "Intersectionality and Social-Reproduction Feminisms: Toward an Integrative Ontology." *Historical Materialism* 24, no. 2 (2016): 38–60.

Ferguson, Susan. *Women and Work: Feminism, Labour, and Social Reproduction*. London: Pluto, 2019.

Foot, Rosemary. *A Substitute for Victory: The Politics of Peacemaking at the Korean Armistice Talks*. Ithaca, NY: Cornell University Press, 1990.

Frank, Rüdiger. "Lessons from the Past: The First Wave of Development Assistance to North Korea and the German Reconstruction of Hamhung." *Pacific Focus* 23, no. 1 (2008): 46–74.

Frazier, Robeson Taj. *The East Is Black: Cold War China in the Black Radical Imagination*. Durham, NC: Duke University Press, 2014.

Friedman, Jeremy. *Shadow Cold War: The Sino-Soviet Competition for the Third World*. Chapel Hill: University of North Carolina Press, 2015.

Ghodsee, Kristen. "Research Note: The Historiographical Challenges of Exploring Second World–Third World Alliances in the International Women's Movement." *Global Social Policy* 14, no. 2 (2014): 244–64.

Ghodsee, Kristen. "Rethinking State Socialist Mass Women's Organizations: The Committee of the Bulgarian Women's Movement and the United Nations Decade for Women, 1975–1985." *Journal of Women's History* 24, no. 4 (2012): 49–73.

Ghodsee, Kristen. *Second World, Second Sex: Socialist Women's Activism and Global Solidarity during the Cold War*. Durham, NC: Duke University Press, 2019.

Gills, B. K. *Korea versus Korea: A Case of Contested Legitimacy*. London: Routledge, 1996.

Gonzalez, Maya, and Jeanne Neton. "The Logic of Gender: On the Separation of Spheres and the Process of Abjection." In *Contemporary Marxist Theory: A Reader*, edited by Andrew Pendakis, Jeff Diamanti, Nicholas Brown, Josh Robinson, and Imre Szeman, 149–74. London: Bloomsbury, 2014.

Goodman, Joyce. "International Women's Organizations, Peace and Peacebuilding." In *The Palgrave Handbook of Global Approaches to Peace*, edited by Aigul Kulnazarova and Vesselin Popovski, 441–60. Cham, Switzerland: Palgrave Macmillan, 2019.

Gore, Dayo F. *Radicalism at the Crossroads: African American Women Activists in the Cold War*. New York: NYU Press, 2011.

Goswami, Manu. "Imaginary Futures and Colonial Internationalisms." *American Historical Review* 117, no. 5 (2012): 1461–85.

Gradskova, Yulia. *The Women's International Democratic Federation, the Global South, and the Cold War: Defending the Rights of Women of the "Whole World"?* New York: Routledge, 2021.

Gradskova, Yulia. "Women's International Democratic Federation, the 'Third World' and the Global Cold War from the Late-1950s to the Mid-1960s." *Women's History Review* (2019): 1–19.
Gray, Kevin, and Jong-Woon Lee, *North Korea and the Geopolitics of Development*. Cambridge: Cambridge University Press, 2021.
Gutkin, Irina. *The Cultural Origins of the Socialist Realist Aesthetic, 1890–1934*. Evanston, IL: Northwestern University Press, 1999.
Halim, Hala. "Afro-Asian Third-Worldism into Global South: The Case of *Lotus* Journal." *Global South Studies: A Collective Publication with the Global South*, November 22, 2017.
Hamm, Kristen Elizabeth. "'The Friendship of Peoples': Soviet Ballet, Nationalities Policy, and the Artistic Media, 1953–1968." MA thesis, University of Illinois, Urbana-Champaign, 2009.
Harrington, Carol. "Resolution 1325 and Post-Cold War Feminist Politics." *International Feminist Journal of Politics* 13 (December 2011): 557–75.
Harsch, Donna. *Revenge of the Domestic: Women, the Family, and Communism in the German Democratic Republic*. Princeton, NJ: Princeton University Press, 2007.
Hartman, Saidiya. "Venus in Two Acts." *Small Axe* 12, no. 2 (2008): 1–14.
Henriques, Michaela Maria Magdalena Schwarz-Santos Gonçalves. "Minding His-Story: Dora Russell's Voice on the Side of Life against the Backdrop of Her Peace Mission in the 1950s." PhD diss., University of Lisbon, 2015.
Herrmann, Anne C., and Abigail J. Stewart, eds. *Theorizing Feminism: Parallel Trends in the Humanities and Social Sciences*. Boulder, CO: Westview, 2001.
Hershatter, Gail. "Local Meanings of Gender and Work in Rural Shaanxi in the 1950s." In *Re-drawing Boundaries: Work, Households, and Gender in China*, edited by Barbara Entwisle and Gail E. Henderson, 79–96. Berkeley: University of California Press, 2000.
Herzog, Philipp. "'National in Form and Socialist in Content' or Rather 'Socialist in Form and National in Content'? The 'Amateur Art System' and the Cultivation of 'Folk Art' in Soviet Estonia." *Nar. umjet* 47, no. 1 (2010): 115–40.
Hirsch, Francine. *Empire of Nations: Ethnographic Knowledge and the Making of the Soviet Union*. Ithaca, NY: Cornell University Press, 2005.
Hong, Young-sun. *Cold War Germany, the Third World, and the Global Humanitarian Regime*. Cambridge: Cambridge University Press, 2015.
Honig, Emily. "Iron Girls Revisited: Gender and the Politics of Work in the Cultural Revolution, 1966–76." In *Re-drawing Boundaries: Work, Households, and Gender in China*, edited by Barbara Entwisle and Gail E. Henderson, 97–110. Berkeley: University of California Press, 2000.
Houten, Christina Van. "Simone de Beauvoir Abroad: Historicizing Maoism and the Women's Liberation Movement." *Comparative Literature Studies* 52, no. 1 (2015): 112–29.
Howard, Keith. *Songs for "Great Leaders": Ideology and Creativity in North Korean Music and Dance*. Oxford: Oxford University Press, 2021.
Hwang, Su-kyoung. *Korea's Grievous War*. Philadelphia: University of Pennsylvania Press, 2016.
Iber, Patrick. *Neither Peace nor Freedom: The Cultural Cold War in Latin America*. Cambridge, MA: Harvard University Press, 2015.
Ilic, Melanie. "Soviet Women, Cultural Exchange and the Women's International Democratic Federation." In *Reassessing Cold War Europe*, edited by Sari Autio-Sarasmo and Katalin Miklóssy, 157–74. New York: Routledge, 2010.

Johnson, Kay Ann. *Women, the Family and Peasant Revolution in China*. Chicago: University of Chicago Press, 1983.
Kadnikova, Anna. "The Women's International Democratic Federation World Congress of Women, Moscow, 1963: Women's Rights and World Politics during the Cold War." MA thesis, Central European University, 2011.
Kang, Liu. "Maoism: Revolutionary Globalism for the Third World Revisited." *Comparative Literature Studies* 52, no. 1 (2015): 12–28.
Kang, Thomas Hosuck. "North Korean Captured Records at the Washington National Records Center, Suitland, Maryland." *Committee on East Asian Libraries Bulletin*, no. 58 (1979): 30–37.
Kang, Xiaofei. "Revisiting *White-Haired Girl*: Women, Gender, and Religion in Communist Revolutionary Propaganda." In *Gendering Chinese Religion: Subject, Identity, and Body*, edited by Jinhua Jia, Xiaofei Kang, and Ping Yao, 133–56. New York: SUNY Press, 2014.
Kaplan, Temma. "On the Socialist Origins of International Women's Day." *Feminist Studies* 11, no. 1 (Spring 1985): 163–71.
Kawashima, Ken. *The Proletarian Gamble: Korean Workers in Interwar Japan*. Durham, NC: Duke University Press, 2009.
Kim, Cheehyung Harrison. *Heroes and Toilers: Work as Life in Postwar North Korea, 1953–1961*. New York: Columbia University Press, 2018.
Kim, Dong-choon. *The Unending Korean War: A Social History*. Larkspur, CA: Tamal Vista, 2009.
Kim, Elli Sua. "Rituals of Decolonization: The Role of Inner-Migrant Intellectuals in North Korea, 1948–1967." PhD diss., University of California Los Angeles, 2014.
Kim, Joungwon Alexander. "The 'Peak of Socialism' in North Korea: The Five and Seven Year Plans." *Asian Survey* 5, no. 5 (1965): 255–69.
Kim, Kyung Hyun. "The Fractured Cinema of North Korea: The Discourse of the Nation in *Sea of Blood*." In *In Pursuit of Contemporary East Asian Culture*, edited by Xiaobing Tang and Stephen Snyder, 85–106. Boulder, CO: Westview, 1996.
Kim, Monica. *The Interrogation Rooms of the Korean War: The Untold History*. Princeton, NJ: Princeton University Press, 2019.
Kim, Seongbo. "The History of the State Socialist System of North Korea Brought to Light through a Wealth of Sources." *Korea Journal* 46, no. 3 (2006): 260–74.
Kim, Seong-nae, "Lamentations of the Dead: The Historical Imagery of Violence on Cheju Island, South Korea," *Journal of Ritual Studies* 3, no. 2 (1989): 251–85.
Kim, Suk-Young. *Illusive Utopia: Theater, Film, and Everyday Performance in North Korea*. Ann Arbor: University of Michigan Press, 2010.
Kim, Sun Joo, ed. *The Northern Region of Korea: History, Identity, and Culture*. Seattle: University of Washington Center for Korea Studies, 2010.
Kim, Suzy. "After Human Rights and the Liberal Order: Toward a New Theory and Praxis of Personhood." *Journal of Human Rights Studies* 1, no. 2 (2018): 65–106.
Kim, Suzy, ed. "Cold War Feminisms in East Asia." *positions: asia critique* 28, no. 3 (2020).
Kim, Suzy. *Everyday Life in the North Korean Revolution, 1945–1950*. Ithaca, NY: Cornell University Press, 2013.
Kim, Suzy. "Mothers and Maidens: Gendered Formation of Revolutionary Heroes in North Korea." *Journal of Korean Studies* 19, no. 2 (2014): 256–90.
Kim, Young C. "The Democratic People's Republic of Korea in 1975." *Asian Survey* 16, no. 1 (1976): 82–94.
Kim, Young-Hoon. "Border Crossing: Choe Seung-hui's Life and the Modern Experience." *Korea Journal* 46 (Spring 2006): 170–97.

Kirasirova, Masha. "The 'East' as a Category of Bolshevik Ideology and Comintern Administration: The Arab Section of the Communist University of the Toilers of the East." *Kritika* 18, no. 1 (2017): 7–34.
Kleeman, Faye Yuan. *In Transit: The Formation of the Colonial East Asian Cultural Sphere*. Honolulu: University of Hawai'i Press, 2014.
Koikari, Mire. *Pedagogy of Democracy: Feminism and the Cold War in the U.S. Occupation of Japan*. Philadelphia: Temple University Press, 2008.
Krylova, Anna. *Soviet Women in Combat*. New York: Cambridge University Press, 2010.
Kuoshu, Harry H. *Lightness of Being in China: Adaptation and Discursive Figuration in Cinema and Theater*. New York: Peter Lang, 1999.
Kwon, Heonik. *After the Korean War: An Intimate History*. New York: Cambridge University Press, 2020.
Lankov, Andrei. *Crisis in North Korea: The Failure of De-Stalinization, 1956*. Honolulu: University of Hawai'i Press, 2005.
Lankov, Andrei. *From Stalin to Kim Il Sung: The Formation of North Korea 1945–1960*. New Brunswick, NJ: Rutgers University Press, 2002.
Laville, Helen. *Cold War Women: The International Activities of American Women's Organisations*. Manchester: Manchester University Press, 2002.
Lee, Christopher J., ed. *Making a World after Empire: The Bandung Moment and Its Political Afterlives*. Athens: Ohio University Press, 2010.
Lee, Im Ha. "The Korean War and the Role of Women." *Review of Korean Studies* 9 (June 2006): 89–110.
Lee, Jae-Bong. "U.S. Deployment of Nuclear Weapons in 1950s South Korea and North Korea's Nuclear Development: Toward the Denuclearization of the Korean Peninsula." *Asia-Pacific Journal* 7, no. 8.3 (February 2009).
Lee, Kwang Ho. "A Study of the United Nations Commission for the Unification and Rehabilitation of Korea (UNCURK)—the Cold War and a United Nations Subsidiary Organ." PhD diss., University of Pittsburgh, 1974.
Lee, Steven Hugh. "The Korean Armistice and the End of Peace: The US-UN Coalition and the Dynamics of War-Making in Korea, 1953–76." *Journal of Korean Studies* 18, no. 2 (2013): 183–224.
Lee, Steven S. *The Ethnic Avant-Garde: Minority Cultures and World Revolution*. New York: Columbia University Press, 2015.
Le Foll-Luciani, Pierre-Jean. "'If Only I Could Have Been a Bomb, I Would Have Exploded': Algerian Women Communist Militants, between Assignation and Subversion of Gender Roles (1944–1962)." *Le Mouvement Social* 255, no. 2 (2016): 35–55.
Lewis, Su Lin, and Carolien Stolte, eds. "Other Bandungs: Afro-Asian Internationalisms in the Early Cold War." *Journal of World History* 30, no. 1–2 (June 2019): 1–246.
Liu, Xiao. "*Red Detachment of Women*: Revolutionary Melodrama and Alternative Socialist Imaginations." *differences* 26, no. 3 (2015): 116–41.
Lomax, Alan, Irmgard Bartenieff, and Forrestine Paulay. "Dance Style and Culture." In *Folk Song Style and Culture*, 222–47. Washington, DC: American Association for the Advancement of Science, 1968.
Lüthi, Lorenz M. *The Sino-Soviet Split: Cold War in the Communist World*. Princeton, NJ: Princeton University Press, 2008.
Ma, Ning. "The Textual and Critical Difference of Being Radical: Reconstructing Chinese Leftist Films of the 1930s." *Wide Angle* 11, no. 2 (1989): 22–31.

Mackie, Vera. "From Hiroshima to Lausanne: The World Congress of Mothers and the Hahaoya Taikai in the 1950s." *Women's History Review* 25, no. 4 (2016): 671–95.

Manela, Erez. *The Wilsonian Moment: Self-Determination and the International Origins of Anticolonial Nationalism*. New York: Oxford University Press, 2007.

Masuda, Hajimu. *Cold War Crucible: The Korean Conflict and the Postwar World*. Cambridge MA: Harvard University Press, 2015.

May, Elaine Tyler. *Homeward Bound: American Families in the Cold War Era*. New York: Basic Books, 2008. First published in 1988.

McClellan, Woodford. "Africans and Black Americans in the Comintern Schools, 1925–1934." *International Journal of African Historical Studies* 26, no. 2 (1993): 371–90.

McDuffie, Erik S. *Sojourning for Freedom: Black Women, American Communism, and the Making of Black Left Feminism*. Durham, NC: Duke University Press, 2011.

McGregor, Katharine. "Opposing Colonialism: The Women's International Democratic Federation and Decolonisation Struggles in Vietnam and Algeria 1945–1965." *Women's History Review* 25, no. 6 (2016): 925–44.

McGregor, Katharine. "The World Was Silent? Global Communities of Resistance to the 1965 Repression in the Cold War Era." In *Truth, Silence and Violence in Emerging State Histories of the Unspoken*, edited by Aidan Russell, 147–68. New York: Routledge, 2019.

McHugh, Kathleen, and Nancy Abelmann, eds. *South Korean Golden Age Melodrama: Gender, Genre, and National Cinema*. Detroit: Wayne State University Press, 2005.

Meng, Yue. "Female Images and National Myth." In *Gender Politics in Modern China: Writing and Feminism*, edited by Tani E. Barlow, 118–36. Durham, NC: Duke University Press, 2003.

Meserve, Walter J., and Ruth I. Meserve, eds. *Modern Drama from Communist China*. New York: New York University Press, 1970.

Mezur, Katherine, and Emily Wilcox, eds. *Corporeal Politics: Dancing East Asia*. Ann Arbor: University of Michigan Press, 2020.

Mezzadri, Alessandra. "On the Value of Social Reproduction: Informal Labour, the Majority World and the Need for Inclusive Theories and Politics." *Radical Philosophy* 2, no. 04 (2019): 33–41.

Mies, Maria. *Patriarchy and Accumulation on a World Scale: Women in the International Division of Labour*. London: Zed Books, 2014. First published in 1986.

Mislán, Cristina. "Claudia Jones Speaks to 'Half the World': Gendering Cold War Politics in the *Daily Worker*, 1950–1953." *Feminist Media Studies* 17, no. 2 (2017): 281–96.

Modern Girl Around the World Research Group (Alys Eve Weinbaum, Lynn M. Thomas, Priti Ramamurthy, Uta G. Poiger, Madeleine Yue Dong, and Tani E. Barlow, eds.). *The Modern Girl Around the World*. Durham, NC: Duke University Press, 2008.

Mohanty, Chandra. "Under Western Eyes: Feminist Scholarship and Colonial Discourses." *Feminist Review* 30, no. 1 (Autumn 1988): 61–88.

Moon, Katharine. *Sex among Allies: Military Prostitution in U.S.-Korea Relations*. New York: Columbia University Press, 1997.

Morris-Suzuki, Tessa, ed. *The Korean War in Asia: A Hidden History*. New York: Rowman & Littlefield, 2018.

Nam, Hwasook. *Women in the Sky: Gender and Labor in the Making of Modern Korea*. Ithaca, NY: Cornell University Press, 2021.

Nash, Andrew. "Third Worldism." *African Sociological Review / Revue Africaine de Sociologie* 7, no. 1 (2003): 94–116.
Olcott, Jocelyn. "Cold War Conflicts and Cheap Cabaret: Sexual Politics at the 1975 United Nations International Women's Year Conference." *Gender & History* 22, no. 3 (2010): 733–54.
Olcott, Jocelyn. *International Women's Year: The Greatest Consciousness-Raising Event in History*. New York: Oxford University Press, 2017.
Park, Alyssa M. *Sovereignty Experiments: Korean Migrants and the Building of Borders in Northeast Asia, 1860–1945*. Ithaca, NY: Cornell University Press, 2019.
Park, Haeseong. "Christian Feminist Helen Kim and Her Compromise in Service to Syngman Rhee." *Korea Journal* 60, no. 4 (2020): 169–93.
Park, Sang Mi. "The Making of a Cultural Icon for the Japanese Empire: Choe Seung-hui's U.S. Dance Tours and 'New Asian Culture' in the 1930s and 1940s." *positions* 14, no. 3 (2006): 585–626.
Park, Sunyoung. *The Proletarian Wave: Literature and Leftist Culture in Colonial Korea, 1910–1945*. Cambridge, MA: Harvard University Asia Center, 2015.
Park, Sunyoung. "Rethinking Feminism in Colonial Korea: Kang Kyŏngae's Portraits of Proletarian Women." *positions* 21, no. 4 (2013): 947–85.
Person, James F. "The 1967 Purge of the Gapsan Faction and Establishment of the Monolithic Ideological System." North Korea International Documentation Project E-Dossier No. 15. https://www.wilsoncenter.org/publication/the-1967-purge-the-gapsan-faction-and-establishment-the-monolithic-ideological-system.
Person, James F. "North Korea in 1956: Reconsidering the August Plenum and the Sino-Soviet Joint Intervention." *Cold War History* 19, no. 2 (2019): 253–74.
Phạm, Quỳnh N., and Robbie Shilliam, eds. *Meanings of Bandung: Postcolonial Orders and Decolonial Visions*. New York: Rowman & Littlefield, 2016.
Pieper Mooney, Jadwiga E., and Fabio Lanza, eds. *De-centering Cold War History: Local and Global Change*. New York: Routledge, 2013.
Pojmann, Wendy. "For Mothers, Peace and Family: International (Non)-Cooperation among Italian Catholic and Communist Women's Organisations during the Early Cold War." *Gender & History* 23, no. 2 (2011): 415–29.
Prashad, Vijay. *The Darker Nations: A People's History of the Third World*. New York: New Press, 2007.
Prashad, Vijay. *Red Star over the Third World*. New Delhi: LeftWord Books, 2017.
Roberts, Rosemary. "Gendering the Revolutionary Body: Theatrical Costume in Cultural Revolution China." *Asian Studies Review* 30, no. 2 (2006): 141–59.
Roberts, Rosemary. "Positive Women Characters in the Revolutionary Model Works of the Chinese Cultural Revolution: An Argument against the Theory of Erasure of Gender and Sexuality." *Asian Studies Review* 28, no. 4 (2004): 407–22.
Ruddick, Sara. *Maternal Thinking: Toward a Politics of Peace*. Boston: Beacon, 1989.
Rupp, Leila J. *Worlds of Women: The Making of an International Women's Movement*. Princeton, NJ: Princeton University Press, 1997.
Ryang, Sonia. "Gender in Oblivion: Women in the Democratic People's Republic of Korea." *Journal of Asian and African Studies* 35, no. 3 (2000): 323–49.
Ryang, Sonia. *North Koreans in Japan: Language, Ideology, and Identity*. Boulder, CO: Westview, 1997.
Sanchez-Sibony, Oscar. *Red Globalization: The Political Economy of the Soviet Cold War from Stalin to Khrushchev*. Cambridge: Cambridge University Press, 2014.
Sanz, Veronica. "No Way out of the Binary: A Critical History of the Scientific Production of Sex." *Signs* 43, no. 1 (2017): 1–27.

Sato, Courtney. "'A Picture of Peace': Friendship in Interwar Pacific Women's Internationalism." *Qui Parle* 27, no. 2 (2018): 475–510.

Schmid, Andre. "Comrade Min, Women's Paid Labour, and the Centralising Party-State: Postwar Reconstruction in North Korea." In *Everyday Life in Mass Dictatorship: Collusion and Evasion*, edited by Alf Lüdtke, 184–201. London: Palgrave Macmillan, 2015.

Schmid, Andre. "The Gendered Anxieties of Apartment Living in North Korea, 1953–65." In *Postsocialist Landscapes: Real and Imaginary Spaces from Stalinstadt to Pyongyang*, edited by Thomas Lahusen and Schamma Schahadat, 281–303. Bielefeld, Germany: transcript Verlag, 2020.

Shen, Zhihua. *Mao, Stalin and the Korean War: Trilateral Communist Relations in the 1950s*. Translated by Neil Silver. New York: Routledge, 2012.

Siefert, Marsha, ed. *Labor in State-Socialist Europe, 1945–1989: Contributions to a History of Work*. Budapest: Central European University Press, 2020.

Skelton, Sophie. "From Peace to Development: A Re-constitution of British Women's International Politics, c. 1945–1975." PhD diss., University of Birmingham, 2014.

Slobodian, Quinn, ed. *Comrades of Color: East Germany in the Cold War World*. New York: Berghahn Books, 2015.

Sluga, Glenda. *Internationalism in the Age of Nationalism*. Philadelphia: University of Pennsylvania Press, 2013.

Song, Jay, and Steven Denney. "Studying North Korea through North Korean Migrants: Lessons from the Field." *Critical Asian Studies* 51, no. 3 (2019): 451–66.

Strauss, Gloria B. "Dance and Ideology in China, Past and Present: A Study of Ballet in the People's Republic." *Asian and Pacific Dance: Selected Papers from the 1974 CORD-SEM Conference*, edited by Adrienne L. Kaeppler, Judy Van Zile, and Carl Wolz, 19–53. New York: Committee on Research in Dance, 1977.

Stueck, William. *The Korean War: An International History*. Princeton, NJ: Princeton University Press, 1995.

Suh, Dae-sook. *Kim Il Sung: The North Korean Leader*. New York: Columbia University Press, 1988.

Suh, Dae-sook. *The Korean Communist Movement, 1918–1948*. Princeton, NJ: Princeton University Press, 1967.

Sutherland, Zöe, and Marina Vishmidt. "The Soft Disappointment of Prefiguration." Lecture at the Centre for Social and Political Thought, University of Sussex, June 2015.

Swerdlow, Amy. *Women Strike for Peace: Traditional Motherhood and Radical Politics in the 1960s*. Chicago: University of Chicago Press, 1993.

Szalontai, Balázs. "In the Shadow of Vietnam: A New Look at North Korea's Militant Strategy, 1962–1970." *Journal of Cold War Studies* 14, no. 4 (2012): 122–66.

Szalontai, Balázs. *Kim Il Sung in the Khrushchev Era: Soviet-DPRK Relations and the Roots of North Korean Despotism, 1953–1964*. Palo Alto, CA: Stanford University Press, 2005.

Tikhonov, Vladimir. "Demystifying the Nation: The Communist Concept of Ethno-nation in 1920s–1930s Korea." *Cross-Currents* 28 (2018): 69–92.

Tikhonov, Vladimir. "The Issue of Factionalism in the Korean Communist Movement of the 1920s–early 1930s." *Marŭk'ŭsŭchuŭi yŏn'gu* [Marxism 21] 15, no. 2 (2018): 152–83.

Tikhonov, Vladimir. "Korea in the Russian and Soviet Imagination, 1850s–1945: Between Orientalism and Revolutionary Solidarity." *Journal of Korean Studies* 21, no. 2 (2016): 385–421.

Tikhonov, Vladimir. "Worldwide 'Red Age' and Colonial-Era Korea: An Attempt at Meta-historical Analysis." *Marŭk'ŭsŭchuŭi yŏn'gu* [Marxism 21] 17, no. 2 (2020): 146–82.
Ueno, Chizuko. "The Politics of Memory: Nation, Individual and Self." *History and Memory* 11, no. 2 (1999): 129–52.
Van Zile, Judy. "Performing Modernity in Korea: The Dance of Ch'oe Sŭng-hŭi." *Korean Studies* 37 (2013): 124–49.
Van Zile, Judy. *Perspectives on Korean Dance*. Middletown, CT: Wesleyan University Press, 2001.
Varga-Harris, Christina. "Between National Tradition and Western Modernization: *Soviet Woman* and Representations of Socialist Gender Equality as a 'Third Way' for Developing Countries, 1956–1964." *Slavic Review* 78, no. 3 (Fall 2019): 758–81.
Vogel, Lise. *Marxism and the Oppression of Women*. Boston: Brill, 2013. First published in 1983.
Von Eschen, Penny M. *Race against Empire: Black Americans and Anticolonialism, 1937–1957*. Ithaca, NY: Cornell University Press, 1997.
Vu, Tuong, and Wasana Wongsurawat, eds. *Dynamics of the Cold War in Asia: Ideology, Identity, and Culture*. New York: Palgrave Macmillan, 2009.
Wang, Zheng. "Creating a Socialist Feminist Cultural Front: *Women of China* (1949–1966)." *China Quarterly* 204 (December 2010): 827–49.
Wang, Zheng. *Finding Women in the State: A Socialist Feminist Revolution in the People's Republic of China, 1949–1964*. Oakland: University of California Press, 2017.
Weigand, Kate. *Red Feminism: American Communism and the Making of Women's Liberation*. Baltimore: Johns Hopkins University Press, 2001.
Wernicke, Günter. "The Communist-Led World Peace Council and the Western Peace Movements: The Fetters of Bipolarity and Some Attempts to Break Them in the Fifties and Early Sixties." *Peace & Change* 23, no. 3 (July 1998): 265–311.
Wernicke, Günter. "The Unity of Peace and Socialism? The World Peace Council on a Cold War Tightrope between the Peace Struggle and Intrasystemic Communist Conflicts." *Peace & Change* 26, no. 3 (July 2001): 332–51.
Westad, Odd Arne. *The Global Cold War: Third World Interventions and the Making of Our Times*. Cambridge: Cambridge University Press, 2005.
Wilcox, Emily. "Crossing Over: Choe Seung-hui's Pan-Asianism in Revolutionary Time." *Muyong yŏksa kirokhak* [Journal of society for dance documentation and history] 51 (December 2018): 65–97.
Wilcox, Emily. *Revolutionary Bodies: Chinese Dance and the Socialist Legacy*. Oakland: University of California Press, 2019.
Willetts, Peter, ed. *"The Conscience of the World": The Influence of Non-governmental Organisations in the UN System*. Washington, DC: Brookings Institution, 1996.
Wittner, Lawrence S. *Rebels against War: The American Peace Movement, 1933–1983*. Philadelphia: Temple University Press, 1984.
Wu, Judy Tzu-Chun. *Radicals on the Road: Internationalism, Orientalism, and Feminism during the Vietnam Era*. Ithaca, NY: Cornell University Press, 2013.
Yamabe, Kentarō. "A Note on the Korean Communist Movement by Dae-sook Suh: With Special Reference to Source Materials Used." *Developing Economies* 5, no. 2 (1967): 405–12.
Yasutake, Rumi. *Transnational Women's Activism: The United States, Japan, and Japanese Immigrant Communities in California, 1859–1920*. New York: NYU Press, 2004.

Yoneyama, Lisa. *Cold War Ruins: Transpacific Critique of American Justice and Japanese War Crimes*. Durham, NC: Duke University Press, 2016.

Yoo, Theodore Jun. *The Politics of Gender in Colonial Korea: Education, Labor, and Health, 1910–1945*. Berkeley: University of California Press, 2008.

Yoon, Duncan McEachern. "Cold War Africa-China: The Afro-Asian Writers' Bureau and the Rise of Postcolonial Literature." PhD diss., University of California Los Angeles, 2014.

Yoshimi, Yoshiaki. *Comfort Women: Sexual Slavery in the Japanese Military during World War II*. New York: Columbia University Press, 2000. First published in 1995.

Yu, Miin-ling. "'Labor Is Glorious': Model Laborers in the People's Republic of China." In *China Learns from the Soviet Union, 1949–Present*, edited by Thomas P. Bernstein and Hua-Yu Li, 231–58. Lanham, MD: Lexington Books, 2010.

Yuval-Davis, Nira. *Gender & Nation*. London: SAGE, 1997.

Index

Abd el Aal, Mahasin, 222
Adams, Doris, 98
Adenauer, Konrad, 63
Adlam, Edith, 98
aesthetics of everyday folk, 169–71, 237–38
   in "age of people's creation," 171–76
   and Choe's dance philosophy, 188–93
   and politics of aesthetics, 176–88
Afro-Asian Conference (1955), 111
Afro-Asianism, anti-colonial, 58
Afro-Asian Peoples' Solidarity Conference (1957–1958), 116–17
Afro-Asian Peoples' Solidarity Organization (AAPSO), 117
Afro-Asian Writers' Bureau, 271n75
Afro-Asian Writers' Conference (1958), 118
agricultural cooperatives, 154
Algeria Solidarity Day, 117
All-China Democratic Women's Federation (ACWF), 65, 111, 113, 272n95
All Korean Women Enthusiasts Congress (1950), 67
American Peace Crusade, 39
American Women for Peace (AWP), 38
Andreen, Andrea, 29, 34, 85, 106, 109
An Kŭm-sŏn, 144–45
An Mak, 187
An Sŏng-hŭi, 175, 182
anti-imperialism, 56–64, 90–93
   and Asia Pacific Peace Conference, 73–81
   and Conference of the Women of Asia, 64–69
   and differing conceptions of peace, 118
   and internationalism, 261n25
   Korean War and, 69–70, 236
   and peaceful coexistence, 125–28
   and People's Congress for Peace, 81–82
   Tricontinental Conference (1966), 231–32
   of WIDF, 33, 55
   and women in revolutionary melodramas, 197–99
   World Congress of Women (1953), 83–90
   World Congress of Women (1958), 121
   World Congress of Women (1963), 124–30

World Congress of Women (1969), 221, 222–23
   and World Peace Council, 69–73
antiracism
   and reinforcement of racialized traits, 82
   of WIDF, 33, 55
Appeal to Women of the Whole World, 29, 128
Armstrong, Elisabeth, 33, 64
arts. *See* aesthetics of everyday folk; dance
Asian-African Conference of Women (1958), 121
Asian-African Conference of Women (1961), 121
Asian-African Film Festival, 117
Asia Pacific Peace Conference (1952), 73–81, 112
Asia Women's Conference. *See* Conference of the Women of Asia (1949)
atomic weapons. *See* nuclear weapons

Bachmann, Ida, 42, 85, 88, 114
Bai Lang, 48–49, 85, 89
ballet, 170, 174, 181, 184–88, 193, 197, 208, 212, 285n74
Barlow, Tani, 209
Bass, Charlotte A., 105
Begum, Safia, 109
Benjamin, Walter, 171–72
Bhattacharya, Tithi, 276n27
Blanco, Elisa, 81
Bolshevik Revolution. *See* October Revolution (1917)
Bouesso, Véronique, 105
Brooklyn Peace Committee, 50
Buchaca, Edith, 65
Bucur, Maria, 17
Bulletin, 249n73
Burnham, Dorothy, 50

Cahn, Hilde, 41
Cai Chang, 68, 102*f*
Canada, 90–92
capitalism, 136, 137–42
Castledine, Jacqueline, 31, 32, 38–39
Cerney, Edwin, 78

321

Cerney, Isobel, 78
Cesarini, Grazia, 19
Chang Kil-ja, 184
Chang Sun-il, 56
Chang Ŭn-dŏk, 131, 164–65
chemical warfare, 45. *See also* germ warfare
Chen, Tina Mai, 196, 211
Chiang Kai-shek, 36
Chi Chŏng-ja, 145–46
child care, 142, 146, 148, 157–58
children, 39, 97, 106–8, 120, 156–57, 229. *See also* maternal feminism; motherhood
China
   Chinese People's Volunteers, 73, 111, 147
   Chinese women withdraw from WIDF, 101, 122, 124–29, 272n95
   classical arts, 182–83
   cultural exchanges with, 183
   Cultural Revolution, 130, 193, 209, 213, 291n52
   dance, 171, 172, 182, 191, 193
   feminism and *The White-Haired Girl*, 193, 196, 203–5, 206–9, 210–13, 266n92, 291n50, 292n59, 292n67, 293n74
   Maoism, 112, 269n44
   opera, 172, 174
   and UN World Conference of Women (1975), 224
Chin Ok-sun, 145
Cho Byŏng-ryun, 161
Chodorov, Marjorie, 47
Ch'oe Chŏng-ok, 154–55
Ch'oe Ho-suk, 155
Ch'oe Kŭm-ja, 229–31
Choe Seung-hui (Ch'oe Sŭng-hŭi), 169–71, 180*f*, 181*f*, 183*f*
   in "age of people's creation," 171–72, 174–76
   dance-drama of, 169–70, 174, 175, 179–82, 188, 192–94
   dance philosophy of, 188–93
   death of, 287n107
   and politics of aesthetics, 176–88
   and sleeve dance, 286n101
   as SPA member, 15
Chollima Movement, 147, 211
Chŏng Ch'il-sŏng, 13, 15, 60–62, 137
Chŏng Chi-su, 184–85, 190, 193
Chŏng Chong-myŏng, 62
Chŏng Ok-suk, 145
Chosŏn dynasty, 7, 144, 161
Chosŏn Nyŏsŏng (Korean women), 5–6, 14, 47, 66, 70, 134*f*, 150–51, 190, 196, 215–16
Cho Yŏng, 64, 262n36

Chung, Joseph Sang-hoon, 280n102
Chung Tai Kim, 225
Ch'unhyang, 160
Clark, Katerina, 200
class exploitation
   and oppression of women, 211–12
   and sexual violence, 207–8
   See also labor
classical literature, moral character of women in Korean, 159–61
clothing, 190–91
Cold War
   effects of "end" of, 234
   Korean War as crucible of, 30
   maternalist strategies to bridge divide caused by, 100–101
colonialism. *See* anti-imperialism; imperialism
"comfort women," 227–32
Cominform, 23, 101, 113
Comintern, 7, 8, 10
Commission on the Status of Women (CSW), 218, 223
Committee of Correspondence, 45
communism
   and anti-imperialism, 59, 63
   WIDF support for, 34–35
communist feminism, 196–97, 206–7
   in anti-Japanese revolutionary melodramas, 197–99
   desexualization in historical trajectory of, 209–13
Communist Party USA, 31, 47
Communist University of the Toilers of the East (KUTV), 9, 10, 246n34
Concha, Eunice Emilia, 21
Conference of Asian Countries on the Relaxation of International Tensions (1955), 111–12
Conference of the Women of Asia (1949), 34, 64–69
Confucianism, 15, 22, 160, 161, 249n71, 288n4
Congress of American Women (CAW), 33–34, 38
Congress of Indonesian Women, 56
Congress of the Toilers of the Far East (1922), 58–62
Constructivist movement, 172–73
Cotton, Eugénie, 13, 19, 32, 34, 45, 52, 84*f*, 103–4, 113, 218, 232
craftwork, 161
creative work, 139. *See also* productive labor
Cuba, 231–32
Cuéllar, Diego Montaña, 77

cult of domesticity, 135, 136
culture. *See* aesthetics of everyday folk; dance; folk culture

dance, 169–71
 in "age of people's creation," 171–76
 ballet, 170, 174, 181, 184–88, 193, 197, 208, 212, 285n74
 Choe's philosophy regarding, 188–93
 creation of sleeve dance, 286n101
 and politics of aesthetics, 176–88
dance-drama, 169–70, 174, 175, 179–82, 188, 192–94. See also *Sea of Blood*
de Alwis, Malathi, 236
December Theses, 10
Declaration of Mexico on the Equality of Women and Their Contribution to Development and Peace (1975), 224, 225
Declaration of Mothers for the Defence of Children, against the Danger of War (1956), 106–8
Declaration of the Rights of Women (1953), 29
de Haan, Francisca, 31
Deng Yingchao, 68, 113
desexualization of women, 196, 209–13
de-Stalinization, 15, 187, 272n94
dialectical realism, 173
Ding Ling, 69, 210
disarmament, 52, 57, 58, 78, 80, 105, 107, 124–28
domesticity, cult of, 135, 136
domestic work, 142–44, 145, 146. *See also* reproductive labor
drambalet, 186
Du Bois, W. E. B., 9, 39
Dulles, John Foster, 57

Ebon, Martin, 292n58
Elshtain, Jean Bethke, 215
Equal Rights Amendment, 31, 34
Equal Rights Law (1946), 163–65
Evans, Ernestine, 59
Evans, Harriet, 291n52
Ezrahi, Christina, 285n74

Fanon, Frantz, 198
Farley, Lin, 233
Fassbinder, Clara-Maria, 108
Fate of One Member of a Self-Defense Unit, The, 197–98
Federation of Cuban Women, 219, 231–32
Federation of Japanese Women's Organizations (Fudanren), 56–57, 115

Federici, Silvia, 276n21
Felton, Monica
 activism of, 52–54
 and Asia Pacific Peace Conference, 47–48, 78–79
 delivers letters from British POWs, 257n96
 on devastation of war, 29
 leaves WIDF, 114
 on Pak Chŏng-ae, 14
 and People's Congress for Peace, 81
 proposes visit to South Korea, 44, 256n82
 retribution against, 46
 third visit with Korean women, 91*f*
 and WIDF, 87
 and World Congress of Women, 85, 89–90
feminism
 depoliticization of, 236
 and gender discrimination, 196
 left feminism, 31
 Maoist, 206, 209–10
 market, 217
 socialist feminism, 252n15
 See also communist feminism; maternal feminism
feminist erasure, 206–9
film cars, 204–6
Five Principles of Peaceful Coexistence, 112
Five-Year Plan (1957–1961), 147
Fleron, Kate, 1, 2, 41, 44, 46, 85, 86–87, 89, 90
Floreanini, Gisella, 97, 98, 107
Flower Girl, The, 193, 196, 197–98, 199, 203–4, 208, 209, 210, 211, 292n67
Flynn, Elizabeth Gurley, 47
Fodil, Abassia, 41, 85, 88
folk culture, 172–76, 179, 191–93
folktales, 159–61, 200, 204, 289n17
Foot, Rosemary, 39
Fourth World Congress of Women (1958), 116
France, 36, 64
Frazier, Robeson Taj, 39

Ganley, Anna, 105
Gannett, Betty, 47
Garland, Margaret, 79, 266n99
gender complementarity, 234–35
gender equality
 and children's early education, 158
 codification of, 31
 and domestic labor, 142–44
 WIDF support for, 35
 in "Women in the Family" report, 221–22
 See also sex difference

Gender Equality Law. *See* Equal Rights Law (1946)
gender inequality
  and communist feminism, 196–97
  and labor, 276n28
  and maternal feminism, 32, 288n4
  and productive labor, 153–54, 279n75
  and reproductive labor, 139–40, 276n28
  and sexed body, 291n52
  and structural violence, 234
gender justice, 250n88
gender mainstreaming, 235, 236
General Association of Korean Residents in Japan (Ch'ongryŏn), 57, 259n5
Geneva Conference (1954), 56, 63, 111
Geneva Conventions (1949), 77, 80, 83
germ warfare, 45, 77, 88
Gerwani, 128
Gills, Barry, 299n102
Goldhamer, Herbert, 39
Gonzalez, Maya, 139–40, 276n28
Gore, Dayo, 39
Gorky, Maxim, 108, 184, 197, 200, 201, 215
Goswami, Manu, 261n25
Gowgiel, Florence, 37, 105, 255n51
Gradskova, Yulia, 254n35
Group of 77 / G-77, 273n119
Guevara, Ernesto Che, 232
Guo Moruo, 68, 76–77

hairstyles, 62
Hannevard, Germaine, 88–89
Han Sŏl-ya, 70, 71, 77, 79
Harlem Women's Committee for Peace and Freedom, 47
Harsch, Donna, 16, 279n75
Hayes, Dorothy M., 105
Hikmet, Nazim, 108–9
Hŏ Ch'ŏl, 68
Hŏ Chŏng-suk, 12, 14, 15, 16, 29, 40–41, 51, 68, 225
Hoang Thiai, 84*f*
Ho Chi Minh, 64
Hong, Young-sun, 63, 83
housewifisation, 135, 136
Howard, Keith, 286n101
Hugel, Cecile, 221, 223
Hungarian Revolution (1956), 113–14
Hwang In-ae, 132

Im Hŏn-yŏng, 289n17
imperialism
  denounced by WIDF, 33, 55
  racism and, 223
  rise of Third World against, 109–10
  and Vietnam War, 229–31
  women's rights and, 227
  See also anti-imperialism
Im Sun-dŭk, 15, 139
International Children's Day, 121
International Council of Women, 249n73
International Federation of University Women, 9
internationalism, 56, 82, 130, 163, 261n25
International Labour Organization, 120
International Woman Suffrage Alliance, 249n73
International Women's Day, 52, 233
International Women's News, 249n73
international women's peace movement
  and left feminism, 31
  and rise of Third World against imperialism, 109–10, 111–18
  and women in definition of peace, 118–22
  Women's Peace Caravan, 98–101
  World Congress of Mothers (1955), 100–111
  World Congress of Women (1953), 29, 83–90
  World Congress of Women (1958), 121
  World Congress of Women (1963), 121–30
  World Congress of Women (1969), 219–23
  World Congress of Women (1975), 226–27
International Women's Year, 223, 233–34

Jackson, Ada, 65
James, Julia, 98
Japanese colonization, 7, 8, 11, 60–62, 197–99, 203, 228–29
Japan Mothers' Congress, 101
Japan Women's Association, 232
Jeanson, Colette, 50
Jiang Qing, 213, 292n58
Joliot-Curie, Frédéric, 70
Joliot-Curie, Irène, 34
Jones, Claudia, 47, 257n102
Joy, C. Turner, 39
Juche ideology, 163, 187, 196, 198, 286n86

Kang Chu-ryong, 11
Kang On-sun, 132
Kang Pan Sok, 165, 216
Kaplan, Temma, 233
Kim Chŏng-ok, 132
Kim Chŭng-nyŏ, 155
Kim Ch'un-hŭi, 132
Kim Eun Su (Kim Yŏng-su). *See* Kim Yŏng-su
Kim Hak-sun, 228
Kim Hong-ok, 64, 262n36

Kim Hwal-lan (Helen), 62, 260n21
Kim Il Sung
    and Choe Seung-hui, 170, 174, 177, 179–80
    Chosŏn Nyŏsŏng's focus on, 215–16
    Juche speech, 187
    and KDWU's promotion of women as communist mothers and socialist builders, 163
    and Kim Jong Suk, 194, 196, 216–17
    and Pak Chŏng-ae, 8, 14
    space for dissenting views under, 15
    state visits of, 236
    and Supreme People's Assembly, 12
    and *The White-Haired Girl*, 210–11
    and women's movement, 16, 165
Kim Im-sŏng, 67, 68–69
Kim Jong Il, 192–93, 293n83
Kim Jong Suk, 194–95, 216–17, 225, 293n83
Kim Kyŏng-il, 247n39
Kim Kyu-sik, 58
Kim Mu-sam, 190
Kim Myŏng-hwa, 194
Kim Ok-sŏn, 228
Kim Ok-sun, 129–30, 162–64
Kim Pong-suk, 228–29
Kim Rak-ju, 146
Kim Saeng-güm, 146
Kim Sang-gi, 148
Kim Sŏng-ae, 165
Kim Sun-ok, 43
Kim Wŏn-gyŏng, 59
Kim Wŏn-ju, 248n60
Kim Yŏng-su, 48, 75–76, 79, 81, 84*f*, 85*f*, 110, 114*f*, 116, 121
Kim Yong-bŏm, 7–8, 9
Kirasirova, Masha, 9, 246n26
kisaeng, 60, 61–62, 164–65
Koguryŏ Kingdom, 161
Kollontai, Alexandra, 200
Ko Myŏng-ja, 245n24
Korean Communist Party (KCP), 8, 10, 12, 246n34
Korean Democratic Women's Union (KDWU), 4–5
    and Conference of the Women of Asia, 65
    emblem of, 157*f*
    founding of, 12
    movement to create model families, 157–58
    National Conference of Women Socialist Builders (1959), 137, 147–48
    National Congress of Child Care Workers (1966), 158
    National Mothers Congress (1961), 137, 156–58

Second Congress, 91*f*
    Third Congress, 162–65
    and WIDF, 41
Korean Democratic Women's Union of Japan, 57
Korean National Peace Committee (KNPC), 70, 71
Korean War, 29–32
    as anticolonial war of national liberation for world peace, 69–70, 236
    Asia Pacific Peace Conference calls for end to, 80
    children lost in, 97
    as crucible of Cold War, 30
    opposition to, 37–49
    reconstruction following, 147
    and WIDF's appeal to maternalism, 49–55
    women as written out of history of, 1–2
    Women's International Democratic Federation's activism during, 32–37
    World Congress of Women's opposition to, 83–90
Korean Women's League, 13, 110. *See also* South Korean Democratic Women's Union
Koryŏ Kingdom, 161
Kosmodemyanskaya, Zoya, 51
Ko Yŏng-suk, 132
Krylova, Anna, 196
Kuoshu, Harry H., 292n59
Kwŏn Ae-ra, 59
Kye Wŏlhyang, 179–80

Laban, Rudolf, 189
labor, 131–37, 165–66
    and aesthetics of everyday folk, 169–71
    as creative work, 139
    gendered division of, 153–54
    and gender inequality, 276n28, 279n75
    nature of, 137–47
    productive versus reproductive, 135–36
    as service and sacrifice, 159–62
    and Third Congress of KDWU, 162–65
    and women as socialist builders, 147–55
    and women as socialist mothers, 156–59
    See also class exploitation; productive labor; reproductive labor
"labor hero," 132–33
Labor Law (1946), 13–14
labor organizing, 4, 10–11, 12, 247n39
Lankov, Andrei, 7
Lansiaux, Marie-Anne, 102
Lansing, Marjorie, 30

INDEX

Law of Equal Rights for Men and Women (1946, Equal Rights Law, Gender Equality Law), 13–14
League of Koreans, 259n5
Le Clerc, Françoise, 65
Lee, Mary S., 225
Lee, Steven, 173
left feminism, 31
Legend of Okryŏn Pond, 187
Leider, Ruth, 47
Leow, Rachel, 58
Lettice, Hilda, 98
Levine, Lillian, 50
Leyden, Elsie, 221–22
Li Soo Wul, 225
Li-thi-Quê, 88
Liu Shaoqi, 292n58
local production, 149–50
Lomax, Alan, 189
López Portillo de Tamayo, Marta, 222
Lunacharsky, Anatoly, 186

MacArthur, Douglas, 43
maidens, militant, 203–6
Mallard, Amy, 47
Manchurian faction, 8
Maoism, 112, 269n44
Mao Zedong, 208, 211, 269n44
March First Independence Movement (1919), 8, 59, 60–62, 260n20
market feminism, 217
marriage, 150–51, 221–22
Marshall, Wynsome, 98
Marx, Karl, 131, 137
Marxism, 112, 144
Marxism-Leninism, 130, 163, 272n94
maternal feminism, 49–55
　Conference of the Women of Asia, 65
　and gender equality, 32, 288n4
　and intervention in Korean War, 30
　rallying of disparate groups around, 109–10
　See also maternalism; motherhood
maternalism
　cult of maternity, 200
　maternal thinking, 252n17
　National Mothers Congress and valorization of, 156–58
　and uniting of women, 119–20
　See also maternal feminism; motherhood
McClellan, Woodford, 246n29
McDuffie, Erik, 39
McKinley, Laura, 226
melodramas, representations of communist women in, 197–99

Mezzadri, Alessandra, 275n13
Midnight Moon Elegy, 179, 182
Mies, Maria, 135, 275n15
militant maidens, 203–6
militant peace, 119, 121, 169
Millard, Betty, 38
minjok, 9, 177, 284n45
Mistral, Gabriela, 118–19
model families, 157–58
"modern girl," 62, 196
Moiseyev, Igor, 185, 283n17
Möller, Ina, 119
Monolithic Ideological System, 24, 165, 174, 192, 199, 215, 218, 237
Mother, 196, 200–202, 208
motherhood
　Declaration of Mothers for the Defence of Children, against the Danger of War (1956), 106–8
　Japan Mothers' Congress, 101
　National Mothers Congress (1961), 137, 156–58
　Permanent International Committee of Mothers, 106
　proletarian, 210
　reconfiguration of, 210, 214–15
　Regulation of Work Hours for Working Mothers, 158
　in *Sea of Blood*, 202
　shared expectations of soldiering and, 215
　and socialist realism, 200
　World Congress of Mothers (1955), 100–111
　See also maternal feminism; maternalism
Mun Ye-bong, 70, 71
Mun Yŏng-sin, 61–62
Murrel, Thel, 50–51

Namp'o Machine Factory, 150
Nasretdinova, Zaituna, 183
Nasser, Gamal Abdel, 113, 130, 274n133
National Arts Festival, 175–76
National Assembly of Women (NAW), 46
National Conference of Women Socialist Builders (1959), 137, 147–48
National Congress of Child Care Workers (1966), 158
National Federation of Indian Women, 56, 115
National Institute of Information on Consumer Products, 131
nationalism, 63, 101, 172, 193, 237
National Mothers Congress (1961), 137, 156–58
National Woman's Party, 31
Neton, Jeanne, 139–40, 276n28
"new women," 62, 210

night work, 31, 119
Noi Donne, 18, 19
nonviolence, 118. *See also* pacifism
novyi byt (new everyday life), 172–73
nuclear weapons, 46, 108–9, 116–17, 120–21, 124, 126, 271n66. *See also* disarmament

ocherk, 173, 283n18
October Revolution (1917), 186, 201, 233
opera. *See* revolutionary opera
Organization of Solidarity with the People of Asia, Africa and Latin America (OSPAAL), 232
Ovsyannikova, Maria, 5, 42, 85–87, 89, 90
O Yi-suk, 142

pacifism
  and differing conceptions of peace, 118, 119
  rejection of, 51, 73
Paek Sin-jŏn, 132
Pak Chŏng-ae, 3–4, 6–13, 14–15, 16
  and Asia Pacific Peace Conference, 74
  birth of, 244n16
  on children lost in war, 97
  concludes KDWU presidency, 162
  and Conference of Asian Countries on the Relaxation of International Tensions, 111–12
  and Conference of the Women of Asia, 66f, 68
  death of, 248n61
  on easing women's domestic burden, 148
  elected to WIDF executive committee, 254n37
  on Korean War, 69–70
  and National Assembly of Women's first meeting, 46
  and peace movement, 71–73
  and Second Congress of WIDF, 35
  and second generation of women leaders, 248n60
  on women in workforce, 148
  on World Congress for Partisans for Peace, 70
  at World Congress of Mothers, 102f, 103f, 105
  and World Congress of Women, 88
Pak Chong-sŏng, 190, 193
Pak Den Ai (Pak Chŏng-ae). *See* Pak Chŏng-ae
Pak Kye-ri, 293n83
Pak Kyŏng-suk, 178f
Pak Suk-hyŏn, 146
Panchsheel Treaty (1954), 112
Pang Chae-suk, 132–33
Park, Sunyoung, 173, 292n62

Pax, 249n73
peace
  Asia Pacific Peace Conference, 73–81, 112
  call for just, 111
  and creation of World Peace Council, 69–73
  definition of, 118–22
  militancy of, 119, 121, 169
  People's Congress for Peace, 81–82
  Women's Peace Caravan, 97–100, 120
  World Congress of Women, 83–90
  See also disarmament; international women's peace movement
peaceful coexistence, 57, 74, 76, 80, 81, 112, 122, 124–28, 237
"Peace in Asia and the Role of Women," 232
Peace Preservation Law (1925), 8
People's Congress for Peace, 81–82
Permanent International Committee of Mothers, 106
Person, James, 248n56
Pieper Mooney, Jadwiga E., 254n35
Popova, Nina, 34, 128–29
Popp, Paula, 98
Popp, Rosaleen, 98
Prashad, Vijay, 262n32
Praskovya, "Pasha" Angelina, 133
Prerret, Odette, 21
prisoner of war (POW), 44, 48, 73, 77, 80, 83
productive labor, 135–36
  experience of reproductive labor and, at National Mothers Congress, 156–57
  liberation of women through entry into, 275n15
  as service and sacrifice, 159–62
  women's double burden of reproductive labor and, 237
proletarian arts and culture, 170–71, 173, 183, 186, 200
proletarian family, 200–201
proletarian internationalism, 130, 163, 183, 212
proletarian motherhood, failed, 210
Public Distribution System, 136, 153

racial division, 82–83
racism, 33, 78, 223, 227, 246n29. *See also* antiracism
Raicho Hiratsuka, 57
Ramelson, Marian, 65
Rape. *See* sexual violence
recycling, 154–55
red labor union, 10, 12, 247n39
red peasant union, 7, 12
red pouches, 154–55

Regulation of Work Hours for Working Mothers, 158
reproductive labor, 135–36
   experience of productive labor and, at National Mothers Congress, 156–57
   and local production, 149–50
   as service and sacrifice, 159–62
   valorization of, 137–47
   and value generation, 275n13
   women's double burden of productive labor and, 237
   See also domestic work
revolutionary model ballet, 193, 197
revolutionary opera, 170, 192, 193, 199. See also *Flower Girl, The*; *Sea of Blood*
Richardson, Beulah (Beah Richards), 39
Ri Sŏk-ye, 185
Ri Su-kwang, 160
Ri T'ae-jun, 71–72
Ri Yong-ak, 52–54
Robeson, Eslanda Goode, 30–31, 65, 105, 117–18
Robeson, Paul, 39, 70, 117–18
Rodd, Nora, 20–21, 48f, 87, 90–92
Rodriguez, Candelaria, 46, 85, 87–88, 89
Roosevelt, Eleanor, 13
Ruddick, Sara, 252n17
Rupp, Leila, 249n73
Russell, Diana, 226
Russell, Dora, 36, 98, 100, 106, 109, 119, 120–21
Ryang, Sonia, 288n4
Ryŏksa Kwahak, 196
Ryo Oyama, 50

sacrifice, labor as, 159–62
San Francisco Treaty (1951), 50, 76
Sauvy, Alfred, 63
Save Our Sons Committee, 37–38, 255n51
Schmid, Andre, 279n83
Sea of Blood, 192–93, 196, 197–98, 199, 201–2, 204, 208, 209, 290n42
self-determination, 9, 35, 44, 58, 83, 113, 136, 198, 234
service, labor as, 159–62
Seven-Year Plan (1961–1967), 150, 158–59, 280n100
sex difference, 196, 206–7, 212–13, 214. See also gender equality; gender inequality
sexism, 132–33, 151
sexuality, 234–35
sexual violence
   and class exploitation, 207–8
   against "comfort women," 227–32
   as concern to leftist women, 218–19

Shanghai Dance Troupe, 210, 213, 293n74
Silla Kingdom, 161
Simch'ŏng, 160, 204
Sin Hyŏn-ok, 88
Sŏ Tong-man, 8, 245n22
socialism
   and productive-reproductive labor binary, 135–36
   reproductive labor and building, 146
   value of gendered labor under, 144
   wages under, 140–42
   women as socialist builders, 147–55
   women as socialist mothers, 156–59
   and women's challenging of traditional class and gender status, 213–14
socialist distribution, 152–54
socialist feminism, 252n15
socialist realism, 172–73, 176, 178, 186, 188, 200–201
social reproduction theory (SRT), 138, 139–40, 276n21, 276n27
Soenito-Heyligers, Trees, 41–42, 128
Sŏng Wŏn-il, 262n36
Soong Ching-ling, 13, 65–66, 76, 81
South Korean Democratic Women's Union, 14. *See also* Korean Women's League
Soviet Union
   controversy over ballet in, 186–87
   cultural exchanges with, 183
   gender equality in, 196
   as multiethnic state, 9, 246n29
   and UN World Conference of Women (1975), 224
   WIDF support for, 34–35
Soviet Women's Committee, 127–29, 223, 254n35, 270n60, 272n96
Stalin Peace Prize, 73
Stern, Charlotte, 47
Stockholm Peace Appeal (1950), 57, 71
Story of Sado Castle, 181–82, 192
Suez Crisis, 113
Supreme People's Assembly (SPA), 12, 15
Sutherland, Zöe, 276n21
Suzuki, Lewis, 78
Swan Lake, 185, 186

Tang Un-sil, 132
Taylor, Valerie, 105
Tereshkova, Valentina, 122
Third World, 32–37, 63–64, 109–10, 111–18, 121, 130, 224, 262n32
Third Worldism, 111–12, 130
Three-Year Plan (1954–1956), 147, 277n47

Tikhonov, Nikolai, 72
Tikhonov, Vladimir, 63
"To the Women of Pyongyang" (Rodd), 92
"tractor girl," 133
trade, 80
traditional values, 119, 161
transmission belts, 12, 163
transversal politics, 31, 234
Tricontinental Conference (1966), 231–32
True Daughter of the Party, A, 193
Truman, Harry, 46
Tsoi, Vera. *See* Pak Chŏng-ae
Turgunbaeva, Mukarram, 183–84

Ulanova, Galina, 184
Umbles, Idell M., 105
Union of Italian Women, 20, 50, 130
Union of Sudanese Women, 115, 222
Union of Vietnamese Women, 56, 219, 229–31
United Nations
    Asia Pacific Peace Conference drafts letter to, 81
    Command in Korea, 51, 83, 235–36
    Commission for the Unification and Rehabilitation of Korea (UNCURK), 51, 235–36
    General Assembly Resolution 3390B, 235–36
    Korean membership in, 227
    and racial division, 82–83
    Security Council Resolution 1325, 232–33
    Special Rapporteur on violence against women, 228
    WIDF expelled from, 36
    World Conference of Women (1975), 223–26
Unrim and Okran, 187
US House Un-American Activities Committee (HUAC), 33, 40
Uzbekistan, 117–18

Vaillant-Couturier, Marie-Claude, 19, 37, 40*f*, 68
Vermeersch, Jeannette, 46, 69, 113
Vietnam War, 36, 64, 219, 221, 229–31, 235
Vishmidt, Marina, 276n21
Vogel, Lise, 138

Waechter, Lilly, 41, 46, 47, 81, 85, 87, 89, 114, 114*f*
wages
    according to industrial sectors, 1955, 141*t*
    under socialism versus capitalism, 140–42
Wang Zheng, 16, 213, 217
Warren, Josephine, 98
waste, reducing or recycling, 154–55

We Accuse!, 42–45, 227
Weigand, Kate, 252n15
Wellman, Peggy, 105
Wheaton, Louis, 78
Wheaton, Tomoko Ikeda, 78
White-Haired Girl, The, 193, 196, 203–5, 206–9, 210–13, 266n92, 291n50, 292n59, 292n67, 293n74
Wigdor, Hazel, 21
Wilcox, Emily, 172
Willcox, Anita, 78
Winter, Helen, 105
"woman question," 31–32, 227
women
    challenge traditional class and gender status, 213–14
    contributions of leftist and communist, 218–19
    in definition of peace, 118–22
    desexualization of, 196, 209–13
    discrimination against, 31, 119
    legal rights of, 14
    as socialist builders, 147–55
    as written out of history, 1–4, 15–17, 234
women, representations of, 194–97, 213–17
    in anti-Japanese revolutionary melodramas, 197–99
    communist, 194–95, 216–17
    and communist feminism, 206–7, 209–13
    and feminist erasure, 206–9
    as militant maidens, 203–6
    as mothers, 200–202
"Women in Society" (López Portillo de Tamayo), 222
"Women in the Family" (Leyden), 221–22
"Women in the Struggle to Win and Defend National Independence, Democracy and Peace" (Abd el Aal), 222
Women of China, 130, 217
Women of the Whole World, 5, 17–21, 37, 47, 115, 249n72
Women's Anti-Fascist Front of Yugoslavia (WAF), 113
Women's International Democratic Federation (WIDF), 4–5
    appeal to maternalism, 49–55
    bias against, 254n35
    Chinese women withdraw from, 101, 122, 124–29, 272n95
    Conference of the Women of Asia, 64–69
    consultative status with UN Economic and Social Council restored, 218–19
    cooperation with press, 19
    council meeting in Helsinki, 114–15, 116

Women's International Democratic Federation
(WIDF) (continued)
First Congress, 35
and gender mainstreaming, 235
governance of, 254n39
and Hungarian Revolution, 113–14
as informal communication channel, 90–92
international women's commission of,
41–46, 47–49
and International Women's Year, 223
opposition to Korean War, 39–50
Pak Chŏng-ae and Yu Yŏng-jun elected to
executive committee, 254n37
rallies with other groups around maternal
feminism, 109–10
reconciliation of Yugoslavian women and,
112–13
revised constitution of, 114–15
Second Congress, 35
stripped of consultative status with
UN Economic and Social
Council, 218
study session "on the protection of
motherhood as a right of women and a
responsibility of society," 119–20
and Third World, 32–37
Women of the Whole World, 5, 17–21, 37, 47,
115, 249n72
World Congress of Mothers (1955), 100–111
World Congress of Women (1953), 29, 83–90
World Congress of Women (1958), 121
World Congress of Women (1963), 121–30
World Congress of Women (1969), 219–23
World Congress of Women (1975), 226–27
Women's International League for Peace and
Freedom (WILPF), 33, 109, 226, 249n73
women's liberation movement, 3, 119
Women's Peace Caravan, 97–100, 120
women's press, 17–21
Chosŏn Nyŏsŏng (Korean women), 5–6, 14,
47, 66, 70, 134f, 150–51, 190, 196, 215–16
Noi Donne, 18, 19
We Accuse!, 42–45, 227
Women of China, 130, 217

Women of the Whole World, 5, 17–21, 37, 47,
115, 249n72
Women United for United Nations
(WUUN), 45
work. *See* domestic work; labor; productive
labor; reproductive labor
workingclassization, 136
World Congress of Mothers (1955),
100–111
World Congress of Partisans for Peace
(1949), 70
World Congress of Women (1953), 29, 50–51,
83–90
World Congress of Women (1958), 116, 121
World Congress of Women (1963), 121–30
World Congress of Women (1969), 219–23
World Congress of Women (1975), 226–27
World Festival of Youth and Students
(WFYS), 177
World Peace Council (WPC), 69–73
World Plan of Action, 224
Writers' Bandung, 118
Wu, Judy, 51
Wyatt, Jane, 98

yangban, 144, 161
Yang Yun-yu, 124–25, 126, 127
Yi Chu-mi, 176
Yi Hyo-jae, 225–26, 232, 296n51
Yŏ Un-hyŏng, 58
Yoneyama, Lisa, 250n88
Young Women's Christian Association
(YWCA), 50, 62
Yugoslavia, 101, 112–13
Yu Ho-jun, 3
Yu Man Oe (Yu Man-ok), 84, 132
Yun Se-p'yŏng, 159–61, 280n103
Yu Yŏng-jun, 13, 15, 35, 64, 68, 110, 254n37,
262n36

Zanti, Carmen, 117
Zetkin, Clara, 135, 233
Ziegler, Gilette, 41, 88
Zuaf, Lelia, 102, 104f